RUN TO GLORY AND PROFITS

RUN TO GLORY & PROFITS

THE ECONOMIC RISE OF THE NFL DURING THE 1950s

DAVID GEORGE SURDAM

UNIVERSITY OF NEBRASKA PRESS
LINCOLN AND LONDON

Portions of chapter 9 originally
appeared as the author's "A Tale
of Two Gate-Sharing Plans: The
National Football League and the
National League, 1952–56," *Southern
Economic Journal 73*, no. 4 (April
2007): 931–46. This content appears
with the permission of the Southern
Economic Association, © 2007.

Library of Congress
Cataloging-in-Publication Data
Surdam, David G. (David George)
Run to glory and profits: the economic rise of the NFL during the
1950s / David George Surdam.
pages cm
Includes bibliographical
references and index.
ISBN 978-0-8032-4696-6 (cloth:
alk. paper) 1. National Football
League. 2. Football—Economic
aspects—United States. I. Title.
GV955.5.N35S87 2013
796.332'64097309045—dc23
2013011615

Set in Minion by Laura Wellington.
Designed by Nathan Putens.

CONTENTS

TABLES

ACKNOWLEDGMENTS

As always, writing the acknowledgements is one of this author's favorite tasks. Many people have assisted me in the preparation of this book.

George Rugg, curator of the Joyce Sports Collection at Notre Dame University, was instrumental in providing team scorecards and other information. Jon Kendle, researcher at the Pro Football Hall of Fame Archives and Information Center in Canton, Ohio, supplied me with minutes of National Football League and American Football League meetings, as well as other information. Their assistance made this book stronger.

I offer my grateful appreciation for the Pro Football Hall of Fame Archives and Information Center's permission to use archival material in this book. I also thank the *Southern Economic Journal* for their permission to reprint large portions of my article on gate sharing in Chapter Nine.

The University of Oregon and Notre Dame University microfilm sections staff helped in locating *The Sporting News* on microfilm. University of Oregon archivists helped me located information on Joe Lillard, an early pioneer of integration in the NFL. Graduate students Ashley Fewins and Nadya Shumilova downloaded and printed key *New York Times* articles. In addition, both were attentive students and a joy to work with.

Alicia Pecha, Nathan Mackey, and Kayla Gump, undergraduate student assistants in the Economics Department at the University of Northern Iowa worked on processing the note cards for this book. Their efforts on a rather tedious task were greatly appreciated.

Farzad Moussavi, dean of the College of Business Administration, and Fred Abraham, head of the Economics Department at the University of Northern Iowa, gave unstinting financial support and encouragement. The University of Northern Iowa generously granted me a summer research grant during the writing stage. The College of Business Administration gave funds for two research trips to Canton, Ohio, as well as financing the index.

Janine Goodwin copyedited the manuscript under the direction of Sabrina Stellrecht at the University of Nebraska Press. Their efforts improved the final version, and I enjoyed working with them.

Sarah Statz Cords compiled the index and, as usual, was a pleasure to work with.

Professor Kevin Quinn of St. Norbert College gave the book a thorough reading early in the process. Two anonymous referees provided useful comments for improving this manuscript.

I also acknowledge three more members of the University of Northern Iowa community. Rosie Lang, dining unit manager at Rialto Dining Hall, has supervised hundreds of delicious meals for a hungry bachelor, as well as being a good friend. Students Jen Bolden and Danielle Enderson proved inspiring with their dedication to scholarship and their friendliness. Ms. Boden will one day join the academy; Ms. Enderson earned a CPA and various honors while rooting for the New England Patriots. I'm sorry there isn't more about your favorite team, Danielle, but they came late in the story.

I thank the surviving members of my dissertation committee, Professors Robert W. Fogel, Nobel Prize winner in economics, and David Galenson for their encouragement over the past twenty-five years. While the NFL is a far cry from my Civil War dissertation, they have maintained an interest in my work. For the sake of Bob, who is a Chicago Bears fan, I trust I have not unduly maligned the Bears in any way.

RUN TO GLORY AND PROFITS

INTRODUCTION

The National Football League (NFL) has longed reigned as America's favorite professional sports league, having surpassed Major League Baseball (MLB) and prevailed against the National Basketball Association (NBA). Success may have spoiled the NFL, as the league has exhibited pompous and arrogant behavior. During the 1976 bicentennial celebrations, the NFL sponsored an essay contest for the schoolchildren of America on the topic "The NFL in American History." Leading historians — including Henry Steele Commager, who retorted, "It has no importance whatsoever" — scorned the league's chutzpah.[1] The league's historical videos are renowned for their overly dramatic narration and unsubtle musical cues.[2] One would think the narrator was describing the titanic struggle between the Red Army and the Wehrmacht instead of the Packers and Chiefs in the retroactively dubbed Super Bowl I. The league's use of Roman numerals to denote Super Bowls has also taken its share of ridicule.

NFL owners, though, have reason to be proud of their league. They collect huge sums of money from television networks. The Super Bowl (at least it is not named the "World Series") is a national — and now a worldwide — event. More Americans watch the game than vote in Presidential elections. The current owners, however, rarely reflect on the league's humble beginnings and adolescence. Even in the 1950s, after thirty seasons of operation, the NFL lacked the glamour and the profits of Major League Baseball. NFL owners barely survived the German- and Japanese-inspired disruption of their league. After World War II, the onset of peace seemed to provide a promise of prosperity as the demand for leisure pursuits increased, but that hope was dissipated when a new set of owners formed a rival league, the All-America Football Conference (AAFC).[3] As late as 1949, famed sportswriter Grantland Rice wrote, "Pro football can never compete with college football. No pro teams can ever match the drawing power of Notre Dame, Michigan, Southern California, SMU, Army and Navy, Minnesota, Stanford and California and Texas, and too many others to mention."[4]

Despite Rice's dismissal, even Presidents of the United States began paying attention to the NFL. The league cheered the news that President Truman would see some contests in the upcoming 1945 season. Now, of course, a presidential phone call to the Super Bowl champions is de rigueur.[5]

The NFL's ascent from obscurity to the front pages of the sports world during the 1950s raises many questions. How did the league achieve prosperity after years of struggle? How did the league defeat the rival AAFC? Sports historians and observers frequently cite television and the league's superior competitive balance (in comparison with Major League Baseball's competitive balance) as critical factors that triggered the league's rise. The league's revenue-sharing, player draft, player reserve clause, and television policies were intertwined with competitive balance issues and are often credited with improving the league.[6] The answers to these questions comprise the subsequent chapters of this book.

The NFL owners' and players' actions are amenable to economic analysis. The owners and players possessed scarce resources (such as capital, labor, and stadium dates) that had alternative uses. All involved had to allocate their scarce resources among the alternative uses in ways that best served their interests and helped fulfill their goals.

While owners, like most businesspeople, were politic enough not to claim they were trying to maximize profits, profit maximization or cost minimization could never be far from their minds given their sometimes slender capital reserves. An owner might, of course, jettison some profits if he thought he would win a championship. In this way, he might be thought a sportsman, the image so beloved by the owners and a number of sportswriters.

Owners almost seemed to take pride in their announced losses. They seemed to espouse the view that there were few more enjoyable ways to lose money than by owning a sports team (which was preferable, apparently, to owning a slow racehorse). The issue of profitability in professional team sports is, to quote Winston Churchill, "a riddle, wrapped in a mystery, inside an enigma." Owners had good reasons to be reticent about profits. They did not want players to have a reason to agitate for higher salaries, and they were wary of attracting and emboldening potential upstart leagues. The drawback to pleading poverty was that such depictions might dampen potential suitors' interests and thereby suppress franchise values.

NFL owners, though, would have had to be spectacularly inept if they failed to make profits, given adequate demand. They held two huge advantages over the run-of-the-mill business owner. Because the league granted territorial rights — barring competition in an owner's territory — an owner could set his ticket prices and behave monopolistically. Such price-setting power should have bolstered profits. Territorial rights afforded protection only within a league; no other league team could enter another team's territory without approval or compensation. Teams in other leagues, though, might enter an occupied territory and risk the legal wrangling. The owners, through their reserve clause and reverse-order draft of collegiate players, squelched competitive bidding for players, thus allowing themselves to suppress player salaries. Both of these advantages, territorial protection and the suppression of the rights of labor, ran counter to the spirit, if not the letter, of U.S. antitrust policies.

If an owner was in a market where the demand was inadequate, these two advantages of price-setting power over ticket prices and superior bargaining power over player salaries might not avail him profitability. Inadequate demand might arise if an owner had too much competition (a rival team contesting the same territory); an inept set of players and coaches; ticket prices that were set too high; an inadequate population base; or if his area had insufficient consumer purchasing power.

The NFL faced competition from the All-America Football Conference and the American Football League, whose owners did not respect NFL territorial protection. Some NFL owners found themselves with rival teams in town, reflecting that western cliché, "This town isn't big enough for the two of us." The owners in the new leagues increased bidding for the limited number of talented players. The NFL owners' profits were thereby doubly squeezed, as their previous advantages became less effective.

While it is understandable that NFL owners would not welcome AAFC and AFL newcomers with open embraces, there was no reason to approve their tactics in combating the new entrants. Antitrust questions arose, so Congress decided to investigate, a backhanded tribute to the league's growing success and popularity.

Since a key element for an owner's success rested upon adequate demand, owners sought ways to increase demand individually and collectively. To boost demand, owners could improve their playing talent, if it didn't cost too much. What was beneficial for one owner might prove injurious to the collective interests of all of the owners, so the league implemented rules ostensibly designed to curb untoward competition for players. These rules pertaining to the reverse-order draft of college players and revenue sharing were not as straightforward as fans and pundits believed. NFL owners are to be congratulated for successfully cloaking exploitive behavior under the guise of "competitive balance" and cooperation.

Other attempts to increase demand were more benign and benefited fans: innovations to distinguish the pro game from the college variety, for instance. NFL owners, while resistant to reintegrating the league with African American players in the late 1940s and early 1950s, eventually tapped into the deep and, initially, cheaper pool of such players. If these players incidentally boosted demand for NFL games, so much the better. In retrospect, television was a major boost to the demand for NFL games, but owners struggled to learn how to effectively harness the new medium.

Players, too, were beginning to act collectively to improve their situation. They, of course, hoped to maximize their earnings while improving working conditions. During the period covered in this book, they had yet to form an effective union, one creating a monopoly of labor.

The NFL's past reverberates today. Owner-player strife has long-standing precedence; for so many years, owners held the whip hand in dealing with players. When players began gaining bargaining parity, owners were seldom gracious about the process. Owners may have believed their own myths about League Think and cooperation, but their actions continued to betray a more accurate depiction of them as a Hydra of conflicting self-interests. Owners pursued their self-interest in multiple ways, from moving their franchises despite opposition by fellow owners to refusing to share more than a pittance of their luxury box revenue. Fans remained loyal despite repeated provocation, because the NFL's product remained so alluring.

It was a good thing that NFL games were such an attractive product; the games have had to continue to enthrall generations of fans despite the exasperating shenanigans of owners and players.

The NFL's rise to prosperity was not inevitable, given the league's struggles against the AAFC and AFL. While the AFL mimicked many of the AAFC's experiences, the new league had a decisive asset that ensured survival: a five-year television contract. The new league's adroit use of its television contract proved an ironic twist. According to most observers of the NFL, its owners' prosperity during the 1950s was due, in large part, to their lucrative television arrangements. Many of these same owners had initially been suspicious of television.

Television loomed large in the December 1958 championship game between the New York Giants, long a power in the league, and the upstart Baltimore Colts. The game has been hailed as, among other things, "The Greatest Game Ever Played." The game was undoubtedly exciting, and it was the first overtime in championship play. Millions of Americans watched the game, and in the days following the game, it remained a topic of conversation. Sportswriter Tex Maule was quick to label it, "The Best Football Game Ever Played." NFL commissioner Bert Bell simply commented, "I never saw two clubs with the pitch of desire and inspiration shown by the Giants and the Colts. Neither have I ever witnessed such tremendous crowd enthusiasm as the fans displayed in the Stadium."[7] Imagine Bell's pleasure upon getting the results from the television returns. Maule's explanation of the game's significance, though, is of value. "The classics of the pretelevision era have been perpetuated only in the minds of the spectators on hand and by the newspaper accounts; this, for the first time, was a truly epic game which inflamed the imagination of a national audience."[8] This, then, was the game's significance. A generation or two of football fans could say, with meaning, "Where were you when Ameche plunged into the end zone?"

By the 1950s, the NFL was winning its struggle to gain public attention, not only in league cities but throughout America. The mass media of radio and television, along with greater newspaper coverage and the introduction of national sports publications, helped to create new legions of professional football fans. Pro football, long the ignored stepsibling of college football, began to rival, if not surpass, the amateur game. League commissioners Joe Carr and Bert Bell worked diligently to publicize the game, but both lacked the promotional ability of later commissioner Pete Rozelle; then again, Rozelle had a higher-quality product to peddle than did Carr and possibly Bell. According to David Harris, Rozelle eventually marketed the game as "an experience." Michael MacCambridge summed up the NFL's enormous burst of popularity in the late 1950s; "the confluence of elements — the Giants' stature, the '58 title game, the Packers' mystique, Rozelle's vision and [Jim] Kensil's [the league's publicity man] implementation of it, the sport's appeal to Madison Avenue — all contributed to pro football moving toward center stage of American sports."[9]

These events are in sharp contrast to the league's first thirty seasons. Early in the league's history, George Halas was ecstatic to read in a newspaper "that his Chicago Bears had beaten the Chicago Cardinals for the championship of the NFL before a thousand or so diehard fans. It was the second sentence, though, which had the Halas heart doing flippity-flops. In unexpectedly extravagant language came the critical appraisal: 'It was a very fine game.' There was no third sentence. That was the entire newspaper account." Halas worked hard, touring "newspaper offices to leave press notices — which never were printed — and complimentary tickets — which no one wanted — even for free."[10]

By the late 1950s, Major League Baseball was nervously watching the NFL's rise. Branch Rickey, who knew quite a bit about making money in baseball and quite a bit about losing money in football, noticed that interest in pro football spilled over into the preseason training camps and encroached upon baseball's former monopoly on summertime sports sections. "Unless we're on our toes, pro football and pro basketball will pass us in both fan interest and at the gate."[11] College football, too, took notice of the NFL's popularity, with Edward "Moose" Krause, Notre Dame athletic director, admitting, "Don't tell me the pros aren't winning the fans away from the college games, because they are. For years the college people have been appealing to fans to attend their games out of loyalty. That's fine. But now we have to offer them something more for their entertainment dollar."[12]

Perhaps a telltale sign of the NFL's prosperity was the now-ubiquitous "economic impact" studies used by proponents of publicly financed stadiums. By 1964 NFL owners Art and Dan Rooney and Pete Rozelle could claim that the NFL pumped real money into cities. Rozelle

> revealed that the Giants, paying the Yankees a percentage rental for Yankee Stadium, paid $90,000 in rental "for just one game" — the 1962 championship game. "You can see," he went on as a low whistle ran over the room, "how football can help pay off your new stadium." He told how pro football can make other businessmen richer. An Atlanta study, he said, found that the average out-of-town visitor to a football game spends $50 on the weekend. Assuming that half of a capacity crowd in Atlanta's planned 57,000-seat stadium would be from out of town, he said, "Visitors would pour $1,425,000 into the bloodstream of that community in one weekend." That was rich enough for Pittsburgh's bloodstream. When Rozelle finished, the businessmen applauded and at the table where Art Rooney sat with members of the Stadium Authority, there were smiles.[13]

Perian (pronounced Perry-Ann) Conerly, who was married to New York Giants quarterback George Conerly, wrote newspaper columns about life in the NFL. She recalled the changing attitude toward her husband's work. "It concerns tone of voice. 'Your husband plays professional football?' has been the stock opening line of new acquaintances since our marriage in 1949. It remains so in 1960. But the exclamation today bears not a trace of pity."[14]

The postwar period was less sophisticated, which is not to say innocent. Perian Conerly recalled Roosevelt Grier's foray into show business. He went on the Dick Clark Show to perform his record release: "Moonlight in Vermont" with the flip side "Smoky Morning."[15] No "Super Bowl Shuffle" or rap at that time. Grier later costarred in "Daniel Boone" with Fess "Davy Crockett" Parker (since Parker sported the same duds, who could tell the difference between Davy and Daniel?).

While Brooklyn priests exhorted their parishes to pray for baseball slugger Gil Hodges during a horrendous slump, the bishop of the "San Francisco diocese granted a special dispensation for the Colt Catholics to eat meat on Friday evening. 'I shouldn't, after what you did to us in Baltimore,' he said gruffly, 'but I will because I don't want your boys to collapse after our boys whip them.'"[16]

In another example of the ways in which the cultural mores of the 1950s and early 1960s differ from those of today, when the Dallas Texans of the American Football League took a flight to Buffalo, the flight attendant ("stewardess" as they were known then) altered the welcoming remarks: "The beautiful blonde and shapely one is me. The other girl is Sherry Hansen. My name is Betsy Lockhart and if we can do anything for you like holding your hand or sitting on your lap, just let us know. And we both will kiss the first one to make a touchdown." After the game, players and the accompanying sportswriters returned to the plane, whereby a sportswriter sprinted up the steps and announced he had scored the first touchdown. No one knew whether the rightful owner of the two kisses, running back Johnny Robinson, witnessed the swindle.[17]

Even the United States' erstwhile foe, the Soviet Union, took note of professional football, though it did not join the fans. The Soviet press had been pillorying Major League Baseball for its violence and mistreatment of blacks. During the early 1950s, the Soviet press addressed American "futbol." According to a *New York Times* article, the Soviets claimed, "futbol" was

> designed to brutalize American youth and prepare it to take its place in an "army of bandits and haters of mankind" under the United States' policy of militarization. The newspaper *Soviet Sport* said that American college "futbol" was one of the chief instruments for inculcating American youth in the spirit of "beastly psychology and racist hatred for other peoples." *Soviet Sport* said that nowhere in American sport was achieved such a measure of "racism, corruption, swindling, defrauding of the spectators, boorishness and harshness" as on the playing fields of American colleges.[18]

Apparently the Washington Redskins were unknown to the Soviets.

As the era neared its end, even the nascent counterculture paid attention to football. San Francisco 49ers quarterback Y. A. Tittle and his receiver, R. C. Owens, devised their "Alley-Oop" pass. The beatniks (forerunners of hippies) considered the play "a sort of mystical experience with the ball being 'the center of a focus of unity' between passer and receiver."[19]

All of the league's success broke up the tight coterie of owners who had struggled to make the league viable. In a telling anecdote, long-time NFL observer, Beano Cook, reflected with Pete Rozelle in 1987: "At one time, a handshake was all that was needed in the NFL. Credit the nuns. Most of the owners were Catholic. They fought like hell with each other but when a deal was made, that was it. A handshake. No lawyers. You know that when Art Rooney gave his word, that was it. Same with the Mara brothers. Now nobody cares except for a few owners. In many ways, the NFL reminds me of the Roman Empire."[20]

Between 1946 and 1960, then, the NFL had been transformed from a league with a modest but growing following in the northeast quadrant of the nation to an enthralling sport entertaining millions of Americans across the nation.

1

THE USURPERS

NFL owners could congratulate themselves for having survived World War II intact, if just barely so. The 1945 championship game garnered the top gross gate receipts in the history of the championship with 32,178 fans contributing $164,542.[1] Although NFL owners claimed chronic losses, the pent-up wartime demand for entertainment induced hopes for better days. Economic profits or the anticipation of such profits inspire envy, and envy triggers entry. The incumbent owners, naturally, were not pleased with the prospect of fighting for fans and for players.

As the war wound down, entrepreneurs began speculating that postwar America would be hungry for professional sports entertainment. Many leagues and franchises were called; few were profitable. Several prospective owners petitioned the NFL for franchises even before the war ended. Major League Baseball and professional basketball owners also faced a clamor for more teams. The NFL owners found themselves battling a formidable challenger in the All-America Football Conference.[2]

A rival league was nothing new for the NFL. The league had survived challenges from fledgling leagues throughout its existence, with "Cash and Carry" Pyle's American League being a typical example. Pyle and George Halas had engineered the lucrative professional debut of Red Grange after his spectacular college career. Pyle wanted part ownership of the Bears, but Halas refused. In retaliation, Pyle formed his American League, drenching all the owners in red ink and bankruptcy. Halas's team barely survived the upheaval.[3]

Many writers have chronicled the inception and demise of the AAFC. Beyond a cursory description of the league's experience, we shall focus on how the NFL battled the new league. Successful companies often face competition, and much of antitrust law concerns the legitimate and illegitimate behavior displayed by incumbents.

The Postwar American Economy

The victorious Americans eagerly looked forward to the end of World War II. While some worried that the transition from a wartime to a peacetime economy might trigger a relapse into another recession or depression, the economy adjusted admirably.

Gross National Product (GNP) seemed to fall and then rebound between 1945 and 1947, but when it is adjusted for changes in the price level, the real GNP fell in both years. Thereafter, real GNP rose continually except for brief, shallow downturns in 1954 and 1958. The general price level rose quickly because of the postwar boom in consumer spending and because of the relaxation of price controls. By the early 1950s, though, the changes in the price level as reflected by the commonly used Consumer Price Index (CPI) stabilized. For the period 1952–56, the index was almost stagnant. The drop in real GNP in 1946, though, was a reversal of a "good news, bad news" joke. The "bad news" was that real GNP dropped (largely because of reduced spending on defense), but the good news was that consumers spent more. The pent-up demand for leisure and consumption began to be satisfied in 1946. Nominal and real spending on spectator recreation jumped in 1946. Motion pictures enjoyed prosperity in 1946 as well. Real spending on sports experienced a burst of enthusiasm in the late 1940s before lapsing into stagnation. Americans began switching from public to private forms of recreation expenditures. Instead of going out to movies and ballgames, Americans chose to remain at home watching television or watching their children play. The demographic changes wrought by the baby boom reduced the number of young single men and women. Reflecting this family emphasis, the only part of the movie industry that did well was the drive-in sector.[4]

Americans purchased automobiles and houses in suburbs in greater numbers. The automobiles gave them mobility and made living in the suburbs more feasible. The growing distance between middle- and upper-middle-class homes and the downtown areas, where many ballparks were located, created a demand for easy freeway access and convenient parking once suburbanites reached the ballpark. The migration of African Americans to northern cities continued after the war, too, changing the racial makeup of many cities. Table 1 shows characteristics of the cities with National Football League teams in 1950, as well as some later NFL locations. These cities typically had SMSA (Standard Metropolitan Statistical Area) median incomes above the national average, so their residents should have been better able to afford tickets to professional sporting events.

The AAFC's Birth

When the NFL rebuffed several prospective owners' applications, Arch Ward, *Chicago Tribune* sportswriter (and later sports editor), encouraged the prospective owners to form a new league. Because of the wartime-imposed limits on many entertainment options, there was a great yearning for entertainment just waiting for the war to end before cascading throughout the industry. Because the war had disrupted the normal transition of players from college to pro careers, there was also a backlog of talent available. Many players, even former NFL players, had ambiguous contractual status. Bert Bell denied that these players were free agents.[5] Owners could also hope that the hike in college attendance caused by the GI Bill would improve the quality and quantity of college talent graduating in the years to come. A visionary such as Paul Brown could quickly build a powerful team from the pool of available players. The new league, indeed, hoped to avoid a bidding war with the NFL over players. They also hoped to stage a game between the champions of the two leagues that would be akin to baseball's World Series.[6] Sports historian Michael MacCambridge believes the NFL's decision to continue operations during the war proved a key element in its struggle against the AAFC, giving the older league the necessary continuity and tradition.[7]

By early 1945 AAFC owners were hiring coaches and signing players in anticipation of debuting in the fall of 1946.[8] They also sought stadium leases.[9]

AAFC owners were, in many cases, wealthier than their NFL counterparts. Hollywood stalwarts Bing Crosby, Louis B. Mayer, and Don Ameche (no relation to the Colts' Alan Ameche) owned the Los Angeles Dons.[10] They attempted to get Bert Bell to form a franchise, and Bell admitted he was tempted. George Halas convinced him that the NFL would make him commissioner, so Bell stayed with that league and became an implacable foe of the AAFC. AAFC commissioner James Crowley, a member of Notre Dame's famed "Four Horsemen," later released information about Bell's interest in owning an AAFC team.[11]

As with their NFL peers, AAFC owners did not own stadiums. While most Major League Baseball teams owned stadiums and could legitimately deny the use of such facilities to potential rivals, NFL owners could not be certain their landlords wouldn't lease stadiums to new teams. The AAFC had access to several large stadiums, and Arch Ward later boasted that AAFC teams played in stadiums with a larger combined capacity than did the NFL teams.[12]

The AAFC exposed some fissures in the NFL's structure. Cleveland Rams owner Dan Reeves was perturbed that his 1945 championship team lost money overall. He was eyeing the burgeoning Los Angeles market for his team. Dan Topping, owner of a dormant Brooklyn franchise that was temporarily merged with Ted Collins's Boston club, was chafing at his inability to field his team in his Yankee Stadium, as he was the sole NFL owner who owned a stadium.[13]

The NFL owners' initial response to the AAFC's announcement of its intention to play in 1946 was ridicule. Outgoing NFL commissioner, Elmer Layden, another of Notre Dame's "Four Horsemen," perhaps viewing the AAFC as akin to the patsies that his Notre Dame team used to play, retorted, "New league? Why they haven't even got a football."[14]

Unfortunately for Layden's prescience, the AAFC may not have had their footballs yet, but they scored a huge publicity coup when disgruntled Dan Topping dropped his team in the NFL to field a new one in the upstart league. Even though the Giants' owners, the Maras, had finally acquiesced to his playing in the Stadium, Topping claimed dissatisfaction with the playing dates assigned to him.[15] Topping announced that his new team, the cleverly named Yankees, would play in Yankee Stadium. Because Topping owned the stadium with his baseball partners Larry MacPhail and Del Webb, the team would earn concessions revenue. Topping gladly paid the $50,000 AAFC membership fee, although some reporters thought that the other AAFC members enticed him with cash contributions. These owners knew that having a franchise in New York City gave their league credibility, as AAFC commissioner Jim Crowley stated: "We were ready to go, anyway, and I think we would have done very well, but getting New York in the league certainly has boosted our stock. . . . Several of our people right now could sell their franchises for considerably more than they paid for them."[16] Topping ungraciously blasted the NFL upon his departure: "[The NFL] is no league at all, it is a racket. I ought to know, I was one of the 6 stooges for the big 4 until I got some brains and pulled out."[17]

The remaining NFL owners derided Topping for being a poor owner who lost considerable money in operating the Brooklyn franchise. Topping's defection left NFL owners reeling. Some observers believed that Ted Collins, owner of the Boston Yanks, might join him in the new league. In the meantime, Topping's defection left the fate of the Brooklyn team in limbo; eventually the Boston and Brooklyn teams merged and remained in Boston for the time being.[18] George Preston Marshall, owner of the Washington Redskins, actually thought it a good thing that Topping switched leagues, as it clarified the NFL's "New York problem." Marshall also sounded conciliatory about the AAFC: "If the other league proves itself, there is that possibility [of a championship between leagues]. If the All-American [sic] Conference is a sound success it will help professional football all around. If it is a failure, it will not hurt anybody but them."[19]

Topping's defection solved a pressing problem for the AAFC, as his became the eighth team in the league, making scheduling easier. Baltimore had originally been granted a franchise but could not get organized in time for the 1946 season. The league set up a fourteen-game schedule, with each team playing a home-and-home set with every other rival, unlike the NFL and its lopsided schedule in which teams fought over the opportunity to play the Bears and the Giants.[20] Because landing a New York franchise was imperative for the AAFC, Topping's new compatriots not only provided financial inducements but also allowed him the right to select one player from each team, exclusive of the top three men named by each club. In return Topping shared the hundreds of players on the reserve list of his old Brooklyn club.[21]

AAFC owners immediately challenged NFL teams to exhibition games. NFL owners recognized the danger of playing even exhibition games with the upstarts. As John McGraw of baseball's New York Giants realized in 1904, playing a championship series with an American League team only served to strengthen the upstarts while possibly damaging the entrenched league. The NFL owners declined such invitations and passed a rule prohibiting their teams from playing exhibition games against any other circuits, aside from one of their own minor league allies, without the consent of four-fifths of the league membership. The AAFC made repeated invitations to the NFL for exhibition or championship games between the leagues, occasionally even trying to embarrass the older circuit into accepting. Later Commissioner Jonas Ingram wired Bell, while releasing the contents of the telegram to reporters before Bell received it: "Since no valid reason has been advanced for the refusal of the National Football League to accept our challenge of Aug. 25 [1947] to a world championship game between your champion and the All-America Football Conference champion, the only conclusion we can draw is that you feel your champion would be unable to defeat ours, or that you feel the All-America Conference is not well established as a major league. In answer to your first assumption, we hereby offer to play our second-place team against your champion."[22]

With Layden's quips about "owning a football" ringing in their ears, the AAFC owners decided that they needed to raid NFL rosters for players. Commissioner Jim Crowley told reporters, "We originally resolved not to tamper with National League players, but since the NFL snubbed us we can see no reason why we can't hire their players." At the time, the AAFC had 150 players under contract but only 4 were former NFL players.[23]

As the 1945 NFL season wound down, AAFC owners began their raiding in earnest. The Chicago Bears lost Edgar (Special Delivery) Jones to the Cleveland Browns. Jones signed a contract to play the 1946 season with the Browns, but he was under contract with the Bears for 1945. The Bears had surreptitiously signed Jones away from the Pacific Coast [Football] League's San Francisco Clippers, who had signed him to play for $500 a game.[24] While the anonymous reporter called Jones a "surprise backfield star," he had only appeared in one game with the Bears before NFL commissioner Elmer Layden ruled that he was suspended for the 1945 season. Cleveland owner Arthur McBride mocked Layden, saying, "Mr. Layden knows now that if we haven't got a football we at least have a player the National League would very much like to have."[25] AAFC owners attempted to entice long-time NFL quarterbacks Frank Filchock and Sid Luckman to defect, but without luck. Luckman admitted, "They [AAFC owners] have been hounding me for the last several weeks, and their offers have been fabulous."[26] Sportswriter Arch Ward wrote that, "In the All-America, these skyscraper checks certainly weren't out of line. The conference teams had to make a big splash quickly, and signing fabulous players was the most effective means to establish a following."[27]

NFL owners faced two disadvantages in battling interlopers. Major League Baseball had tight control over thousands of players, whom they could threaten with such reprisals as blacklisting. Because the NFL had few minor league affiliations, individual teams did not control hundreds of players.[28] An upstart football league could also gain instant credibility by signing top college prospects. It was easier to induce these highly publicized football players to sign contracts with a new league, whereas established baseball owners didn't have to worry much about a new league reaping much publicity by signing college All-American baseball players.

The Fight for Players

Because player salaries stagnated during World War II in real terms (adjusted for changes in the price level), player salaries were very low. The Philadelphia Eagles and Cleveland Rams claimed that their payrolls were $123,500 and $128,000 respectively. The Rams claimed that the $128,000 payroll was 25 percent higher than any previous payroll, and they expected to pay $190,000 in salaries for 1946. Sportswriter Stanley Frank reported that team payrolls were remarkably similar across teams, quoting Elmer Layden's survey showing a spread of only $19,000 across teams in 1941. The last-place Chicago Cardinals allegedly paid their thirty-three players a combined $45,000 that season.[29] Bert Bell told reporters that AAFC competition raised NFL team payrolls by an average of $100,000 per season. The AAFC owners could offer hefty percentage increases in the nominal salaries and still pay players less in purchasing power (real salaries) than they earned in 1941. Between 1941 and 1946, the Consumer Price Index rose by roughly 33 percent. The index rose another 23 percent by 1950.[30]

Although the salary increases seemed dramatic, they can easily be exaggerated unless adjusted in real terms.

AAFC teams quickly signed such NFL standouts as the Chicago Bears' Norm Standlee, Lee Artoe, Ace Parker, and Parker Hall. These signings helped bolster the new league in the public's opinion.[31] The raiding even included a coach; Washington Redskins coach Dudley Sargent DeGroot signed with renegade owner Dan Topping. DeGroot had coached the Redskins to an Eastern Conference title.[32] Historian Craig Coenen believes that the AAFC owners used their deep pockets to obtain their fair share of collegiate talent to go with the dozens of former NFL players they had signed.[33]

Desperate to stanch the flow of players to the AAFC, the NFL owners, along with their minor league allies (the Pacific Coast [Football] League and the Dixie League), reiterated their five-year ban from organized football (thus implying that the AAFC was "unorganized football") for any players who played for the AAFC. The owners cleverly interpreted the ban to be effective not upon signing a contract with the AAFC but upon actually appearing in a game, thereby allowing erring players to return to the friendly embrace of the NFL.[34] AAFC commissioner James Crowley warned AAFC players not to be duped by NFL salary offers designed to entice them back into the fold. Crowley claimed, "These offers sound fine on the surface, but most of them carry a clause which makes them cancelable on forty-eight hours' notice."[35] Commissioner Bell lifted the suspension of players banned for breach of their contract or their option clause in November 1949; his action may have been prompted by the William Radovich case.[36]

Both leagues began cloak-and-dagger operations, relying on secrecy to protect their chances of signing talented collegians. The AAFC proposed a "secret" draft. The owners tweaked the NFL by claiming their draft was superior to the NFL one. The AAFC owners planned to solicit information from college coaches as to which of their players would be interested in pursuing a professional career. An AAFC coach, Brooklyn's Mal Stevens, told reporters, "There's no sense in publicizing a list of players who have no intention of entering the professional field. The National League has conducted this draft system mainly to advance its own game by flaunting names of college stars before the public eye."[37] The NFL held its draft on

January 11, but withheld the names of the players. The owners continued hold secret drafts throughout the duration of the interleague strife.[38]

While football owners could count on losing thousands of dollars in the internecine struggle, they might have remembered that only the lawyers are certain winners in such disputes. When the NFL Boston Yanks decided to retaliate for the AAFC's raids by pursuing and signing Notre Dame quarterback Angelo Bertelli, the Los Angeles Dons quickly filed a lawsuit, just one of many filed by football owners during the AAFC-NFL struggle for players. The case drew interest because the Yanks claimed the Dons used underhanded tactics to sign the youngster. Bertelli himself claimed the AAFC team used "fraud and misrepresentation" when inducing him to sign the contract. He alleged that the Dons' agent did not divulge whom he represented (yet he signed the contract anyway). The Dons argued that Bertelli was a "unique" talent who was comparable to Sammy Baugh and Sid Luckman, and that he was irreplaceable, while the Yanks were put in the odd position of stating he was "just another outstanding passer." The Dons argued that they had given Bertelli $1,000 to sign the $10,000-a-year contract while he was still in the Marine Corps. Bertelli admitted signing the contract but returned the bonus before signing with the Boston Yanks. The court ruled that Bertelli had to play with the Dons. Rather than prolong the legal proceedings, Collins assented to the court's decision and encouraged Bertelli to play for the Dons. Under those strained circumstances, Bertelli played one full season with the Dons before playing three games with the Chicago Rockets.[39]

Both leagues considered setting up affiliations with professional teams in smaller cities. On occasion, NFL owners had discussed creating minor league systems similar to baseball's. Given the ephemeral nature of the postwar boom in spectator sports, it was just as well that they didn't invest too much in such teams. The owners' real purpose was to stash their redundant players without exposing them to teams in the opposing league.[40]

The legal threats and counterthreats occasionally led to bizarre rumors. The Cleveland Browns signed fullback Gaylon Smith and tackle Chet Adams, formerly of the Los Angeles Rams. At one point, a rumor circulated that the Browns would send Ted Fritsch back to Green Bay provided the Rams didn't sue over Adams and Smith. The Packers would send a "name" player to the Rams. Not only was the "player to be named later for a lawsuit to be dropped" novel, it was an interleague trade, something that Bert Bell quickly said was "absolutely out of the question."[41] Fritsch rejoined the Packers after telling the Browns he didn't want to play for them (maybe he saw how good Marion Motley was). The lawsuit over Chet Adams ended in the Browns' favor, although the judge's legal reasoning was of interest. Judge Emerich B. Freed "ruled the Cleveland Rams had ceased to exist as of the date of the transfer of their franchise to Los Angeles and that Adams's obligations under the contract became impossible of performance."[42] If his interpretation was correct, the ruling should have send shudders down the spine of any owner considering relocation, as it threatened to grant free agency to all of his players.

Major League Baseball owners watched pro football's turmoil with interest. Some baseball owners stood to benefit from the new league, as they rented their stadiums to the new teams.[43] Baseball owners, though, worried about the potential court challenges to clauses in player contracts, especially the reserve clause.

Other Fields of Struggle

At the NFL meetings, the owners ousted Elmer Layden and installed Bert Bell as commissioner.[44] Part of the NFL owners' rationale for ousting Layden was their desire to get a hard-boiled leader. Bell might have seemed an anomalous choice, given his earlier flirtation with the AAFC, but he immediately denied that the league was interested in cooperating with the AAFC: "I've got no time to worry about the All-America Conference or any other league."[45] The NFL owners were not interested in sharing their hard-won glimmer of prosperity with a bunch of nouveau-riche owners.

Some sportswriters believed the AAFC had a good chance of succeeding and cited the league's careful preparation. NFL owners had traditionally pled poverty. As a way to discourage potential entrants, such a strategy of modesty made sense, but it didn't work. Sportswriter Stanley Frank disputed the NFL's sob stories about losses, writing, "It was inevitable that a second league would make a play for the swollen profits in pro football, given greater allure by the current sports boom." He repeated the AAFC owners' claim that they were willing to lose $300,000 over the first three years as evidence of their determination.[46] The AAFC owners attempted to ensure that talent was somewhat evenly distributed. The owners also proved visionary in negotiating a $250,000 travel deal with United Air Lines.[47]

The NFL had several weapons at its disposal. The established league could use its schedule to hamper AAFC efforts. Bert Bell, NFL schedule maker by default, could arrange to give New York, Chicago, and Los Angeles the most attractive home dates in order to encroach upon rival AAFC teams' attendance in those cities. Since the NFL never had balanced schedules, its owners easily acquiesced to the gerrymandered scheduling. The New York Giants got seven home games in their eleven-game schedule, including three on the same Sundays as the AAFC New York Yankees and another pair of games on the same weekend (the Yankees sometimes played on Saturday). In a show of bravado, Tom Gallery, Yankees official, chortled, "We will play in direct competition with the Giants, Sunday for Sunday. Let the fans decide which teams they want to see." Unfortunately for the Yankees, the Giants drew over 190,000 fans versus the Yankees' 101,000 during the four weekends; both teams won their divisions.[48] The Chicago Bears got six home games, while the Chicago Cardinals, perennial second bananas of the Windy City, received just four home games. The Los Angeles Rams only got five home games.[49] The NFL used its established publicity contacts, and the league's publicity director, George Strickler, urged team public relations men to cooperate fully with media personnel at an April meeting. Some owners groused at the AAFC's publicity successes. George Halas told his fellow owners that the Chicago newspapers and Associated Press favored the AAFC Chicago Rockets over the NFL teams in the city.[50]

At least Dan Reeves's transfer of his Rams to Los Angeles gave the NFL a chance to compete for the lucrative Southern California market. There was an existing professional team, the Hollywood Bears, competing for playing dates at the Los Angeles Coliseum. If one of the leagues had gotten first choice of desirable playing dates, they might have been able to cripple the other Los Angeles rival. The Rams struck first, signing a three-year contract calling for a rental price of 15 percent of the gate plus a $6,500 per game cleanup fee. The Coliseum commission had yet to decide whether to accept the application of the AAFC's Los Angeles Dons. The commission ruled that only six professional games could be played between the last week of September and the first week of December. The Rams got five of the dates, which essentially froze the Dons out of the Coliseum. The Coliseum Commission claimed its decision to allow just one pro team use the facility was based on its concerns for the University of Southern California and the University of California, Los Angeles football programs. Before NFL owners could congratulate themselves, the Dons' owners, Hollywood big shots with political clout, began to fight back. They eventually got five playing dates at the Coliseum without having to fall back to using Gilmore Stadium (with a limited seating capacity of twenty-five thousand) or the Rose Bowl. In the event, the Dons might as well have played in Gilmore Stadium, since the club, even with a winning record, was hard pressed to attract thirty thousand fans for any of their games.[51]

The AAFC Debuts

The AAFC opened play on Friday, September 6, 1946, when the Cleveland Browns shellacked the Miami Seahawks 44–0 in Cleveland before sixty thousand fans. The game proved a harbinger of sorts, as the Browns ran off seven wins in a row before losing back-to-back games against the California teams. The Browns became the league's marquee team and garnered national publicity. Paul Brown was hailed as a genius, and NFL owners may have privately been glad they didn't have to send their best club, the Chicago Bears, to do battle against the Browns. The Browns' last two regular-season games against the Seahawks and Dodgers demonstrated the league's weakness: the combined total attendance for the two games was less than twenty-four thousand.[52]

Despite the lopsided results, *Newsweek* reported that the league ended its first season in "fairly good shape. Only three of its teams probably will make money—the Cleveland Browns, the New York Yankees, and the San Francisco Forty-Niners—but except for the badly clipped Miami Seahawks, the others are by no means breaking their backers' bankrolls."[53] The Seahawks, in fact, were in dire straits. James Crowley reported that the team's owners had not met the league's "indebtedness clause," and that the league had to cover the last two months' payroll. The Seahawks owners failed to post the $100,000 guarantee. A week later, the league awarded (actually reawarded) a franchise to Baltimore. The terms included Baltimore paying $100,000 and posting a $250,000 guarantee.[54] The Brooklyn Dodgers were losing money rapidly, despite having a natural rivalry with the New York Yankees. Reporters estimated that the Dodgers lost $250,000 in 1946.[55] The league's championship game between the Cleveland Browns and New York Yankees in Cleveland was not as lucrative as hoped, perhaps because the Browns were 13.5-point favorites. The NFL Championship Game between the Giants and Chicago Bears pulled in fifty-eight thousand fans, some seventeen thousand more than the AAFC game. The Browns, apparently confident of their ability, had challenged the eventual NFL champions to a game, but Bert Bell push the kibosh on the idea, arrogantly stating, "The winner of [our] game is the only world champion that we recognize." Bell didn't sense the irony of how small the NFL "world" was.[56]

Arch Ward, one of the visionaries who inspired the AAFC's founding, boasted that the league's inaugural season was a "tremendous show," especially in comparison the NFL's history of franchise instability.[57] The AAFC owners anticipated losses in 1946, and he claimed that they had expected $100,000 losses per season for each team for the first three seasons. He thought Cleveland, New York, and San Francisco actually made money in 1946, with the Browns being able to pay coach Paul Brown over $50,000 for his efforts.[58]

While the AAFC got off to a reasonable start, its best hopes for survival were to reach an accommodation with the NFL and to somehow improve its weak teams. Replacing Miami with Baltimore did not improve competitive balance, but the Baltimore fans appeared more enthusiastic than those in Miami. The NFL owners, some of whom had precarious finances, maintained a solid front of opposition to any agreement with the AAFC, but neutral observers believed professional football would be best served by a setup similar to Major League Baseball. One writer said the interleague struggle was eroding player discipline: "If you don't like what I [a disgruntled player] am doing, you can be saved the trouble from now on, because I am going to the other league."[59] AAFC commissioner Jim Crowley stated that he approached Bert Bell regarding a meeting to hammer out an agreement for both leagues to respect each other's player contracts, but

Bell denied this. He might have been encouraged to do so by rumors that some AAFC signees were reconsidering and wanted to return to the NFL.[60]

The Protracted Struggle

Some NFL teams were struggling, and there were reports that Art Rooney was peddling the Pittsburgh Steelers. Since many teams were doing poorly on the ledgers, peace rumors flourished.[61]

But peace was not at hand, and team owners resumed competing for players. The NFL began raiding AAFC rosters, although not always successfully. Both sets of owners eyed Army's duo of running backs, Glenn Davis and Doc Blanchard, especially when rumors floated that the Army might allow the two players four-month leaves to play football. The AAFC, recognizing the publicity coup of signing the players, encouraged the Brooklyn Dodgers to trade their draft rights to Blanchard to San Francisco, which already had rights to Davis. The AAFC's machinations were futile, as the secretary of war denied the football players' applications for leaves.[62]

During the AAFC's second season, when reported attendance remained stable across the league and actually increased for some teams, some NFL owners took to disputing the upstart league's attendance figures. Baseball owners were notorious for issuing exaggerated attendance figures when competing with rival leagues. Tim Mara of the New York Giants called the AAFC "the biggest flop in American sports promotions." He claimed that the receipts of a Yankees-Browns game at Yankee Stadium would fall far short of the $70,000 predicted. Maher and Gill list the November 23, 1947 game between the two teams as having 70,060 in attendance.[63] Such a crowd would almost completely fill Yankee Stadium. Experienced sportswriters should have been able to ascertain whether the announced attendance was grossly inflated, although, of course, they lacked the ability to gauge how many fans attended with complimentary tickets.

Although most of the AAFC teams were stabilizing during 1947–48, the Chicago Rockets continued to limp along. The franchise was inept on the field and had trouble getting over five thousand people to attend for some of their games against other lackluster AAFC teams. The Internal Revenue Department was unhappy with the Rockets, too, as the team's unpaid withholding taxes alone reached $25,596. The league eventually assumed ownership of the franchise and began looking for new owners.[64] The Rockets' prospects were not helped by the Cardinals' brief period as a contending team in the NFL.[65]

By the end of the 1947 season, sportswriter Ed Prell wrote, "The All-America Football Conference . . . definitely has carved out a permanent place of itself in major league sports." Prell believed six of the teams were close to breaking even or making a profit, although Brooklyn and Chicago were obvious weak links. The league had a total attendance of two million for exhibition, regular-season, and championship games, although some or even many of these may have been attendees with complimentary tickets. The league's ability to generate crowds in excess of fifty thousand was impressive, though. Prell thought the Los Angeles Dons and New York Yankees were enjoying larger crowds than their NFL rivals in those cities.[66] Commissioner Admiral Jonas Ingram confirmed that Brooklyn was in good standing and that Branch Rickey was willing to take over if the current owners so desired. Rickey did, indeed, step in; he took over the team in January 1948, without responsibility for the team's indebtedness. Ingram also expressed hope that new ownership would take over the Chicago Rockets. A few months later, the league took over the Baltimore Colts when the club's president admitted the team did not have sufficient funds to guarantee operation for 1948 despite relatively healthy gates in 1947. Sufficient funding was found to maintain Baltimore, and the team was able to participate in raiding NFL rosters by signing a New York Giants running back.[67]

Rickey did show initiative in his ardent pursuit of University of Mississippi quarterback Charlie Conerly: "I offered the boy more than a $20,000 bonus, and a four-year contract at $20,000 per year. I never offered any baseball player that kind of money." Rickey admitted that he may have overbid for Conerly. Despite his lavish wooing, Rickey lost out to the New York Giants, who offered much less money. Rickey, always cash-conscious, was bemused by Conerly's decision.[68] The Giants were desperate for a quarterback after the suspension of Frank Filchock, and sent halfback Howie Livingston and an unnamed player to the Washington Redskins for draft rights to Conerly. While Conerly never achieved All-NFL status, he was a mainstay in the team's resurgence. Livingston became a journeyman running back.[69]

The AAFC and NFL manipulated their college drafts again in 1947. The AAFC tried to redress the competitive imbalance by having its top teams participate in the first round and then defer drafting for most of the remainder of the first ten rounds. The championship game participants, the Browns and the Yankees, only took four selections each in the ten rounds. The usual secrecy pervaded the draft. The NFL, meanwhile, had its plans for an early draft postponed because of a playoff game between the Eagles and Steelers.[70] The AAFC's efforts may have contributed to the Baltimore Colts' improved record in 1948, but Chicago and Brooklyn continued to languish despite additional reinforcement in the form of twenty players transferred from stronger teams to the three struggling clubs. Commissioner Ingram lauded the contributing clubs: "The determination and unselfish cooperation of the representatives of the various clubs during the meeting was impressive."[71]

Shirley Povich wrote that while the Baltimore Colts were avidly seeking quarterback Bobby Layne, many of their compatriots were not going into the player market with "much enthusiasm." In a volte-face, Admiral Ingram chided wealthier AAFC teams for not doing more to help Baltimore and Brooklyn with players. The admiral became petulant and exclaimed, "They can get a new commissioner if they don't adopt some of my suggestions for the good of the league. So far the temptation to load up with all the talent they can get and turn nothing loose to a weaker club has been too great for some of our owners. I thought I was working with smarter people."[72]

Sportswriter Herman Goldstein reported signs of improved competitive balance, based mostly on Baltimore's improvement, but Ingram's complaint about competitive imbalance was accurate. The Brooklyn and Chicago clubs had three wins between them, while Cleveland and San Francisco won twenty-six of twenty-eight games. None of the other clubs had winning records.[73]

Peace Feelers

At the end of the 1948 season, owners renewed interest in a settlement. While NFL stalwarts George Halas, George Preston Marshall, and Tim Mara remained staunch foes of conciliation, some of their peers began to waver. Philadelphia Eagles owner Alexis (Les) Thompson told *Sport* magazine writer Al Stump, "We'll either get smart and make peace with the All-America Conference — or we'll all go bust." Stump observed that the two leagues' rivalry benefited football fans and players, as it meant more games and higher pay. He worried, though, that those gentlemen funding the party had little patience and had dwindling wherewithal with which to continue. Thompson pointed out that San Francisco 49ers owner Tony Morabito averaged thirty-five thousand in attendance and still lost almost $150,000 in two years (left unsaid was how Thompson knew how well or how poorly an owner in the rival league was doing). Thompson said he purchased the Eagles in 1940, and the team sold seventy-one season tickets and attracted fewer than five thousand people per game that season.[74] He claimed that frugality limited his loss that season to $50,000. In 1947 the Eagles had a title-winning team that sold twenty thousand season tickets and averaged thirty thousand per game in attendance, but "the final figures showed an even greater *deficit* than in 1941!"[75] (italics in original) Thompson claimed that only the Bears, Giants, Redskins, and Browns earned profits in 1947. Aside from the issue of two teams competing in the same city (such as in New York, Los Angeles, and Chicago), the key issue revolved around a common draft. Thompson said he proposed such a draft, but none of the other NFL owners would even second his motion.[76]

Thompson halted his peace-seeking efforts when, at a meeting between owners of each league held in his office, Dan Topping loudly proclaimed that the Giants stood to lose $200,000 during the season, a statement that enraged the Giants and Thompson. NFL owners may have felt emboldened by rumors that Paul Brown was considering resigning as coach of the Cleveland Browns. They interpreted this rumor as an indication of Brown's loss of faith in the league.[77] Another swirling rumor, contradictory to the previous one, claimed that the NFL would admit Cleveland and San Francisco while allowing the Boston Yanks to move to New York. Obviously such a move required the approval of the Giants' Maras. As rumors go, this one was actually prescient of the final outcome.[78]

A few months later, Thompson renewed his efforts to promote peace: "I'd be a fool, if I didn't try and resolve a situation in which most of us are losing money [a reported $32,000 in 1947]." His proposal again revolved around a common draft pool, but George Preston Marshall was having nothing to do with the plan. In a revealing statement, Marshall thundered, "But less than a third of our budget goes to players' salaries. Cutting them won't solve the problem. The real trouble . . . is simple: not enough people will pay enough money to see pro football."[79] The interesting aspect of Thompson's efforts was his claim of having lost $32,000 while playing in an uncontested market and winning a championship. Thompson was reputedly wealthier than many of the owners, so a $32,000 loss shouldn't have threatened his solvency. Surely he could have outlasted the flagging AAFC. Conversely, those NFL owners without a championship team and without deep pockets may well have been losing greater sums and may have been becoming fatigued.

There were signs that the AAFC owners were flagging. A Cleveland Browns official admitted that the Chicago Rockets required a $300,000 infusion of cash from Cleveland, New York, and Los Angeles in order to finish the 1948 season.[80] Despite this admission, the AAFC declared it would operate with eight teams in 1949. Los Angeles Dons owner Benjamin F. Lindheimer reported that league attendance fell by 5.4 percent between 1947 and 1948 but claimed this was "less than the average drop for sports and amusement industry as a whole."[81] A group of Dallas investors expressed interest in fielding a team if the Chicago Rockets folded. To guard against teams becoming bankrupt at midseason, AAFC officials required evidence that each team had at least $200,000 in "free and unpledged cash."[82]

Sportswriter Jimmy Powers, though, believed until late 1949 that the AAFC was viable and excoriated Tim Mara's refusal to settle with the upstarts.[83] Bert Bell said there was "no truce" between the two leagues, but on the next day he announced that the two groups of owners would meet. Alexis Thompson still advocated peace, and this time George Halas joined in by calling for a "sensible solution."[84] The meeting between AAFC commissioner Jonas Ingram, an AAFC committee, and the NFL officials foundered on the fate of the Baltimore and Buffalo teams. Both teams refused to go quietly into football oblivion. The NFL indicated it would accept only Cleveland and San Francisco. One can imagine that NFL owners coveted the San Francisco franchise as a traveling partner to the Los Angeles Rams, and the Browns' status as a premier team made them attractive. NFL owner Ted Collins wanted to relocate his franchise to New York and play in Yankee Stadium (presumably after merging ownership with Dan Topping). Other AAFC owners hoped to buy partial ownership in NFL teams. Brooklyn was not involved; as the franchise had lost heavily, it was not attractive to the NFL.[85] Sportswriter Dan Daniel attributed the failure of negotiations both to Tim Mara's antipathy toward Dan Topping and to George Preston Marshall's refusal to countenance a franchise in Baltimore, which he considered a violation of his territorial rights. Marshall reputedly shouted, "There can be no peace as long as Baltimore remains." Marshall also implied that he couldn't understand how Tim Mara could consider letting the Boston team play in New York.[86]

Because peace promised financial relief, if not prosperity, both sets of owners continued to meet. The owners continued to pursue their individual self-interest as the spirited bidding for collegiate talent erupted again. Some observers felt that even if a complete accord could not be reached, a truce involving a common player draft would be an astute move.[87]

Dan Topping reiterated his plans to have professional football at Yankee Stadium in 1949, whether it was his Yankees team or another team, presumably the Boston Yanks. In the intertwined world of professional sports, Horace Stoneham, who was the landlord of the football New York Giants and the president of the baseball New York Giants, was encouraging Topping to resolve the strife, as he felt having three football teams in the city was one team too many. Both Topping and Chicago Rockets president R. E. Garn indicated that they would either fold or remain in the league, whichever would best serve their fellow AAFC owners. The Mara brothers agreed to let Ted Collins move his Boston Yanks to New York and play either in Yankee Stadium or at the Polo Grounds. Branch Rickey and his football Brooklyn Dodgers were an unknown factor. Rickey had failed to replicate his baseball success in Brooklyn with the pigskin Dodgers and was bleeding money.[88]

Scheduling difficulties had precluded an earlier attempt by a team to share New York City with the Giants. Brooklyn Tigers owner Arthur Friedlund had offered the Giants $250,000 to share the city by playing in Yankee Stadium. Because the baseball Yankees did not permit NFL games until the baseball season was over, the Tigers' proposal was not feasible.[89]

While these negotiations were taking place, Eagles owner Alexis

Thompson was fielding offers to sell his team. He wanted $250,000 and was dealing with a group of sixty buyers headed by Jim Clark, a Philadelphia politician.[90]

Rumors of peace persisted throughout January 1949. The eventual solution that was adopted after the 1949 season was essentially agreed upon, but the Baltimore-Washington situation remained unresolved, as did the turmoil in New York City. Eventually, the Brooklyn Dodgers merged with the New York Yankees (how jarring those headlines must have seemed; a Dodger-Yankee is redolent of that staple of the 1950s B movie, a scientific experiment gone horribly wrong), and the AAFC owners decided to continue for another year. The Chicago owners were undoubtedly sacrificing money for the sake of loyalty to their fellow owners. Branch Rickey, still keen on professional football, admitted, "This new team will be as much Brooklyn's as New York's. The fact that financial support was poor in Brooklyn must be traced to the poor team we gave the Brooklyn fans. . . . I'm certain they will travel to the Stadium."[91] Rickey's prediction proved chimerical.

As the peace embers flickered, owners began pointing fingers. Buffalo owner James Breuil blamed George Marshall and Tim Mara because of their refusal to accept continuation of the Buffalo Bills and Baltimore Colts. Breuil revealed that Marshall was willing to let the Colts' owners buy into the Redskins, but at a "ridiculous figure." The Maras were willing to let Breuil buy into a merged team comprised of Collins's Yanks and Topping's Yankees. Breuil turned down the offer, since he wanted Buffalo to remain in professional football. Given the weakness of the Yanks and Yankees, his decision was probably astute. Bert Bell denied Breuil's allegations and stated that Tim Mara wasn't at the meeting, nor did Marshall obstruct anything. "In accusing Mara and Marshall of blocking so-called 'peace,' Mr. Breuil is speaking strictly for Buffalo consumption."[92] The NFL owners may still have felt they had little to lose by waiting out the faltering AAFC and then bringing in the two or three most desirable teams.

When the Dodgers and Yankees merged, the putative beneficiary was the new, resurrected Chicago Hornets, formerly the Chicago Rockets. The Dodger-Yankee team took seven of the Dodgers' players and the remaining twenty-nine went to bolster the new Hornets. While the Brooklyn–New

York team went 8-4, the Chicago team staggered to a 4-8 record in 1949. The two teams occasionally had crowds of thirty thousand, but almost as often had crowds of less than fifteen thousand. Reflecting the AAFC's parlous state, the owners voted to trim playing rosters from thirty-five to thirty-two players.[93]

Sportswriter Grantland Rice, famed for the "Four Horsemen of the Apocalypse" image of Notre Dame football, excoriated the owners for failing to come up with an agreement. Rice thought that two leagues in a setup similar to baseball's would have been good for the game. Rice quoted Steelers owner Art Rooney, who indicated he would not operate the Steelers in 1950 unless a deal was made. Rice also thought NFL owners would not be sorry to see the Los Angeles Rams (and Dons) disappear, citing the expense of traveling to Los Angeles. Another reporter, though, contested Rice's dismal depiction of Pittsburgh; Pat Livingston claimed in October 1953 that "so solidly had [coach Jock Sutherland] built the Steelers that, even during the battle between the National League and the All-America Conference, the Steelers made money each year of the costly war."[94]

The 1949 season began inauspiciously. Attendance was off, and sportswriter Harry Sheer wrote, "Gate receipts are dangerously off, wavering towards red-ridden books — and we didn't mean Joe Stalin's library. As of today, only two of the total of seventeen clubs are reasonably certain of clearing 1949 in the black [Bears and Redskins]."[95] Sheer went on to quote a football owner truism, "One bad Sunday can put you into the red for the entire year." He also listed the expenses of running a team; they totaled $600,000, including $60,000 for sundry items. He figured that NFL teams needed twenty-five thousand paid admissions per game and AAFC teams needed thirty thousand to break even and noted the importance of season-ticket receipts, of which the Bears and Redskins were the chief recipients.

The Peace Accord

"Give peace a chance" surfaced again even before the end of the 1949 season. A Chicago newspaper claimed the two leagues would merge into a twelve-team circuit, but both commissioners, Bell of the NFL and O. O. (Scrappy) Kessing, denied the rumor.[96] Paul Brown, though, couldn't resist using the rumors to castigate George Preston Marshall as the real culprit for the failure to reach an agreement. Brown claimed he heard Marshall tell struggling owners they should "get out of football"; he also said that Dan Reeves "spoke scathingly to me of what he thought of George Preston Marshall for holding up the peace, and by so doing driving other club owners to the wall." Brown believed that Bert Bell misled reporters when he told them that nine NFL owners opposed including Baltimore in any settlement, but this may have been in response (and in resignation) to Marshall's insistence that he would never accept a Baltimore club. In a subsequent article, Cleveland owner Mickey McBride echoed Brown's statement, as he was certain the Tim Mara would prove reasonable. McBride claimed his payroll went from $180,000 in 1946 to $270,000 in 1949, although part of this rise no doubt emanated from the continued success of his team.[97]

Marshall's intransigence, even in the face of the unanimity clause, should have been resolvable. Economists would suggest a side payment to him to acquiesce in the "violation" of his territorial rights, and, in fact, months later, the Baltimore owners made a payment to Marshall, although the other owners could have pooled money to placate him. In fact, Marshall himself pointed the way to a resolution. By December 1949 he was willing to negotiate with the Baltimore Colts if they would satisfy NFL admission requirements and pay the Redskins for trespassing upon his territorial rights.[98]

A week later the owners agreed to a settlement. Thirteen teams would comprise the National-American League, an unwieldy title that would quietly revert to the National Football League in 1953, along with the elimination of the American and National Conferences, renamed as the Eastern and Western Divisions. Baltimore, San Francisco, and Cleveland joined the ten NFL teams. The Chicago Hornets disappeared without a struggle. The Los Angeles Dons merged with the Rams, while the Bills' owner, James Breuil, purchased an interest in the Cleveland Browns. Ted Collins purchased Dan Topping's New York Yankees and merged them with his transplanted New York Bulldogs. In return for acquiescing to the Bulldogs' invasion of their territory, the New York Giants were to receive six players from the former Yankees. The thirteen remaining teams retained rights to their current player rosters. They conducted a draft of college players from a common pool, although both leagues had drafted some players in early drafts. The fate of the players on the teams that folded remained undecided.[99]

The Aftermath

In the aftermath, some observers gave Horace Stoneham, owner of baseball's New York Giants, credit for the agreement. Stoneham, as landlord for the football Giants and potentially for the New York Bulldogs, wanted peace so that professional football would survive and gate receipts at games in New York City would increase. He summoned Bert Bell and J. Arthur Friedlund, the AAFC representative, to his office. From there, they got Marshall's assent to allowing Baltimore into the league. Marshall ignored rumors that he had blocked any agreements in the past because of his refusal to countenance a Baltimore franchise and said, "My only comment on the settlement, is that I'm glad Baltimore at last gets a chance to get into major league football." Of course he demanded and received an indemnity from the Baltimore owners, but he proved coy in responding to a reporter's query about the nominal fee: "You're from Washington. You ought to know that anything under one billion dollars is considered nominal in this town."[100] Baltimore agreed to indemnify Marshall $100,000 for "invading" his territory. After the Colts lasted just one season in the NFL, Marshall refunded $50,000 to Abraham Watner, the Colts' owner.[101]

Tim Mara explained the financial aspects of the agreement. NFL owners were concerned about the Los Angeles Dons and Chicago Hornets because of those teams' low average net ticket prices of $1.61 and $1.82 respectively. Mara claimed that teams needed to both attract large crowds and also get an average net ticket price of $2.50 to be successful. (He politely declined to state another obvious reason for not wanting the Dons and Hornets: they competed with NFL teams in those cities.) He detailed how the NFL owners warmly embraced the San Francisco franchise because it would enable owners to mitigate the cost of traveling westward.[102] Assuming the Giants had to play a fixed number of road games, though, his analysis is flawed. The owners should have been concerned only about the cost difference between going to Los Angeles and going to another league city.

Mara also thought the merger was good because the players would be concentrated on thirteen instead of seventeen teams. He hoped this would result in more evenly matched teams than in the past, as he feared a repeat of the AAFC experience, in which the Browns' dominance appeared to hurt everybody's gate, even Cleveland's. He lauded Bert Bell's efforts and claimed five of the ten NFL teams were in the black for 1949.[103]

Ted Collins was excited about being able to shift his team to the Yankee Stadium, while his New York counterpart, Jack Mara, chortled, "Of course, we're happy about the 'war' being over. Now, maybe, the football writers can write football instead of finance." Topping explained that he had learned that "baseball and football could not be operated by the same organization and, as everyone knows, baseball is the primary interest of the New York Yankees." Bert Bell had to dampen enthusiasm about the agreement by stating there would be no championship game between the Cleveland Browns and the eventual NFL champion in 1949, because the league constitution barred such games.[104]

All would not continue to be sweetness and light between the New York owners, with a dispute brewing over the six players from the defunct Yankees. Topping later stated that he had long been willing to step out of football and become a football landlord at Yankee Stadium if it meant peace.[105] Collins and the Maras argued over which "six players" the Giants would get. Bert Bell finally resolved the issue by having the two teams alternate choosing players until the Giants got their six.[106]

After the Browns defeated the 49ers in the AAFC Championship Game, Paul Brown groused about the proposed conference alignments. He didn't think Cleveland would fare well at the (visiting) gate playing Detroit, the Chicago Cardinals, Los Angeles, Baltimore, and San Francisco.[107]

Brown's remark indicated that while peace was at hand, settling the details remained contentious. Owners began jockeying for the best schedule matchups. Some teams wanted to retain old rivalries. Many of the established NFL teams wanted to avoid the West Coast road trips. Because there were thirteen teams in the league, setting up balanced divisions was impossible. For businessmen with limited valuable time, NFL owners (and their newfound AAFC chums) were willing to spend hours and days haggling over relatively minor points. Brown's boss, Mickey McBride, whined, "Unless we get what we need in personnel to fill our gaps plus a place in the division with the better clubs, then we'll not be interested in the new league and we'll be out of business." His dream division lineup included the Eagles, Redskins, Bears, Giants, and Lions.[108] Bell ultimately stepped in and arranged the divisions and schedule. The Baltimore Colts were designated as a swing team, the one team that would play each of the other twelve teams. The divisional lineups were similar to those stated in the original merger agreement, and to the lineups that Bell had planned from the beginning.[109]

The owners finally settled on a method for distributing players. Bert Bell's brother, John, a distinguished jurist who might have been concerned about potential antitrust issues, advised "definitely against the distribution of, or the making of any list pertaining to the distribution of any players on the reserve list of Buffalo, Chicago Hornets, Los Angeles Dons, or the New York Yankees with the exception of those members of the New York Yankees team who had been turned over by the terms of the Agreement by Mr. Topping to the Commissioner's office."[110] The college draft would include professional players who were members of the New York Bulldogs, while other professional players who had been members of now-defunct AAFC teams or who had been cut as rosters were adjusted would be placed in a separate draft pool.[111]

The last AAFC commissioner, O. O. Kessing, could not accept reality and expressed his displeasure of the agreement, and he hinted that the AAFC would continue playing. He wanted two separate leagues that would meet in a championship game. Some of the former AAFC teams did not give up hope of joining the NFL. Buffalo fans sought to demonstrate their support for the Bills by purchasing five-dollar and ten-dollar subscriptions to fund a resurrected team. Bert Bell, while claiming admiration and respect for the Buffalo fans' enthusiasm, put off the franchise with vague promises of future consideration. His statement, "While I don't say Buffalo will get a franchise, I certainly can't say that the city won't," was a masterpiece of doublespeak.[112] Buffalo residents contributed more than $250,000, and the committee in charge of bringing pro football back to the city raised its goal to $500,000 to ensure solvency. Bert Bell announced that NFL owners would consider adding Buffalo and Houston. Glenn McCarthy, a Houston oilman, headed the group seeking a Houston club, although he also claimed that he was willing to buy the Cleveland Browns and move them to Houston. Bell's announcement included two conditions: "First, that the new franchises gain unanimous approval from the thirteen NFL owners, and second that they would fit into the schedule." He claimed that making a schedule for thirteen teams was easier than for fourteen and fifteen, and said that scheduling sixteen teams "is like 'rolling off a log.'"[113]

Bell later told Buffalo fans that it wasn't the franchise money that mattered but season ticket sales, so in a Pavlovian response, Buffalo fans signed fourteen thousand season-ticket pledges. Bell probably knew that Buffalo would not get unanimous support from the owners, particularly the New York Giants' owners; he also probably knew a blunt denial of their application could raise the ire of prominent politicians in upstate New York. The league turned down a motion, made by George Preston Marshall, to expand to fourteen teams. Some of those dissenting (Los Angeles, San Francisco, and both Chicago teams) stated they were concerned about the problems of a fourteen-team schedule, which seems disingenuous given that a thirteen-team schedule meant imbalanced conferences and bye weeks.[114]

Even with peace, AAFC and NFL participants could not resist hurling brickbats at each other. Otto Graham joked that the AAFC absorbed the NFL in the merger and that the Browns would "do all right" in the NFL, while blaming Marshall for the delay. Marshall, never one to avoid an opportunity to make an ill-humored insult, retorted that the Graham might not "be able to hold a job in the new league." Since these insults occurred at a league function, one is entitled to wonder whether the exchange was rehearsed. Sportswriter Shirley Povich had an astute reading of the situation: "If Marshall didn't [enjoy the exchange], he will start taking some satisfaction out of the episode next season when he counts the gate receipts of the Redskins-Browns game."[115]

The big losers were fans of the now-defunct AAFC teams in Los Angeles, Chicago, Buffalo, and New York City. Players were also big losers. There were now fewer roster slots among the surviving teams; in addition, the common draft meant there was less competition for draft choices. Sportswriter Stan Baumgartner noted the immediate drop in salary offerings: "Before the peace, [Leon] Hart was said to be asking $25,000 a year. Now he will be lucky to get $15,000." He predicted that players would "be thankful" to get $200 a game. Bert Bell announced, "Players' salaries will be predicated strictly on the financial condition of the clubs and the patronage of the league."[116] Bell, however, received a salary boost and a contract extension for his efforts.

Sportswriter Joe Williams sounded a note of optimism as the 1950 season opened:

> If pro football is ever to establish itself as a major sport on a sound finan-
> cial basis, it would seem now is the time — granting the world does not
> come apart at the seams in the meantime. . . . Artistically, pro football
> should reach an all-time peak this season. Peace was desirable and to
> an extent will prove profitable at the gate, but no guarantee came with it
> that there no longer will be deficits. There never has been a season in 30
> years of trying that pro football, as a league operation, made money. In
> this respect it is an operation without precedent in the history of sports.

Williams said that Tim Mara admitted that the Giants have "done little better than break even for his 26 years in the league."[117]

Even before the 1950 season began, a dubious nostalgia for the AAFC arose. George Preston Marshall lamented the demise of the AAFC because the leagues' strife had created reams of publicity. Some of the other owners agreed with him and lauded his suggestion of putting a league publicity office in New York City.[118]

How good were AAFC teams? No one knows for certain, of course. One clue rested with reporters' summation of top playing talent. For two seasons, the Associated Press named All-Pro teams. The writers named six NFL and five AAFC players for 1948. In 1949 seven NFL players were among the eleven on the "first team" and six were among the eleven on the "second team" in *The Sporting News*' postseason honors.[119] These results implied that football writers thought AAFC teams at least had some excellent individual talent.

Why the NFL Triumphed

The NFL was unable to keep the AAFC from getting sufficient numbers of quality players. Its secret draft and threats of blacklists failed to deter players from signing with AAFC teams. The NFL's attempt to use the schedule to weaken AAFC New York, Chicago, and Los Angeles franchises had limited success. While the AAFC's Chicago team staggered throughout the four seasons, this may have been because of its poor record on the field and its misfortune in having to face resurgent Bears and Cardinals. New York and Los Angeles proved contested battlegrounds throughout the four seasons.

Perhaps the NFL benefited more from AAFC defects and missteps than from any of its own stratagems. The AAFC was not helped by instability at the top; it employed new commissioners on an almost yearly basis. The NFL benefited from Bert Bell's strength and pugnacity. The Cleveland Browns' dominance, while creating national attention for the league, proved a mixed blessing. As half the teams in the league were consistently weak on the field, the viable franchises struggled to survive. If anything saved the NFL, it was Paul Brown's genius, in that the competitive imbalance weakened some of the AAFC teams. The AAFC's personnel remained proud of their efforts, as reflected in the preface to the league's posthumous publication reviewing the 1949 season: "That the performances of AAFC players and teams may be available to the present generation of writers and commentators, and that they may be preserved for future football historians, this supplement to the *1949 Record Manual* is published."[120]

2

PROSPERITY AND ITS DRAWBACKS

The NFL's success against the AAFC should have ushered in an era of prosperity. Prosperity, though, was not without risk, including the risk that prosperity would attract interlopers. The NFL would face threats to its hegemony within a decade of defeating the AAFC.

The Canadian Threat

Major League Baseball had withstood a challenge from Mexican millionaires right after World War II. Just as they were ready to bask in newfound prosperity, the National Football League owners found themselves fighting football owners from Canada.

The Canadians played a slightly revised game of football, with a ban on blocking in the open field, three downs for a first down, and the "rouge," a special kick play, being the main differences.[1] The Canadian teams had a quota on American players. Because the crowds were smaller, Canadian owners could not and did not want to field teams entirely composed of higher-salaried American players.[2]

Almost as soon as the AAFC and NFL reached an accord, Canadian owners began raiding American rosters. The early 1950s witnessed Canadian signings of several prominent American players. The Americans responded by challenging the Canadian contracts in the courts and, eventually, by raiding Canadian rosters. Los Angeles Rams four-time All-NFL tackle Dick Huffman; New York Giants defensive guard and captain Don Ettinger; Chicago Cardinals center Bill Blackburn; and Philadelphia Eagles end Neill Armstrong signed contracts with Canadian teams after the 1950 season. Quarterback George Ratterman became the epitome of a roving player. The New York Yankees inherited Ratterman from the defunct AAFC Buffalo team. Ratterman signed a contract with the Montreal Alouettes before completing his pro career with Cleveland. The Rams and Yankees quickly filed restraining orders to prevent their players from going north. Armstrong reportedly returned to the Eagles briefly after paying a $2,000 fine, while Ratterman decided to quit the Alouettes despite a $20,000 contract.[3]

The raids continued throughout the 1950s. While the Canadians' actions were not a serious threat to the NFL, their player raids gave players leverage in their ongoing salary struggles with NFL owners and kept player salaries from dropping by as much as owners desired. For African American players, Canada promised to be an alluring haven. There was less institutionalized prejudice, and black players could find offseason jobs, even teaching and coaching in white schools.[4] Bert Bell's assessment in 1955 was accurate: "[Canadian teams have] taken about forty or fifty American players, but if a ballplayer don't [sic] want to play for you, what good is he? Our owners get sore, the same as I would if I was an owner. I don't want to lose anybody, either, but we've got all the good players we need, and the world isn't coming to an end."[5]

Bell explained that the American owners particularly disliked the Canadian tactic of enticing players currently under contract with NFL teams, although he probably also meant American players without a signed contract but still under their option year. He explained, "We do not want to lose outstanding players, but if they outbid us we have no complaint. . . . A highly-publicized college star is of value for advertising purposes during the training season, but if he flops in exhibition games, he is worth little." He denied that the NFL maintained a blacklist of players who had jumped leagues. Some sportswriters believed that there were plenty of good players available, so the Canadian raids didn't affect the quality of play in the NFL.[6]

At first individual NFL teams contested the Canadians, but by 1954, the league waged a collective effort to stymie the Canadian raids. American owners were angry at having lost some of their top collegiate draft picks to the Canadians, such as the Baltimore Colts' loss of Billy Vessels and the Philadelphia Eagles' loss of first draft choice Johnny Bright. Vessels claimed the Colts offered him just $6,500, while Edmonton offered at least $10,000; in addition, he got a job selling leases for the Imperial Oil Company.[7]

Bell hired a former Canadian player and coach, later identified as Robert Snyder, to educate American college players about conditions in Canada. The Canadians cried, "Foul!" at this "propagandist," who denigrated Canadian football to American players. Bell blandly replied, "If he means we are telling the American players the truth about Canadian football, then we've hired a propagandist." This hired mouth emphasized the friction between Canadian and American players, friction which arose from the Americans' heftier paychecks.[8] Darrell Royal, who was coaching for Edmonton and who later gained renown as the University of Texas football coach, said the NFL was "putting on a front" with their propagandist.[9]

The leakage of established NFL stars included the Cleveland Browns' Mac Speedie and Philadelphia's Bud Grant. The British Columbia Lions' signing of Arnie Weinmeister, perennial All-Pro tackle of the New York Giants, ignited renewed hostilities. Weinmeister claimed the Giants told him after he signed his 1953 contract that the team planned to replace him in 1954. Weinmeister reportedly earned $11,000 playing for the Giants, making him one of the highest-paid linemen in the game. The Giants maintained, of course, that Weinmeister was legally their player under his option year.[10] Bert Bell coolly dismissed the importance of the Weinmeister signing, using his educated voice for once, "C'est la guerre," before lapsing into slang: "The war is on — and we'll give it to 'em with both barrels. We have been willing to go along, live and let live. But now they have fired the big shot and we'll let 'em have it."[11] George Preston Marshall was more sanguine: "Canada doesn't have the parks nor the population for operating football as the National League operates. The only way they can wage war is definite financing by individuals who are willing to absorb big losses for the sport of it. A few tough years and those fellows will toss in the sponge. If we start going after their men, we'll make 'em curl up."[12]

NFL retaliation took the form of raiding Canadian teams. The New York Giants signed Alex Webster and Tex Coulters away from the Montreal Alouettes. Webster had never played in the NFL, while Coulters had previously played six seasons with the Giants. The Chicago Cardinals signed Canada's Most Outstanding Player of 1954, Sam Etcheverry, but they had to wait until 1961 for him to play for them.[13]

The NFL had to take the Canadians more seriously after Canadian owners signed a television contract with the National Broadcasting Company (NBC) worth a few hundred thousand dollars. The television contract bolstered the Canadian teams' finances. Most of the teams were civic institutions similar to the NFL's Green Bay Packers. As sportswriter Keith Munro described it, "If there are profits, these are plowed back into the sport. If there are losses, there is usually a millionaire handy to take up the slack."[14] The television money enabled the Canadian teams to upgrade their playing talent by making additional raids on NFL rosters and talented collegians. Munro estimated that ninety Americans played in Canada during 1953 but expected that number to rise.

While officials of the two leagues occasionally met to resolve differences, the negotiations were hesitant and were marked both by suspicion and by the difficulty in resolving the lawsuits currently wending their way through the court systems. Bell emphasized that the key issue for the NFL was preventing "contract jumping" and honoring the option year.[15] Even with an agreement regarding players currently under contract, the Canadian teams would still be able to compete for prized collegiate players.

Toronto and Vancouver proved stumbling blocks to an agreement. Toronto was unwilling to relinquish any players it had signed who were under contract or option with NFL teams, especially one Tom Dublinski; Toronto's intransigence irritated the other Canadian owners.[16] In frustration, the Canadian Big Four League, comprised of eastern teams, decided to rescind its decision to honor player options. Canadian teams quickly signed Gil Mains of Detroit and Don King of Cleveland. Bert Bell had promised that Montreal rather than Detroit could have Gordon Malloy, a disputed collegian, but when the Canadian teams launched their latest raids, Bell revoked the deal and awarded Malloy to the Lions.[17]

With the leagues unable to reach an accord, individual team owners began negotiating agreements. Bell encouraged NFL owners to do so in the hope that enough Canadian teams would sign such agreements to exert pressure on the holdouts. Washington and Calgary signed a "no raiding" agreement. George Marshall agreed to call off a damage suit filed in the wake of the Dick Modzelewski and Bob Morgan signings, while Calgary agreed to pay the Redskins a "substantial sum" to settle the suit. Washington agreed to let Morgan play for Calgary, while Calgary agreed to nullify the contract with Modzelewski. The plan worked to the extent that the Western Interprovincial Football Union, four western teams, amended its bylaws to prevent any of its clubs from signing any NFL player under contract or option, which was the NFL's goal.[18]

The NFL gained an impressive legal victory the next month. Former Chicago Bear Frank Dempsey signed a contract with the Hamilton Tiger-Cats. The federal court awarded the Bears $100,000 and an injunction prohibiting Dempsey from playing for the Tiger-Cats. The two teams quickly settled for a nominal sum. With this legal precedent, Canadian signings of established NFL players became rarer as few NFL players completed their option year, a fact that would hinder true free agency in the years ahead.[19] The Canadians also lost a lawsuit concerning Tom Dublinski. The court ruled that the player had breached his contract with the Detroit Lions when he signed with Toronto. The judgment enjoined him from playing for Toronto until 1956 and ordered Dublinski to pay the costs of the court action: $19. The Lions did not fare as well in subsequent rulings, and Dublinski never played in the NFL. Eventually a Canadian court awarded a judgment of $6,950 against Dublinski in favor of the Lions.[20]

Rumors of peace persisted throughout 1955 and into 1956. By February 15, 1956, Bert Bell and Ralph Cooper, chairman of the Canadian Football Council, came to an agreement to recognize and respect each other's contracts. The remaining issue concerned what to do about players previously "stolen." As with the Korean War problem of how to return prisoners of war, the NFL wanted forty-five players returned, while Canada wanted thirteen back. Students of Cold War movies might envision a hypothetical exchange of players across a bridge on the international boundary.[21] Even after the agreement, NFL owners distrusted their Canadian counterparts, so they implemented an early draft for college players. It was slated for November 26, before the regular season ended and before the correct draft order was established. George Preston Marshall criticized the precipitous draft and stated his belief that the Canadian teams offered little competition for collegians, given the Canadians' parlous financial situation.[22]

NFL owners eventually accommodated the Canadians to the extent of allowing a Canadian League game to be played in Philadelphia before the NFL regular season. The game was played in order to raise money for charity, although some observers thought it possible that it would draw a larger crowd than had ever attended a regular Canadian game.

The Canadians employed more than 150 American players in 1959, and they continued to pay higher salaries than their American counterparts, although none of the newspaper articles ever explicitly stated whether the contracts were in Canadian or American dollars. One player said, "Up here, football's fun."[23]

As with the short-lived Mexican League baseball effort, which never endangered Major League Baseball, the Canadian football teams never directly threatened the NFL. The main effects of the Canadian and Mexican leagues on American leagues were to bolster player salaries and to raise questions about player contracts.

The American Football League

In the wake of the successful 1958 championship game between the Giants and Colts and the near-decade of relative prosperity, NFL owners could be forgiven for feeling smug. Their success, though, sparked a new conflagration that threatened to immolate their prosperity.

While the NFL was solidifying its popularity, Major League Baseball was scrambling to adjust to the new realities of postwar America's population shifts. Both football and baseball owners, however, were slow in recognizing the burgeoning population centers in the West and South. Growing cities and their citizens craved the "big league" cachet. The Major Leagues were wary of antagonizing Congress and triggering scrutiny of antitrust issues; they hoped the relocation of five teams would placate the restless legislators. When the baseball Dodgers and Giants left New York for California, they created a void that tempted entrepreneurs. William Shea and Branch Rickey immediately saw that there were enough open cities to form a new baseball league.

NFL owners, with their stable franchises (aside from the Chicago Cardinals) were also complacent with regard to expansion. No doubt the owners were hesitant to upset their prosperity. The addition of new teams was fraught with risks. New, weak teams would dilute the established teams' ability to draw fans to every game. New teams meant more competition for players.

Economists and business professors have coined the term "spatial pre-emption" to describe a situation in which incumbent firms fill enough market niches to prevent the entrance of new firms into the industry. Breakfast cereal companies may market unprofitable cereals in an effort to plug any possible openings for a new competitor. Sports leagues, too, can practice spatial preemption by putting a team into almost every large city capable of supporting one. Leagues have sometimes found that having multiple teams in very large cities such as New York or Los Angeles will keep a rival league from placing a viable team there.

During the 1958 hearings, legislators queried NFL commissioner Bert Bell about the possibility of expanding the league or creating a new league. The legislators clearly wanted more professional football teams, although, at the height of the Cold War, it is odd that legislators cared so much about football. Bell, who had been having confidential conversations with Lamar Hunt of the nascent AFL, blurted that there was a new league in the offing. No doubt he figured such news would placate the legislators just enough to quell talk of further expansion. Bell's enthusiasm for the new league, which included claims that the NFL would welcome it, was either a calculated ploy to use the AFL or a somewhat desperate attempt to deflect demands for expansion. Bell told the legislators that he had talked to every NFL owner and none objected to a new league.[24]

The new league Bell referred to was the brainchild of Lamar Hunt. Hunt, a wealthy Texas oilman (perhaps that is redundant), had been rebuffed in his efforts to buy an existing NFL franchise in the hope of relocating it to Dallas. He was not alone in his frustration at not having gotten an existing or an expansion team. Hunt expressed an interesting philosophy to his fellow owners. The league minutes read:

> Mr. Hunt then stated that he did not feel that the new League desired to engage in a war with the older established National Football League. He reiterated his belief that the representatives in the American Football League were primarily interested in bringing professional football to their respective cities, and that if any one representing any of the six charter members of the American Football League had as his primary motive making a great deal of money out of football, or spending exorbitant

sums in the establishment of its team, such thinking was contrary to the express beliefs of the majority of the representatives.

He went on to emphasize equalization of all teams.[25]

The AAFC owners had supposedly possessed deep pockets that had enabled them to absorb losses for some time. The AFL owners included some oilmen with even deeper pockets than their AAFC predecessors. Sportswriters took note of the hundreds of thousands of dollars the owners had to sink into their teams in order to get players and to set up their franchises. The NFL, in response to the AFL, also welcomed a Texas oilman in Clint Murchison Jr., owner of the Dallas Rangers (Cowboys).

Professional team sports owners are reluctant to reveal their finances. When they are negotiating with a prospective buyer, they must, of course, open their financial records. Hunt had seen enough financial statements to have a good sense of the economics of an NFL team. He would put his knowledge to good use. On a plane ride, after being turned down yet again, Hunt put down some prospective financial figures on an airline napkin.[26] He then queried some prospective owners and NFL commissioner Bert Bell.

The fledgling AFL needed a presence in New York City. The league didn't have the mixed blessing of getting an existing NFL team to switch allegiance, so the new league needed a brand-new team. Harry Wismer, a sports announcer associated with the Washington Redskins and senior vice president of the Texas American Oil Corporation, seemed just the man to establish an AFL presence in the Big Apple. Wismer boasted that his group was prepared to spend $1 million to organize the team. The reader should note that such losses were not as bad as they might seem, since joining the NFL would have cost hundreds of thousands of dollars in expansion fees (although some of those fees might have been categorized as player purchases that could later be claimed as tax deductions). An NFL expansion team, of course, would get the "priceless" privilege of hosting known NFL teams, while all the AFL teams were nonentities. Although any AFL New York team could forget about playing in Yankee Stadium, the old Polo Grounds were available and rumors of a new, publicly financed stadium in Flushing Meadows held promise for any new team in the city.[27]

The AFL quickly arranged stadium leases. They would share three stadiums with NFL teams: the Los Angeles Coliseum, the Cotton Bowl in Dallas, and Kezar Stadium in the California Bay Area. The AFL teams in Dallas and Oakland had priority in the selection of the playing dates.[28]

As the new league coalesced, the members paid $25,000 each "as an evidence of firm faith." Each member also posted bonds of $125,000 and put into escrow some $500,000. Hunt stated, "None of us feels that we will achieve boundless success overnight. We are going into this on a sensible basis, with the idea of putting thought and money into it to succeed. . . . Everybody is prepared to face the prospect that we may have one or more losing seasons before we go over the top. The financial end is firmly held."[29]

The NFL's intransigence with regard to expansion encouraged adventurous parties to suggest new leagues. Bell claimed three new professional football leagues were in the works: Hunt's American Football League, the Trans-America League, and the International League. He singled out Hunt's group as having the best chance of success.[30] The *New York Times* reported the formation of the American Football League on August 15, 1959. Bell had earlier said the NFL would honor the American's contracts, and Hunt stated that the new league would honor the NFL's contract, although the AFL promised to compete for collegiate talent. Hunt also indicated that he asked Bell to be commissioner of all pro football, but Bell turned down the request, saying he was too busy handling NFL business.[31]

Some witnesses before a congressional committee were not as optimistic as Bell regarding a new league. Longtime player Chuck Bednarik expressed his doubts that a new league would be viable. He thought "there wouldn't be enough good ballplayers to put on a good show for the public." He didn't think there were even enough good players for the NFL to expand by two or three clubs.[32] Bednarik's worries about the supply of players was a long-standing argument by entrenched owners. Major League Baseball owners chided Branch Rickey's and William Shea's proposed Continental League, claiming the new teams would not have rosters of well-known players. Sportswriters philosophized that any prospective league would be stymied by its lack of credible players. Of course, once the established leagues approved expansion, the player shortage suddenly evaporated.

Confronted with the specter of a new rival, NFL owners pulled their old tricks out of the closet. In many ways, the AFL challenge was, as baseball's Yogi Berra is alleged to have said, "déjà vu all over again." The NFL resorted to secret drafts, chicanery over stadiums, tough talk, refusal to play the new teams, denigration, and other tricks. But the NFL's most promising tricks included expansion and a clumsy "divide-and-conquer" attempt. Bell continued to issue pious declarations of welcome: "There is room in this country for more pro football teams and the public demands 'em. There are plenty of good players for the teams." Bell did worry that the oil millionaires who comprised the bulk of the AFL owners would spend lavishly and might start raiding NFL rosters, despite their promises not to.[33] Sportswriter Joe King, remembering the frenetic bidding war during the AAFC's existence, wrote, "It is going to be fun getting out of college with an All-America football diploma this year, because there is fresh money in the pro player market. . . . An NFL source estimates that the few top prizes winding up collegiate careers this season will go for the huge sum of $30,000."[34]

The NFL had eleven solid franchises. The Bidwell family had been determined to stay in Chicago, even though their Cardinals were a lackluster franchise. By the late 1950s, though, Mrs. Bidwell considered moving to one of the growing cities in the West and South, and she worried that expansion would reduce the roster of attractive cities.[35]

The NFL announced its plans to expand shortly after Hunt and the AFL revealed their plans to start playing in 1960. Just as Major League Baseball had co-opted several of the proposed Continental League's cities, Bell and the NFL owners told reporters of their plans to expand into Dallas and Minneapolis–St. Paul. The NFL owners' plan jeopardized the AFL's Minnesota plans by enticing the Minnesota group of investors into switching leagues. The group holding the AFL franchise in the Twin Cities initially vowed that they would not shift to the NFL.[36] A few months later, Oakland became the eighth member of the AFL, beating out Atlanta. AFL commissioner Joe Foss urged AFL owners to help stock the Oakland franchise.[37]

The timing of the NFL's decision to expand to Dallas and Minneapolis–St. Paul seemed suspicious to some observers. George Halas headed the league's expansion committee. Groups representing Houston, Dallas, Miami, Buffalo, Louisville, Seattle, Minneapolis, Boston, and Denver had made attractive offers throughout the late 1950s, but Bert Bell and the NFL owners remained adamant that no expansion would occur "until weaker current members got well."[38] The league had given no indication of being willing to expand in the foreseeable future until the AFL's formation.

Lamar Hunt felt that the NFL expansion was trespassing on AFL territory and did not shy away from confrontation with Bell. Hunt claimed the cities were AFL "private property," while Bell blandly said the NFL considered them "open" to anyone. The fact that Dallas was Hunt's chosen city was not lost on anyone. Hunt blasted the NFL's overture to the Twin Cities: "The NFL is doing anything it can to prevent this league from getting off the ground, but we are in business."[39]

The NFL's offer ended up persuading the Twin Cities group to switch. The AFL initially resisted the switch but later succumbed to the inevitable and granted them permission to withdraw.[40] The bitterness over the Dallas–Twin Cities brouhaha would lead to the AFL's antitrust lawsuit against the NFL in the years ahead. Joe Foss mocked Bert Bell's testimony before the Senate Judiciary Committee the previous summer, in which Bell had claimed benign intent toward the AFL.[41] Foss, unlike his AAFC counterparts, proved better able to convince allies in Congress to investigate the NFL's activities. He had been the governor of South Dakota and had allies in the national Democratic Party, including Senator Estes Kefauver, chairman of the antimonopoly panel. Kefauver issued a statement saying he would hold hearings if the NFL tried to "push around" the AFL.[42]

Because the AFL did not have access to a large pool of players without current contracts, such as the one that existed after World War II, none of their teams could create a powerhouse similar to the Cleveland Browns. While the Browns might have been the best team in professional football in 1946, no AFL team could come close to such a boast in 1960. Many of the AFL's top players were, at best, NFL castoffs, including George Blanda (who later demonstrated his ability to lead NFL teams to victories).

The AFL held a draft of collegiate players in November 1959. Since there were no previous league standings, the owners drew lots to determine the order of selection. In order to promote competitive balance, "The selectors filled all eleven squad positions for each team in their first draft rounds."[43] The AFL held its draft before the NFL did so that AFL owners could use their head start to sign top collegians before the NFL could even contact them. The AFL draft was complicated by reports that the Twin Cities owners were going to shift to the NFL. Lamar Hunt was quoted as saying that owners anticipated that payrolls would amount to $350,000–$400,000 per club, roughly the same as NFL payrolls.[44] The league held a second draft of college stars in December. Hunt noted that the NFL teams typically had openings for a limited number of rookies each season, although he was too optimistic in citing a figure of just twenty players. His main point, though, was well taken: the AFL would have no difficulty getting enough college graduates to fill their rosters, even if many of these players were not widely known.[45]

Despite the early AFL draft, the NFL competed successfully with the AFL, getting a bare majority of its first-round choices. The Chicago Cardinals drafted George Izo, a Notre Dame quarterback, as the second pick in the draft, after the Rams selected Billy Cannon. Within five minutes of drafting Izo, the Cardinals announced they had signed him. Shortly thereafter, the Rams introduced Cannon and announced they, too, had signed their first-round draft pick, leaving the AFL's Houston owner, Bud Adams, gnashing his teeth. George Halas drafted "Dandy Don" Meredith in the third round on behalf of the prospective NFL Dallas team. The Dallas owner signed Meredith, thereby frustrating the AFL Dallas entry.[46]

There was controversy surrounding the signing of Cannon because the Rams had allegedly signed Cannon before he played in Louisiana State University's bowl game; the allegation proved true.[47] Judge William J. Lindberg ruled that the Rams contract was not valid, so Cannon played for the Oilers. The judge chided Rams general manager Pete Rozelle for taking advantage of an "exceptionally naïve . . . provincial lad untutored and unwise in the ways of the business world." Clearly, no one came out of the affair looking very good. This was probably Rozelle's biggest lapse of integrity in an otherwise admirable record.[48]

In a similar case, another judge freed Charlie Flowers, a University of Mississippi fullback, from a contract with the New York Giants. Again the judge characterized the player as "naïve." The Giants tried to sign Flowers before his team's participation in the Sugar Bowl. Sportswriter William Briordy reported that the Giants wanted Joe Foss to tell the Los Angeles

Chargers that their contract with Flowers had been invalidated. As further proof of their arrogance, John V. Mara and Wellington T. Mara included a statement: "It is our opinion that every city is a one-team city."[49] As in the battle for players with the AAFC, NFL owners proved sore losers. An NCAA council accused the NFL and AFL of signing college players before completion of their college eligibility. Rozelle claimed the NFL had adhered to a policy of protecting colleges and athletes by refusing to sign players before their classes were graduated, but his actions in the Billy Cannon case left his credibility in question.[50]

The AFL's secret draft of November 1961 resulted in an admission that the league had violated an agreement with the American Football Coaches Association not to sign any player before he had played his last college football game. In the ensuing brouhaha, Pete Rozelle threatened retaliation, piously maintaining that the AFL's act "has brought discredit upon professional football as a whole in the eyes of the colleges and the public." Foss declared the secret draft null and void, and thereby triggered a tempest when New York Titans owner Harry Wismer refused to accept the nullification and tried to sign the six players the Titans had selected. Wismer was not pleased when Buffalo picked Ernie Davis in the redraft.[51]

In normal years, the NFL's slots for rookies were limited, so the AFL found plenty of college players available. The NFL could have attempted to keep more players under contract by increasing its player roster limit. The league increased the limit from thirty-three to thirty-five for the 1957 season. The owners voted to increase the limit to thirty-six for 1960.[52]

While the NFL sniffed at the AFL player pool, a sportswriter suggested that the new league could reach parity relatively quickly: "Starting from scratch, the AFL teams naturally won't immediately match NFL standards of play. But it shouldn't take long for the new circuit to become truly major league."[53] Even with topflight talent, coaches needed time to mold their players into cohesive units. One reporter predicted that the AFL "might even produce a more wide-open game — possibly with more scoring. This is not because they have better runners, passers or receivers; it is because it is almost impossible to develop a cohesive, intelligent and dependable defense using 11 players who met as strangers on the opening day of training camp."[54]

In the perpetual squabbling over players, Pete Rozelle claimed that AFL owners were tempting NFL players to play out their option year prior to switching leagues. He labeled this "tampering." Bert Bell and Rozelle frequently boasted before Congress that the NFL-style reserve clause was far more liberal than Major League Baseball's, so, in a sense, they were being hoisted on their own petards.[55] Rozelle expressed hopes that Joe Foss would keep his AFL owners in line regarding signing players. Rozelle also told his owners to keep him informed as to whether any AFL team raided their players.[56]

Joe Foss boasted that the AFL had signed 400 players without triggering a price war with the NFL. He stated that contracts ranged from $6,000 to $15,000, with most being between $6,500 and $8,250. Foss and Hunt took pains to prevent a player war.[57]

In addition to competing for collegiate players in order to stymie the AFL, NFL owners tried to buy off Hunt and K. S. (Bud) Adams, owner of the Houston franchise, by offering to let them join the NFL. Hunt was determined to bring in all of the AFL teams and not just a few, as occurred with the AAFC. The NFL sorely underestimated the oil businessman's determination and his loyalty to his fellow AFL owners.[58]

AFL owners pondered various legal issues. Would they be able to enforce a blackout of NFL games in cities where an AFL game was being played?[59] The big legal showdown, though, came from the NFL's threatened and eventual move into Dallas. Joe Foss told reporters, "We would not consider it a kiss of love if the NFL expanded into Dallas. It would be a clear sign they intended to continue their scorched-earth policy that caused us to surrender the Minneapolis–St. Paul territory." Foss reiterated the AFL owners' decision not to tamper with NFL players.[60] AFL owners, though, did not get the congressional chest-thumping they hoped for; Senator Kefauver declined to schedule hearings on the NFL's move into Dallas, although he warned the NFL to treat the AFL with fairness: "I'm for expansion of football, but it is not a question of rights. It is a question of who has the better product in a city, if he produces it fairly, without monopolization and without pushing anyone around." Paul Dixon, the committee's attorney, cited George Preston Marshall's claim that NFL proponents of expansion were out to wreck the AFL. Marshall initially opposed expansion but voted for it when the AFL became public. As Dixon put it, "Is this a bona fide expansion or not?"[61]

While the AFL owners blustered about seeking redress from Congress or from the courts, newly minted NFL commissioner Pete Rozelle retorted, "They moved into our territory in New York and in Los Angeles and in San Francisco (Oakland). Why shouldn't we be allowed to move into Dallas?"[62] Foss eventually convinced the Department of Justice to study the Dallas situation in order to see whether there was an antitrust violation. The AFL alleged that the NFL made indirect threats to players in the form of a blacklist and claimed the new league would "go down the drain was soon as we pull the plug." They claimed the expansion was motivated by an attempt to stymie their league. Hunt and several of the AFL owners had been told, when seeking to purchase an NFL expansion team, that "expansion is several years away." Foss told the Department of Justice that "the N.F.L. was very quick to react to this threat of monopoly. [The NFL] employed three main tactics — first, to entice away A.F.L. members by promising them N.F.L. franchises; second, when this technique did not prove entirely successful, to franchise teams in cities on top of the existing A.F.L. teams, and third, to impede the new league in its efforts to obtain suitable players and coaches." Foss also included George Preston Marshall's outspoken remarks as evidence.[63] A month later, Foss announced that the AFL would seek an injunction against the NFL. He quipped, "We couldn't sit idly by and let them cut us off at the knees."[64] NFL owners, though, had other reasons to worry. For the first time in nearly a decade, their league showed a decrease in per-team attendance during the 1960 season.[65]

The AFL filed a $10 million antitrust suit against the NFL on June 17, 1960. The complaint reiterated the accusations made to the Department of Justice.[66]

The NFL's attorneys first attempted to get the suit dismissed and then claimed that the NFL's actions had not damaged the AFL. An NFL attorney used a dubious argument in which he suggested that the fact of the AFL's survival implied that the NFL had not tried to kill it. NFL witnesses cited the fact that the City of Houston denied the NFL's application to lease its stadium as the precipitating factor for the NFL placing a franchise in the Twin Cities. Dallas Cowboys owner Clint Murchison Jr. admitted that he had offered to split the NFL expansion franchise with Lamar Hunt, or even to turn it over to Hunt completely. George Halas testified that the NFL's decision to expand into Dallas and Minneapolis–St. Paul was not in response to the AFL's formation but due to a long-considered desire to expand.[67] Judge Roszel C. Thomsen eventually ruled that the NFL did not have a monopoly in professional football, so he acquitted the NFL of the charges leveled by the AFL. He stated that the AFL failed to prove that the NFL had monopoly power and that they had "undertaken some course of action to exclude competition or prevent competition." The judge stated, "Neither rough competition nor unethical business conduct is sufficient. . . . The requisite intent to monopolize must be present and predominant."[68]

Joe Foss naturally projected an air of optimism, even in the wake of the adverse judicial ruling. He told reporter Al Hirshberg that the eight AFL owners were committed to each other and would not desert and join the NFL if so invited. Foss also mentioned that the AFL was considering expanding, although one of the requirements would include the preseason sale of twenty thousand tickets. He admitted that none of the current AFL teams had such a healthy ticket base, although some had fifteen thousand. "We want all our teams to be healthy before taking new ones. We certainly want to expand — always have — but it must be an orderly expansion."[69]

The AFL, perhaps foolhardily, continued to challenge the NFL to a championship game. While the new league could hope to gain credibility from such a game, the challenge was not without risk. Had the NFL champion demolished the AFL's champion, the public's perception might have been fatally damaged. Of course, had an NFL champion played poorly or even lost, the AFL would have had priceless credibility. It was during this controversy that Pete Rozelle quipped, "It's an incongruous proposal. You don't consider playing games with people who are suing you for $10,000,000."[70]

The AFL had one asset the AAFC lacked. Unfortunately for the AAFC, television had not yet proven to be the ally of professional football that it would become in later years. Television provided no lifeline for the AAFC. The AFL exploded a bombshell in April 1960, when it announced a national television deal with the American Broadcasting Company (ABC). The deal was potentially worth $2,125,000, or $125,000 per game. Reporter Richard Shepard stated, "This is believed to be the first time that a major professional league has negotiated a broadcasting contract for all of its teams." The setup included blackouts in the area where a game was being played. Individual teams were free to arrange any radio broadcast rights and local television rights.[71] At a stroke, it became more credible that the AFL was here to stay. The league also realized Pete Rozelle's and Bert Bell's dreams of a national television contract before they could get one for the NFL. The new league, of course, had an advantage in that its teams hadn't signed individual television contracts that might have caused teams with more lucrative contracts to balk at a national one.

The AFL suffered losses and experienced disappointing attendance during its first season, but the owners' wealth and the assured television money buoyed them. Owners could hope to field better teams as their talent base converged with that of the NFL, assuming, of course, that AFL owners signed their share of each college class. Sportswriter Roy Terrell predicted, "The AFL will perform on a level with the National Football League within three years; within five, it will challenge the NFL to a postseason game for the championship."[72] Terrell pointed out that in addition to the television money, some of the teams had an adequate base of season-ticket holders. Denver had a smaller season-ticket base but owned its own stadium, so it didn't pay explicit rent (although it surely incurred maintenance and repair expenses). Terrell concluded that the NFL's success had created an audience for professional football that surpassed that of the late 1940s, so the AFL had an advantage over the AAFC: "The trouble then was that there actually weren't many pro football dollars. Today there are, and it is to the rival NFL that the AFL owes a deep vote of thanks."[73] Some of the owners could also look forward to lower expenses in subsequent years, as they had paid for expansion of some of the stadiums. While these owners may have expensed the entire cost during the first season, economists and accountants would argue that the cost should have been spread across a number of seasons, reflecting the continuing use of the expanded stadium. Terrell cited the AFL's 60-40 percent gate-share rule, which was similar to the NFL's (assuming the 15 percent off-the-top deduction for stadium rental), and its equal sharing of the national TV deal as factors that might maintain some parity between teams.[74]

Crowds at AFL games could, on occasion, give too rosy a view of the league's prosperity. Several owners gave away tickets or sold discounted tickets. Lamar Hunt admitted the league needed exposure: "We have to change the football habits of the people here [in Dallas], so we have to induce them to come to our games however we can." Hunt, of course, was in competition with the NFL's Dallas Cowboys. His crosstown rivals groused, "Exposure can kill people." Fortunately for Hunt's Texans, the Cowboys were terrible on the field.[75] In New York City, Harry Wismer's AFL Titans were doing poorly. The team announced that its opening day paid attendance was just six thousand. The team did not announce paid attendance or a turnstile count thereafter. Oakland suffered from scanty attendance, selling just forty-two hundred season tickets instead of a hoped-for twenty thousand. The Raiders admitted that their losses might have amounted to $400,000.[76]

Eventually the AFL's Los Angeles and Dallas franchises would relocate to San Diego and Kansas City. The San Diego movement was temporarily slowed when team owner Barron Hilton arranged to get the capacity of San Diego's Balboa Stadium increased.[77]

Readers probably know the denouement of the two leagues' struggles. The two leagues agreed to a merger in 1966, with Pittsburgh, Cleveland, and Baltimore eventually switching to what is now known as the American Football Conference to balance the conferences at thirteen teams each. The AFL promised, among other things, to pay $18 million in indemnities. While the indemnities may seem harsh, they were payable over a number of years. In addition, the current rate for expansion teams was not that different than the prorated indemnity.[78]

Conclusions

The AFL's experiences differed from the AAFC's. The AFL did not benefit from a backlog of players with ambiguous contractual status, as had the AAFC. NFL owners underestimated Lamar Hunt's determination and his loyalty. The AFL owners had the crucial advantage of guaranteed television money to bolster their shaky gate revenue. The television contract granted them a national audience. In addition, these owners were riding professional football's wave of popularity in the late 1950s. That popularity might not have been sufficient to support two leagues in the 1940s. The AFL also did not suffer from a dominant team. The NFL owners' usual tactics of trying to control the player supply, conducting secret drafts, and refusal to play teams in the new league failed to eradicate the AFL. The NFL, like Major League Baseball, failed to practice spatial preemption in time to prevent talk or the formation of a new league. NFL owners eventually swallowed the bitter pill of expansion, which was not appetizing; expansion meant diluted rivalries, games with new weak clubs, and increased competition for top players. The NFL's belated expansion failed to head off the AFL.

3

MEASURES OF THE NFL'S POPULARITY

After a harrowing fifteen years of economic woes and real (not football) war, NFL owners looked forward to a prosperous peacetime economy in 1946. The owners had reason to hope for a surge in the demand for professional football. What happened to NFL gate receipts, salaries, and profits during the postwar years? Since gate receipts were the primary source of revenue for NFL owners, this chapter examines them. The chapter shows that gate receipts should have been increasing between 1946 and 1960, and owners should have had the ability to pay higher salaries to players and to reap profits.

Attendance

Team gate receipts depended upon attendance and ticket prices. Most historians have cited attendance while neglecting ticket prices.

The NFL suffered a decline in attendance after the initial postwar boom, despite increasing the number of games from ten to eleven in 1946 and from eleven to twelve in 1947 (table 2). The league's jump in 1950 was the result of adding three new teams, while the drop in 1951 could be attributable to the demise of the original Baltimore Colts. This assumes that the 1946 figures were not too greatly exaggerated. Thereafter, the league stabilized at twelve teams playing twelve games each. The first unambiguous increase in attendance after the postwar boom occurred in 1952. During the 1950s NFL commissioner Bert Bell proudly announced almost yearly increases in the league's total attendance. The 1960 increase was due to the addition of the Dallas Cowboys, not to any general increase. By 1960, though, league attendance showed a healthy gain even from the postwar boom years of 1946–47, a rebound that was not shared by Major League Baseball.

Sports researchers have grown wary of pro sports attendance figures. All attendance figures are not created equal. Major League Baseball attendance figures in the *New York Times* exemplified the ambiguity between total and paid attendance. Because of the various sports leagues' revenue-sharing rules, the owners had to supply accurate counts of paid attendance to visiting teams and to the league office. In leagues such as the NBA, where there was no gate sharing, teams had to supply accurate information on gate receipts because they had to pay a percentage to the league office. NFL teams based their gate-sharing rules and funding of the league office on gate receipts and not on attendance. The league would, on occasion, announce paid attendance to the public while requiring attendance reports from its members.

In addition to the possible discrepancy between total and paid attendance, teams charged different ticket prices or sold different proportions of seats in various classifications (general admission, reserved, box). Coenen claimed that large-city teams sold a lot of cheap seats at a dollar or less per seat or less during the early history of the league.[1] Changes in ticket prices affected gate receipts in conjunction with attendance. If a team raised its ticket prices and only lost a few customers, its gate receipts would increase (this is what economists label the price elasticity of demand, that scourge of undergraduate economics classes). Examining attendance is, therefore, just a starting place in the discernment of a league's popularity.

Maher and Gill present game-by-game attendance for NFL games, which underlie the data shown in table 2. Their figures do not always coincide with information published in team media guides. In most cases, the divergences are small, but for some games, the difference in attendance ran into the tens of thousands. The NFL reported "paid attendance" to Congress in 1957; these league-wide figures usually run one hundred thousand to two hundred thousand less than the season totals shown by Maher and Gill, implying that their figures included people admitted for free or on discounted tickets. The Maher and Gill figures do coincide with the general description provided in contemporary newspaper accounts.[2]

Historian Craig Coenen described how, in the NFL's early days, owners gave out large numbers of free tickets or discounted tickets, such as Ladies' Day tickets, to swell the crowd.[3] The New York teams sometimes played doubleheaders with a high school game opening the afternoon. Unfortunately, most of the crowd left after the high school game and before the NFL game. Lest the reader find such doubleheaders strange, we note that the New York Knicks basketball team used the same promotion, sometimes with the same embarrassing result.[4]

Football entrepreneurs inflated attendance figures in the hope of enticing more fans, who presumably gauged an event's worth by its reported attendance. Sports leagues have traditionally exaggerated attendance when fighting a rival league. Sportswriters often waxed indignant or cynical about this chicanery. Tim Mara complained that the AAFC's attendance figures were "absolutely false. The All-America Conference has lost so much money [that] it is the biggest flop in American sports promotion."[5]

Unlike baseball, in which teams infrequently sold out their stadiums, some NFL teams, such as Pittsburgh and Washington, played in stadiums with such small seating capacity that owners of such teams had difficulty cashing in on a successful and popular team unless they raised ticket prices. Most owners, especially those selling a large proportion of season tickets, could not raise prices during the season. The potential for ill-will undoubtedly constrained owners from exploiting unexpected increases in popularity by raising ticket prices within seasons.

George Preston Marshall moved his team from Boston, where fan indifference or antipathy meant small crowds, to Washington DC, where he proved adept at promoting the team and putting a quality team on the field. After the war, the team wasn't so talented. The stadium, small to begin with, was in a decaying part of the city. Since Marshall continued to fill the stadium, perhaps he was content to field mediocre teams.[6]

Major League Baseball enjoyed a surge in attendance as the war wound down, and the NFL's 1945 season also seemed to be a harbinger of flush times. The league's attendance of 28,636 per game broke all records.[7] Owners bemoaned rising player salaries immediately after the war. Attendance jumped 30 percent between 1945 and 1946, though, indicating that the owners might have had sufficient revenue to meet increases in salaries, especially if they had raised ticket prices in 1946.

Of course, other entrepreneurs suspected that the burgeoning demand for entertainment meant that the time was ripe for starting new professional sports leagues. Despite the internecine feud with the AAFC, NFL per-game attendance jumped, just as did Major League Baseball's. Even the competition in Los Angeles, Chicago, and New York did not erode the NFL's per-game attendance, although one wonders whether the NFL exaggerated its figures to appear victorious in the interleague struggle. The AAFC stole some of the NFL's luster when the Cleveland Browns attracted over sixty thousand paying customers to their home debut against the Miami Seahawks; the attendance was the largest ever for a regular-season professional game. The Cleveland Rams had not approached this figure during their championship run of 1945, peaking at about twenty-nine thousand for a game with Green Bay, although the Rams' championship game set a record for gate receipts at $162,000. The Bears/Giants championship tilt of 1946 promised to far surpass the Rams' gate receipt record if the weather held. In fact, the game filled the Polo Grounds with over fifty-eight thousand fans and gate receipts were $282,955.25.[8] The attendance boom persisted in 1947, and the Los Angeles Rams showed their revenue potential when almost seventy thousand fans packed the Los Angeles Coliseum for a game with the Chicago Cardinals.[9] AAFC owners, too, had tantalizing glimpses of pro football's potential, as games in the Los Angeles Coliseum and Cleveland rivaled sellouts at Yankee Stadium.[10] College football also enjoyed a surge in popularity during the immediate postwar years, a surge that outlasted the pros' boom, which ended with the 1947 season.[11]

While NFL owners could congratulate themselves on a popular 1946 season, there were ominous trends. America's most popular mass entertainment — motion pictures — was nearing its apogee in terms of the proportion of Americans attending movies. A significant downturn, which began before the widespread diffusion of television, awaited the industry. Major League Baseball enjoyed a five-season boom before a retrenchment occurred. Television was a symptom of a transformation in American leisure from a desire for public leisure, such as motion pictures and spectator sports, to private leisure, enjoyed in the expanding suburbs, car trips, and home entertainment.

The NFL's skidding attendance figures in 1948 and 1949, if they were not triggered by increases in ticket prices, augured ill for NFL bottom lines. Sportswriter Tommy Devine blamed not only competitive imbalance, but the pros' passing game: "Forward passing is a spectacular phase of football but the pros may be giving the fans too steady a diet."[12] The Bears-Cardinals rivalry, though, heated up as the heretofore hapless Cardinals fielded their strongest editions. The 1946–48 home-and-home series between the two crosstown rivals almost sold out each of the six games.[13]

The postwar doldrums were apparent in various cities. The situation in New York was deteriorating. The teams sharing the city were all struggling at the gate. The Giants' mediocrity following their 1946 championship game appearance did not help them pull in fans. The Giants and the AAFC Yankees both won their division titles in 1946. The Giants attracted almost twice as many patrons as the Yankees did that year; this was the only season the two teams each played seven home games, as the Giants would thereafter have six home games versus the Yankees' seven in 1947–48. The next season the two teams flip-flopped in terms of attendance, as the Yankees continued to win while the Giants collapsed. The Giants' attendance collapse continued during 1948–49, and both teams sported losing records. The Yankees reported larger crowds in 1948, although Tim Mara disputed their announced attendance. The Yankees' rebound on the field was matched by a reduced total attendance, but part of the reduction may be attributed to the shorter season. Over the four seasons, the two teams' announced attendance figures were closely matched, with the Yankees having 760,000 and the Giants 828,000. Overall the Giants did better, despite the fact that the Yankees had a better record and two additional home games in 1947–48. The Brooklyn Dodgers and New York Bulldogs played before tiny crowds and were not factors. Sportswriter Tom Meany detailed the scanty crowds at many games in the metropolis. He pointed out that the Maras blamed Dan Topping for the fiasco, since the AAFC would have been stillborn had Topping remained in the NFL.[14]

What effects did AAFC teams have on NFL teams in other shared cities? The Chicago Bears and Chicago Cardinals fared well at the gate during the struggle with the AAFC. The Cardinals had their best run of success on the field during the struggle, and the Bears continued their winning ways. By contrast, the Rockets were mediocre at best and inept at worst. With two strong teams in the NFL, the Rockets' 195,000 attendees in 1946 was a credible showing. The team had its best record that season at 5-6-1.

When it had successive 1-13 records, the attendance dwindled, but it still rivaled the Cardinals' usual attendance marks. All things considered, the Rockets left a tantalizing promise of what might have been had the team been stronger. The Bears and Cardinals declined on the field after the merger, and the Cardinals' attendance sank.

The struggle in Los Angeles was bitter. While the Rams drew 901,000 during the four seasons, the Dons were close with 857,000. The two teams sported similar records the first three seasons they shared the city. The Rams suffered an attendance relapse in 1950 despite winning the division again. The team blamed the televising of its home games for the debacle. The team's attendance rebounded in 1951 and remained among the league leaders for the remainder of the period studied.

The Washington Redskins seemed immune to the comings and goings of the Baltimore Colts. While the team's attendance fell slightly between 1945 and 1946, so did its record. Washington's attendance rebounded somewhat in 1947, even though it now faced competition in Baltimore and its record continued to regress. In the two seasons that the Colts were dormant before their 1953 return (1951–53), the Redskins' attendance was stable. The Redskins had a 6-5-1 record in 1953–54, their best record in several seasons, so the Colts' revival may have forestalled any gain in attendance for Washington.

The NFL's absorption of three AAFC teams did not immediately restore per-game attendance, but hopeful signs abounded. An exhibition game between the Redskins and Rams at the Coliseum brought in ninety-five thousand fans; this was surely an auspicious start to the 1950 season. Bert Bell chortled at a luncheon, "I believe that nine of the thirteen teams in the league will make money this year. The fact that every team has been strengthened will be an important factor."[15] Despite Bell's optimism, the NFL saw attendance fall by 7 percent midway through the season. Bell attributed the decrease to Los Angeles' ill-fated experiment with television. The televising of home games coincided with a drop in attendance of sixty-six thousand for the first three games, despite the team's similar performance in the 1949 and 1950 seasons. The New York Yankees showed considerable improvement, earning six more wins in 1950 than in 1949, but the team's attendance remained scant. The Detroit Lions, also showing improvement, blamed their indifferent fan support upon inadequate newspaper publicity. Truly this was a season of discontent for league owners.[16]

Bell, of all people, used a variation of inadequate publicity to explain the situation. After pointing out that the league was better balanced and stronger than ever, he mused, "I cannot understand the small turnouts. Some blame it on television, but though I am against television, I do not think that is the reason. I feel that the owners missed the boat because of their policy on publicity." While Bell operated the league out of Philadelphia, he suggested the league needed to put its news releases on the wire services coming out of New York and Chicago: "More small towns would then be informed of what's going on, and it's no secret that many of our fans are from out of town." He further suggested going to a round-robin system rather than the home-and-home within-conference schedule. Even though he disliked television, he added, "Continued small attendance may compel us to seek revenue from that medium, which will result in even smaller turnouts. Our stadiums may have to be turned into studios."[17]

Tim Mara and the Giants must have been disappointed with attendance after they regained their monopoly of the city. When the Yankees folded, the Giants' attendance went up thirty-nine thousand between 1949 and 1950, but they won four more games in 1950 than they had in 1949. The New York Bulldogs provided scant competition. After the Bulldogs left the city, the Giants' home gate increased from 174,000 to 203,000 between 1951 and 1952. The Giants' record was worse in 1952, which might have muted any attendance gain from the Bulldogs' relocation. The Giants would not regain their popularity until 1956.

In the case of Los Angeles and New York, then, the surviving NFL teams did not gain many of the fans who had attended AAFC games in those cities. Overall attendance at professional football games remained lower for most of the 1950s than it had been during the immediate postwar years.

The NFL could take solace in the fact that an attendance downturn appeared to be general for sports. Major League Baseball saw a drop of 2.75 million in attendance after the peak in the late 1940s, signaling a decade-long funk. The motion picture industry, too, continued its decline, although the drive-in theater sector was growing rapidly, belying the "television killed the movies" thesis. College football attendance fell during the 1950 season, but pundits claimed television was hurting attendance. The East and Pacific Coast regions suffered the biggest relative drops, while the South and Southeast had increases. Although attendance began rebounding from the 1949 total, much of the resurgence occurred at a few top-ranked schools.[18] Television's effect upon attendance will be examined in greater detail in chapter 11.[19]

Although the 1950 season proved disappointing, it did end on a bright note. The league launched the Pro Bowl, pitting All-Star teams comprised of players in each conference against each other. While the game did not sell out the Los Angeles Memorial Coliseum, almost fifty-four thousand people attended the game, which was sponsored by the Los Angeles Newspaper Publishers' Association.[20]

The 1950s witnessed a continual increase in the league's total attendance. Bell generally told owners at their winter meeting that the attendance was higher than the previous year. The increases were not dramatic but steady.[21] A *New York Times* reporter mentioned the difference between the paid attendance and total attendance in 1954: 2,415,948 total versus 2,219,167 paid.[22] The Los Angeles Rams were one of the main reasons NFL attendance was so healthy. The owners underestimated the team's drawing potential when Reeves first proposed moving west. The visitors' shares from playing in Los Angeles eventually far surpassed almost any city in the league, and the talk of subsidizing travel expenses seemed silly in retrospect.[23]

Burgeoning demand for tickets was reflected in advance sales. By 1956, the Detroit Lions were looking to exceed their record total of 36,000 season tickets, and they were not alone. The Bears hoped for $600,000 in advance sales, while the Giants were selling tickets at "a 50 percent higher clip than in '55."[24] San Francisco and the Chicago Bears each exceeded 30,000 season-ticket sales before the 1958 season. The twelve teams sold over 250,000 season tickets for 1958. Sales of these tickets alone exceeded 1.5 million, or more than the entire 1945 league attendance.[25] Three teams reported season-ticket sales in their media guides. Baltimore's season-ticket sales rose from 15,755 in 1953 to 45,644 in 1960, while Detroit's went from 8,685 in 1950 to a peak of 42,154 in 1958. The 49ers' sales of season tickets fluctuated but rose to 20,737 in 1957. Reporter Art Morrow concluded an article on the attendance figures with, "Even if the National League should reach an attendance of 3,000,000 this year, it would not represent the pot of gold at rainbow's end. The end of the rainbow is not in sight."[26] Even the Packers began selling 30,000 season tickets by 1960, although they sold only 10,000 or so season tickets for their Milwaukee games.[27]

While the game's popularity began spurring talk of expansion, Bell dampened the enthusiasm by repeating his mantra, "We won't be ready to do that until the lowest two clubs in our Eastern and Western setups can each win four or five games. Then we'll know there's enough talent around for us to expand without spreading material too thin."[28]

The league's popularity occasionally raised hackles. *San Francisco Examiner* reporter Rube Samuelsen quoted fellow columnist Prescott Sullivan, who irritated 49ers owner Tony Morabito by chiding him about the lack of cheap seats at Kezar Stadium. Morabito charged $3.75 for all but 4,500 out of 60,000 seats. The cheap seat section, which Sullivan nicknamed "County Jail Number Three," was a "heavily-policed, fenced-off, escape-proof cheaper section."[29] $3.75 was a relatively low price by 1957.

Crowds grew by roughly 5 percent during the 1957 season. Tex Maule suggested that the "ability of the underdogs to whomp their betters regularly may insure an even bigger increase in the burgeoning crowds." A 49ers-Rams game packed the Los Angeles Coliseum with over a hundred thousand fans—almost a season's worth of fans for some teams: at that time, it was the largest crowd ever for a regular-season game.[30] Green Bay opened a new stadium, and their attendance rose to thirty-one thousand per game at those games. Since the Packers played three of their games in Milwaukee, though, the team's overall home attendance increase was diluted. Milwaukee, wild over their baseball Braves, was blasé about the Packers. The league edict requiring Green Bay to play three games annually in Milwaukee would be rescinded in the future.

Bert Bell credited television for the league-wide increase in attendance, as it made the NFL game "known to millions of fans who hitherto had not viewed it. Obviously, he pointed out, many of these new fans were attending games."[31] Detroit, too, became NFL football–happy, especially since the Lions had spent much of the 1950s winning a preponderance of games after three last-place finishes in the late 1940s. For the 1957 league championship game against the Cleveland Browns, 55,263 people paid up to ten dollars each to watch the Lions rout the Browns.[32] No one would have guessed that, for all the talk of competitive balance, the Lions would never again appear in a championship game.

The Lions' success, albeit their final one, contrasted sharply with the performance of the Chicago Cardinals. After back-to-back conference titles in 1947–48, the Cardinals became the NFL equivalent of baseball's Washington Senators (or Kansas City Athletics). The 1950s were unkind to the team. From 1950–59, the Cardinals sported only one winning record (1956) and could only aspire to mediocrity. Continued high draft picks could not resuscitate the team, and its record contradicted the league's boast of competitive balance through the reserve clause, revenue sharing, and the reverse-order draft. The Cardinals struggled to attain one hundred thousand home paid attendees, and the annual game with the Chicago Bears provided the only significant sustenance. It would be unkind to suggest that most of those in the crowd for the Bears-Cardinals games at Comiskey Park or Soldier Field were Bears fans. Cardinals owner Violet M. Wolfner, the widow of the former owner, stubbornly refused to move her team. She insisted that her husband had planted a team in Chicago before the Bears, so if anyone vacated the city, it should be the Bears.

In addition to the mess on Chicago's South Side, Bell and Rozelle had to worry about the small stadium capacities in Washington DC, Philadelphia, and Pittsburgh (less than thirty-eight thousand each), lest a permanent disparity in attendance develop. Wolfner's Cardinals, at least, played in a large stadium. Baseball's Pittsburgh Pirates had long complained about the paucity of parking at Forbes Field. The Eastern Conference's combined home attendance was in glaring contrast to the Western Conference, and Bell had to worry about the long-term ramifications.[33]

Few, if any, NFL owners or officials attained the legendary status that baseball owner Bill Veeck Jr. achieved in the art of promotion. George Preston Marshall may have come closest. He hired a band and pulled off various promotional events. Sportswriter Hugh Brown characterized Marshall as "loco as a fox when it comes to beguiling the fans." Somehow Marshall enticed Washington DC residents to embrace the transplanted Redskins. In one example of his promotional efforts, he arranged a special train to take thousands of Redskins fans to a game against the Eagles in

Philadelphia: "For approximately $11.40, [Marshall] provided the fans with a train ride both ways, a bus to the ball park, and a turkey dinner with all the trimmings."[34] As early as 1947, Marshall was selling out Griffith Stadium. His season ticket sales exceeded thirty-one thousand, which was almost 90 percent of the stadium's capacity: "Visiting teams were able to pick up a check for their exact money split the Wednesday preceding their Sunday engagement as the Redskins advised fans without tickets not to bother coming to the ball park because there would be no room."[35] While Marshall was unable to sustain such popularity, he was able to sell almost twenty thousand season tickets a year in the late 1950s, even though the team rarely contended.

The Eastern Conference's attendance bright spots were Cleveland and New York. The Browns were perennial contenders throughout the 1950s, and the Giants, while up and down, were consistently contenders in the latter half of the decade. When the two teams collided, whether at Yankee Stadium or by the shore of Lake Erie, large crowds showed up. A chart in *The Sporting News* revealed the disparity between East and West. Seven NFL teams attracted over 275,000 in attendance in 1958, led by the Rams' 450,000. The other five teams all drew fewer than 170,000 and included four Eastern Conference teams. Because of the NFL's scheduling, the Eastern Conference teams were at a disadvantage in getting road revenue. This point will be developed further in the chapter 9. At least the Pittsburgh Steelers could hope that a move to the University of Pittsburgh stadium would boost the gate in comparison with Forbes Field, while Green Bay would expand its stadium to seat over thirty-eight thousand people.[36]

The flush times continued into the 1959 season, which would again set a new attendance mark for the eighth straight season. Season-ticket sales remained strong. As shown earlier, however, there was a danger in Bell's ebullient annual announcement of record-setting attendance. *Sports Illustrated* football columnist Tex Maule saluted Bell's and the NFL's sagacity: "The mushrooming success of pro football, built solidly on a sensible TV program, wise distribution of talent and intelligent promotion, has encouraged a group of optimistic people, headed by Lamar Hunt of Dallas to plan another league."[37] Although the NFL could hardly keep the large crowds and packed stadiums a secret, they could have remained mum or evasive about league profits. While Bell and the owners did not usually divulge exact numbers, the congressional committees required them to submit several seasons' worth of detailed financial information. Reporters described the financial figures in some detail in *The Sporting News* and other newspapers. Between the published sources and the owners' statements that implied prosperity, the Lamar Hunts of the nation felt encouraged to look into professional football. At one point during the 1959 season, Bell did admit that he suspected attendance was reaching a "saturation point" and that the owners "would do well to equal last year's crowd."[38]

Even the competition from the newly formed AFL did not derail NFL attendance. The Colts, Giants, Lions, 49ers, and Rams sold a combined total of over two hundred thousand season tickets heading into the 1960 season.[39] However, the expansion Cowboys, whether because of AFL competition in the city, a terrible team, or the surfeit of college football in the area, did not prove appealing to the fans. Early on, the Dallas team tried to boost the gate and create new fans by hiring a *reel* cowboy legend—Roy Rogers. Rogers and his wife, Dale, appeared at a Cowboys game. The reporter made no mention of Roy's horse, Trigger, but since the couple entered the stadium "in a gleaming white convertible," one may assume Trigger remained in his stable. In an early example of baby-boomer boorishness, many children in the audience showered the Hollywood stars with "paper cups, many with ice and soda pop still in them. Rogers's expensive cowboy costume was ruined and a large chunk of ice clipped Dale just below the eye." Rogers, justifiably angry, did not croon, "Happy trails to you," but hectored the crowd via the public address system: "Somebody has been throwing things and I don't appreciate it." Forty-three youths were arrested and taken to the police station. Reporter Walter Robertson described how the arrests set "off a loud cry from indignant parents who thought they should have been notified before their children were hurried away to jail."[40] The promotion failed to fill the stadium. The Cowboys might later become "America's Team," but they certainly weren't Roy Rogers's team. Dallas' doldrums continued the next season.

If Bell was correct that NFL teams were reaching the saturation point in terms of attendance, the league's ceaseless quest for revenue might have turned toward increasing ticket prices or developing an even greater reliance upon television revenues. Pete Rozelle recognized the importance of marketing and began developing lucrative sources of income from bobble-head dolls, pennants, and other sports bric-a-brac. In this, he was probably more astute than Bert Bell.

Ticket Prices

Attendance gains were accompanied by higher ticket prices, as NFL owners hiked their ticket prices immediately after the war. These factors should have triggered a rapid increase in revenue.

NFL teams raised ticket prices throughout the 1940s and 1950s, according to information gleaned from media guides and programs. Table 3 summarizes the trends in ticket prices. Teams playing in stadiums with small capacities, such as Green Bay, Pittsburgh, and Washington, tended to compensate by having higher ticket prices. Information on ticket prices in the media guides and programs during the 1940s is scant. Each of the three teams reporting ticket prices during the early 1940s raised prices immediately after the war. The Giants raised their box and reserved prices by 21 and 36 percent respectively between 1943 and 1945. The Redskins more than doubled their prices between 1943 and 1950.

In the wake of the AAFC surrender, NFL owners got additional good news. The federal government was considering a reduction in the admissions tax, which the government had initially enacted during World War I and had reinstated in 1932. The owners voted that each owner could decide whether to adjust ticket prices or not.[41]

Teams raised the prices of box and reserved seats during the 1950s. These are nominal ticket prices, unadjusted for changes in the price level. For the period from 1951 to 1959, for example, the Consumer Price Index changed by 12 percent, so about half the change in box prices of four dollars to five dollars during that time period would simply have kept pace with inflation. Most of the teams' ticket prices rose faster than changes in the general price level, but these increases were on the order of 10 to 20 percent in real terms. Fans generally believe that teams only raise ticket prices and never lower them. Between 1953 and 1954, though, six teams dropped some of their prices, usually by twenty to thirty cents per ticket. Green Bay's and the New York Giants' drops were temporary, and prices bounced back the following season. Baltimore, Detroit, Pittsburgh, and

Washington may have taken a few seasons to restore prices. The Detroit Lions officials told their fellow owners at the February 1, 1957 meeting that they planned to raise their ticket prices for 1957. Several other owners mentioned they were considering similar actions.[42]

Were teams participating in the championship game likely to raise ticket prices in the subsequent season? The evidence is mixed. Using sources underlying table 3, we find that only two teams definitely raised their ticket prices after winning the NFL Championship Game (one team's ticket pricing was unavailable)in the years between 1948 and 1959. Of the losing teams in the NFL Championship Game between 1951 and 1959, three definitely raised their prices the following season (once again, one team's ticket pricing was unavailable).

With the growing importance of season-ticket sales, owners passed a rule stating that the discount for season tickets could not be greater than 20 percent. Hence a six-game season ticket for $4 seats could not be priced at less than $19.20. Most owners did not give discounts for season tickets.[43]

The NFL naturally charged more for tickets to its season-ending championship games; oddly, they mandated that teams charge regular-season prices for any playoff games to resolve ties in the standings. At the January 24, 1947 meeting, the owners voted to revise their bylaws pertaining to the championship game. They agreed to assess prices based on stadium capacity. For smaller stadiums (defined as less than forty thousand), the price was four dollars, while owners playing in larger stadiums (more than forty thousand) could charge three dollars. These prices rose during the 1950s, but the owners continued the policy of setting higher prices for games in smaller stadiums, although this was no longer defined by the forty-thousand rule. In this way, they hoped to level the gate receipts for any particular game. By 1958, the NFL's popularity enabled it to charge ten dollars per ticket for its championship game in New York; the price remained at ten dollars for the 1961 game in Green Bay.[44]

Conclusion

Rising per-game attendance coincided with rising ticket prices to boost revenues. The NFL owners should have enjoyed growing gate receipts during the postwar period, setting a foundation for better financial statements.

4

PROFITS AND LOSSES

The NFL owners' public pronouncements regarding profits were almost uniformly grim for many seasons. NFL owners reported chronic losses before and during World War II. They claimed they remained in business because of their love of the game. Although profit figures can be manipulated (both legally and illegally), we can deduce some general trends from attendance figures and ticket price information. Franchise sale values are another guide to past and expected future profits. An industry characterized by chronic losses should find itself with few prospective buyers for franchises and with occasional bankruptcies. Because of rising ticket prices and increased attendance in the late 1940s, nominal team gate receipts should have been higher and thus able to sustain higher player salaries and other expenses.

Stadiums

Potential profitability depended on a number of factors, including an owner's playing venue. NFL owners differed from MLB owners in a crucial way: NFL owners rarely owned a stadium. Most of them rented stadiums from municipal authorities, universities, or Major League Baseball owners. Football owners typically paid a rental based on gross receipts, often at the rate of 15 percent as reflected by the league's revenue-sharing rules, so their profit/loss statements showed an explicit rental expense. Had the owners possessed stadiums, they might not have the explicit rental expense but would, instead, have had depreciation and maintenance expenses. In addition, baseball owners had large amounts of capital tied up in their stadiums. Of course, some baseball owners earned revenue by hosting college and professional football games.

Because the baseball season overlapped the beginning of the football season, stadium availability in the early part of the NFL season proved to be a headache. Bert Bell worked long hours trying to arrange the schedule, and stadium availability was a crucial piece of the puzzle. The NFL's New York teams had to worry that the baseball Giants, Dodgers, and Yankees might participate in the World Series, as they so often did during the postwar years.

Major League Baseball owners' stock of stadiums gave them an advantage in deterring new teams and leagues from moving into their territory. Unless there was an alternative stadium in a city, the existing MLB team could deny any other team the use of the sole viable playing site. The NFL owners had much less leverage, so their ability to use stadiums to deter entry was limited.

Baseball owners also benefited from concessions sales at their stadiums, an income which they did not share with their football tenants. Some NFL owners got small amounts of income from selling programs and scorecards. In later years, when NFL and AFL owners became adept at wringing better rental terms from stadium owners and managers, especially with publicly owned stadiums, they began to get concessions and parking revenues.

Dan Topping, new one-third owner of the baseball Yankees, hoped to have his Brooklyn Tigers NFL team play games in his Yankee Stadium. The baseball Brooklyn Dodgers were only willing to grant the Tigers a one-year lease on Ebbets Field because Branch Rickey was hoping to get into professional football and the Dodgers were hoping for greater income from renting Ebbets Field for other activities. Topping's purchase of the baseball Yankees raised some questions. A New York Times reporter saw potential for trouble for the NFL's New York Giants if an AAFC team was to rent Yankee Stadium. He claimed the Yankees got very little net revenue from hosting college football games. The Yankees were among the last group of teams to install lights for night baseball, although such lights would be useful during late afternoons in autumn. Topping did not like the way negotiations went with the Maras' New York Giants team; eventually, he bolted for the AAFC.[1] Across the East River, former baseball Philadelphia Phillies owner William D. Cox and a partner were arranging to rent Ebbets Field for their AAFC Brooklyn Dodgers team.[2]

Several NFL teams played in stadiums with seating capacities of less than forty thousand. If the team had an outstanding season, its revenue potential was crimped. While Green Bay, with its small population base, understandably had a small stadium throughout the team's first thirty-five years, the team officials knew their days in the NFL might be numbered if they couldn't generate larger crowds and larger visitors' shares for their rivals. By 1956 the team floated a referendum for a $960,000 bond issue to finance a new or remodeled stadium seating thirty-two thousand. Verne Lewellen, the Packers' general manager, told reporters, "Pro football is big business. We can't get along with our present inadequate, wooden stands seating about 24,000. Gone are the days when our minimum guarantee to a visiting team was $5,000. It's $20,000 now."[3] Bert Bell added pressure on Green Bay voters by urging them to vote for the referendum; he ominously mentioned "firm offers for a franchise from many cities whose stadiums can accommodate large crowds."[4] Bell's heavy-handed tactics presaged owner antics of the 1980s, when owners played musical chairs with vacant stadiums. Green Bay voters overwhelmingly supported the referendum, and the new stadium opened in 1957.

The New York Giants switched from the Polo Grounds to Yankee Stadium for the 1956 season. The Maras were gratified when over forty-eight thousand people ventured to the new venue, the largest opening — day crowd for the franchise. The October 21 date, though, reflected one drawback. The baseball Yankees, participating in yet another World Series, had forced Bert Bell to schedule the Giants' home opener late in the season. The Giants' move to Yankee Stadium proved successful, and the team signed a ten-year lease in 1961. The team averaged over fifty-three thousand per game in attendance during its first years in the stadium. One reporter thought the New York Yankees baseball team cleared $1 million in rental fees, which was possible as the Giants paid 15 percent on gross gate. If tickets cost about four dollars each, that figure could have been reached.[5]

Pittsburgh switched to another ballpark in 1958. The Steelers and the baseball Pirates were dissatisfied with aging Forbes Field. The stadium was small and lacked convenient parking. The Steelers wanted to switch to the University of Pittsburgh's stadium. The proposed move wasn't universally favored, as many in the collegiate athletic world disliked professional sports.[6]

George Preston Marshall's Washington Redskins played in Griffith Stadium. Marshall probably worried about the deteriorating neighborhood surrounding the stadium; Washington Senators baseball owner Calvin Griffith certainly did. Given the two owners' ambivalence about African Americans, the changing complexion of the neighborhood made them long for a shiny new stadium located elsewhere in the city. Marshall would eventually get his wish (a stadium with twenty-two-inch-wide seats, a modern lighting system, and lack of obstructions from pillars and posts), while Griffith moved to the Nordic Twin Cities.[7]

In many of these cases, NFL owners, like their baseball peers, worried about inadequate parking and amenities. By the 1950s most of Major League Baseball's stadiums were pushing forty years or more in age. The growing cities of the West and Southeast boasted gleaming new stadiums with ample parking. Baseball and football owners eyed these stadiums keenly.

The nascent AFL wanted a New York franchise and needed a stadium. While Dan Topping's dream of filling Yankee Stadium caused him to switch to the AAFC, the AFL Titans moved into the New York Giants' former venue, the smaller Polo Grounds. The team considered Ebbets Field, but Harry Wismer decided to use the Polo Grounds until the proposed new stadium in Flushing Meadows opened. The Titans' proposed lease for Flushing Meadows Stadium (later renamed Shea Stadium) was a reasonable $5,000 a game or 10 percent of the gross, whichever was larger.[8]

Profits

Sports economists have learned one truism: beware of false profits. Readers living in the new millennium will surely have no difficulty in accepting that truism. The antics of Enron and other corporations, with their dubious accounting practices, have left some heretofore respected accounting firms in tatters.

While 1950s sportswriters and readers may have been more accepting of published profit figures than we are now, the truism holds for professional team sports in the middle of the twentieth century. The data the owners supplied to Congress appears to be accurate. The owners may have worried about lying to Congress, so they sent in the real numbers.

The gate-sharing and league fee rules afford checks on the revenue figures. Even if these figures are accurate, though, care has to be taken in analyzing the net income (profit) figures.

Owners often had other business interests aside from football. In some cases they could shunt expenses and revenues from company to company. They could put kin on payroll, or pay themselves a fancy salary, if doing so was beneficial from an income tax standpoint. For new owners, the player depreciation allowance rule created paper losses that reduced an owner's income tax liability from the team or from another business interest. In an era when the income taxes on businesses and corporations ran about 50 percent, businessmen had an even greater incentive to expense everything possible than they would have had when the tax was much lower. Since football owners rarely owned a stadium, they usually didn't incur the issue of expensing stadium improvements.

For these and other reasons, an owner could legally massage his net income figure to his best advantage. Most owners also learned the art of modesty. Unless they were fighting a rival league and needed to impress the public with their team's popularity, most owners realized that boasting about profits was not only bad manners but poor public relations. Owners might not lie directly, but they might utter some vague ambiguity about "being in the black" or "breaking even." In some contexts, owners preferred to exaggerate losses, especially if they were hoping to get an antitrust exemption, a publicly financed stadium, or some other subsidy.

Owners complained about rising costs, even aside from player salaries. Of course they faced rising costs. Everyone in the economy faced higher prices as the wartime economy, with its accompanying price controls and shortages, changed over to peacetime production. The real question was whether the owners' expenses were rising faster than the general price level. Even if such expenses rose faster than the general economy, such a rise might have reflected prosperity. Teams might have chosen to house their players in nicer hotels, taken first-class train tickets, provided more uniforms, and offered other amenities. Owners might have hired additional office workers to help with the burgeoning ticket sales; innovative owners might have begun hiring publicity and promotion staff to boost the gate even more.[9] While payrolls increased above wartime levels, even an increase of $150,000 per season per team should not have triggered catastrophic losses, given the increase in ticket prices and attendance.

The NFL's profit experiences during its struggles with the AAFC and AFL must remain conjectural, barring publication of team ledgers.[10] Sportswriters reported fabulous losses. Bert Bell seemed to take perverse pride in pointing out the league's chronic losses, even before the AAFC debacle. His predecessor, Joe Carr, set the tone: "No owner has made money from pro football but a lot have gone broke thinking they could."[11]

When the 1948 Philadelphia Eagles, NFL champions, failed to post a profit, many wondered whether this augured doom for the league. Michael MacCambridge relates that the Eagles had revenues of $624,782 and $709,920 in expenses, with player payroll accounting for $268,819.[12] The Eagles' real problem, though, was a lousy home schedule. Four of their home games drew fewer than twenty-three thousand apiece, with the finale against the hapless Detroit Lions failing to fill half the seats. The marquee games against the Chicago Bears and Washington Redskins (the only two teams with winning records venturing to Philadelphia that season) played to capacity crowds, and it is likely that many fans could not get in.[13]

MacCambridge detailed Dan Reeves's initial lackluster success on the West Coast. Reeves's Rams, who won the championship in 1945, did not reproduce their success on the playing field in Los Angeles until 1949, when they returned to the top of their division. MacCambridge believes the team lost $161,000 in 1946 and $184,000 in 1947. He states that because the team had to pay an additional $5,000 per game ($30,000 for the season) in guarantees to visiting teams, its losses were increased. The Rams' attendance figures belie the dismal 1946 profit picture. The team had 134,308 more total home attendees than in 1945 and almost twenty thousand more road attendees (it played four home games in 1945 and five in 1946), so Reeves should have had considerably more revenue with which to pay the increased visitors' guarantee and player payroll. Even if the team averaged just $1.50 net from each additional home attendee and $0.50 for each additional road attendee, this meant over $211,000 more in gate receipts. If Reeves's increased travel costs were $30,000 and were added to the $30,000 in greater visitor's shares, he would still have had $150,000 to offset increased payroll costs (assuming the attendance figures were accurate). Reeves might have been able to sustain such publicized losses longer, but his five-year tax write-off from the government's "hobby" law was expiring.[14]

A whirlwind tour through the *New York Times* and the *Sporting News* provides a portrait of what the public heard about the poor, struggling NFL. AAFC owners' 1946 losses might have been inflated by start-up costs as teams established their business operations. In the event, AAFC owners were not shy about proclaiming their losses. Tony Morabito, owner of the San Francisco 49ers, said he lost $100,000 in 1946 despite a winning team.[15] One particularly gloomy assessment quoted an AAFC partisan, who claimed, "We're in a helluva lot better situation for playing poker than the National is. They're going to lose Green Bay, Pittsburgh, the New York Bulldogs and also the Chicago Cardinals . . . if this war continues."[16] The partisan's perspicuity proved erroneous. However, the partisan proved accurate about Ted Collins and the now Boston, then New York Yanks/ Bulldogs.

Tom Meany said, "One million dollars will go down the pro football drain at the Polo Grounds, Yankee Stadium and Ebbets Field." He did not divulge the source for his extreme pessimism, stating laconically, "Because they guard their figures with the secrecy of a guy in the numbers racket, the exact losses of the three local professional football teams will be difficult to determine." He did at least try to use the declines in attendance to measure the shortfall in gate receipts, so his estimates were not completely fabricated. He noted that the AAFC Yankees siphoned off some 2,300 season-ticket holders from the Giants due to Yankee Stadium's amenities, which included the Stadium Club, a forerunner of luxury boxes. The Yankees also did not pay explicit stadium rental, since their owner also owned the stadium.[17]

The Chicago Bears were enjoying the postwar period. After winning their division in 1946, the team finished second by just one game in each of the following three years. The crosstown Cardinals won the division in 1947 and 1948, and the teams' rivalry fueled large crowds; almost every game between the two teams between 1946 and 1949 drew in excess of fifty thousand. Francis J. Powers and Ed Prell chronicled the Bears' success, stating the team had $490,000 in advance ticket sales in 1948.[18]

In the case of Pittsburgh, Les Biederman wrung his hands over the team's inability to make large profits despite seven straight sellouts at Forbes Field and a rare winning team in 1947. The trouble was that Forbes Field seated only thirty-five thousand or so. Owner Art Rooney bemoaned the increase in player payroll from $51,000 in 1941 to $230,000 in 1948. He also cited increased taxes and increased transportation costs (rising from $5,700 in 1941 to $72,000 in 1948).[19]

In an era before domed stadiums with climate control, teams fretted about inclement weather during late November and December. League championship games demonstrate the volatility in attendance due to the weather. Officials printed 77,600 tickets on the off chance that the 1945 game between Washington and Cleveland would fill Cleveland's Municipal Stadium, but only 32,178 fans showed up.[20]

Craig Coenen believes the two professional football leagues lost a combined $8.5 million during the struggle. His table 4.6 is based on information in the *Philadelphia Inquirer* (December 25, 1949). Because of the losses, Art Rooney claimed he "would not operate a team in 1950 unless the NFL makes peace with the AAFC."[21]

The *Philadelphia Inquirer* article is of interest. Table 4 shows the reported losses of NFL and AAFC teams. The article did not include figures for the four profitable NFL teams. NFL owners had claimed they rarely made profits before 1946. Given the small crowds attending Boston/New York, Detroit, and Green Bay games between 1946 and 1949, their losses are hardly surprising. The AAFC losses are more difficult to explain. The Brooklyn and Chicago teams obviously suffered from low attendance, although their losses were considerably greater than Detroit's or Green Bay's. Cleveland's financial loss, which occurred despite its huge attendance, is a mystery. Three of the four NFL teams not reporting losses averaged roughly thirty thousand fans per home game, a level easily exceeded by Cleveland and San Francisco. Cleveland and Los Angeles may have charged lower ticket prices on average than other teams, eroding some of their attendance advantage.

The New York and Los Angeles teams' reported losses are surprising, given their above-average home attendance.[22] The Los Angeles teams did incur somewhat higher transportation costs, but these costs were on the order of tens of thousands of dollars per year, hardly enough to create the $2.25 million combined loss claimed. Tim Mara and Dan Topping, owners of the Giants and Yankees, may have inflated their attendance figures or issued an inordinate number of complimentary tickets.

Even though the 1950 season was disappointing in many respects because league attendance did not improve as much as anticipated, *Sporting News* writer Ed Pollock suggested that attendance and gate receipts were up 47.2 percent, so ten of the thirteen teams would show profits. He admitted that whatever profit the teams made during the season was a paltry amount, not enough to offset the $8 million in losses during the previous four seasons. Pollock's article, though, was a mishmash of numbers and "guesstimates." His twin 47.2 percent figures were based on assuming the same ticket prices between seasons. He later used per-team attendance figures, which revealed a much more modest increase of 10.4 percent. He quoted one owner as saying, "I worry all season about losing $150,000 to make $25,000." Apparently the owners hadn't been able to trim payrolls much.[23] Pollock's optimism aside, other owners continued glum in subsequent seasons. In 1952 Art Rooney moaned, "As I see it, we'll have to cut operating expenses. We're getting the top dollar now for tickets. And the players are not over-paid when you consider that they could make big money in other lines." Rooney estimated owners needed around thirty thousand paid attendance per game to break even. Given that some owners played in stadiums with a seating capacity of barely more than thirty thousand, they were living on the brink if thirty thousand was, indeed, the break-even point.[24]

In a sense, NFL profitability approximated a zero-sum game. There were only so many wins available in any given season (ignoring ties), so teams that improved did so to the detriment of other clubs. When Detroit improved with the addition of Bobby Layne, Leon Hart, and Doak Walker, their profit picture improved considerably. The team greatly benefited by playing in a spacious stadium that seated almost sixty thousand people, which they filled on several occasions.[25] The Lions created a reservoir of fan goodwill, reflected by its growing numbers of season-ticket holders.

When the Miller brothers purchased the New York Bulldogs and moved them to Dallas, they anticipated $800,000 in expenses for their first season and $500,000 thereafter.[26] If the brothers truly expected such expenses, then the disaster that befell them can be attributed to their overly optimistic attitude regarding revenue (which they sorely lacked).

As the 1950s proceeded, sportswriters began portraying the NFL as prosperous. Their fascination with attendance and profit figures did not diminish. Some noted Bert Bell's Cassandraesque warning about the need to maintain vigilance with regard to expenses. On one occasion he claimed, "I don't know who made money or who didn't. I didn't see the books."[27]

During the television antitrust trial over which Judge Allen K. Grim presided, Bell pled poverty in public. He claimed that only four clubs made "real money" during the 1952 season, while six lost money. He suggested roster reductions, food and hotel allowance decreases, and a reduction in the visiting team's guarantee as cost-cutting measures. He did not explain how the last would help the league as a whole, since the visiting team's guarantee was just a redistribution of revenue, not a collective expense. He said that the league needed to consider eliminating the point after touchdown to save on $17 footballs, which would save $6,000. The owners agreed that if they lost the case, they would need to reduce salaries by 20 percent immediately.[28]

With Grim's decision safely in the past, league owners were more willing to admit, or at least not to deny, that prosperity had arrived in the NFL (aside from Chicago's South Side with the woebegone Cardinals), and readers could now revel vicariously in the NFL's "biggest dollar profit in history."[29] Writers predicted an impending attendance of three million for a season. Bell's pay and his extended contract also reflected the league's success.[30]

In analyzing that success, sportswriter Roger Kahn suggested that the public's acceptance of NFL football as the premier football game helped greatly. The pro game's growing popularity antagonized some college officials, who wanted to retaliate by not hiring coaches from the NFL. Kahn considered the pros' handling of television superior to that of the NCAA.[31]

When the congressional antitrust subcommittee began investigating the NFL in 1957, Bell made sure that NFL owners, while not claiming insolvency, did not appear too prosperous. His *The Story of Professional Football* claimed the average team made just $50,000 in profits or $600,000 collectively, "while the Federal government collected more than $900,000 in admission taxes — approximately 33 percent more than the combined net income of the twelve clubs comprising the National Football League." Bell's case was helped by Sam Fox, a professor of accountancy at the University of Illinois. Professor Fox analyzed the data presented to Congress in 1957. He chided the league for its poor rate of return on sales (2 percent): "In any business, that would be a poor return on investment, and when you figure the most profitable franchise had only a 2 percent return on sales, it is indeed anything but a good business venture by any business criteria or standards." He concluded that "the average club owner has to virtually be a millionaire or he couldn't conceivably carry on. No businessman following principles of business policy would ever dream of investing, or should we say highly speculating on a franchise under such conditions. . . . If you haven't got millions to lose don't go into the football business."[32] Professor Fox's analysis raises some questions, though. First, why use return on sales? The net income to investment ratio would seem a better measure. NFL owners had little investment in physical capital. During this time period, few had invested more than a few hundred thousand dollars in their franchise in terms of franchise purchase prices or prior losses. Second, rising franchise values suggested that current net income or anticipated future net income were positive; that the purchase had great tax benefits; or that the owner was willing to pay for the enjoyment and satisfaction of owning a professional sports team.

The owners sporadically paid dividends to shareholders and to themselves. Cleveland Browns owner Arthur "Mickey" McBride told reporters that he had "never taken a penny out of it. Sometimes the team, as a corporation, has made a little money. Not much, just a little. But personally I've never tapped it." McBride's fellow owners appear to have felt the same way. The league reported almost $2 million in net profit after taxes for the 1952–56 seasons, but owners disbursed less than $225,000 in dividends.[33]

Whatever the interpretation of the figures, the data supplied to Congress in 1957, which covered the 1952–56 seasons, is a unique trove of information. The NFL was experiencing prosperity and losses were becoming rare. The Chicago Cardinals were the "sick man of the NFL," to use a Eurocentric political term. Unless the Cardinals' owners were extremely liberal in defining expenses, their losses appear real. Because the team's attendance marks were low, the losses seem consistent. The formerly penurious Detroit Lions and Los Angeles Rams were now well-to-do, joining the San Francisco

49ers in boasting the league's healthiest income statements. Former Eagles owner Alexis Thompson had complained about his inability to earn a profit, even when his team won a championship. The Eagles continued to struggle. The Eagles, Steelers, and Redskins, while enjoying decent crowds, simply could not make large profits, given the capacity of their stadiums, unless they could raise ticket prices and gain more revenue by doing so. Their teams were generally mediocre during the mid-1950s, and when an attractive opponent, such as the Browns, visited, the low seating capacities prevented these owners from cashing in to offset crowds of fifteen to twenty thousand for most league games.

Using the data shown in tables 2 and 5, there was a strong correlation, of course, between attendance and net income before taxes.[34] The losses all occurred with attendance of 170,000 per year or less. The break-even point appeared to be centered on 150,000, although the Chicago Bears barely broke even in 1952–53 with attendance well in excess of 200,000. A handful of teams made profits even when their attendance fell below 150,000. The Green Bay Packers earned decent profits in 1954–55 with tepid attendance.

If we use a figure of 170,000 as a break-even point, the AAFC's situation becomes clearer. The league struggled in 1946 but is unlikely to have lost large sums of money in 1947 and 1948. Some of the 1946 losses may have been due to start-up costs. The 1949 season was probably the worst season aside from 1946. Even in 1949, though, if 170,000 was a break-even point, several of the teams were reasonably close. Of course, the ticket prices may have been lower in 1946–49 than they were for the NFL during the mid-1950s, while the player salaries may have been similar or slightly higher in the earlier period.

Revenues

A team's profit and loss were closely related to its gross operating income. The correlation between the two variables was about 67 percent. The gross operating income, while widely dispersed, showed less disparity between teams than in baseball's American League, where the New York Yankees routinely had three to five times as much gross operating income as the team with the least income. The NFL did not suffer from a New York state of mind. The Giants were not among the highest collectors of gross operating income, and even the Washington Redskins usually collected more. The San Francisco 49ers had considerably more gross operating income than any team in the league, but they did not dominate on the playing field.

A team's gross operating income consisted of home game receipts (less visitors' and league's shares), away game receipts, exhibition game receipts, concessions receipts, and "sale of television and radio rights." Tables 6–11 show the relevant data, as well as measures of the distribution. Since most NFL owners did not own the stadium they played in, they received little concessions revenue. Cleveland, Detroit, and Washington's concessions revenue consisted mostly of program sales. The Lions, Redskins, Browns, Steelers, and Packers reaped $382,000 in total concessions receipts across the five seasons reported to Congress, with no team earning more than $43,000 for any given season.

Home game receipts provided almost half of the teams' gross operating income, while away game receipts provided another fifth. Receipts from sale of television and radio rights provided about 13 percent of gross operating income. San Francisco and Chicago led the league in home game receipts during this period. These two teams sometimes had four times as much in home game receipts as the team with the lowest amount. Table 8 demonstrates that teams had large differences in home game receipts per attendee, which reflects either different ticket prices or a mix of seats sold, including general admission, reserved seats, and box seating. The home game receipts per attendee figure understates the average ticket price, since the numerator does not include the visitor's share, league's share, or ticket taxes. Since these were generally proportional, the home game receipts per attendee figure yields rankings similar to those of an average ticket price. The Steelers and Redskins appear to have offset their limited seating by collecting higher receipts per attendee. According to table 3, the two teams had higher ticket prices than most clubs in 1952, and the Steelers maintained the highest prices in 1956. On the other end of the scale, the Lions and Rams packed in a lot of fans but collected relatively little from them. The Bears and 49ers appear to have attracted good-sized crowds and extracted high amounts.

The distribution of away game receipts was much tighter than for home game receipts. The top:bottom ratios for away games were roughly half those for home games. Unlike Major League Baseball, in which fans demonstrated a marked preference for winning teams such as the Yankees and Dodgers, the effect of winning upon road attendance was less pronounced in the NFL. The Cleveland Browns were very successful in this time period, but they did not lead the league in road receipts. Of course, the Browns played in a conference with relatively poor-drawing opponents. The greater proportion of season-ticket holders also muted any preference for watching visiting teams with winning records.

NFL teams played a variety of preseason exhibition games. For some teams, the games proved highly lucrative. Rams owner Dan Reeves confided to sportswriter James Murray that these games "make the difference between profit and loss."[35] Washington Redskins minority owner Harry Wismer told reporter Al Silverman, "The owners have secretly told me that they make more than enough in the exhibitions to carry them through the year." Silverman included exhibition game receipts originally reported by Joe Williams of the New York *World Telegram and Sun* for 1956, but these figures are far higher than those presented to Congress; in many cases, the reported exhibition game receipts exceeded teams' home game receipts. Silverman claimed that only George Preston Marshall publicly repudiated the figures.[36] Readers will note that observers often said that television revenues made the difference between making a profit and incurring a loss, but it is clear that two or three revenue streams were interchangeable in making such a difference.

Most discussions of NFL revenue sharing and equity neglect the wide disparities in exhibition game receipts. The San Francisco 49ers and Los Angeles Rams dominated this source of revenue, with the two teams often combining for more than a third of total league exhibition-game receipts. The Baltimore Colts and Green Bay Packers were swamped in the contest for exhibition-game revenues. While teams may have arranged some form of sharing (or perhaps they simply arranged home-and-home swaps), there was scant mention of sharing in the league constitution and bylaws. Since San Francisco often earned $300,000 more from this source than did Green Bay and Baltimore, they had a significant advantage in earning profits and perhaps in fielding strong teams. Naturally, teams chose to schedule games only with the most attractive teams, and this preference meant the less attractive teams had to scramble for exhibition games. Bert Bell told the owners of stronger teams to try and help the weaker teams by scheduling exhibition games with them.[37]

Bell and Rozelle worried about growing disparities in television revenues. While there were some ten-to-one disparities between teams for a particular season, the distribution was not as uneven over five seasons as it was in Major League Baseball. The New York Giants held an advantage over Green Bay, but the disparity was less than for the baseball Yankees versus the Baltimore Orioles (formerly the St. Louis Browns). Rozelle, however, presented information early in his tenure as commissioner that showed a widening gap in television revenues.

By the end of the decade, teams were beginning to approach $1 million each in gate receipts. Austin Gunsel, interim commissioner, reported gate receipts of $11,374,194.36 for 1959, based on a 9-percent increase of $1,024,513.85 from 1958 figures.[38] Green Bay, with its new stadium and winning record, boasted its first season with over $1 million in total operating income. The team received just $108,000 in radio and television revenue. The club showed a $131,883 profit for the season, almost doubling its surplus held at year's end from a year earlier.[39]

Certainly the league's revenue streams seem puny in contrast to those of later years, when television contracts grew exponentially and crowd sizes continued to grow. David Harris points out that by the 1974 meetings, owners could congratulate themselves on revenues averaging $6.2 million and operating profits nearing $1 million each. Even given the rise in the general price level between, 1956 and 1973, for example, the revenue streams had advanced rapidly.[40]

Expenses

At the end of World War II Arthur Daley made some estimates of NFL expenses in anticipation of the AAFC's debut in 1946. Daley reported:

> It's generally estimated that the first $40,000 taken in at the gate goes for operating expenses. . . . Tack on an extra $10,000 for a transcontinental jaunt and add to that sum a vastly higher payroll for the [AAFC] and it can't possibly be a paying proposition. Gilmore Stadium in Los Angeles

seats 28,000 and Ebbets Field approximately 35,000. Someone ought to try them on for size. . . . Larry MacPhail discovered that with the Yankees during the baseball season when an incredible string of rainy Sundays cut at least 100,000 off his attendance figures. With a ten-game schedule instead of one of 154 games that could be fatal.[41]

Even after the NFL's first two appearances before the subcommittee, Bell was still preaching economy. Joe King wrote, "The commissioner is prepared to show his owners how closely some approached the brink of comparative catastrophe, even in the prosperous season, how rapidly red ink could shower upon at least a third of the league, and why this time of plenty is the provident occasion to set up safeguards against bad fortune in the future."[42] Perhaps Bell was being cagey. He undoubtedly knew that many wealthy businessmen across America desired pro football teams of their own and that the NFL owners were lukewarm at best about expanding. By poor-mouthing the league in public, Bell may have been trying to discourage potential entrants. Even in the euphoria of "The Greatest Game Ever Played," Bell cautioned owners that, "Just because we had this kind of attendance and money, it still isn't any bed of roses. Unless a team sells 25,000 season tickets it can run into rough times."[43]

Bell's pessimism persisted. A month later he bemoaned the impending Justice Department antitrust case, rising operating costs, player salaries, and other factors: "Only a few years ago, our bylaws stipulated that the entire cost of four officials at each game should not exceed $35,000 the season. Last fall, our costs for five officials was $85,000, including their fees and travel expenses."[44] Bell also urged owners to economize on hotel and food bills: "They don't have to stay at the best hotels and eat the most expensive food. They can stay at respectable, clean, good eating places."[45]

Bell told the owners that while television receipts were becoming vital, television affected attendance to the detriment of the typical regular-season game and to the benefit of games with bearing on determining the title. This dichotomy threatened the league's stability, as weaker teams found themselves declining. Bell suggested the owners cut expenses, possibly by reducing the player limit from thirty-three to thirty, eliminating specialists, and redressing competitive imbalance by giving the weaker teams castoffs from the stronger teams. The owners could try to manipulate the schedule by arranging more topflight contests, but, of course, there were only so many of those to go around.[46]

NFL teams had disparities not only in gross operating income but also in gross operating expenses (table 12). Measured by the top:bottom ratio, gross operating expenses had a slightly tighter range than gross operating income. The Packers and Eagles, though they were faltering at the gate, managed, at least, to keep their expenses within their operating income. Several of the teams incurred five-year gross operating expenses close to $4 million, or $0.8 million per season.

Gross operating expenses consisted of administrative salaries, "other expenses," and player salaries. Stadium rental fees may not appear in "other expenses," as owners may have deducted them at the conclusion of each game. Although owners complained about salaries — and salaries may have been the largest single expense — salaries comprised just over a third of the gross operating expenses. Salaries, however, comprised a smaller proportion of the expenses in 1956 than in 1952, as "other expenses" and "administrative expenses" rose faster.

Administrative expenses might have been what owners could use to adjust net income (table 13). The Philadelphia Eagles did not bother to pay much in administrative salaries, but Los Angeles and Detroit led the league in such salaries. If an owner chose to take a large salary, he could reduce his profit or even incur an apparent loss. By paying himself a larger salary than before, therefore, an owner might try to evade the tax on team income while incurring more personal income tax, or, if he found it more beneficial, he might cut his salary and report more team income and less personal income.

"Other expenses" constituted about half the total expenses. These expenses rose by 40 percent over the five-year period, well above the change in the general price level (table 14). Only the Detroit Lions appeared immune to the increase in "other expenses." If new owners used the depreciation allowance for players, their "other expenses" would have increased. Five teams were purchased in the postwar period: the 49ers in 1947, the Lions in 1948, the Eagles in 1949, and the Browns and Colts in 1953. The player depreciation allowance ran for five years, so the 49ers would have depleted their allowance by the beginning of the 1952–56 period. The Lions and Eagles did not show any discernible reductions in their "other expenses" in the fifth or sixth year after their deductions expired; if anything, the Eagles' "other expenses" increased in 1954–55. The Browns showed a jump in their "other expenses" in 1953, but there is no way to ascertain the change in the Colts' expenses. For most teams, stadium rentals may have been a large item, perhaps the second-largest expense, even if it was not shown in the overall expenses they gave to Congress. Owners often paid up to 15 percent of the gross gate receipts after taxes for stadium rental.[47] Detroit's low "other expenses" figure is a mystery, given how well the team fared at the gate.

Owners often complained about transportation expenses throughout this period. They sometimes predicated scheduling, relocation, and expansion decisions upon transportation costs. The New York Bulldogs were assigned to the Western Division for the 1950 season in order to avoid having the two New York City teams in the same division. To assuage owner Ted Collins, the other owners approved a $12,500 subsidy to cover his added transportation costs.[48]

The Chicago Bears and Chicago Cardinals bickered about switching divisions, mostly to avoid the West Coast trip. George Halas opposed having permanent divisions, unless, of course, his team was placed in the Eastern Division. Halas assumed that his Bears were such strong draws that the other Western Division teams wanted the Bears in their division: "To use the Bears as a drawing club for the Western Division is a disadvantage of the Bears. If no Eastern clubs are played outside of the Yanks it is detrimental to us. We may be a drawing power for a short time and for the two Coast Clubs to want us now is natural but if they have to exist only by virtue of having the Bears they are in pretty bad shape and they should strengthen some other way."[49]

By 1959 sportswriters were speculating on the finances of the impending AFL. Tex Maule again provided detailed lists of estimated expenses, while Howard Roberts discussed the cost of player uniforms and training camp expenses.[50]

Player Salaries

NFL owners inculcated manners in their players. Along with such topics as politics and religion, they wanted their players to consider discussing player salaries among themselves to be taboo. The less players knew about what their teammates and rivals were making, the easier it was for the owner to tamp down salaries. Football quarterback Norm Van Brocklin a congressional committee that he was paid $21,000 in 1957, but that he did not know how his salary compared with those of other players: "The practice in professional ball is, at least with the Rams, not to find out what your teammates are making; they just do not talk about it."[51]

While today's fan can revel in copious salary information, caution should always be used. Owners and players have motives for distorting salary figures. Unless the source has examined team payrolls or contracts on file at the league office, any secondhand reports are suspect. The press, though, might give general clues as to player salaries.

During the postwar period, most NFL players earned less than $20,000, so exaggeration in either direction would have been, at most, a few thousand dollars. The 1952–56 team salary information provided by the owners to the 1957 congressional hearing on organized professional team sports is likely to be accurate, although, even here, care has to be used. Some teams included coaches' salaries in the team payroll.

The NFL had never been known for munificent salaries, aside from Harold "Red" Grange, but he was a highly publicized college star and was cleverly marketed. Many of the early NFL players did not have college backgrounds; as the league solidified and the Great Depression cut opportunities even for men with college degrees, a greater proportion of the league's players were college graduates. Historian Steven Riess shows that by the 1930s almost five out of every six players had college degrees, and a majority of them had grown up in white-collar households.[52]

Historian Craig Coenen believes average NFL salaries were about $8,000 in 1949 and $8,400 in 1956. He claims that after adjusting for inflation, "players' real wages were actually less in 1959 than they had been ten years earlier."[53] His basic surmise that player salaries did not keep pace with growing revenues is likely true, but his sources are not sufficient to prove the point. He based his claim upon information from the Green Bay Packers and upon player Norm Van Brocklin's article on player rights, among other sources. The Packers, being a public entity, released annual profit-and-loss statements. Between 1949 and 1959, the team's income rose from

$560,000 to $1,351,000 (not adjusted for changes in the price level); their experience is not likely to be representative of NFL teams, as they finished last in 1949 and were resurgent in 1959. Coenen's salary figures for 1956 appear to be too pessimistic, according to payroll information contained in the 1957 hearings of the U.S. Congress antitrust subcommittee.[54]

An article in the *Sporting News* pointed out that the income tax laws changed after the end of World War II. Players would see a 10-percent reduction in their income tax. The writer pointed out, "For the club owner, the revised setup is of far more striking vitality. Elimination of the excess profits tax means there is a basic levy of 40 percent as against the wartime imposts of 80, or even 95, percent. This arrangement leaves the club owner with a far greater financial elasticity in his relations with his payrolls. It also places at his disposal more funds for the acquisition of manpower."[55]

Because the NFL did not have a minimum salary rule for much of the postwar period, we cannot depend on a fixed minimum. Bert Bell and the owners asserted before Congress that no player received less than $5,000 for an entire season, but their testimony may have been self-serving.

Readers also have to remember that the general price level rose between 1941 and 1946 and continued to rise at a healthy clip until the early 1950s. Owners and reporters wrung their hands over the run-up in salaries in the wake of the AAFC-NFL competition for players. A large proportion of the salary increases, therefore, simply restored the purchasing power of player salaries, though there might have been some increase in real, inflation-adjusted salaries. Had there been no AAFC, increased gate receipts and inflationary pressure would likely have boosted nominal salaries. The battle with the AAFC gave NFL owners a more sympathetic reason to bemoan salary increases.

The NFL's boast that most of its players were college-educated (if not necessarily graduates), and were therefore not ruffians, was two-edged. College graduates had higher earning potential than the general labor force. NFL owners, like their professional basketball peers, could not afford to slash salaries too much, as players would choose alternative employment. The NFL's rosters were usually 33 to 40 percent larger than Major League Baseball rosters, but three times larger than NBA rosters. With only twelve or fourteen games on the schedule and, in some cases, with limited seating capacity, an NFL owner's ability to pay salaries was constrained. When the NFL held a monopoly (1950–59), collegiate players who wanted to play in the NFL had no choice but to acquiesce to whatever the team drafting them was willing to pay or to go to Canada. The players themselves recognized the negative effect this had on their starting salaries, although some didn't think it mattered much. A congressional committee member, citing the tens of thousands of dollars in bonuses untried baseball prospects received to sign with teams, asked Chuck Bednarik, "Don't you think if there were no player draft, the bonuses to football players to sign would be much higher?" Bednarik replied, "Well, I don't think a football player goes into football with the idea of staying in the game for 15 or 20 years, or with the object of making a lot of money. Football is more hazardous than baseball and there is no such thing as bonus." Bednarik admitted that he had been fortunate in that two teams from different leagues held draft rights to him, so "I could dicker with both, and get that extra buck. A man has to prove himself in football." Bednarik proved an exception to his own rule by playing fourteen seasons.[56]

As well as being limited to just one suitor, NFL players were discouraged from employing agents or legal counsel during negotiations. George Halas told the antitrust subcommittee a story: "A player came in and I gave him a pretty substantial increase. It was a salary up to about $12,500. And he said, 'Gee, I would like to have a little more.' Well, I said, 'All right, we will make it $13,000.' Well, he said, 'Gee you know,' he says, 'I think any number with 13 is bound to be very unlucky, and it may affect me.' So I gave him the $14,000. Do you think for a minute that I would grant anything like that to any outside representative or a counsel? No chance."[57] Owners liked their players ignorant.

Red Grange probably held the record for highest nominal salary when he parlayed his spectacular 1925 college season into a half-season with the Chicago Bears and several exhibition games. A decade later, Art Rooney of the struggling Pittsburgh Steelers paid Byron (Whizzer) White $15,800 during the Depression; that would have been over $25,000 in 1949 dollars. White opted to play the 1938 season and led the league in rushing (though his presence did not improve the Steelers' record), because he could defer his Rhodes Scholarship until January 1939. He later served on the United

States Supreme Court; Supreme Court justices earned $20,000 per year in 1938.[58] Sammy Baugh recalled that George Preston Marshall signed him for $8,000 in 1937, fresh out of college.[59]

After World War II owners and players apparently were expecting to see salaries resume at prewar levels, even though the Consumer Price "All Items" Index rose by 22 percent between 1941 and 1945; this may have been understated because of the widespread price controls. Scattered remarks in the press implied that players averaged roughly $3,000 each.[60] Sportswriter Stanley Frank claimed that NFL payrolls in 1941 ranged from $45,000 to $64,000, with most starting players earning between $2,000 to $3,000 and some stars making in excess of $10,000.[61] Philadelphia Eagles general manager and backfield coach Charley Ewart hoped that an AAFC merger or demise would bring salaries back to pre-1946 levels. He claimed that top-of-the-line players might not see their salaries diminished, but for "second and third stringers, those men whose pay was inflated $2,000 to $3,000 a season by competition, things will have to come back to normal. Each team carries about 15 men who see little action, but who get two or three thousand dollars inflation wages. Cut these down to proper figures and you will save 30 to 45 thousand dollars."[62] Ewart's comments, though, ignored the change in the general price level. Between 1945 and 1949, the Consumer Price Index had jumped another 32 percent. The index, therefore, had risen 62 percent between 1941 and 1949. A starting player making $4,000 in 1941 would need to earn $6,480 to maintain his earning power in 1949. If Ewart had gotten his wish, player salaries might have fallen below the prewar level in purchasing power or in real terms. His claim, though, seems absurdly high. Suppose the salaries trebled between 1941 and 1949: in that case, using the 62-percent jump in prices, players' purchasing power would have increased by 85 percent, which would have been a good boost but hardly the exponential jump it was made out to be.

Cleveland Browns owner Arthur "Mickey" McBride told reporters his team payroll went from $150,000 in 1946 to $240,000 in 1947 and to $297,000 in 1948. He declared that his team needed to gross $1.1 million in revenues to break even. Note that, if it had been true, McBride's claim would have meant that player salaries would have comprised less than 30 percent of team revenues, a figure that, while higher than Major League Baseball's

18 to 22 percent of total expenses during the mid-1950s, was not inordinate; baseball salaries during the 1920s and 1930s comprised roughly one-third of club expenses. In any event, since most NFL teams paid around 15 percent for stadium rental, player costs and stadium rental still comprised less than 50 percent of gross receipts. Reporters did not ask what happened to the remaining 50 percent.[63] Alexis Thompson complained that the payroll for his Eagles was $190,000 in 1946, while Dan Reeves claimed his payroll for the Rams went from $128,000 to $170,000 after the team's championship season in 1945.[64]

Bert Bell claimed, "Our salaries have increased 400 percent in the past ten years, due to the balanced power of our clubs." He did acknowledge the role of rising gate receipts in boosting salaries.[65] Bell later stated, "During the same 12-year period [last twelve seasons], average income of league players has increased approximately 325 percent." A good proportion of this 325-percent increase, of course, would have been needed to keep pace with the change in the general price level (roughly 48 percent between 1946 and 1958). He went on to slyly denigrate the players' efforts: "The salary of a league football player, who devotes only 2 months full time and 3 months part time to playing football averages over $9,200 per season."[66] In another case, sportswriter Tom Meany may have exaggerated the amount of the football Brooklyn Dodgers' player payroll: "The Brooklyn football payroll is greater than the baseball payroll. This is the most expensive football team Brooklyn ever has fielded." While the second half of his statement may well have been true, it is difficult to see how the football team could have had a larger payroll than the baseball team, which was one season removed from a National League pennant. Even in the 1930s, the baseball Dodgers' team payroll hovered around $250,000; in 1948 prices, this would have been much higher.[67]

With the absorption of a few AAFC teams by the NFL, observers figured that the players' heyday was over. A writer for *Time* magazine cited Arthur McBride, owner of the Browns: "Some . . . players who got $10,000 and $12,000 this year will be playing for half that—or less—next season." The writer also cited high draft choice Leon Hart's diminished bargaining leverage.[68] Writer Joe Williams practically chortled, "Headline backs have been pulling down $20,000, faceless guards $10,000." He also pointed out that Leon Hart, who had hoped for $25,000, had to reduce his demands. Williams also made a spurious comparison with baseball: "A Joe DiMaggio starts out in big league baseball at $10,000 or less. Pro footballers were shamelessly undersalaried before the challengers came along. They've been crazily overpaid ever since and my philosophy in this respect happens to be that the hired hands are worth all they can get. But when salaries spiral to a point which is all out of reason and general bankruptcy threatens, then it's either revision downward or close up shop."[69]

Tim Mara thought salaries needed to come down, especially because he claimed that revenues fell during the AAFC-NFL contretemps. Mara also claimed that players did "less work in today's fast-action specialized football than they did 10 and 15 years ago, and an owner must have 32 good men, if he can find them, and cannot get along with 15 to 20." However, Mara indicated that "salaries were never the crucial make-or-break expenses in recent years. A team dropped much more through poor scheduling, involving extraordinary travel, and with a losing team, than it did through inflated salaries."[70] Owners frequently bemoaned transportation costs, but these typically ran far lower than player salaries.

NFL salaries were comparable to the NBA salaries, but top players' salaries in both leagues fell far behind those of baseball players Joe DiMaggio, Ted Williams, and Stan Musial. Major League Baseball, of course, still generated greater revenue streams. Professional wrestlers could make far more than the best NFL star during the late 1940s and early 1950s, with Lou Thesz reputedly making $250,000 a season. Even top women professional wrestlers could hope to pull in $30,000 a year.[71]

Because of competition from Canada, which erupted almost immediately after the end of the AAFC-NFL strife, the downward pressure on salaries was diminished.[72] The eventual resumption (if, indeed, there had been a diminution) of growth in gate receipts also cushioned player salaries.

Two seasons after the merger, two Detroit stars, quarterback Bobby Layne and halfback Doak Walker, reportedly made $15,000 each. Layne apparently received a similar salary when he played for George Halas and the Chicago Bears. Layne's salary demonstrates the confusion inherent in discussions of player salaries. An article in *Time* magazine claimed that Layne signed with the Bears for a $10,000 bonus and a salary of $18,000, with promised raises of $1,000 per season; in other words, more than $15,000. Walker mentioned that his contract expired in 1952: "That gives me three years. After that, football may have to yield to business." He already had business interests in the Dallas area, including a sporting-goods store and a filling station.[73] Walker represented the type of player Bert Bell extolled. These players intended to use their NFL earnings to establish a nest egg for business investments. They did not intend to make the NFL a career. Walker played for only six seasons.

Quarterback Y. A. Tittle received between $15,000 and $20,000 from the San Francisco 49ers. Reporter William Worden commented that this was "for about five months' work," as though an entire season of professional football were a cushy job. Tittle, like many of his peers, worked at another job in the off-season; Tittle worked in an insurance office.[74] NFL star quarterbacks were exceptions to Bell's "three- (or four)-and-out" characterization of NFL players' experiences. Tittle played seventeen seasons, surpassing Sammy Baugh's sixteen and Charlie Conerly's fourteen.[75]

Tittle's teammate Hugh McElhenny's salary was up to $12,000 in 1953, but he still augmented his NFL salary by moonlighting. Author Dave Newhouse describes how McElhenny attended team practices in the morning and then headed for "his second job at Granny Goose Foods, maker of a popular brand of potato chips."[76]

While quarterbacks likely received the top salary on many teams, other skilled-position players earned comparable amounts. Frank Finch wrote in 1954 that Elroy "Crazy Legs" Hirsch pulled in nearly $100,000 "for the past few years."[77]

NFL linemen (both on offense and on defense) and defensive players generally received lower salaries than the offensive backs. While it is difficult to measure contributions to a team's record by players at different positions, offensive backs certainly garnered more glory and attracted the fans. *Sports Illustrated* football columnist Tex Maule wrote, "This attitude [of the obscurity of defensive players] was, unfortunately, reflected in pay checks; the five-figure incomes were reserved for pro quarterbacks, ends and halfbacks."[78]

Player salaries increased by 36.7 percent between 1952 and 1956. Gross operating income and home game receipts rose even more rapidly, 48.6

percent and 43.1 percent respectively (away game receipts increased by 50 percent). Player salaries as a proportion of gross operating income or home game receipts fell, even as the league began to stabilize and even prosper.

Team payrolls were remarkably similar across teams. As table 15 shows, in none of the five years did the team with the largest payroll exceed the team with the smallest payroll by even 50 percent. Baseball's American League had a somewhat higher proportional spread between the top and bottom payrolls, but the payroll disparities in the American League just before 2000 dwarf the disparities in the NFL of the 1950s.[79] When the Lions and the Browns won the league championships in 1953 and 1954, their payrolls were not inordinately large.

Creighton Miller, legal counsel for the Players Association, testified before Congress: "According to statistics, the average professional football player's salary from 1946 to 1949 increased from $4,000 to $8,000. . . . The player's average salary at the present time, according to Commissioner Bell, is between $8,500 and $9,000 per season, which means that since 1949, during a period which found the owners enjoying greatly increased revenues, the average player's salary was increased by no more than $1,000 in this 7-year period." Kenneth Harkins pointed out that the NFL owners submitted payroll figures suggesting that average player's salaries rose from $7,458 in 1952 to $9,216 in 1956. Miller, himself, did not have access to player salary data, and he admitted that his figures of $4,000 to $8,000 was taken from a January 3, 1949 article in *Time* magazine.[80] Kenneth Harkins queried Miller as to why player salaries did not keep up with net income and revenues, and Miller stated, "Without question, the fact that there is no other league with whom or to whom the player may bargain is certainly a factor that . . . would allow the club owner to pay the player whatever he wants to pay him. There is no competitive bidding."[81]

Teams sometimes used novel tactics to compensate players without raising salaries. In a move that may have been meant to keep salaries down, the AAFC Brooklyn Dodgers announced a profit-sharing plan. Given that the Dodgers floundered, the plan undoubtedly did so as well.[82]

What the owners gave, they could take away. Coach Curly Lambeau fined the entire Green Bay team one-half of one game's salary (about 4 percent of their season salary) for a poor showing against the resurgent Chicago Cardinals.[83]

Coaches typically earned more than all but the best players. Detroit Lions coach Gus Dorais was dismissed at the end of the 1947 season. The *New York Times* reported he had had a five-year contract at $27,000 per year. His successor, Alvin McMillin, was to receive $30,000 per season as general manager and coach.[84] A few years later, the Los Angeles Rams signed Sid Gillman to a four-year contract estimated to be worth $25,000 per annum, while Buddy Parker reportedly earned $30,000; his salary was tied in part to club earnings.[85]

Players participating in the NFL Championship Game earned a share of the gate receipts and television money (table 16). Since the attendance and gate receipts varied considerably across seasons, players had only a rough idea of what this added income might be. For some players, the added income represented a proportionally significant boost to their salaries. Cleveland Browns players received almost $2,500 each for winning the 1954 championship game. The next year they hit the championship game jackpot. The game was played in Los Angeles and the attendance was double that of the previous year's championship game in Cleveland. Because the television money did not double between years, player shares did not double, but at $3,500 per player, they were still a handsome amount.[86] All-Star players also received money from playing in the postseason Pro Bowl.[87]

Players, especially those in New York, began getting endorsement offers. Players also received trivial sums for allowing their likenesses to be placed on bubblegum cards. Bert Bell let the players' association take over the contract with Topps Gum. The royalties amounted to about $50 per player.[88]

If NFL players' real salaries stagnated in the second half of the 1950s, relief was on the way. The American Football League promised to boost salaries in the same way the AAFC had. Just a little competition made a significant difference in salaries. One report stated that the AFL intended to establish a minimum salary 10 percent higher than the NFL's $6,500 minimum (compare this to the $5,000 established in 1958–59). The AFL owners also promised to pay their game officials "substantially more than in the NFL, which was said to have $3,000 per season as the highest salary."[89] AFL owners were also willing to pay more for general managers and coaches. Barron Hilton, president of the Los Angeles Chargers, offered ex–Notre Dame coach Frank Leahy $50,000 to be general manager of the Chargers. This reported figure, however, was twice what the New York Titans offered Steve Sebo to be their general manager.[90]

By 1962 sportswriters were tossing around salary figures in excess of $30,000. Joe Foss told Al Hirschberg that the AFL's average salary was $10,000 and that Billy Cannon got the top salary at $33,000.[91] Earlier, Murray Olderman had reported that Giants' quarterback Charlie Conerly was "somewhere in the $30,000-a-year range."[92]

Player Limits

The NFL played their rules concerning the limit on the number of players on a roster like an accordion. They increased and decreased the limit to suit their needs. The ostensible purpose of changing the player limits, in addition to the obvious need of adjusting to two-platoon or wartime football, was to trim player payrolls or to diminish the pool of players available for a rival league. Assuming that the players eliminated from a reduction in the roster limit were the worst players, who were typically the least paid, such savings were probably minimal, perhaps $4,000 to $6,000 per player cut, depending on the minimum salaries being paid.

A more useful aspect of the player limit, though, was to deny players to a rival league. The AAFC, Canadian, and AFL teams needed players, and NFL rosters were handy places to find good and not-so-good players.

The NFL owners decided to leave their player limit at thirty-three instead of raising it to thirty-five, as suggested, by George Preston Marshall (who usually pushed for cost-control measures) at the January 1947 meetings. The owners reversed themselves six months later and increased the limit to thirty-five for the first three games and thirty-four for the remainder of the season. Two years later, when peace seemed at hand, the owners pushed the limit back to thirty-three. The limit seesawed back and forth; it was down to thirty-two for 1950 and back to thirty-three in 1951. The decision to restore the limit to thirty-three in 1951 was in response to the Korean War draft of young men, which took some NFL players.[93] Bell, worrying that the signs of prosperity after the AAFC merger were ephemeral, urged the owners to cut their rosters to thirty men for the 1953 season, primarily through the elimination of the "injured reserve" list. They rejected his proposal, as they feared to make any moves that "would give their fans the idea they were cheapening their product."[94] Two years later, the owners considered increasing the limit to thirty-five players for the first two games, giving coaches more time to evaluate their marginal players. The next year, George Preston Marshall was advocating for a thirty-five man roster, and the proposal passed in 1957.[95] The NFL owners later raised the limit to thirty-eight in order to create a reservoir of players for the new Minnesota Vikings team, with the intent of dropping the limit back to thirty-five in 1961. The increased limit also served to deny some players to the AFL. The league dropped the limit back to thirty-six in 1961.[96]

Conclusion

Yes, NFL owners faced rising nominal and real costs during the postwar period. Their revenues, however, outpaced their costs, so by the mid-1950s most owners were enjoying a measure of prosperity, if they had not been doing so already. The salary increases from the competition with the AAFC appear to have persisted into the 1950s. The owners certainly had the wherewithal to pay these salaries, and might have been able to pay even higher salaries, given the rising revenues.

5

THE PERILS AND TRIUMPHS
OF NFL OWNERSHIP

Owning an NFL team might seem to be a glamorous experience. A capitalist manufacturing door knobs or cardboard boxes may be the envy of her industry, but outside of trade journals she reaps scant public acclaim. Owning a championship sports team (even if it is not profitable) brings the owner publicity and, starting in the late twentieth century, a Gatorade or champagne dousing. During the postwar years, owning an NFL franchise was fraught with risks. Many franchises faltered, usually due to inadequate demand relative to expenses. In order to boost the bottom line, some owners opted to move to cities which they hoped would bring in better money.

If the overall demand for pro football had risen, owners might have decided to create "expansion teams." Expanding into viable locations carried an important advantage, as it could deny outposts to any rival league that might arise. Economists call filling most or all of the viable locations to forestall the entry of a new league spatial preemption.

Although several AAFC and NFL teams went bankrupt, NFL owners began to see handsome offers for their teams by the mid-1950s.

Franchise Sales

While profit figures can be massaged to tell an intended story, franchise sales prices give another indication of past profits and perceived future profitability. As the old caveat goes, "Past performance does not imply future performance," so a team that was unprofitable might still have seen a jump in its franchise value if a new lucrative television contract came along or if tax laws changed, among other factors.

Readers are also cautioned to interpret fabulous rates of appreciation in the context of changes in the general price level (inflation), general market rates of return, and the risk both of accrued losses and of bankruptcy. Readers should also understand the magic of compound interest. The "rule of seventy-two" is a good rule of thumb: it states that you can predict how fast an asset will double in price by dividing seventy-two by the market rate of return (interest on a high-quality bond would suffice as a proxy for a rate of return on a relatively safe investment). If the general rate of return is 6 percent per annum, then a typical asset would double in value every twelve (72/6) years; for a rate of return of 9 percent per annum, a typical asset would double in value every eight years (72/9).[1] If owners lost money for several seasons, this would, in effect, be similar to increasing the original purchasing price when figuring out the rate of appreciation. Since the NFL had to resuscitate a couple of franchises after the settlement with the AAFC, owners could not be certain that their investment in a team would prove profitable. For instance, Ted Collins claimed to have lost $720,000 in the four years he operated a team in Boston.[2]

Economists James Quirk and Rodney Fort compiled a list of NFL franchise sales (table 17). Quirk and Fort showed that after World War II the NFL had the most stable turnover ratio and that a majority of teams sold had losing records at the time of their sale. On average, NFL teams had the highest rate of appreciation among professional team sports leagues, with annual rates of appreciation hovering around twenty percent. Their data ends with 1990.[3] The events of the late 1940s and early 1950s, though, demonstrated that owning an NFL team still entailed some risk.

The pioneering NFL owners, while not poverty-stricken, certainly would have made no one's list of "America's Wealthiest." For those owners who had few, if any, assets out of football, the game was a true labor of love. After many of the tank towns dropped out, wealthier owners in New York and some larger cities moved into the NFL. Craig Coenen states that by 1943, millionaires owned nine of the eleven teams. Of the teams that lacked well-heeled owners, the Green Bay Packers were, and continued to be, an anomaly. The team was owned by the community, and when there was a lack of money, townspeople anted up. To forestall the team's relocation to Milwaukee, the Packers' board of directors decided to sell nonprofit voting stock.[4] The other anomalous team, the Chicago Bears, was run by George Halas. Halas practiced a wary frugality and, as with some of baseball's player-turned-owner entrepreneurs, used his superior football knowledge to survive, even when surrounded by owners with deeper pockets. He eventually died with considerable wealth.[5]

Sufficient wealth alone did not ensure that a given person could purchase a team. While David Harris and Michael MacCambridge paint wonderful scenes of owners' eccentricities and foibles, NFL owners did, in fact, care with whom they associated. The owners amended the "Membership" section of the constitution and bylaws to require a ten-twelfths vote to approve any transfer, sale, assignment, retirement or cancellation of a franchise at the January 1960 meetings. The former rule had required unanimity.[6]

The NFL owners hung on grimly throughout the Depression years. In an early demonstration that NFL franchises were stabilizing and gaining value, Fred Mandel, a department-store owner in Chicago, purchased the Detroit Lions for $200,000, which was $180,000 more than the previous owner had paid in 1934.[7]

Bert Bell purchased the NFL Philadelphia franchise in 1933. Although Bell was a scion of wealth, his family's fortunes had collapsed during the stock market crash. Bell bought the franchise for $2,500, but he needed help from his wife and a friend to scrape up the sum. Bell sold his team to Alexis Thompson for $160,000 in 1940. Thompson lost money annually, and his experiences mirrored that of fellow Philadelphia team owners Connie Mack (baseball's Athletics) and Gerald Nugent (baseball's Phillies). Eddie Gottlieb later became a fourth owner (basketball's Warriors) struggling to survive in the city. Thompson watched his losses escalate during the AAFC era.[8] James P. Clark supposedly offered Thompson $300,000 for the team in 1948. Had Clark paid $300,000 for the team, which had won the championship in 1948 but reputedly continued to incur a loss, readers might surmise that Thompson roughly doubled his money in eight years. The remarks about inflation (prices rose considerably during the wartime and postwar years) and previous losses apply here. After holding out for $300,000, Thompson finally sold to Clark's syndicate for a reported $250,000.[9]

World War II quickly threatened to swamp the owners. Bell's Eagles and the Pittsburgh Steelers merged for one season, while the Boston Yanks and Brooklyn Tigers considered merging for the 1945 season. Considering the franchise instability, the owners voted in April 1945 to change the constitution so that no more than twelve and no fewer than ten clubs could comprise the league.[10] Mandel found that owning a team during wartime was not a profitable venture. In addition to his purchase price, he apparently poured in hundreds of thousands of dollars. He indicated his willingness to sell his franchise late in 1947, but negotiations did not go smoothly. Mandel later indicated he would retain the team for at least another season, having already turned down an offer of $175,000. Shortly thereafter, he sold the team to a syndicate headed by D. Lyle Fife. Reporter Joseph Sheehan cited rumors that Mandel asked for $350,000 but received closer to $200,000. Given the war and postwar inflation, $200,000 represented a depreciation in real (adjusted for inflation) terms.[11]

The New York Yankees baseball club purchased the New York Yankees football club in 1947, making Topping (and his partners) the head of both franchises. The football Yankees were not a successful team.[12]

The nascent AAFC also saw franchise ownership turnover. The struggling football Brooklyn Dodgers club needed to find new ownership, as well as to post a $200,000 bond as evidence of its ability to meet its expenses in 1948.[13] After the AAFC merged with the NFL, Buffalo owner James Breuil exercised his option to buy into the Cleveland Browns. He purchased a 25 percent share by sending three players to Cleveland; his remaining players were drafted by the other teams. A similar deal had been offered to Ben Lindheimer, owner of the defunct Los Angeles Dons, in 1949, but Lindheimer had rejected the offer, saying he wanted eight instead of three players to be awarded to the Rams.[14]

Owning an NFL franchise came with no guarantees. When the AAFC and NFL reached a settlement, the Baltimore Colts had refused to go quietly into pro football oblivion. The team's owner, Abraham Watner, got his wish and got a berth in the NFL. He may have wished that he hadn't, as the team won just one game in 1950 and floundered. Watner asked for an infusion of talent from the other teams but was rebuffed. He turned his franchise back to the NFL amidst pending lawsuits involving the city of Baltimore and players. He got a partial refund of the indemnity he paid to George Preston Marshall and $50,000 for his player contracts.[15] The Dallas Texans' owners joined the unhappy group of AAFC losers. The Chicago Cardinals survived only through the masochism and deep pockets of their owners.

Even glamorous teams faced changes in ownership. Arthur (Mickey) McBride decided to sell his Cleveland Browns team to a syndicate of Cleveland businessmen in 1953. McBride received $300,000 upfront and an additional $300,000 later. Two years later, Saul Silberman sold his half of the team for $575,000. Art Modell later put together a deal to buy the team for $3.925 million in 1960; the *New York Times* reported the price as $4 million.[16] These figures, if true, represented a fine rate of appreciation, especially since the inflation rate was low between 1953 and 1960. As a comparison, the Milwaukee Braves, a wildly successful baseball franchise, sold for $5.5 million.[17] The NFL was catching up to Major League Baseball!

Cleveland's record franchise price was soon superseded. Edwin W. Pauley purchased 37.5 percent of the Los Angeles Rams on December 16, 1947. Two years later, Hollywood icons Bing Crosby and Bob Hope each purchased 10 percent of the Rams. No purchase prices were reported.[18] The Rams' principal partners, Dan Reeves, Ed Pauley, Hal Seley, and Fred Levy, feuded and eventually ended up seeking legal action. At one point, Reeves's partners made an offer: they would buy him out for $1 million or he could buy them out for $2 million. Reeves didn't have $2 million, but he refused to sell for the $1 million. After years of wrangling, Pete Rozelle stepped in. He told the owners to make offers. Reeves offered to pay $7.1 million, while the co-owners offered $6.1 million. After paying his co-owners $4.8 million for their shares, Reeves was the sole owner of the club.[19]

When New York Giants owner Tim Mara died, sportswriter Joe King recalled that the owner had turned down an offer of $1 million for the team. King believed the franchise was worth much more in 1959. Since Mara claimed losses during much of his ownership, ascertaining any rate of appreciation would have been difficult.[20]

Harry Wismer, part owner of the Washington Redskins, decided the money was greener in the other league and launched the AFL's New York Titans. The NFL and AFL naturally took a disapproving view of such shenanigans. New commissioners Pete Rozelle and Joe Foss ordered Wismer to divest his 26.25 percent interest in the Redskins by December 8 or face a public sale. Wismer blamed Marshall for his tardiness in divesting, claiming that the curmudgeon had told potential buyers that Wismer was asking for too much money. Wismer was hoping to get $350,000, although he said

Marshall had ruined a deal for $300,000 the previous year. The story ended happily for Wismer, as William B. MacDonald agreed to the $350,000 purchase price. Wismer was now the AFL's headache; he went on to infuriate AFL commissioner Joe Foss on occasion.[21]

A letter in the Philadelphia Eagles' team folder at the Pro Football Hall of Fame in Canton, Ohio, dated December 19, 1962, discussed a potential sale of the Eagles for a purchase price of $4.5 million, with $2.75 million of the price attributable to player contracts (for purposes of depreciation) and $450,000 for the Franklin Field lease and coaches' contracts. The team would be sold in 1963 for over $5 million.[22]

Franchise Relocation

The postwar NFL did not play the franchise musical chairs game to the same extent as did Major League Baseball (six of sixteen teams) and the National Basketball Association. The NBA was experiencing a shakedown similar to the one the NFL had endured during its first two decades. The NFL, of course, had franchise turmoil due to its struggles and the eventual merger with the AAFC.

Cleveland Rams owner Dan Reeves was disgruntled. His 1945 Rams won the league championship, but Reeves claimed to have lost money that season. In a sense, he was unlucky to have won the franchise's first championship just as the war ended. He did not enjoy the peak of the postwar attendance boom. His Rams had just four home games out of ten regular-season games in 1945, and the team had fewer than eighty thousand in home attendance that season. The Cleveland Browns had four crowds in excess of sixty thousand in 1946, and, even allowing for possible inflation of the attendance figures, the Browns clearly enjoyed greater fan support. The reader is entitled to speculate, therefore, whether Reeves's decision was premature. Then again, the possible confrontation with the Browns in Cleveland might have proven even more disastrous for the Rams than the 1945 season. The AAFC's formation and its incursion into Cleveland gave Reeves an added excuse to move his franchise.

Professional sports leagues usually have clauses in their constitutions stipulating unanimity or a supermajority of support for a proposed transfer. Law professor Jeffrey Glick justified the legitimacy of such clauses, as relocating a team might cause "serious hardships for the other league members both in terms of travel schedules and costs . . . by balancing the interests of all teams in site selection, a legitimate restraint can promote on-field competition in locations acceptable to both participants, create a marketable product and thereby promote economic competition."[23]

The shimmering image of playing in the Los Angeles Coliseum, with its vast seating capacity, lured Reeves. Reeves's fellow owners feared that his proposed relocation would prove deleterious to them. The crux of the matter was whether the increased gate receipts in Los Angeles (compared with those in Cleveland) would compensate for the increased travel costs. In addition, train travel to Los Angeles from Chicago took two days, although most teams would opt to fly. Reeves, being the sole West Coast club owner, would bear the brunt of the increase in transportation costs. His fellow owners recognized that the nascent Cleveland Browns represented a true threat to the Rams' viability in Cleveland, and they were loath to let the AAFC get the initial foothold in the burgeoning southern California territory. Reeves even offered to pay his peers a higher guarantee ($15,000) for their visitor's share. Four owners voted against the transfer, stymieing it. Dan Topping's defection to the AAFC gave Reeves credibility when he announced in response, "Consider the Cleveland Rams out of football." Reeves's threat was silly, but the owners didn't want another publicity fiasco similar to that of Topping's defection. George Halas, George Preston Marshall, and Charles Bidwill switched their votes, and Reeves had his permission.[24]

For years, teams continued to complain about having to play in Los Angeles, and some fought being placed in the same division. The joke would be on them, as the Rams' drawing power made the West Coast jaunt lucrative. Years later, Bob Burnes related how the Rams and 49ers had proven "a ten-strike for professional football. It has proven to be a financial bonanza, comparable in its way to the every-day's-a-holiday situation in Milwaukee baseball." Displaying prescience, Burnes wrote that Major League Baseball owners were envious of football's West Coast success; Walter O'Malley and Horace Stoneham would transform envy into action.[25]

George Preston Marshall's experiences in Boston were similar to those of Dan Reeves in Cleveland. Marshall's team won the 1936 division title, but he claimed he lost $85,000. He blamed the Boston press for giving scant coverage to his team. Attendance was so bad that he agreed to play the Green Bay Packers at the Polo Grounds instead of in Boston.[26] Marshall decided Boston fans were unwilling to support his NFL team, so he relocated the team in 1937.

The second Boston incarnation under owner Ted Collins failed, too. Collins appeared to have a reverse Midas touch when it came to football (he was a self-made man in the radio industry), and between being unable to please fans and increasing salaries, found himself sandwiched and losing money. By 1948 Collins was eyeing New York City. The New York Giants, of course, were lukewarm about his intentions, especially since his team might have to share the Polo Grounds with them. The other owners were probably glad to see Collins vacate Boston, given its paltry visitor's shares. Collins claimed to have lost $800,000 during his five seasons in Boston, but, according to Joe King, he was able to write off much of his losses against his income tax; by 1950, his ability to write off further losses was gone. The Maras grudgingly agreed to share their territory with the Yanks. They charged Collins between $100,000 and $250,000 for the invasion and gave him the leftover Sundays on the schedule at the Polo Grounds. Collins hoped that Yankee Stadium would become available for his use. Even when Yankee Stadium became available at $50,000 annually, the Giants still had the first choice of Sundays; between that and given the baseball Yankees' habit of being in the World Series, Collins sometimes only got a handful of games there.[27]

Even with the AAFC New York franchise out of the picture by 1950, Collins fared poorly in the big city, and he stated he needed six "equitable" home dates at Yankee Stadium in order to continue operating the team. Collins was willing to relinquish his franchise, and the league paid him $100,000. Collins agreed to accept a $200,000 settlement with regard to the Yankee Stadium lease. The Giants' Tim Mara agreed to waive the balance of the territorial rights indemnity settlement, quipping, "I would have given Collins more if he had asked."[28] Reporter Ed Prell wrote that Collins had failed to give two teams their visitor's guarantees and had been delinquent in his payments to the league. Prell described the meeting transferring Collins's ownership as a "star chamber session." Since Collins gave up, his losses were probably real.[29]

Collins's team had a brief burst of semi-success in 1950, when the team went 7-5 and had sportswriter Joe King gushing, "This season he has a glamour team," but the clock struck midnight and the Bulldogs reverted back to being losers.[30] The NFL owners considered moving the team to Baltimore for a second try.

Two young Texans with a gift of gab stepped forward to resuscitate the team for the 1952 season. The Miller brothers, who were not stereotypical Texas oilmen but textile manufacturers, wanted to relocate the team to Dallas. While most NFL owners were hardly progressives with respect to racial mores, they recognized the potential problems of having a team in the Deep South, especially one with some African American players on its roster, including Buddy Young, George Taliaferro, and Sherman Howard. The Detroit Lions worried about losing lucrative exhibition games in Texas, so they opposed the move; the Chicago Cardinals also opposed the deal, seeing one more potentially lucrative city occupied. Despite these concerns, the owners accepted the Miller brothers' offer of $300,000. According to reporters, the league kept $100,000 and turned the remainder to Dan Topping to settle the Yankee Stadium lease agreement, which contradicts the league's annual $25,000 payments reported in the league meeting minutes. Bell expressed optimism: "We are interested only in the right group and the right site for our franchises and Dallas appears to qualify on both counts."[31] While Bell waxed optimistic, sportswriter Joe King sounded a sour note: "[Financial losses] could happen in Texas, too, no matter how strongly the fans support the team at the start with their Lone Star 'nationalism.' Nobody ever loved a loser, not even Texas fans, and that's the hazard for Miller in a risky business." King also pointed out that Collins had traded several draft picks for immediate help that proved ephemeral.[32]

Joe King was prescient. The brothers' efforts to obtain local Southern Methodist University star Doak Walker failed, and their promotional gimmicks could not overcome a rotten team and the popularity of college football. The Miller brothers hemorrhaged money by ten-gallon hatfuls, with the team unable to even cover visiting teams' expenses. King claimed that the popularity of local college football siphoned off fan dollars, but the team's ineptness undoubtedly was a crucial factor. By midseason, the Miller brothers were begging to be relieved of their franchise. Suitably chastened after reportedly losing almost $250,000 in less than a season's time, the brothers forfeited the franchise to Bert Bell and the NFL owners, who surely gnashed their teeth at having been persuaded to sell the franchise to the brothers. Then again, in the wake of the collapse of the New York Yanks, the league wanted a twelfth team for 1951.[33]

One of the team's trustees observed that "sufficient financial backing had been obtained to operate the club on a long-range basis but that 'interim financing' could not be obtained for several reasons. These included legal technicalities that prevented the franchise from being sold at this time. Some forty bondholders have, in effect, a mortgage on the club."[34] Once again the NFL was on the hook for player salaries and other expenses. Bell stripped Dallas of its remaining home games. He used language from the league's constitution to explain his actions: "I have determined that the Dallas Texans Football Club, Inc., is guilty of acts detrimental to the NFL, namely a refusal to continue to operate the club and field a team throughout the balance of the 1952 season. The franchise . . . is hereby canceled and forfeited and the player contracts, including the reserve-player list, are hereby taken over by the NFL." Despite these failings, Bell remained gracious toward the Miller brothers (or perhaps he was a gifted actor): "I think you were a wonderful sport. I want you to know that I will never forget that you and your brother and Harlan Ray dug into your own pockets to pay the Los Angeles Rams their $20,000 guarantee."[35]

Demonstrating that hope does spring eternal, at least in professional football, another group of Dallas investors expressed interest in buying the team. Bell rebuffed their efforts when they balked at paying the $200,000 to cover Ted Collins's Yankee Stadium lease settlement.[36]

Baltimore fans refused to relinquish their dreams of an NFL team. During the Dallas fiasco, the directors of the former Baltimore team were preparing to sue the NFL and Abraham Watner for the loss of the franchise. With the Dallas franchise in tatters, Bell decided to offer Baltimore another chance. The team, however, had to sell at least fifteen thousand season tickets ($250,000) before the beginning of the season. Michael MacCambridge characterizes the city's efforts to sell the requisite number of seats as "one of the early signs of a phenomenon that pro football would see frequently in the coming decades: sport fans convinced that the very existence of a franchise gave the city itself a measure of national prestige and identity." Such filmmakers as Barry Levinson (*Tin Men*) and John Waters (*Hairspray*) may have contributed more to the city's cachet, however. The ticket-sale drive was successful; all the franchise needed, in a reversal of the usual order of things, was an owner. Bell persuaded his friend Carroll Rosenbloom and some associates to pay $200,000 for the franchise, with just $25,000 down (this sounds similar to a used-car pitch: "Just $25,000 down and you can drive away this refurbished franchise!").

Fans could be forgiven for thinking that Baltimore was simply Dallas relocated, especially as the Dallas players became Baltimore players. Technically, the Baltimore team was an expansion team, as the Dallas franchise was left dormant. The NFL achieved its goal of getting the City of Baltimore to drop its lawsuit against the league and Abraham Watner.[37]

During the congressional inquiry into professional sports, the NFL placed the agreement between itself and Baltimore into the evidence. The Baltimore owners agreed to pay the league $200,000 in cash, with $25,000 immediately and the remainder in payments stretching until January 12, 1959. The franchise also got a first pick in the January 1953 draft, in addition to a group of players. This time the Baltimore franchise took hold.[38]

The Boston/New York Yanks, Baltimore Colts, and Dallas Texans were weak teams, and folding or relocating them made sense. Some relatively prosperous teams were also candidates for relocation, as investors in cities across America eagerly sought NFL franchises. George Preston Marshall claimed that a group of Louisville, Kentucky businessmen and the Kentucky State Fair and Exposition offered him "the most fantastic offer ever made by a community to acquire a professional sports team." The Kentucky gentlemen offered an expanded stadium with somewhat greater capacity than Griffith Stadium where the Redskins played; a guaranteed season ticket sale of twenty-five thousand for the first three years; stadium rental of 6 percent of the gross (instead of the 15 percent charged by baseball's Washington Senators); and 100 percent of all concession income except parking, of which the Redskins would get 20 percent. Marshall received no concession income at the time. Marshall was probably sorely tempted, but he said, "If it's still laying around four years from now, when our lease on Griffith Stadium expires, we definitely will consider it."[39] Louisville's offer presaged the almost annual ritual of NFL owners playing off their cities against other cities in the stadium game.

When Marshall rebuffed the Louisvillians, they turned their attentions to the Pittsburgh Steelers and Philadelphia Eagles. The Steelers played at Pittsburgh's Forbes Field. Art Rooney was also tempted by the Louisville offer: "I'm interested and I've already had my office in Pittsburgh wire these people that we'll be happy to talk with them."[40] Unlike Marshall, Rooney had no stadium lease; his had expired. Rooney complained, "We have the highest overhead in the NFL. Our rental at Forbes Field is the highest in the league. Even when we sell out the 34,000 seats we have a hard time making ends meet." The Louisville group enticed Rooney with the promise, "Our stadium will be enlarged to seat around 47,000. Our parking facilities are the best in the world with a tremendous capacity of 27,000 automobiles." The Pittsburgh Pirates baseball team quickly allied themselves with the Steelers, claiming both teams needed a new municipal stadium. Pirates vice president Thomas P. Johnson told reporters, "I'm glad the issue arose. What we need in Pittsburgh — both the Steelers and the Pirates — is a municipal stadium we can both use." Louisville representative Bill Henry made a similar pitch to the Eagles (who paid 12 to 14 percent of gross receipts in rent), although he guaranteed them only fifteen thousand season tickets.[41] The parking situation reflected the changing reality of professional team sports. A greater proportion of fans were driving to the games instead of using mass transit. Parking facilities became paramount.

Rooney was in the happy position of being wooed by two suitors, as he reported that a Buffalo, New York group was also hoping to land his team. The Buffalo group's offer included the low rental rate of $1,000 per game. Rooney said he was currently paying 15 percent of the net gate after taxes; he also paid maintenance costs, which averaged $6,000 a game.[42] Rooney hung on in Pittsburgh. The city built Three Rivers Stadium a decade later.

As early as the transfer of the New York Yanks to Dallas, sportswriter Ed Prell wrote that the Chicago Cardinals remained the league's weakest link. Every professional sports league has its downtrodden, financially weak team. The NFL's prosperity during the 1950s did not extend to the Chicago Cardinals: as table 5 demonstrates, the Cardinals reported persistent losses during the mid-1950s. They were the only team to do so. Prell thought that the Cardinals, even after a couple of rare winning seasons, would forever remain Chicago's second team, behind the Bears. Because of the television blackout, neither team could televise its games effectively; therefore, both lost out on this revenue source. Prell thought the Cardinals might either merge with the Bears or relocate. The team's long-time owner, Charles Bidwill, died in the 1940s, and his widow, Violet, then married Walter Wolfner. Wolfner disputed Prell's concerns: "I'm sure Chicago can support two big league football teams."[43] Violet apparently developed an antipathy toward George Halas, and some observers felt her obstinacy in remaining in Chicago, despite attractive offers to relocate, stemmed from her determination to spite the Bears' owner. By the late 1950s, after a lengthy run of mediocre teams, the Cardinals were playing to small crowds. This, of course, antagonized the other owners, who took in small visitor's shares.

Violet wanted the Cardinals to transfer from Comiskey Park on Chicago's South Side to Northwestern University's Dyche Stadium north of the city, but Bell refused to countenance the move. The longstanding agreement had been that the North Side was Bears territory, while the South Side belonged to the Cardinals (similar to the territorial split between Al Capone and the rival bootlegging gangs). Bert Bell told owners that "this is the toughest decision I have ever had to make. This is my decision on the territorial rights between the Cardinals and the Bears." Bell decided in favor of the Bears. Halas told his fellow owners he would supply copies of the agreement between Bidwill and himself regarding territorial rights, the so-called Madison Street agreement.[44]

The Cardinals started playing games at Soldier Field. With two teams in the city, the television blackout made a national contract less attractive to television networks. The Cardinals' refusal to move was, therefore, adversely affecting the other eleven owners. The Wolfners' intransigence in refusing to sell or relocate would cause the NFL headaches for years.[45] The Cardinals refused to leave the lucrative Chicago television market without compensation.

Because the collective gains of relocating the Cardinals far outweighed the benefits of remaining in the city, the other NFL owners agreed to subsidize the Cardinals' eventual relocation to the amount of $500,000. George Halas and the CBS television network also agreed to help subsidize the move.[46] Halas, of course, gained by having the Chicago market to himself, in addition to the opening up of television rights; CBS gained by being able to telecast games into Chicago. The Cardinals agreed to move to St. Louis (creating confusion, since the baseball Cardinals were already a city institution), pending a satisfactory stadium lease at Busch Stadium and television arrangements. A *New York Times* reporter wrote that the $500,000 was, in part, to reimburse the Wolfners for money they paid to improve Soldier Field. St. Louis also promised twenty-five thousand season tickets for the first season. In addition, the Wolfners were buoyed by the hope of a new and larger stadium in St. Louis. The St. Louis interests behind the new stadium realized they needed two tenants to make the project viable, so landing a football team was imperative. The Cardinals faced a tepid response in St. Louis and would remain mired in mediocrity. They opened their new home with a gate of twenty-six thousand fans, including only fifteen thousand season-ticket holders.[47]

The Green Bay Packers remained an anachronism. Throughout the 1950s, observers wondered when the team would relocate. Bob Burnes wrote, "Even if everybody in town turned out for every game, it would scarcely be enough."[48] The team struggled throughout the 1950s, but new coach Vince Lombardi rapidly transformed the franchise and ended talk of relocation.[49]

Expansion

Although the relocations of teams sated a few cities' appetites for NFL football, there were more investors clamoring for teams than there were willing sellers. Legislators pressured Major League Baseball to occupy the growing cities across America, and while the American League in particular bungled its franchise relocations and expansion, the movements satisfied the legislators.[50] With the NFL growing in popularity, congressional pressure was building for the NFL to move into more cities. The NBA had yet to reach the popularity of its older peers, and the congressional committee did not seem as anxious to have NBA teams occupy their cities.

When grilled by the congressional committee, Bell claimed there weren't enough good players to supply more teams.

CHAIRMAN (EMANUEL CELLER): Is there enough football talent to support two more teams, say, or a league?

MR. BELL: My contention is when the last 2 teams in each conference win 3 or 4 ballgames for 2 years, there is enough material — provided they get that first selection choice for 2 years — to establish two other teams. Last year was pretty close to it. I think it is inevitable that it is going to happen.[51]

Craig Coenen describes the NFL owners' hesitation regarding would-be owners. They raised the league entrance fee in 1940 from $10,000 to $50,000 in order to dissuade the casually interested. Coenen thought many of these investors were "boosters," who thought having an NFL team would prove their city to be "major league."[52] While NFL owners might have been flattered by the attention and gratified at the potential appreciation in their franchise's value due to unmet demand, additional teams meant diluted voting power for the original owners and a potential weakening of traditional rivalries. In the crowded northeast quadrant of the country, any expansion threatened to violate some existing owner's territorial rights. Some NFL officials, including Curly Lambeau, considered expanding to twelve teams for the 1946 season, but the idea was stillborn. On occasion, existing professional football teams in such leagues as the Pacific Coast [Football] League asked to be granted spots in the NFL, but the league only promised to consider their applications in the future. Bell told San Francisco Clippers officials that they would be given preference if the league ever expanded, but he remarked that the difficulty in creating a suitable schedule was a key obstacle to expansion. The Clippers' case was likely doomed by the NFL's hope of acquiring the AAFC San Francisco 49ers in an eventual merger. Throughout the 1950s, the NFL owners rebuffed potential owners.[53]

When the NFL responded to the AFL's formation by announcing plans to expand, the process was hardly straightforward. George Preston Marshall, whose territorial ambitions rivaled those of the staunchest imperialist, opposed Dallas because he viewed the entire South as his territory, given his televising of Redskins games throughout the region. Marshall also disliked Dallas's putative owner, Clint Murchison Jr., because of his past dealings with the young man. Murchison had previously tried to buy the Redskins and move them to Dallas. While Marshall may strike most readers as an irascible, penny-pinching, bigoted owner, he had a sentimental side. Murchison held a trump card in his efforts to land a Dallas expansion team. One of Marshall's innovations was to provide live music at his games. The team even had a fight song, "Hail to the Redskins," which Marshall adored. As David Harris relates — and he was not writing fiction — Marshall had fired the song's composer from his post as leader of the franchise's in-house band, and in a fit of pique the bandleader had sold the rights to the tune to a Murchison crony. When Murchison threatened to deny the Redskins the use of their theme song, Marshall relented and the Dallas Cowboys were born on January 28, 1960. Not counting the price of the song, the franchise cost Murchison $600,000.[54]

In response to congressional pressure in 1957, Bert Bell encouraged NFL owners to expand, but he encountered opposition to his efforts. Bell thought adding two teams would be wise, but unless the schedule was lengthened, the intraconference home-and-home series would have to be junked. The clubs in the NFL's Western Conference were not keen on breaking up their lucrative schedule. Bell blasted the Western Conference's owners: "They must think of more than the chance to get money — they must think of satisfying the fans. I can tell them from experience that fans can get sick of any team, and will demand variety. The fans are not satisfied to see a team from the other section only once every six years and in several cases only once every 11 years, on the present schedule." Bell identified Buffalo and Louisville as prime candidates for expansion.[55]

George Preston Marshall opposed Bell's plan. He conceded that some current teams might be forced to relocate because of small crowds and inadequate parking and that Louisville and Buffalo were attractive sites. He denied Bell's claim of selfishness: "I don't believe there's anyone in the NFL piggish on the subject of money. They wouldn't be in it if they were." Marshall's main concerns revolved around television money and increased competition for players. The owners voted down both proposals — immediate expansion and removing the interconference home-and-home schedule — at the January 1958 meetings; they did agree to form a committee to investigate expansion. Bell told owners at the January 1959 meetings that he had an offer of $650,000 for an expansion franchise: "This offer comes from a man who would have everyone's approval. He has no tax angle. I am sure you would all want him. He is a very high-class, high-type man." Bell wasn't pushing for action; he just wanted owners to know that quality buyers were clamoring for NFL franchises.[56]

The NFL committee on expansion, chaired by George Halas, recommended that Houston and Dallas be added to the league for the 1961 season. As Lamar Hunt observed, the timing of the committee's findings were suspicious: "I think that he [Halas] must have been poorly advised in making this statement because the Senators or Congressmen from Colorado, the state of Washington, Minnesota and Florida are not going to be happy about it all, as you can imagine. They were aware that the National League has been trying to sabotage the formation of this league and I think their reaction is going to be very strong."[57] Hunt's political acumen failed him this time. When Major League Baseball thwarted the Continental League by announcing expansion for 1961 and 1962, legislators applauded the move, even though it killed the Continental League.

While Hunt fumed and the NFL committee switched its sights to Minneapolis–St. Paul, some NFL owners remained opposed to expansion. Marshall, citing the league constitution's clause requiring unanimous approval for new franchises (although owners could change the bylaws with ten votes out of twelve at the January 1960 meetings), insisted he would not give his assent. In a stunning piece of revisionism, Marshall said, "The AAC [AAFC] was the best thing that ever happened to us. We got a lot of publicity out of it and, though the venture lost $14,000,000, we gained two pretty good franchises, Cleveland and San Francisco. If the proposed new league become [sic] a success, stayed in existence three to five years, it could provide excellent possibilities for the NFL." Marshall thought the two leagues might eventually play a championship game and, at worst, the NFL could absorb the best survivors of the AFL as it had done with the AAFC.[58]

Marshall notwithstanding, the other owners were now intent on expansion. Art Rooney suggested, "Minneapolis and Dallas very well could be voted franchises in January [1960], and we could then look ahead to perhaps taking in two other teams — Houston and Buffalo, or maybe Miami — in

'61 or '62. The owners of the new franchises would be able to pay their $600,000 [franchise fee] to the league over a period of years, because we'll have made certain they are financially stable. In return for their $600,000, they'll get players off our rosters."[59]

Nothing was simple in the NFL. While the NFL pondered expansion, Bert Bell died. The owners squabbled while choosing a successor. Halas reputedly orchestrated the transfer of the Chicago Cardinals, the expansion, and the selection of Pete Rozelle. Halas remained neutral on the subject of selecting the new commissioner, but his machinations stamped him as the football equivalent of Talleyrand. Tex Maule supplied a detailed look at Halas's efforts.[60]

Expansion became a reality when the NFL owners, Marshall included, voted 11–0 to approve admittance of the Dallas Rangers (Cowboys) and Minneapolis–St. Paul, with the Cardinals abstaining. The Dallas team paid $50,000 as the franchise cost, but spent $550,000 in "buying" castoffs from the existing NFL teams' rosters. The league voted that the Eastern Conference could decide whether they wanted Dallas or Minneapolis in their conference, which was a sop to the Maras' desire to have Baltimore transferred to the Eastern Conference.[61]

Pete Rozelle urged owners to establish a generous player stocking plan, so Dallas could be reasonably competitive from the outset. The expansion Cowboys paid for the right to select three players made available from each of the twelve NFL teams. Minnesota would get a similar pool of players the following years. Dallas got to choose its three players from an offering of eleven from each rival, while Minnesota chose its three from a set of eight. Pete Rozelle characterized the plan as "intelligent, well-thought-out." Vikings owner Max Winter grumbled, "I'm not at all happy about the league giving us the choice of three out of eight players." The Vikings, however, got to participate in the college draft before taking the field, an opportunity Dallas did not receive. Hall-of-Fame quarterback Fran Tarkenton was among the Vikings' college draft choices.[62]

The NFL's initial experiences with expansion were dismal. While the NFL liked to boast about its competitive balance, the owners proved ungenerous with their offerings. Dallas went 0-11-1 in its debut, while the Vikings did a little better at 3-11. By comparison, baseball's New York Mets gained infamy by finishing 40-120 in their first season. While the Mets continued to wallow in futility, the Vikings sported a winning record in 1964. The Cowboys won the Eastern Conference in 1966. At the time, though, Joe King wrote that, "Expansion is a four-headed embarrassment at this point because of the Dallas failure, because of the necessity of avoiding another flop with Minneapolis, because of the disturbance of the divisions and because of the strain they put on an already jam-packed schedule. All those points are pieces of the one puzzle. The failure of the Dallas Cowboys to win was a stunning shock to the NFL moguls, who believed they had equipped the new entry in modestly-successful style." King used the decrease in attendance across seventy-two games to make a comparison with 1959. He also cited the likelihood of continued stagnant or dwindling attendance per game, due to the unattractiveness of playing such weaklings as Dallas and Minnesota.[63]

The owners' decision to extend the regular season to fourteen games instead of twelve for the 1961 season was one important legacy of expansion. The AFL already played a fourteen-game schedule.[64]

Conclusion

The NFL's prosperity brought pressure to winnow out or transfer its weakest franchises. With the second rendition of the Baltimore Colts, the league enjoyed stability for several seasons. While the twelve owners were hesitant about relocating existing franchises or expanding, they eventually did so in response to the AFL and television.

6

ANTITRUST ADVENTURES

A legacy of the NFL's struggle with the AAFC was the publicity surrounding player rights, territorial rights, and other antitrust issues. Prior to the AAFC-NFL strife, the NFL attracted scant attention from Congress or from the Department of Justice. Professional football's internecine strife and resulting prosperity came with an unanticipated cost: federal scrutiny. The congressional committee members were particularly interested in the owners' territorial rights protection, the reserve clause, the reverse-order draft, and television policies. Were these potentially anticompetitive actions necessary to maintain the league? The owners argued that instead of being anticompetitive, these measures were needed to promote competitive parity; a neat piece of logistical jujitsu . . . if true.

The Unique Nature of Professional Sports Leagues

Professional sports leagues have a unique feature in that, while there is competition among teams, there must also be cooperation. It takes two to tangle, to misquote an old bromide. Bell put it thus: "Professional teams in a league, however, must not compete too well with each other in a business way. On the playing field, of course, they must compete as hard as they can all the time. But it is not necessary and indeed it is unwise for all the teams to compete as hard as they can against each other in a business way."[1]

Professional sports leagues are, therefore, mixtures of cooperation and competition. They are, in fact, cartels. Cartels normally run afoul of U.S. antitrust policies. Unlike a cartel of manufacturers, for example, the owners in a sports league must have minimal amounts of cooperation in setting schedules, standardizing playing rules, and establishing championships.

These rules — known as single-entity cooperation — benefit owners and fans alike. Such cooperation is unlikely to trigger antitrust scrutiny.

Most sports league owners, though, go beyond single-entity cooperation and into the realm of joint-venture cooperation. As Rodney Fort puts it, "Once owners act together in pro leagues to set the stage for competition on the field, they may also act together to raise profits for member owners. All cooperative actions that do not make play happen are called joint ventures."[2] The owners' actions which are designed to boost their collective profits via price-fixing, territorial rights, the reserve clause, player drafts, and national T V contracts are violations, indeed blatant violations, of antitrust policies. The owners and their hired commissioners must step nimbly to persuade legislators to acquiesce to such shenanigans. N F L commissioner Bert Bell stressed to the congressional committees investigating professional team sports that the league rested upon what we could refer to as the "three R's": the reserve clause, the reverse-order draft, and revenue sharing. Of course, the owners also wanted territorial rights and were willing to give the league commissioner power to act unilaterally in some situations.

With the growth of large-scale operations such as railroads and manufacturing, nineteenth-century Americans worried about the concentration of economic power in the hands of the few. The Sherman Antitrust Act of 1890 and the later Clayton Act (1914) created a framework for dealing with monopoly power, although such authority was only fitfully applied for decades after passage of the acts.

In the wake of baseball's Federal League battle with the entrenched National and American Leagues, the Baltimore club filed suit against the other two leagues. The Supreme Court argued that baseball wasn't interstate commerce and, hence, did not fall under the antitrust laws. This antitrust exemption made baseball owners the envy of the professional sports world. Later legal scholars and justices have questioned the correctness of the Supreme Court's ruling.[3]

Due to the popularity and publicity of professional sports, politicians quickly became fans, supporters, and, occasionally, foes. Congressional committees dealing with monopoly power began holding almost annual inquiries. While only occasional legislation ensued, the implicit threats contained in legislators' remarks and advice caused team owners to react.

Football, basketball, and hockey owners were hoping for at least a partial antitrust exemption. Their league presidents and commissioners employed a "Chicken Little" approach, claiming that without antitrust protection, the professional sports sky would fall. While baseball owners were sympathetic toward their fellow owners, they were also leery of being too involved in the legislation.[4] Baseball owners worried that a strong legal challenge to their antitrust exemption, whether indirectly (through an assault on their interpretation of the reserve clause) or directly, might end their privileges.

The NFL's Approach to Antitrust Legislation

The NFL, through Bert Bell, eventually opted to concentrate on getting legal protection through a partial antitrust exemption for their reserve clause, the reverse-order draft of college players, seventy-five-mile territorial rights, and the commissioner's power to issue unilateral edicts.

The NFL owners, when it suited their needs, claimed that their version of the reserve clause differed from Major League Baseball's. Baseball owners claimed that the clause was perpetual, so a player was tied to a team for his professional career unless sold, traded, or released. The baseball owners had yet to impose a reverse-order draft for amateur players (a large proportion of whom were recently high school graduates who might not have reached majority and therefore could not sign a legally binding contract). Football owners claimed their version of the reserve clause was a one-year contract with an option year that bound a player for a second season at no less than 90 percent of his contract salary. They claimed that players who played out their option year were free agents. Bell and the NFL owners claimed that without an antitrust exemption, their league was in danger of being bankrupted by player lawsuits or by an extreme competitive imbalance that would destroy weaker clubs.[5]

The reverse-order draft of amateur players is an egregious violation of both players' and owners' rights to negotiate. Football, basketball, and hockey owners piously contended that the draft promoted competitive parity between teams and made for a better product. The competitive balance argument was, at best, a flimsy fig leaf covering their naked desire to tamp down player salaries. They rarely commented in polite society that the draft gave the lucky owner leverage versus the young player, as the player could only negotiate with the team that drafted him. Such a draft in another profession would incite outrage. The Big Four accounting firms cannot get together and assign negotiating rights for promising young accountants to individual firms.[6] Professional sports owners have succeeded in glamorizing outright exploitation, as the weeks leading into the draft and the draft itself are high drama, replete with endless analysis. Baseball owners, for once, were envious of football owners' ability to sign top rookie talent for modest amounts. During the 1950s, baseball owners were finding the free market for amateur players distasteful. Some owners and officials, such as Branch Rickey, made impressive leaps in logic by claiming that paying large bonuses demoralized youngsters.

While it is understandable that a professional sports league would offer its members some protection from encroachment upon their territory by other league members, the question of whether the territorial protection applied to owners of teams not in the league or whether the territorial rights could be used to deter entry by rival leagues was a key antitrust issue. International waters might be a few miles offshore in extent, but professional sports owners demanded and enacted protection encompassing a seventy-five-mile radius. Territorial limits applied to television broadcasts, too. The history of professional team sports, though, includes several cases of blatant disregard for the territorial limits, even within leagues; sometimes the disputes would be settled with cash indemnities.

When Bell testified before the congressional committee, the following is what the committee members found with regard to territorial rights:

> The amended 1957 Constitution and By-Laws, Article IV, Membership, Section 9 "Territorial Rights": Territorial rights will be 75 miles from the limit of a League city and where League cities are within 100 miles of each other, than half the distance between the two cities, except in the case of the Green Bay Packers' franchise, whose territorial rights shall include the area defined above plus the entire Milwaukee County in Wisconsin.[7]

Bell's and the owners' rationale for the rule included contradictions. Bell testified that:

If a club did not have a protected territory, another team might move into the same city. That is why our bylaws provide reasonable safeguards to protect our teams. For example, 2 franchises in 1 city require the unanimous consent of all teams. Adding a new team or teams to the league may create a serious scheduling problem, and, therefore, we require unanimous consent before granting any new franchise and, of course, only after a complete investigation by the commissioner of any and all new prospective owners has been completed. In addition, the approval of 10 out of 12 teams to the sale or transfer of any existing franchise is required.[8]

Two teams operated in relative amicability in the city of Chicago, well within the seventy-five-mile radius. Owners were prepared to countenance exceptions to the territorial limits. Washington, somewhat less amicably, demanded and received an indemnity from the incoming Baltimore Colts. The league introduced a letter between Washington owner George Preston Marshall and the renewed Baltimore franchise detailing their agreement, which consisted of four $25,000 payments made between January 3, 1953 and July 1, 1954.[9]

Some congressional committee members wanted to cut the territorial limit to thirty-five miles, but Bell would have none of that. He claimed that reducing the territorial limits in the face of television technology would "knock that attendance off because the fellow will get in his car and drive 35, 40, or 50 miles, but the closer the picture on TV, the smaller the attendance." He cited the case of Philadelphia and Atlantic City, sixty-five miles apart: "We believe that 75 miles is fair — we went through all this with the television and radio people, in the court with Judge Grim and the Federal Government, and I think we established with Judge Grim that it was reasonable."[10]

The owners pursued one other antitrust exemption. Professional sports leagues cannot stand too much competition. In some cases, owners who pursue their self-interest can prove detrimental to the collective. One of the roles of a league commissioner or president is to resolve these dilemmas (which are, in essence, the famous Prisoners' Dilemma found in game theory). In a Prisoners' Dilemma situation, all actors rationally follow their best strategy, but the net result is that the collective group is worse off. Another example of the usefulness of a firm hand concerned scheduling games. NFL owners perpetually bickered over favorable schedules, so they opted to let Bert Bell do it. The owners wanted to authorize their commissioners to issue unilateral decrees in the best interest of the league (owners).

The Legal Wrangles Confronting the NFL

Even before the NFL was involved in congressional hearings regarding antitrust issues, the owners were entangled in several lawsuits. Many of these lawsuits concerned disputes between owners and their players.

Owners wanted antitrust exemption for their treatment of players. Whether it was due to the sophistication of veterans after World War II or the prevalence of college graduates in the NFL, football players sought redress for perceived wrongs.

Fullback Ralph Ruthstrom filed suit against George Preston Marshall and the Washington Redskins in 1949. The Redskins suspended Ruthstrom in 1947, so he requested a release in order to play with the AAFC Buffalo team, but his release wasn't issued until 1948. Marshall said the player left without permission, like a truant schoolboy. Ruthstrom filed suit for $4,100, saying the Redskins prevented him from making a living playing football. Unfortunately for Ruthstrom, Judge David A. Pine was not convinced and denied the lawsuit via a directed verdict. In addition to denying his claim, the judge ordered Ruthstrom to pay the Redskins the $41.80 they claimed he owed them from a loan they made him.[11] Score one for the NFL.

The NFL's chief argument in a television case (which will be discussed in greater detail later) presided over by Judge Allan K. Grim, was to hope to tag along with baseball's exemption by claiming that "professional football is not a trade or commerce within the meaning of the Sherman Anti-Trust Act" and that anything else, such as television or radio broadcasting, was incidental.[12] A second aspect of the television lawsuit that would be referred to during the hearings was the cost of defending the league in court against antitrust charges. Bell claimed the television lawsuit had already cost the league $50,000, even with the league's attorneys charging only "humble fees."[13] An attorney for the NFL told reporters that a government victory in the lawsuit would be the "death knell of pro football," thereby setting another precedent for NFL behavior in subsequent antitrust discussions. Bell followed the next day by testifying that "professional football could not survive with unlimited radio and television broadcasts of games." Although government attorneys got Bell to back down on his "could not survive" claim, he was persuasive enough that Judge Grim gave the league his blessing for blackouts of telecasts of live games in the home team's territory.[14] Score two for the NFL.

Bell's later claim that the NFL would be harassed by lawsuits if it did not get antitrust protection had some credibility. The Liberty Broadcasting System, miffed that the NFL did not grant it telecasting rights, filed a 2.1 million dollar lawsuit against the league, claiming antitrust violations. Liberty had also filed a lawsuit against Major League Baseball. One could view the company's penchant for filing lawsuits as sour grapes, since other broadcasting companies had won the rights to telecast baseball and football games. Baseball owners settled the lawsuit for $200,000, but Bell was adamant: "We settle with no one."[15]

The league faced a far more serious lawsuit when William Radovich succeeded in getting his case heard by the Supreme Court. Radovich was a seven-year veteran of professional football. He played five seasons with Detroit before finishing his career with the AAFC Los Angeles Dons. The San Francisco Clippers of the Pacific Coast League considered hiring him for the 1948 season but backed off, because, according to Radovich, NFL owners had blacklisted him: "Claiming that the reserve clause prevented him from selling his services where he wished and from making a living in his profession, Radovich sued the Lions and the National Football League for $105,000 damages. He charged attempts to monopolize interstate commerce in the business of professional football." A Ninth Circuit court quoted the Supreme Court baseball ruling when it ruled that his case was outside the scope of the Sherman Act. The court also advised: "If Congressional indulgence extended to and saved baseball from regulation, then the indulgence extended to other sports."[16] Score three for the NFL, but the Ninth Circuit court's ruling was subject to further scrutiny, a judicial form of a play under review.

The Supreme Court ruled that "Radovich is entitled to an opportunity to prove his charges and refused to grant professional football immunity from the antitrust laws. Of course, we express no opinion as to whether or not respondents have, in fact, violated the antitrust laws, leaving that determination to the trial court after all the facts are in."[17] The NFL asked the court to reconsider but were rebuffed. Radovich and his attorney planned to demonstrate that the NFL differed from MLB because the reverse-order draft stripped the player of most of his freedom of choice.[18]

The Radovich case threatened to fracture the sports leagues' united front. Early in the case, Commissioner Bert Bell informed NFL owners that baseball commissioner Happy Chandler had told him the baseball owners wanted the NFL to settle the case.[19] A subsequent Major League Baseball commissioner, Ford Frick, refused to comment on Bert Bell's questioning of "the right of baseball to remain immune from antitrust laws after the Supreme Court had ruled professional football a 'business,' which he considered discriminatory. The baseball owners worried about the upcoming hearings and scheduled a special meeting to discuss the matter."[20]

The Supreme Court's ruling inspired legislators to action. Representatives introduced bills addressing professional sports and antitrust issues. A California Republican representative, Patrick J. Hillings, was not shy in explaining why he introduced his bill: it would help the West Coast get major league franchises. Another Republican representative, Kenneth B. Keating of New York, called for a congressional investigation of what he termed "abuses" in pro football. The next day a Democratic representative, Oren Harris of Arkansas, introduced a bill that would have exempted all four sports from antitrust laws. His fellow Democrat, Emanuel Celler, castigated Harris for taking a "step backward" before introducing his own bill.[21]

In preparation for the hearings, the NFL "bombarded Congress with a forty-three-page brochure entitled, 'The Story of Professional Football in Summary.'" While Bert Bell was not the suave, polished, personable master of publicity that Pete Rozelle would be, he was pugnacious and, even more important, confident in the justness of the NFL's cause. He saw to it that the owners were depicted as being in football as an avocation, a hobby, and claimed that profits were incidental. He also mentioned that the federal government collected $900,000 in admission taxes on pro football games.[22]

The Congressional Hearings

Congress investigated Major League Baseball during a 1951 hearing. In 1957, the Antitrust Subcommittee of the Committee on the Judiciary had decided to hold hearings involving the four major professional team sports leagues, with Emanuel Celler chairing. Kenneth Keating stated the purpose of the 1957 hearings: "These bills would place the ordinary commercial activities of professional team sports under the antitrust laws, but would specifically exempt from antitrust enforcement certain practices considered essential to the successful operation of these sports." Different bills were circulating: some sought to "blanket professional sports under the antitrust laws," while others would have provided complete exemption. Keating opposed giving a complete exemption, as did Celler.[23] Congress held hearings almost annually thereafter, with the NFL involved in the 1957, 1958, 1959, 1961, and 1964 hearings. One of the 1959 Senate bills would have allowed professional sports leagues to enforce territorial limits, although the limits would have been thirty-five miles instead of the seventy-five miles most leagues wanted.[24] Readers who wade through the thousands of pages of testimony may be disappointed that relatively little legislation resulted.

Bell would repeat the gist of his 1957 testimony again in 1958 and in 1959. He wanted protection for the reserve clause, the reverse-order draft, territorial rights, and the commissioner's power: "If any of these should now be held by the courts to be an unreasonable restraint of trade, organized professional football, the highly competitive and colorful sport that we know today, would come to an end. It would inevitably revert to its former state when four top clubs won most of the games and the public refused to support the poor teams which were unable to acquire good players."[25] Bell told the 1957 committee that the NFL was "still a comparatively small operation." He reported that in 1956, the twelve teams had less than $13 million in combined gross receipts and player payrolls of $3.75 million, or roughly 30 percent of receipts.[26]

Bell's testimony occasionally raised the hackles of some of the committee members. He constantly referred to the players as "boys" and claimed he sided with them instead of the owners, because "they're younger and don't know the angles." Emanuel Celler, exasperated, retorted, "Are they college graduates?" Bell continued to maintain that college graduates did not know the angles.[27]

Kenneth Harkins, a government attorney, promptly pinned Bell. He asked Bell whether any courts had found "the four phases of professional football activities for which you request an antitrust exemption" to be violations of the antitrust laws. Bell could only answer no. Harkins then retorted, "Is it your view that if Congress were to exempt these activities at this time, that that exemption would amount to an implication that these activities were unreasonable and unlawful before they were exempted?" Bell replied, "Well, I do not believe that if Congress enacted a law, that it should revert back." Harkins continued by getting Bell to admit that the league had changed its reserve clause in 1947 to the current one year and one option year instead of the permanent baseball-style reserve clause out of fears that the original contract might not pass muster in a court. Bell also admitted that the owners had changed the option-year salary clause to 90 percent instead of 100 percent.[28]

Harkins later took exception to Article 16, Section 1 of the league's bylaws: "The minimum price for reserved tickets for any regularly scheduled championship games [regular-season games] shall be $1.50 plus tax and a minimum of $1 plus tax for all unreserved adult tickets." Harkins asked Bell whether he was aware that price-fixing was prohibited under the antitrust laws. When Bell admitted that he was aware, Harkins asked whether the NFL was asking for an exemption for price-fixing. Bell answered, "I believe it is in the best interests of the player, and the best interests of the league, and in the best interests of the public." Harkins pointed out that the bylaws covered fixing prices of the "world professional football championship games" and the special arrangement between the Baltimore Colts and Washington Redskins under which Baltimore could not sell tickets for less than the Redskins and vice versa (which apparently meant the two teams had to agree in setting prices). Bell said the meaning of these bylaws was this: "They want the lowest price established. They don't want to compete against each other. We are endeavoring in every way to increase salaries and go along with the players in everything we do. We don't believe that two teams in the same locality, one team selling a seat for 75 cents and the other selling a seat for $4 — we believe it will hurt both of them."[29]

The NFL Players Association's counsel, Creighton Miller, testified that he thought football merited exemption from the antitrust laws when such restraints "foster equal playing competition among league rivals and consequently permit the sport to engage in the operation as a business. Football is unquestionably a unique business because it necessitates cooperation among competitors in order to produce a marketable product. That product is competition." He supported the reserve clause because "elimination of the reserve clause with no substitute would remove the abuses attendant thereto and would probably temporarily increase players' salaries, but, if the rich clubs thereby destroyed competition by competitively being too superior, it might act as a cure that killed the patient." Miller mentioned that some safeguards might be designed to ensure fair treatment of players.[30]

In a strange coincidence, economist Simon Rottenberg had recently published a pioneering article in the *Journal of Political Economy*. Rottenberg described the unique aspect of professional team sports leagues — a mixture of competition and cooperation — and concluded that competitive balance was unlikely to differ greatly under either a reserve-clause or a free-agency regime.[31] Unfortunately, the congressional committee did not ask him to testify.

The NFL arranged for compliant players, both former and current, to testify that the reserve clause was necessary.[32] Red Grange, Chuck Bednarik, Sid Luckman, Norm Van Brocklin, and George Ratterman testified. While all acknowledged the "need" for the reserve clause and the reverse-order draft, they were more willing than the baseball players would be the following year to ask for modifications and a right of appeal. Ratterman proved an interesting witness, as he had played in the AAFC and had flirted with playing out his option year.[33]

In 1957 Bell and Miller concluded by stating they would be pleased if Congress enacted any one of four nearly identical bills.[34] Congress did not pass any of the proposed bills, and Bert and the league's attorneys would reprise their testimony in 1958, 1959, and so on.

During the 1958 hearings Senator Estes Kefauver queried Bell about his claim that without an exemption the NFL would be bankrupted by lawsuits. Bell cited the Radovich and Liberty Broadcasting suits, as well as a threatened Players Association lawsuit. Senator Kefauver did not appear sympathetic: "Just threatening you with a suit does not cause you very much trouble, if the suit is not brought, does it?" Bell, undaunted, retorted, "No, it does not, but it causes you a lot of anxiety about what it may cost you if it is brought."[35] In retrospect, Bell's testimony during the 1958 hearings that "the National Football League would be glad to have Judge [Allan K.] Grim's decision [regarding television blackouts] written into this bill if that would be satisfactory to baseball, basketball, and hockey" would cause some discomfort when the NFL sought an exemption allowing a national television pact.[36] Wyoming senator Joseph C. O'Mahoney, at least, was impressed by Bell's testimony. He told Bell and the committee that he was pleased with the NFL's reserve clause, as it gave players "a real freedom of contract." Bell took the opportunity to say the NFL's reserve clause was "the greatest bargaining situation in the world for a ballplayer." He claimed that the Eagles' Pete Pihos once asked him for advice in negotiating with the team. Bell told him to tell the Eagles' management that he would play out his option, which forced the Eagles to bargain. He cited another player, George Kennard, who did not play during his option year and became a free agent. He went back to play with the Giants because he was familiar with their style.[37]

The committee members asked Bell about compliance with the previous hearing's suggestions. Paul Dixon, Senate counsel, asked Bell whether the league had changed its bylaws regarding "minimum ticket prices." Bell took the opportunity to point out that not only did the owners change the minimum-ticket-price clause but also the lottery bonus pick in the draft. The owners also made explicit the fact that a player had a right to waive his hearing in front of the commissioner and could go to court. He concluded by stating obsequiously, "We would be happy with anything that would keep us out of the courts and spell out the things that we have to have. I understood the Celler bill approved the selection of the college players, territorial rights, and so forth. I said before, we can live with television the way we are. We have no objection. It is up to you gentlemen as to what you want to give us. We are thankful to have the hearings." Although he was obsequious before the congressional committee, Bell boasted to owners of the efficacy of their lobbyist.[38]

Bell's 1959 testimony included the big news that a new professional football league was afoot. He claimed to have discussed the possibility with the NFL owners and that not one objected. He also told the committee that the "new league would be free to compete for players against teams in the present league."[39] Bell again reiterated the league's satisfaction with Judge Grim's decision.

A proposed Senate bill had a stipulation that the reverse-order draft, if given antitrust protection, would require that "no player could be subject to our player selection system unless he had previously given his written consent to be subject to this selection system." Bell interpreted this to mean that if a player refused to sign he was a free agent. Bell naturally opposed such a clause. Senator Kefauver asked Bell whether many players would refuse to sign the consent. Bell answered, "It brings about intricate problems. People where they play, coaches and others may say to them, 'Don't allow yourself to be selected because, if you do, you will have to play with that team, and otherwise you might be able to get where you want to and you will get more money and at least you can't lose anything by holding out.'" Bell argued that this would create competitive imbalance, as players would gravitate to wealthier teams. Senator Kefauver rebutted Bell's pessimism: "This doesn't prevent you from trading players and equalizing player strength. All my bill is intended to do is to try to give an individual player some rights by requiring him to give you a written statement that he will be subject to the draft." Bell refused to concede the point and continued to assert that "written consent" would lead to competitive imbalance.[40] He also stated, "I personally think that large bonuses are a very terrible thing. I think that the ballplayer that plays on that field and puts the fans in the stands is the fellow that should get the increases in salary; not the fellow that you guess may make good in 2 or 3 years while the other fellows that are producing take less money."[41]

Paul Dixon, at least, began to strip away the fallacies in Bell's arguments regarding the efficacy of the player draft and of the reserve clause in promoting parity. Bell bragged that eight different teams had won championships between 1945 and 1957 and claimed that about sixty rookies made the NFL rosters each season. Dixon asked, "Is it your contention that this equalization is coming through the addition of five ballplayers to each team each year?" Bell replied, "The five right ballplayers, the five best college football players. The one first goes to the lowest club and then the next lowest club and so on." Dixon recalled the testimony of three college football coaches that they did not think they could choose the five best players. Bell admitted, "Some of them [highly touted college players] don't succeed and sometimes your 15th choice of a guy that never went to college will become a great player."[42] Bell liked to claim that pro football was a temporary avocation; players stayed a few years, acquired savings, and went into business. He said repeatedly that the average career was three and a half years. Dixon pointed out that drafted players rarely got any money unless they made the team: "Therefore the club isn't taking any gamble. The boy is taking a gamble there, isn't he?" Bell replied, "The club is taking the gamble to the extent that if they pick the wrong player, and he doesn't make the team, they are not going to do very well. . . . But the player isn't taking much of a gamble either when he can find out in 8 weeks if he can make the ball club and establish himself in business in the town where he is playing." Bell admitted the rookies got only $50 per preseason game.[43]

Spurned players could seek employment on football teams in lesser leagues. There had been professional and semiprofessional football leagues throughout America for decades.[44] In the postwar period, many small-city businessmen sponsored teams. The Pacific Coast [Football] League (PCFL) was a long-standing professional football league, one that hired African American players and sometimes paid salaries comparable to those of the NFL. The *New York Times* ran sporadic articles immediately after the war discussing the possibility of NFL teams creating farm systems. A few NFL teams negotiated links with teams in other professional leagues. The NFL's dalliances with so-called minor league teams, however, may have been carried on with an eye toward other potential suitors: AAFC teams. One of the NFL's stratagems in its attempts to thwart the AAFC was to control ever-greater numbers of players, barring the AAFC from the key input. One may view the NFL overtures to other professional teams from this perspective.

Team owners in the lower professional football leagues could hope to align themselves with the NFL and get protection and respect for their player contracts, preventing costly player contract-jumping and raiding.[45] The NFL owners recognized the outside owners' territorial rights, at least when it was convenient to slap the AAFC. When the Cleveland Rams transferred to Los Angeles, the NFL paid an undisclosed indemnity and agreed to set up a professional organization similar to baseball's National Association of Professional Baseball Clubs, involving the NFL and three football minor leagues, the Pacific Coast [Football] League, the Dixie League, and the American Association. The NFL agreed that the San Francisco Clippers of the PCFL retained exclusive territorial rights to the city. Reporter Roscoe McGowen surmised that by making that agreement, the NFL was implicitly reserving San Francisco as NFL territory. Since the NFL had no plans to move into the Pacific Northwest or mountain states at that time, it grandly awarded the Pacific Coast [Football] League territorial rights to Washington and Oregon, and also to California, Nevada, Arizona, New Mexico, Utah, Idaho, and Colorado, the latter territories being the ones the United States had extracted from Mexico a century earlier. McGowen stated that many of the American Association teams had been "farms" of the NFL in 1942, but he didn't elaborate.[46]

Encouraged by the NFL's attention, the three leagues formed the Association of Professional Football Leagues in March 1946. J. Rufus Klawans told reporters that the association's purpose was to create uniform operation of leagues and "involves recognition of player contracts so there will not be any 'jumping' of players. This action, of course, helped the NFL stymie the AAFC's efforts in getting players. It also involves recognition of territorial rights of all member leagues." Klawans admitted that the NFL hadn't joined but he noted that it had been invited to join, as had the AAFC.[47] These smaller leagues may have been emboldened (and perhaps misled) by the apparent sports boom in postwar America. The American Football [minor] League decided to expand from eight to fourteen teams, possibly at the behest of the NFL owners. A month later, franchises in this league were already being transferred or sold, and not because of prosperity. Before the summer ended, league president Joe Rosentover issued a revised and shrunken 1947 league schedule. He also intimated that the league would be comprised of seven teams. A later report indicated that the league and the Pacific Coast [Football] League were having difficulties in 1948.[48] Paraphernalia from teams in these leagues must be collectors' items, indeed.

The NFL's friendliness with the PCFL, the Dixie League, and the American Association dissipated in the wake of the AAFC's demise. These "minor leagues" experienced financial troubles as the 1940s ended, and often came to the NFL meetings to beg for help. NFL owners sometimes farmed out players to teams in these leagues. The NFL owners initially agreed to help underwrite the financial losses of two PCFL teams in Los Angeles because these two teams had helped fight the AAFC Los Angeles Dons. In later years, however, the NFL owners' willingness to help lesser leagues vanished. Rufus Klawans, owner of the San Francisco Clippers in the PCFL and league spokesman, eventually sought admission into the NFL, essentially abandoning his fellow PCFL owners. At the January 1948 meetings, Bell "told the [NFL] member clubs that in his opinion the NFL agreements with minor league affiliates meant very little to the NFL and that the minor leagues were handling their affairs in a very unsatisfactory manner both as to finances and to the character of ownerships. . . . He would agree to any request for cancellation of our agreements with our minor league affiliates. There were no objections expressed by the members."[49]

While lower-level professional football leagues continued their shadowy existence throughout the 1950s, the NFL does not appear to have had maintained many formal ties with them. A decade later, the NFL's lack of connections with or ownership of outside teams redounded to its benefit, as congressional committee members had one less reason to view the league as exploitive. Bell pointedly told the committee in 1958, "I should like to point out that the National Football League has no minor-league affiliations and never had any affiliation with the now-defunct former rival, the All-American Football Conference. Nor has our league ever had any affiliation with the Canadian League." A year earlier, committee cocounselor Kenneth Harkins asked Bell whether there were any football minor leagues. Bell recollected that there was a new one forming in Phoenix. He said the NFL sent them a copy of its bylaws and constitution. He added, "They asked me if we had any objection to their going into any of our league cities, and we said 'No.'"[50] Bell claimed that since NFL football was not a vocation but a means to an end for its players, the idea of a major league–minor league setup similar to Major League Baseball's was not feasible. Playing careers simply were too short. Bell opined, "I think if a kid can't make it in 8 weeks' tryout after he has been to college, he ought to get a job elsewhere. But that is not a criticism of baseball, because they play 10 to 12 years in baseball."[51]

During the 1964 hearings the main reference to outside professional football leagues related to the United Football League, whose commissioner, George T. Gareff, testified as to the potentially deleterious effects arising from the proposed NFL-CBS national television deal. He testified that the televised NFL games were "going to destroy about three clubs in my league that play on Sunday night." The UFL played on Sunday so as to not interfere with high school or college football games. He had hoped to arrange a major league–minor league agreement with the NFL but had heard nothing; he ascribed this to the NFL's wariness of entering into any agreement that might run afoul of antitrust strictures. He urged the committee to pass Senate Bill 2391 to limit the NFL's televising.[52]

Television (and Radio) and Antitrust

As early as 1951 Bert Bell was raising the issue of television and the government's attitude toward it. George Preston Marshall volunteered, "All the lawyers in America have worked on this and baseball has signed an agreement with the government. . . . The government contends that we must follow the rule on baseball. We are a monopoly because we control more than 75 percent of all professional football played according to them. We come under their jurisdiction the same as baseball due to radio and television."[53]

The Liberty Broadcasting System filed an antitrust suit against the NFL and nine of its clubs based on the allegation that the league "illegally adopted and maintained, throughout the United States of America, a system of authorizing the broadcasting of professional football game in such manner as to restrain trade unlawfully in broadcasting and to maintain a monopoly of the broadcasting" in the home territories of NFL teams.[54] LBS had declared bankruptcy before filing the lawsuit, and readers may speculate whether the company's officers were fishing for settlement money. Immediately upon serving Bell with a copy of the complaint, the Dallas, Texas attorneys representing LBS did in fact suggest a settlement, which Bert Bell spurned.

Gordon McLendon, LBS's founder, had testified against the NFL in the television antitrust suit presided over by Judge Allan K. Grim; in fact, Bert Bell and the NFL owners presumed McLendon had instigated the federal investigation. McLendon had created a network of four hundred affiliated radio stations. His network "re-created" professional football games for radio audiences between 1947 and 1949 before broadcasting live in 1950 and 1951. He had NFL permission for all these broadcasts. Strangely, he said that only two games were sponsored, including an NFL title game in 1951. He said the company broadcast thirty NFL games in 1951. When Judge Grim questioned him as to the effects of radio broadcasts on professional sports, McLendon became expansive. While admitting he could not describe television's effects, he claimed, "Speaking for radio I can say that absolutely, it has not hurt the attendance at professional football games. Radio created more interest in football and other sports." NFL defense counsel Bernard Nordlinger induced McLendon to admit that he had sought to buy an interest in the Dallas Texans NFL team (luckily for him, he did not get it) despite "his alleged objections to the league's broadcast and telecast rules and despite McLendon's pending $12,000,000 suit against Major League Baseball for alleged use of similar rules."[55]

After the usual jockeying between attorneys, Judge Allan K. Grim asked federal counsel W. Perry Epes, "Does it make any difference to you whether television might kill professional football?" Epes apparently realized that he might have overstated his case, but he recovered, replying, "That is not the question here Your Honor, but legally, economic justification is not a defense in an antitrust suit." "Then your answer is No": to which Epes could only nod in agreement.[56] Judge Grim's exchange with Epes may have presaged his thinking about the case and his ruling.

The government attorneys established that the "public's right to open television of football games was 'one of the fundamental problems of this case.'" The government also strove to demonstrate that there was widespread interest in telecasts of professional football games. To bolster the second contention, James. W. Seiler, director of the American Research Bureau, testified as to the size of the audience watching various shows. Bernard Nordlinger, representing the NFL, quickly attacked Seiler's credibility, with the attorney maintaining "that a statistician couldn't possibly have the technical and other knowledge to give opinions on the feasibility of telecasting games in certain territories and on the financial benefits to sponsors of the presence or absence of restrictions."[57]

McLendon was not the only station owner disgruntled at having been shut out of NFL telecasts. A Pennsylvania television station owner testified that the NFL forced him to cancel telecasts of five games because his station was seventy-four miles away from Philadelphia. The president claimed that such "betrayal" of the audience's trust would force him out of business, but he admitted under cross-examination that his station was, in fact, still in business.[58]

The NFL's defense was that a government victory in the antitrust suit would sound the "death knell" of the NFL or cause a nationwide blackout of broadcasts and telecasts. Judge Grim denied the motion to dismiss the case, replying that he "wished to hear the entire case before making a decision." An NFL attorney, Francis Myers, a former U.S. senator from Pennsylvania (and likely a personal contact of Bert Bell's, as Bell also hailed from a prominent Pennsylvania family) argued that the government was trying to force NFL team owners to provide "a free seat, mind you even though the granting of that free seat might empty our ball parks, bankrupt our clubs and thus eventually assure those 160 million Americans watch a Western movie rather than a football game," and that buying a television or radio did not entitle a consumer to receive NFL games for free (free, that is, except for the cost of listening to and/or watching commercials). The Los Angeles Rams' experience with and without television in 1949–50 was a key piece of evidence that telecasts hurt NFL gate receipts.[59]

Bert Bell was the primary defense witness. He asserted that unrestricted radio and television would not only diminish live audiences but would force major pay cuts for players: "We would not be able to sell admission tickets in sufficient quantities to pay high salaries." Without high salaries, Bell said, the quality of play would suffer, and fans would stop attending games. Bell thus appropriated the domino theory from its political and military users. Bell believed fans would wait until the day of the game to decide whether to attend or whether to watch on television, and that bad weather would dampen attendance: "Stations and networks are perfectly free to bid for the [telecasting and broadcasting] rights, and the only restriction is that the commissioner must approve all sponsors and announcers. That is only a protection for the league and the public, because he will not deal with anyone who might be detrimental to the game." Bell later backtracked on his dire claims. Attorney Epes asked Bell whether Major League Baseball had rung its death knell when it repealed rule 1-D, which governed broadcasts and telecasts. Bell admitted it hadn't, but added, "But it will."[60]

Bell also testified that he opposed closed-circuit or pay-TV broadcasts, especially if they led to the hypothetical situation in which boxing or other sporting events would be held in a studio and staged solely for television audiences. "I hope I am not in sports if that day ever arrives." When Bell stepped down, an advertising executive described how the NCAA could get $2.5 million for telecasts. In a prescient statement, he told the court that the NCAA's deal was "exclusive and on a national basis": he continued by saying if "pro football could be telecast similarly he could see no reason why it couldn't demand the same price."[61]

The NFL presented evidence from the NCAA's ongoing struggle with telecasts. The NCAA attempted to control telecasts of games, but the two cases were not identical, given the hundreds of college football programs whose territories overlapped. Paul B. Schetsley of the National Opinion Research Center testified to the effect of television on college football (the NCAA paid his organization to conduct the study). Paul Schissler, director of special events for the *Los Angeles Times*, operated the newspaper's annual charity game between the Redskins and Rams. He testified that the game's lowest attendance in the eight years the game had been played occurred the one time the game was televised.[62]

Perhaps more relevant was the testimony of New York Giants president John Mara. Under cross-examination by W. Perry Epes, Mara claimed he would want "a guarantee to cover a complete sell-out for every game," as compensation for granting television rights. Epes forced Mara to admit that the Giants rarely sold out. According to Mara, the Giants made $49,000 in profits in 1952 and received $50,000 for radio rights and $108,000 for television rights, with Miller Brewing and Atlantic Refining sponsoring the broadcasts. Mara stated that the club had stopped televising home games after 1948, when they had determined that the telecasts hurt home attendance. He went on to state that between 1946 and 1948, when the number of television sets went from 30,000 to 400,000 in New York City, bleacher attendance fell from 3,600 to 1,400. Mara later admitted that the fall in bleacher attendance might have been because the team performed poorly in 1948. Bleacher sales bounced back in 1950, when the team improved. Clearly, the conflation of attendance, television, and team record resulted in an ambiguous picture. Mara wanted the seventy-five-mile blackout because "we spend a lot of money building up fan interest within a seventy-five-mile radius of New York City. We consider that Giants' territory. We want the fans to see and hear the Giants' games to arouse and keep their interest in our team. Then, too, we want to give the sponsor a break. The sponsor is entitled to an undivided audience for his advertising. We don't want any other team televising in our territory when we are at home."[63]

George Preston Marshall took the offensive. In his testimony, he claimed that the government was trying to create a monopoly rather than eliminate one: "The only complaints the Justice Department has received about our radio and television policy has been from a few men in radio and television who are not getting a piece of the pie and want to muzzle [sic] in. The people have not complained. I challenge you (government counsel) to prove that the public objects to our radio and TV policy." Epes told reporters that he could not identify the complainants to the Justice Department but said there were "many complaints, not one or two." Unlike most owners, Marshall bragged about not having had "a losing season financially in the last sixteen years, but that without radio and TV receipts, Washington would have been in the red in ten of those years."[64]

Another NFL owner testified as to the beneficial effects of broadcasts and telecasts. Nicholas Kerbawy, general manager of the Detroit Lions, told the court that the team made $114,000 in profit in 1952 and that it received $113,000 from radio and television programs.[65] Kerbawy also cited a drop-off in ticket sales for a Rams-Lions playoff game when a rumor arose that the game was to be televised in Detroit.[66] An anonymous reporter wrote, "Judge Grim found it hard to believe [Kerbawy's claim that] the team had lost money in fifteen of the last seventeen years and survived. He questioned Kerbawy closely concerning this, but got from the witness only the bare facts. Kerbawy said he didn't know how the franchise kept going." The Lions' general manager said the club's present ownership lost $222,000 during its first three years of operation, but recovered most of that in the 1951 and 1952 seasons. Later that day, Philadelphia Eagles president Frank L. McNamee claimed television had a drastic effect on attendance, but he admitted that "in 1948, when a snowstorm blanketed Shibe Park before a title game between the Eagles and the Chicago Cardinals, he stayed home and watched it on television."[67]

NFL officials would use many similar arguments and tactics in subsequent court fights, including hyperbole ("death knell"), facts with ambiguous interpretation (lone attendance changes without context), and the argument that the NFL was not "commerce."

Unlike the audience of *Dragnet*, who always heard the narrator intone, "In a moment, the results of that trial," the NFL had to wait eight months for Judge Allen K. Grim's decision. Grim issued a twenty-one-page opinion, but the key aspect of his decision was that "the league could restrict telecasts that would interfere with gate receipts of a specific game but that it could not interfere with telecasts or radio broadcasts that would not affect attendance."[68] The NFL owners could congratulate themselves on winning the main battle: the right to a television blackout within a seventy-five-mile radius of a home game. Judge Grim denied Bell's power to "approve or disapprove all contracts made by the league teams for the telecasts or broadcasts of their games." The judge rejected the league's argument that it was not subject to the antitrust laws because it was not engaged in interstate commerce. He did provide the league a handy defense by ruling that the restriction of telecasts "was necessary for the league's existence and therefore was not an unreasonable restraint."[69] Grim's decision gave the NFL a basis and a precedent from which to attempt to expand their exemptions from antitrust laws. In a later case, in which the NFL wanted an exemption to launch a national TV deal, the league used Grim's ruling as a rationale. Bell and the owners decided not to appeal Judge Grim's ruling, feeling that half a favorable ruling was better than none.[70]

In the wake of Grim's ruling, an ironic development occurred. The DuMont Network, which telecast NFL games, went bankrupt, perhaps demonstrating that Liberty Broadcasting System might have fared poorly had it won some telecasting rights. The NFL was not yet the audience magnet that would ensure profitability and survival of its television network partner.

The NFL remained wary of congressional and judicial intervention. Interim Commissioner Austin Gunsel decided to partially lift the blackout of the Giants-Browns championship game rematch in December 1959. The game was played in Baltimore; under normal circumstances, Washington DC would have been blacked out. Gunsel, however, decided to forestall any protests concerning a blackout from Washington DC residents and legislators by permitting the game to be televised there. He told the owners, "I cannot help but believe that the decision which was made in this instance may possibly have forestalled anti-trust action on the part of the Department of Justice and I might say that, as a matter of fact, I was contacted by attorneys from the Department, who were doing so at the request of Attorney General Rogers, who, I was advised, had received many complaints about our policy."[71]

Conclusion

The NFL owners and their commissioners failed to get their antitrust exemption, but they prevailed sufficiently in their court fights to avoid disruption from these legal challenges. The owners reaped later benefits by cultivating sympathetic legislators. The owners were a few years away from their greatest legal triumph, when Pete Rozelle did an end run around Judge Grim's quashing of a lucrative national TV deal with CBS. The league's fight to get a national TV contract approved under an antitrust exemption will be covered in the chapter on television.

7

COMPETITIVE BALANCE
AND ITS SOURCES

In the battle for football fans' patronage, NFL owners first had to convince the public that their brand of football was the best. They did so both by innovating with respect to the rules and by boasting of having the best football players. However, the owners struggled to persuade the public that NFL teams were superior to any college team.

In addition to demonstrating top quality, all sports leagues have to worry about excessive competitive imbalance, which might discourage fans from attending games. The NFL has long had a reputation for being the most balanced of the American professional sports leagues. NFL commissioners have frequently boasted of the league's superiority in this respect, compared primarily with Major League Baseball. No NFL team has sustained championship dominance as baseball's New York Yankees once did. Bell and the owners used competitive balance as a rationale for some of the league's policies.

If competitive imbalance was damaging, the owners had no one to blame but themselves. During the postwar period owners dictated all player movement and signings, aside from a few cases of a released player becoming a free agent. NFL owners implemented some rules ostensibly designed to promote parity, although economists suspect that other motives lurked behind the expressed ones. Economists are dubious about the suggested palliatives; for example, they doubt the effectiveness of the reserve clause and reverse-order draft in correcting or preventing the woes of competitive imbalance. Historian Craig Coenen believed the influx of millionaire owners helped promote parity, although it is more likely that such owners simply stabilized the league.[1] While most industries are characterized by the winnowing of the weak, modern sports leagues often prefer to maintain weak clubs. One method of helping teams in small cities survive is cross-subsidization, which is typically achieved through revenue sharing. The league reputedly had a generous revenue-sharing system, but gate-sharing rules reflect the tension within a professional sports league. Because of the complexity of revenue sharing, the topic is covered in a subsequent chapter.

Competitive Balance

Among sports fans and commentators, competitive balance is similar to the weather: lots of people talk about it, but few know what to do about it. Economists and statisticians who study competitive balance within sports leagues have not defined what optimal competitive balance would be. Few people would consider a league where every team wins half its games as ideal. Such a league would be similar to a coin-flipping league. While most readers would find a coin-flipping league painfully dull, we shall return to this hypothetical league later in the chapter.

In Major League Baseball, the New York Yankees' dominance from 1949 through 1964 may have alienated American League fans. Even the Yankees saw attendance at Yankee Stadium stagnate in the early 1960s. The cry, "Break up the Yankees," is well known. What is interesting is that two teams—the Boston Celtics or the Los Angeles Lakers (formerly the Minneapolis Lakers)—have won half the NBA Championships from 1946 to the present. Fans don't seem as insistent on breaking up the Celtics and the Lakers. While the NFL has had dominant teams, many of these teams flagged within a decade and were supplanted. This millennium's New England Patriots, who were dominant during the first decade, eventually lapsed, as did the Green Bay Packers, the Miami Dolphins, the Pittsburgh Steelers, and the Cleveland Browns before them. On the other end of the continuum, though, such teams as the New Orleans Saints (sometimes referred to as the "'Aints") and the Detroit Lions have lain dormant for years, if not for decades, the two teams' recent success notwithstanding. Detroit languished despite annual high picks in the college draft. To call Detroit "mediocre" would be a slur against the term. At best, one can only claim that the reverse-order draft, revenue sharing, and schedule gerrymandering have given teams an *opportunity* for parity but not a *guarantee* of parity, and perhaps that is the way it should be. We will examine the effectiveness of these measures in subsequent chapters.

Bert Bell, the NFL's commissioner during the postwar era, often boasted that the NFL had better competitive balance than did Major League Baseball (he did not condescend to compare the NFL with the NBA). On multiple occasions, he claimed that he worked to help "weak teams" via the schedule, the draft, and other mechanisms. The league's slogan, "On any given Sunday," epitomized the league's obsession with competitive balance. Bell's successor, Pete Rozelle, also proclaimed that the rapid turnarounds of the Philadelphia Eagles and the Green Bay Packers, both of whom went from last to first in their respective divisions between the 1958 and 1960 seasons, demonstrated the efficacy of the league's efforts to promote parity.[2]

Football historians are unanimous in citing the league's superior competitive balance compared to baseball and basketball. They took football's superior competitive balance as an accepted fact and rarely bothered to provide comprehensive analysis. Bert Bell provided historians with much of their information regarding competitive imbalance. He testified before Congress that four teams — Chicago, New York, Washington, and Green Bay — dominated the league's championship games. Michael MacCambridge pointed out that these clubs filled nineteen of the twenty slots in the championship game between 1937 and 1946 — the Cleveland Rams being the exception.[3] The AAFC's lack of competitive balance allegedly doomed that entity, as Bell put it, "Cleveland predominated. They were hand-picked throughout the services prior to the war, and came in there with the greatest aggregation of football players ever accumulated, in my opinion, on one team."[4] The Browns' four-year .898 win-loss record in the AAFC contrasted with three teams' records of .250 or worse (table 18). Sportswriter Hal Lebovitz insinuated that the other AAFC teams were catching up to the Browns, but if so, it was too little too late.[5] But even Browns fans tired of the lopsided competition. By 1949 the Browns' home attendance was less than half the 1946 level.

Some observers wondered whether the Browns were really good, or whether the other AAFC teams were just inept. Sportswriter Franklin Lewis stated, "If the Browns can keep it up against the old National League titans, they'll be universally accepted as one of the great teams of all time. If they flop, their glittering AAC record will be discounted as so much trash."[6] Lewis got a partial answer to his question when the Browns whipped the defending NFL champions, the Philadelphia Eagles, by 38–10 in the opening game of the 1950 season, but writer Harry Warren maintained that other sportswriters remained skeptical.[7] Presumably the remaining skeptics were convinced when the Browns eked out a 30–28 victory over the Los Angeles Rams in the championship game, albeit on their home field.[8]

Measures of Competitive Balance

Economists use the concept of standard deviation in discussions of competitive balance. While readers may not have spent time calculating this basic statistic, the concept is straightforward. Suppose all the teams in a sports league are evenly matched in that either team has an equal likelihood of winning a particular game. (For simplicity's sake, we will ignore any home-field advantage.) Any given contest would resemble tossing a fair coin: perhaps the home team wins if the coin lands "heads," while the visiting team wins if the coin lands "tails". Using today's NFL with its sixteen-game schedule, each team in a hypothetical perfect-parity league would expect to win eight games on average. The last two words — on average — are crucial. If you invited your friends to a "fantasy football league" comprised of coin-flipping contests, not all of you would win exactly eight games. Most of you would win close to eight games, but by sheer luck, some of you might win more than ten or fewer than six games. This variance in the expected number of wins mimics a professional sports league.

Statisticians use the standard deviation to measure the variance about the mean of a distribution of events. For a sixteen-game season, the standard deviation about the eight-win mean (a .500 record) is two wins in either direction: winning six to ten games would be within one standard deviation of the mean (a win-loss percentage of .375 to .625). Roughly two-thirds of the teams would fall within this range if the league is truly similar to a coin flip. About 95 percent of the teams would be within two standard deviations of the eight-win mean, or between four and twelve wins (a win-loss percentage of .250 to .750.[9] The fewer the games, the wider the standard deviation will be. For the NFL's twelve-game season played during the 1947–59 seasons, the standard deviation for a perfect-parity league would have been .144. Major League Baseball's 154-game seasons during the 1950s would have had a standard deviation of 6.2 games (or .040). Since it is unlikely that professional sports leagues have perfect parity, the actual standard deviation will differ from the idealized (perfect parity) standard deviation. To compare win-loss distributions across leagues or sports that play varying numbers of games, economists use a ratio of the actual standard deviation to the idealized standard deviation.[10]

Table 19 shows that the NFL's ratio of actual to idealized (perfect parity) standard deviations were smaller than the AAFC's in each of the four seasons that the two leagues competed. By this measure, Commissioner Bell's boast rings true. As economists James Quirk and Rodney Fort demonstrate, the NFL has traditionally had the lowest ratio of the four major professional team sports: NFL, MLB, NBA, and NHL.[11] Table 19 shows that the difference between the AAFC's ratios in 1946 and 1949 were not very different from the NFL's ratios in 1948 and 1949. While the NFL's ratio diminished temporarily in 1952, it bounced back up to AAFC levels in 1953. The table also shows that the AAFC's per-game attendance compared favorably with the NFL's rates.

One difficulty of using the actual ratio of standard deviation to idealized standard deviation is that the ratio is showing a snapshot of a particular season. If the NFL boasted a lower ratio than, for example, baseball's National League during the 1950s, perhaps the same NFL teams came out on top year after year. The next aspect to consider, then, is whether there was churning of teams, or whether teams showed upward and downward mobility. Table 19 shows that nine teams won an NFL Championship over the fourteen seasons under study. The Chicago Cardinals played in a championship game. Only the Pittsburgh Steelers, Washington Redskins, and San Francisco 49ers failed to attain the championship game during the fourteen seasons (ignoring, of course, the short-lived 1950 Baltimore Colts, the Boston/New York Yanks, and the ill-fated Dallas teams). Table 20 shows NFL teams' records across fourteen seasons. Clearly the fortunes of the Cleveland Browns and the Green Bay Packers argue against long-run parity. Since the average football player played for less than five seasons, there must have been an almost complete turnover of players across these fourteen seasons. Between 1946 and 1959, nine of the sixteen MLB teams appeared in the World Series (although if we extend the record to 1945 through 1961, we would pick up the Tigers, Cubs, Reds, and Pirates as World Series participants, and the Redskins and Green Bay in the NFL's Championship Game). The Cleveland Browns, though, won all four AAFC Championships and participated in the NFL's Championship Game in its first six (and also seven of its eight) seasons in the league.

Table 20 reveals, as one would expect given the NFL's twelve-game season, that teams' win-loss percentages fluctuated, sometimes wildly. Every NFL team experienced at least one losing and at least one winning season between 1946 and 1959. Ten teams experienced at least one season of three wins or fewer; nine teams won at least nine games in one season. The Pittsburgh Steelers were paragons of consistency with their relatively stable win-loss records.

Not only did teams fluctuate from being conference leaders to being cellar dwellers, their ebbs and flows could be astonishingly rapid. Eight of the teams experienced drops of 4.5 or more wins (thanks to ties) between two consecutive seasons; eight teams also experienced gains of 4.5 or more wins between two consecutive seasons. Three teams had big gains and losses across three consecutive seasons. The Boston/New York Yanks (Bulldogs in 1949) went from 1-10-1 in 1949 to 7-5-0 in 1950 and back down to 1-9-2 before folding. The perennially strong Cleveland Browns suffered just one losing season in their first ten seasons in the NFL: 5-7-0 in 1956. The team sported identical 9-2-1 records in 1955 and 1957, showing that the losing record was an aberration. The 1954–56 Detroit Lions went through a decline and rise similar to that of the Browns. While such volatility could occur in a perfect-parity league, NFL teams' experiences suggest that the league was not in perfect parity.

Even if NFL win-loss records displayed smaller ratios of actual to ideal standard deviations than did records in other leagues, another measure displays the league's imbalance. In the twelve seasons between 1999 and 2010, only three NFL teams have scored more than twice as many points as they allowed during a season: the 1999 St. Louis Rams (2.174), the 2007 New England Patriots (2.150), and the 2000 Baltimore Ravens (2.018). The 2007 Patriots compiled a 16-0-0 regular-season record (the undefeated 1972 Miami Dolphins had a scoring ratio of 2.251, better than the 1948 Browns, who had an identical record). Table 21 demonstrates that such measures of superiority and inferiority were more common in postwar professional football, especially given that there were fewer teams in the 1950s than there are today. The Cleveland Browns not only won a high proportion of their games between 1946 and 1954, they frequently scored more than twice as many points as their opponents, indicating the prevalence of routs. The Browns wiped out most of their rivals in their inaugural season, as the team scored three times as many points as it allowed.[12] While NFL owners consoled themselves with the thought that their teams were, top to bottom, superior to the AAFC teams, the Browns' ability to compile similar win-loss records and similar scoring margins argues against the NFL's conceit. The Browns' contemporaries in Philadelphia, the NFL champion Eagles, compiled similarly gaudy scoring ratios in 1948 and 1949.

The competitive imbalance is also reflected in the preponderance of NFL and AAFC teams with the worst scoring ratios between 1946 and 1959. Seven of the nine teams with the worst ratios played in the two leagues before the football war ended. With the winnowing of the first Baltimore Colts, the Dallas Texans, and the New York Yanks, the surviving teams appear to have been more evenly matched. Between 1955 and 1959, just one team displayed such a scoring ratio disparity.

These tables demonstrate that Bell was correct on two measures. The NFL had lower standard deviation ratios and more churning than did the AAFC. Bell was incorrect in that the NFL did have teams that were just as relatively inept as those in the AAFC. Some NFL teams were chronically strong or weak, arguing against the realization of his vision.

The Green Bay Packers were an anomaly in the NFL. Sports economists generally anticipate that teams playing in the largest cities such as New York, Chicago, and Los Angeles will have greater revenue potential than teams in smaller cities such as Pittsburgh, Cincinnati, or, especially, Green Bay. The disparities in potential revenues lead to greater odds against teams in the smaller cities being successful over time. After the shakeout of teams in smaller cities and towns during the 1920s and early 1930s, the Packers were the sole small-town survivor. Curly Lambeau proved to be an astute coach and selector of talent, so the team defied its small population base and was one of the four most successful teams up until the end of the war.

After the war, though, some fans believed that Lambeau was not keeping up with the evolution in professional football. Reporter Jack Sher detailed the team's success: a 198-80-21 win-loss record, six championships, and a points scored–points allowed mark of 4,897–2,581.[13] The team led the league in home and road attendance in 1945. Sher described the close relationship the townspeople had with the players, many of whom remained in the area to open businesses.

The Packers conformed to economists' predictions after the war, and their record sank. The Packers played in a small stadium and began playing half their home games in Milwaukee at the league's behest (without much improvement in attendance). Some owners, such as the Eagles' Alexis Thompson, complained about Green Bay and its paltry gate receipts, where "visiting clubs take a financial licking at Green Bay because of the small population and small stadium."[14] By 1950, the team was teetering financially, and pundits often predicted its demise, but the owners of other NFL teams, especially the old guard, retained a nostalgic fondness for the franchise. Pete Rozelle liked to point to Green Bay as exemplifying the NFL spirit of sharing revenue. Sportswriter Dan Parker was caustic: "The case of Green Bay is ridiculous, Bert Bell, and you know it. . . . It doesn't belong in the National Professional Football League anymore than Kalamazoo [a calumny against Kalamazoo?]. . . . It is not a Major League City."[15]

By 1955 Bell and owners were citing "upsets" in demonstrating that parity was better than ever: "There is nothing freakish and little surprising about these so-called upsets. Rather, they are signs that things in the NFL are returning to normal. There hasn't been normalcy since World War II, you know. . . . The have-not clubs of late, which had done so well before World War II, were bound to come back. Right now, I'd say our league is better balanced in players and better off financially than ever in its history."[16] At the end of the 1955 season, *Sports Illustrated* writer Alfred Wright claimed that "the entire league has never been better balanced. In both 1955 and 1956, every team won between three and nine games. If this wasn't quite the goal Bell wanted — every team winning at least four games in a season for two seasons — it was close."[17]

The Detroit Lions bounced from 9-2-1 in 1954 to 3-9 in 1955 and to 9-3 in 1956. While sportswriter Watson Spoelstra was uncharitable in characterizing the team's dismal 1955 season: "The Detroit Lions are cha-grined and embarrassed by the biggest flop the National Football League has ever known," he admitted that the team suffered from retirements (Les Bingaman), defections to Canada (Tom Dublinski), a bad trade (LaVern Torgeson), and injuries. He added that the Lions' misfortunes served to make the Browns' run of success more amazing. Another reporter attributed the Lions' collapse in 1955 to "softness at the middle of the defensive line," which the Lions remedied by acquiring Ray Krouse from the New York Giants.[18] While Detroit's experiences may have exemplified the upward and downward mobility desired by Bert Bell, it also merely demonstrated that, to a surprising degree, the NFL resembled a coin-flipping contest. The Lions' draft choice in January 1956, the second choice in the regular draft, was Howard "Hopalong" Cassady, who did not rush for any touchdowns during his rookie season. The first-round choice was not responsible for the Lions' resurgence; instead Tommy Devine cited Bobby Layne's "comeback" season and productive play by five rookies, four returning servicemen, and a returnee from Canada. He also credited coach Buddy Parker for obtaining Ray Krouse.[19]

A *Newsweek* story attributed the growing parity, in part, to specialization.

> To a large measure, these sudden and swift changes of fortune which help explain pro football's continually growing appeal (attendance this season is up almost 10 percent), are closely interwoven with specializa-tion. Where the difference between two individual halfbacks may be enormous, the differences among two sets of 23 specialists (two platoons and a place-kicker) tend to be small, particularly in an era when scout-ing techniques are standardized. . . . The league in fact was so close that it was as hard to pick a loser as a winner. "The way it is now," said coach Parker of the Lions, "we just don't have any last-place clubs in this league any more."[20]

Bert Bell, of course, gave the player draft the credit for the parity and the accompanying prosperity. "That's why people come out to see the pros play — they know a game between *any* two teams in the league can go either way easily."[21]

If the relative closeness of competition during the 1955–57 seasons was attributable to the reverse-order draft, then Bell and the pundits had some explaining to do when the win-loss disparities widened again in 1958. Green Bay sank to one win and one tie. In 1959 the Giants became the first team to win ten regular-season games since 1953, while the Cardinals and Rams won just two games each. Heading into 1959, however, Bell was enthusiastic about a resumption of better attendance through parity; he even suggested that improved parity could open up the possibility of expansion.[22]

Comparative Quality

During the NFL's infancy, few people bothered to ponder the question of whether the NFL teams were as good as top college teams. Did the NFL play the "best" football?

Because most of the early NFL players did not play college football, those pundits and fans who cared to ponder the difference between pro and college games could claim that college players were superior. When Arch Ward of the Chicago *Tribune* suggested a game between the reigning NFL champion and a group of college All-Stars, he bestowed credibility upon the pros and ignited a debate concerning the pros' relative quality of play. Previous exhibition games between pros and collegians, including games between Notre Dame alumni and the New York Giants and Chicago Bears, had not resolved the question.

Ward got his newspaper to sponsor the game between the Bears and a group of newly graduated collegiate All-Americans. The NFL and Halas considered the ramifications of such a well-publicized game. A loss might hurt the league's credibility, but the game itself promised to put the NFL in the limelight. The two teams fought to a 0–0 tie before almost eighty thousand patrons. The game became an annual event. By 1945 the pros had won seven games, lost three, and tied two.[23] Of course, the pro team had an advantage in being an existing, cohesive unit, while the college players, many of whom were getting ready to start NFL training season, were individual talents. Arthur Daley suggested that the college players approached the games in a "carefree manner" while the pros had to take the game in stride "because they still have another four months of even more violent league football confronting them."[24] The NFL teams began dominating the series, and by the late 1950s the question was moot.

After the war, several NFL owners began campaigning to end the game with the College All-Stars. Owners worried about their draftees getting injured in the game. They also disliked the fact that league rules stipulated that league recruits who were invited to participate and didn't play were barred from preseason exhibition games with their clubs.[25]

A variation on the games between the College All-Stars and an NFL team was to pit a good pro team against a good college team. At the end of 1945, some people lobbied for a game between Army and the Cleveland Rams. Both sides scorned the idea. John Lardner reported that Steve Owen, the New York Giants' coach, disdained the idea and declared that professionals should never play the collegians in football, "the implication being that the pros do not wish to have murder on their souls."[26]

Army coach Red Blaik stirred controversy by denigrating professional football in an article in *Collier's*, a weekly national magazine. Blaik admitted that a good pro team would be able to beat a good college team, but he expounded, "I think a good pro team might get itself up to beat a good college team in a single game. But if the pro team were put into a league with good college teams . . . it would have to learn to play football the way the colleges do or it wouldn't stand a chance. A fiery team like Tennessee would cripple a pro team. . . . Football is a Spartan game in which youth, spirit and condition count heavily. The colleges have the boys in their best years. Few of them ever play as well after they become professionals."[27] Blaik's basic arguments were that the pros lacked both the spirit and physical conditioning of the collegians; the pros placed too much emphasis on the passing game; pro players were past their prime; pros were too lazy to play good defense; and pro teams played schedules interspersed with weak teams.

The Sporting News ran observations from various football observers; most of these observers thought Blaik greatly mistaken, including his former star Glenn Davis, who stated, "I have found pro ball to be a much more demanding sport than the college game. . . . Since the pros skim the cream of the crop each year from the college ranks, it is only natural to find much better teams in pro ball."[28] Paul Brown told reporters that his 1942 Ohio State team, which was considered the national champion by some, was a "darn good team, but my Browns would have beaten it, 50 or 90 to o, whichever it preferred."[29] Sportswriter Joe Williams took the nuanced view that such exhibition games never could produce a conclusive answer.[30] Johnny Lujack used a variation on the "any given Sunday" theme: "The weakest team in our National League could beat the Army on any given Saturday." Lujack cited the greater sophistication of the pros' defensive schemes.[31] Bob Zuppke, who coached George Halas at Illinois, believed that many collegians hadn't fully matured by the time they graduated. He characterized the pros as "post-graduate play."[32]

By the 1950s few people other than Red Blaik dared to question the NFL's superiority.

Player Movement

Branch Rickey, not known as a lavish spender, blurted at a Brooklyn football luncheon that he'd be willing to "pay $100,000 for a great passer, but not a dime for a poor one."[33] Rickey certainly did not mean he'd be willing to pay $100,000 in salary (unless it was over many seasons), but that a top quarterback who transformed a mediocre team into a crowd-pleasing winner was worth a considerable amount. A winning team meant different amounts of added revenue to different NFL teams. A team playing in a stadium seating only thirty thousand might not see its revenue increase much with a winning team, whereas the New York Giants, playing in either the Polo Grounds or Yankee Stadium, might see its crowds swell by ten or twenty thousand per game with a winning team. In economic parlance, the quarterback's marginal revenue product—the change in a team's total revenue from using a player—could be greater with a team in a larger city than one in a smaller city. Economists Ronald Coase and Simon Rottenberg independently predicted that resources such as players should move to where their marginal revenue product is highest. Rickey's point was that a good quarterback might boost Brooklyn's revenues sufficiently to justify paying a $100,000 price for him.

In the NFL's early days, player movement was characterized by a primitive free-for-all attitude. Owners occasionally loaned players or tampered with players, who still retained college eligibility (perhaps they learned their tricks from college coaches). In one notorious case, when New York Giants quarterback Harry Newman was injured in 1934, whom was Tim Mara going to call? He called his buddy, Art Rooney, owner of the Pittsburgh Pirates (later Steelers). Rooney obliged by sending Warren Heller to the rescue. Mara hoped Heller could adequately pilot the team in a key showdown with the Boston Redskins. The Redskins' owner, George Preston Marshall, immediately protested. The brouhaha demonstrated how haphazard the league was in 1934. Pittsburgh had completed its season, while the Giants still had three regular-season games left. League president Joe Carr initially upheld the trade, but he faltered when it became clear that a majority of the owners opposed the trade. Mara backed down. To forestall a repeat of such shenanigans, owners enacted a trading deadline — no trades after the fifth game of the season — and eliminated the section in the bylaws that covered player loans. Although released players could be claimed on waiver in the usual reverse-order fashion, no players could be traded or loaned to another team.[34]

Paul Brown, a highly successful high school and college coach, spent the war years coaching the Great Lakes football team. He knew players from the Big Ten, from the various service teams, and other sources. He spent the interval between the formation of the AAFC and its debut signing players. He signed Otto Graham before the war ended. He was willing to sign African American players Bill Willis and Marion Motley to pro contracts.[35] Brown's acumen is perhaps best reflected by the fact that twelve of his players were still with the team when it transferred to the NFL.[36]

Teams could improve their on-the-field product by drafting, buying, trading, acquiring players on waivers, or signing the occasional free agent. With the upheaval in franchises, both AAFC and NFL teams received players through special dispersion drafts of players from teams that became defunct. In some cases, when the AAFC and NFL merged, surviving NFL teams got an influx of talent.[37]

With the diminution of the number of teams between 1949 and 1951, surviving teams were able to acquire reinforcements from defunct teams via a special draft. To bolster weaklings Baltimore and Green Bay, NFL owners awarded five extra choices in this special draft. The two clubs' combined win-loss records improved by one game between 1949 and 1950, despite the extra choices in the special draft and the first and third choices (after the bonus pick) in the college draft.[38]

In the wake of the Frank Filchock and Merle Hapes gambling scandal, the New York Giants found themselves without a quarterback. The team floundered for a few seasons while searching for a capable replacement for Filchock.[39] If the Coase Theorem had held, it should have been a simple matter for the Giants to purchase a fine quarterback from a team in a small market, given the arbitrage opportunity. The Giants' resurgence coincided with an influx of talent from the defunct New York teams in the wake of the AAFC collapse. When the Giants slipped again after some conference titles in the late 1950s, they used trades to rebuild, getting veterans Y. A. Tittle, Del Shofner, Bob Galters, Erich Barnes, and Joe Walton. The Giants were wheeler-dealers and had made trades with eleven of thirteen rivals in a seven-year period.[40]

On occasion, teams traded players at their peak. The AAFC Brooklyn team dispatched Glenn Dobbs, the league's Most Valuable Player in 1946, to Los Angeles for hotshot prospect Angelo Bertelli, whose publicity was great. The Dodgers then swapped Bertelli to Chicago for Bob Hoernschemeyer. The Chicago Rockets, plagued by ineptitude and bad luck, suffered bad luck on this trade, as Bertelli proved injury-prone. Sportswriter Ed Prell characterized the Dobbs/Bertelli transfer as the "biggest deal in pro football history."[41] Dobbs played a few more seasons but failed to attain All-AAFC status again, while Hoernschemeyer later enjoyed two All-NFL seasons as a back.

A majority of top players, as defined by being named All-Pro at least once between 1950 and 1960, played for multiple teams. About one-quarter of the migratory players switched teams in the wake of team failures or through the AAFC-NFL agreement. The have-not teams, the Chicago Cardinals, Green Bay, Pittsburgh, and Washington, did obtain some All-NFL players, although some of these players were at the end of their careers. These four teams did not suffer the net loss in quality players that their have-not peers in Major League Baseball suffered during the same years.[42]

The Chicago Bears stockpiled quarterbacks, corralling an "'L of a group" in established star Sid Luckman, January 1946 draftee Johnny Lujack, and December 1947 draftee Bobby Layne. Layne and Luckman are in the Pro Football Hall of Fame. Reporters thought Halas was paying the trio more than $60,000 combined in salaries. Halas used the same lure that baseball's

New York Yankees used in recruiting players: the opportunity to play for the championship. He used the pitch to lure Lujack away from the crosstown Chicago Rockets.[43]

Bobby Layne may well have been the most-traveled Hall-of-Fame quarterback in history, with the exception of George Blanda. Chicago wangled a trade with Pittsburgh for the Detroit pick — number one in the regular draft — that they used to select Layne. George Halas had selected Johnny Lujack two drafts prior with a number-four pick. With Sid Luckman and Johnny Lujack, Halas decided that Layne was expendable, so he sent him to the New York Bulldogs for about $50,000 and two first-round draft choices in the January 1950 and January 1951 drafts. Some reporters thought the $50,000 was the highest price ever paid for a player, but given the volatility of the general price level between 1922 and 1950, this might at best have been the most dollars only and not the most in terms of purchasing power.

Bulldogs owner Ted Collins was desperate to build a winner. When Collins surrendered his franchise, commentators thought the Layne deal had been a spectacular bust for Collins. The irony was that George Halas may have been a loser, too, as he could have used a quarterback with Layne's ability during the 1950s. The two draft choices ended up being Chuck Hunsinger and Billy Stone, who between them gave the team seven seasons' worth of halfback play. Collins then sent Layne to Detroit for $37,500, where he became a Hall-of-Fame quarterback. The Lions used six rookies in 1953 and five in 1954 to become the conference champions in both years. Les Bingaman was the sole player remaining from the last-place club.[44] Layne wound up his career with Pittsburgh, having been traded there for Earl Morrall and two draft choices. He therefore played for all three teams that possessed the draft pick with which the Bears selected him.[45]

Another Hall-of-Fame performer, running back Ollie Matson, was involved in a nine-for-one trade (Matson being the one). Matson had been a Chicago Cardinals star through their lackluster seasons, but they decided to dispatch him to the Los Angeles Rams in 1959. Los Angeles got one good year out of Matson. The key player for Chicago was tackle Frank Fuller.[46]

The second Baltimore Colts club used clever drafting and a remarkable free-agent signing to vault to the top of the league. President Don Kellett and coach Weeb Ewbank drafted L. G. Dupre, George Shaw, and Alan Ameche, as well as picking up the cast-off Johnny Unitas as a free agent.[47] Joe King called the Colts' rise a tribute to a "spend and win" process. When the Colts drafted Ameche, Shaw, and Dupre, Ewbank told Kellett the three would be costly to sign, but Kellett approved the expense.

Another key decision for the Colts was a gigantic five-for-eleven trade made with Cleveland in 1953. The Browns, trying to maintain a championship run, acquired Mike McCormack, Don Colo, Tom Catlin, John Petitbon, and Herschel Forester and sent Bert Rechichar, Carl Taseff, Don Shula, Gern Nagler, and Ed Sharkey to Baltimore. Rechichar and Taseff were still with the club in 1958. Because the Colts had Shaw at quarterback, they were merely looking for a backup when they signed Johnny Unitas as a free agent. The club also retained Gino Marchetti, Art Spinney, Art Donovan, and Jim Mutscheller from the old Dallas roster. They selected star receiver Raymond Berry in the twentieth round, not as the twentieth pick, as one might surmise, given his stellar career. They added Lenny Moore with a first-round pick. Club owner Carroll Rosenbloom realized early on that the fans' early enthusiasm for resurrecting the team might be ephemeral: "We had no right to expect that the fans would continue buying so many tickets year after year unless we produced. I went on the assumption that we might not have nearly so many season sales in '54 if we did not do a job in '53."[48]

Because of the Colts' success, the team easily surpassed the baseball Baltimore Orioles in popularity among the city's residents; the Colts kept Baltimore fans' loyalty for years. When the Orioles were unexpectedly fighting the Yankees for the American League pennant in 1964, a Sunday doubleheader on September 20 attracted fewer than nine thousand fans. Joseph Durso wrote, "Natives explained the lack of interest by pointing out that the Baltimore Colts were playing on TV."[49]

The Green Bay Packers, whether by choice or by necessity, acquired twelve players who had been cast off by other clubs.[50] The Packers' rise to glory coincided with the hiring of Vince Lombardi as coach. Since most of the team's successes occurred after the period examined in this book, little more will be said about the way the Packers supplanted the Browns as the glamour team.[51]

The Chicago Bears had a lackluster record during the early 1950s. The retirement of Sid Luckman and an injury to Johnny Lujack rendered them weak at quarterback. Owner-coach George Halas also emphasized the team's losses of players in the wake of the AAFC-NFL settlement: "This is the severe personnel losses we sustained during the negotiations, which led to the collapse of the All-America conference. In order to hasten the AAFC's end, the Bears surrendered disputed draft rights to at least twenty players who had been picked as future pro stars during the 1947–50 period." According to Halas, this collection of players included Billy Grimes and George Taliaferro, who ended up with Cleveland and New York.[52]

Browns' Dominance

The Browns' core of stars remained remarkably stable, but, ultimately, Paul Brown had to reload. At the end of the 1952 season, though, he still had Otto Graham, Mac Speedie, Dante Lavelli, Marion Motley, Bill Willis, Lin Houston, Frank Gatski, Lou Groza, and George Young as seven-year play-ers.[53] Graham, Groza, Lavelli, Motley, and Young are in the Pro Football Hall of Fame.

Historian Michael MacCambridge points out that when the Browns joined the NFL, Paul Brown recognized that some of the NFL teams were using many of the same methods he did in building their teams, includ-ing an emphasis on scouting and on innovations in tactics. Brown was, to an extent, the victim of imitators.[54] Quarterback Otto Graham proved the mainstay of Brown's success; Brown never won another champion-ship after Graham retired. While the coach recognized running back Jim Brown's abilities and those of many other talented players, he was never able to replace Graham. His Cleveland teams still posted winning records but failed to win titles.[55]

The Browns played in their eighth consecutive championship game in 1953. While the team still retained a core of veterans, they added sev-eral rookies, including Chuck Noll, Don Steinbrunner, Gene Donaldson, and Doug Atkins. The following season, the team got off to a slow start before winning back-to-back titles. During the slow start, team captain Don Colo attributed part of the difficulties to the loss of Blanton Collier, the defensive coach, who had been with Brown throughout the team's reign.[56] Brown lost eleven players from the 1953 team, and some observers predicted the team's run of success was over; Brown got veterans to plug up holes, and the team kept winning. As Brown entered the 1955 season, with Graham back at the helm after a brief retirement, he admitted that the next ten seasons were going to be harder: "It has become progressively more difficult to win." He cited luck as a factor, too: "Things are beginning to get flimsier and flimsier. We've continued to draft last or second-last so long that things may be catching up to us." Reporter Herman Goldstein observed that the Browns "have never been too successful in their drafting." In the most recent draft, Brown had lost draftees to Canada and to court action, and only two of their first ten 1955 selections were on the team. Goldstein said Brown obtained necessary reinforcements through trades, picking up Don Colo, Mike McCormack, Bob Gain, Darrell Brewster, Dub Jones, and Don Paul. By the 1955 season, only Graham, Groza, Lavelli, and Gatski were left from the 1946 team; Brown had acquired eighteen of the thirty-three players from other clubs. Franklin Lewis observed, "Brown has shown an aptitude and a determination for trades that set him apart from almost any other manager-coach in sports. . . . Brown manages to trade men in their prime and get back others equally fit, mentally and physically. Of course, a player coming to the Browns has all the best of it at the outset. He's joining a team that's always in a championship game. He perks up."[57]

An example of Brown's "aptitude" was his trade of Marion Motley to the Pittsburgh Steelers for Ed Modzelewski. Motley had one season left, while Modzelewski played five seasons for the Browns. Lebovitz mentioned that the younger player, a Steeler first-round pick, had spent time in the army, had been injured, and had signed a lucrative contract; the last two factors may have been paramount in the Steelers' decision to trade him. An earlier example had occurred after the 1948 season, when Brown traded draft rights to center Alex Sarkisian to the New York Yankees for veteran tackle Derrell Palmer; Sarkisian never played pro ball, while Palmer played five seasons with the Browns.[58]

At the end of the 1955 season, Brown admitted that he had had a goal from the beginning of his pro coaching career. He wanted to win ten straight division titles: "It was a goal I aimed at, but I didn't think it could be done."

Brown cited the return of Graham for an extra bow and the acquisition of Ed Modzelewski as key factors in keeping the streak alive.[59]

The Browns' streak of division and conference titles ended the following season. Graham's retirement was the key. "The team seemed to sense his presence, his rhythm, his confidence." Babe Parilli and George Ratterman were veteran quarterbacks, but they may have peaked at being good backups. Brown also cited the draft's leveling influence.[60] Since his team went 5-7, it held a middling pick in each round. Even though Brown needed a quarterback, some quarterbacks—including Len Dawson and John Brodie—were taken ahead of Cleveland's fifth pick (sixth overall), so the team took Jim Brown. Cleveland made the playoffs the next two years, after which the team began a gradual decline.

Using the Schedule to Foster Win-Loss Parity

Most fans take scheduling for granted. At the beginning of the season, they may glance at the schedule and plan their autumn activities. NFL owners, though, displayed a keen and ruthless interest in the schedule. In some cases, they had to. Why? The schedule affected each team's attendance and league standings, if not the actual competitive balance. Given a choice, most owners would opt for a lopsided set of tough opponents who drew well rather than for a group of patsies who promised to be stepping-stones toward a division title but whom the fans disdained. George Halas testified once that something had to be done, since teams only wanted to schedule attractive opponents.[61] As a result, some teams rarely played each other. Like students at a junior high dance, some teams had to shoo away partners.

Boston/New York owner Ted Collins blamed Bell's scheduling for his team's inability to break even. Because he moved into New York City, he had to synchronize his games with the New York Giants, who had the first pick of playing dates. In addition, the Yanks were placed in the division with western teams, hiking his transportation costs. Collins's pleas to be placed in the same division as the Giants failed.[62]

Bert Bell and the owners loved to present themselves as "sportsmen" and not as profit maximizers (not that many businesspeople present themselves as profit maximizers). Bell told the Senate antitrust subcommittee, "The only thing I claim about them [the owners] is that they are in love. They get in love with their ball club and they get in love with certain schedules and so forth."[63] "Contentious" hardly described the owners' wrangling over the schedule. It consumed days of meetings; it was a free-for-all that wasted time, created rancor, and injured the league collectively. Bert Bell's recurring headache, and perhaps his most valuable service to the league, was his work on the schedule. Season after season owners would argue and fight over the schedule, sometimes for days. The bickering over the schedule usually consumed more time and effort at the winter meetings than any other topic.

While the owners usually let Bell arrange the schedule as a last resort, they probably knew implicitly that a neutral authority was best for setting up schedules. Why they took years before formally making it the commissioner's duty remains unclear.[64]

The owners' arguments regarding scheduling spilled over into establishing divisions. Since the NFL used a home-and-home intradivisional schedule, the assignment of division rivals was important not only for win-loss records but also for attendance. Being placed in a division with rivals playing in large stadiums could be a lucrative advantage that might, over time, carry over to a team's ability to field a strong roster. The New York Giants, for instance, were wary of losing the Chicago Bears as a division rival. If the Bears were in the opposite division, they might only play against the Giants in the Polo Grounds (or, later, Yankee Stadium) once every five or six seasons. When the AAFC folded, and when the NFL expanded in 1960, setting the division lineups was a protracted process.

Since the league office got 2 percent of the gate receipts, league officers had an incentive to arrange the schedule to maximize revenue, although this might have clashed with the desire to promote parity. Reporter Stanley Frank thought this motive explained why the league's "Big Four" — Chicago, New York Giants, Washington, and Green Bay — "get none the worst of it in the allocation of dates."[65]

Bell had to be part baseball prognosticator, part diplomat, and part juggler to construct the league schedule. Before each NFL season, he had to ponder whether a baseball team owning a stadium in which an NFL team played was likely to appear in the World Series. Bell hoped that baseball owners might rescind their rule prohibiting NFL games in their stadiums before the baseball season ended.[66] The two Chicago teams did not want to play in the city on the same Sunday; this was also true during the years when two clubs shared New York City and when Baltimore and Washington were in the league.[67] Owners disliked long home stands or long road trips, but sometimes they were stuck with them because of stadium availability.

The NFL's early days were marked by haphazard scheduling. In true bush-league fashion, the league's teams played varying numbers of games. As late as the early 1930s, George Preston Marshall recalled that teams played different numbers of games, leading to chaos when it was time to determine the league champion. Marshall said, "In 1932 the Bears won seven, lost one and tied six, and Green Bay won ten, lost three and tied one. The vote was to ignore ties and base percentage on wins and losses." While the Bears and Packers each played fourteen games, the other teams played either ten or twelve games. Marshall, new to the league, proposed the heretical idea that all teams should play the same number of regular-season games, but it would not be until the 1936 season that all teams played the same number.[68]

Bell claimed to have had a guiding philosophy in formulating the schedule: he used the schedule to keep teams in contention for as long as possible and to create as many attractive matchups as possible.[69] Major League Baseball adhered to a straightforward, balanced round-robin schedule; each team played its seven rivals twenty-two times each during the season. Well before the NFL formally instituted measures to pit weak teams against other weak teams and strong teams against other strong teams, Bell tried to do so on an informal basis to help promote parity. Sportswriter Tex Maule lauded Bell's ability: "He has done this so adroitly that the conference champions are seldom decided before the last Sunday of the season."[70] When the New York Giants faltered on the field and in the stands during 1953, Bell arranged for the team to play two early games with the weak Chicago Cardinals and Baltimore Colts the following season. His philosophy was to "give as many teams as possible a good standing as long as possible."[71]

An examination of the 1953–58 schedules, though, casts doubt upon Bell's claims. Because there were only twelve interdivisional games in each season during the late 1950s, Bell's ability to manipulate the schedule was constrained. Two of these games went to Chicago Bears-Chicago Cardinals and Baltimore Colts-Washington Redskins matchups. Bell did not consistently match last-place teams (or first-place teams) against each other for the remaining ten interdivisional games. The average difference in win-loss percentages for the ten games was not too different than it would have been had the interdivisional games been assigned randomly.

Michael MacCambridge lauded Bell for implementing his philosophy, in contrast to his predecessors Joe Carr and Elmer Layden, who acquiesced in schedules that favored the strong: "The owners who had the staying power were the ones who came away with the decent schedules, complained Art Rooney. 'The guys who snuck out to get some sleep or go night-clubbing wound up getting murdered the next season because when they weren't there to defend themselves, we'd give them all the dates we didn't want.'" Other owners complained that the league's "old guard" collaborated to each other's benefit.[72] In the league's early days, teams in smaller towns sometimes opted to play a preponderance of games on the road, games in which the visitor's share was greater than a home gate. Craig Coenen believes Joe Carr used the schedule to weed out weak franchises in smaller communities.[73]

Bell told reporters that teams preferred getting attractive opponents in November: "Late November is the time that a team makes money or finishes in the red. Two last-place teams playing for no reason to run out the schedule won't draw flies. But even a cellar club can do well if it has the potential champion or a great contender on the book on those days."[74]

Bert's informal attempts to match weak versus weak and strong versus strong became routine by the late 1970s.[75] The NFL now designates two games of each team's sixteen-game schedule to promoting parity, opposing first-place to first-place teams down to fourth-place to fourth-place teams.

The league's home-and-home series within divisions or conferences irked some observers, who felt that a round-robin schedule would have been more equitable. The NFL's schedule meant that some teams did not meet for several consecutive seasons. These observers appreciated the AAFC's round-robin, home-and-home schedule. Bill Stern acknowledged, however, that the AAFC schedule was simplified by the fact that only two of its teams played in baseball parks.[76]

NFL owners were not shy about proposing changes to the schedule. George Preston Marshall favored splitting the ten teams into two leagues, although there would be interleague play. How his plan differed from the division or conference setups was difficult to discern. At the 1947 meetings, Marshall resurrected his proposal for the formation of two leagues, rambling on almost incoherently. The gist appeared to be that if there were two leagues, cities with two teams could place one team in each league, which he thought would be beneficial. The owners typically did not like to have both New York teams or both Chicago teams in the same division, but Marshall's plan was odd at best. Detroit owner Fred Mandel wanted a round-robin schedule, but Marshall scorned such a system.[77]

Creating a schedule for the 1947 season exemplified the difficulties involved. There were ten teams and an eleven-game season. The odd number of games created an immediate problem: who would get six home games? During the 1946 season, teams had between four and seven home games. The owners decided that the five teams that had shown the best attendance in 1946 would get six home games each.[78]

Green Bay's Curly Lambeau made an eminently simple suggestion to resolve the home date impasse: increase the season to twelve games. Why didn't they think of that before? Bell, while he was in favor of the increase, warned that because of baseball's later-than-usual conclusion to its season, there might not be sufficient open stadium dates for the NFL to squeeze in an extra game. To ensure fairness and to bring some structure to the scheduling process, Bell suggested a five-year cycle of intersectional games to accompany the home-and-home series within divisional rivals. Under this setup, every team would visit each of the NFL parks at least once every five seasons.[79]

The westward movement of teams caused consternation in the NFL. Many of the eastern teams did not want to incur the added expense of traveling west. The fixation on transportation expenses may have exemplified the still-precarious nature of the league. Teams tried to avoid playing the Los Angeles Rams as if they were a pack of pariahs. The result was that the Rams didn't get to play New York and Washington very often over the years.[80]

The AAFC-NFL merger brought new complications. There were thirteen teams in 1950, which meant bye weeks would be required for teams. The divisional alignment was even more contentious. Eastern teams still wanted to avoid traveling to Los Angeles and to San Francisco. George Halas, in particular, was adamant about his desire to stay within the friendly confines of the northeast quadrant of the country. He suggested a "compromise." If the crosstown Cardinals would agree to making the westward trip to play the two California teams every other season, then he, Halas, might accede.[81] Years later, Bell would muse, "These two franchises [Los Angeles and San Francisco] have saved the National Football League. It's a very funny thing. The eastern and Midwestern clubs all used to want to skip dates on the West Coast. Now, just the opposite is true. They want to go out there and pick up those big checks in Los Angeles and San Francisco. It's like the gold rush to the Coast all over again."[82] Since there were an odd number of teams, Bell designated the Baltimore Colts as a "swing team." The Colts would play each of the other twelve teams once, while its placement in a division remained undetermined.[83]

Bell's schedule for 1950 opened with a bang. The AAFC and NFL champions from the previous season, Cleveland and Philadelphia, could not play a game after the 1949 season, so Bell matched them in the 1950 season opener.[84]

When Baltimore dropped out of the league, leaving twelve teams, the owners again reached a stalemate regarding division alignment. Again, they passed the problem on to Bell. Bell put forth his four-year plan in which interdivisional pairings rotated and every eastern team ventured westward at least once every four seasons. Bell's plan also maintained the Chicago and New York intracity rivalries, as well as Marshall's desired Baltimore and Washington matchup. These pairs would play home-and-home series each season. In addition, every team would get a game in New York during the 1951 season.[85] Bell gave the owners a choice of sorts. They could vote on the schedules he prepared. Bell explained, "If any of the proposals I make receives eleven votes it will go into the books as a permanent set-up. If these eleven votes do not come, then I will make up the alignment and schedule as I see fit and it will be in effect one year." The Cards and Bears switched divisions for one season, so that the Bears would be spared the California trip.[86] Halas fought hard to avoid going to California and to avoid losing dates with longtime rivals New York Giants and Washington Redskins: "We have played some of our most thrilling games with those clubs."[87]

When Ted Collins surrendered his New York Bulldog franchise after the 1951 season and the team moved to Dallas for one season before moving to Baltimore, Bell was confronted with another headache. Baltimore didn't really fit into the Western Conference. Some owners objected because of increased transportation costs (although Baltimore was more convenient for many teams than Dallas had been), but otherwise an eastern club would have had to switch conferences, which none wanted to do. The Chicago Cardinals were the logical choice for such a change, but Bell and the other owners disliked the idea of having both Chicago teams in the same division. As usual in the NFL, another factor made agreement possible. Along with the Baltimore situation, owners were considering setting up a five-game preseason exhibition schedule comprised of interconference pairings. The two issues were tied together, and everyone got something they wanted, ensuring passage of the schedule and of the conference alignment. Baltimore remained in the Western Conference by an eleven-to-one decision; Philadelphia opposed the alignment for unstated reasons. Owners were so pleased with the arrangement that the following year they put it into the constitution and bylaws. At last there was an end to the annual squabbling over playing dates.[88]

While owners professed satisfaction with and gave permanence to the divisional alignment and systematized scheduling, disparities in attendance between conferences raised the troubling specter of lopsided revenues and team strengths. Los Angeles, San Francisco, Detroit, Baltimore, and the Chicago Bears were either more popular or benefited from larger stadiums than their peers in the Eastern Conference, while Washington, Pittsburgh, Philadelphia, and the Chicago Cardinals either were unattractive teams or were constrained by small stadiums. Joe King noted that in 1956 visiting teams took home checks for $50,000 or more in fourteen games. Eight of those games "were in the Rams-49ers-Bears-Lions orbit. Only two such checks were paid out in eastern parks, both by the Giants. . . . The Giants passed out $291,000 to clubs visiting Yankee Stadium and received only $191,000 in return on the road." At the other end of the attendance spectrum, "In the East last year, there were 16 payoffs under $25,000 and just two in the West!"[89]

Although Pittsburgh's move to the University of Pittsburgh's field and

Philadelphia's switch to the University of Pennsylvania's Franklin Field and out of Connie Mack (Shibe Park) Stadium promised to redress the imbalance to some degree, there wasn't much hope of correcting the imbalance without a realignment (switching Baltimore and the Cardinals would have made a difference).[90] Halas had earlier expressed little sympathy for Eastern Conference owners: "'They should take advantage of their own rivalries and stop looking goggle eyed at the larger attendance in the west.' He pointed out the easterners have two advantages over the west — lower traveling expenses and higher television receipts."[91]

The NFL's two-step expansion program to fourteen teams necessitated significant changes to the schedule. The NFL had, of course, had experience with a thirteen-team roster during its 1950 season. Dallas became a swing team for a year. The long-term issue was whether Minnesota and Dallas would end up in the same conference. Since the two teams were unlikely to be attractive draws for some years to come, such an outcome had drawbacks. Because the league hoped to maintain its intradivisional home-and-home series, the season needed to be extended, and the owners approved a fourteen-game schedule. By this time Bert Bell was no longer around to manage things, but he had left a system for resolving scheduling difficulties amicably and without wasting days in argument.[92]

Conclusion

The NFL's vaunted competitive balance was, to some degree, illusory. At best, the reverse-order draft and schedule manipulation gave all teams a chance to remain competitive year after year. The reality was that some teams languished consistently, while other teams flourished. In some seasons the NFL's competitive balance, as measured by the ratio of the actual standard deviation to the idealized one, was not too different from the AAFC's. The NFL, though, had more churning at the top than had the AAFC, as no one team won more than two championships in a row.

8

THE PLAYER DRAFT

Bert Bell maintained before Congress that, at a minimum, the NFL owners wanted an antitrust exemption for their player draft. Bell believed the exemption was necessary to ensure his holy grail, competitive balance. Detroit scout Bob Nussbaumer's statement, made when the Lions had had a run of success but were beginning to deteriorate, must have rung in Bell's ears: "It's finally catching up with us. You need good, fresh material each year — and we just haven't been getting it."[1]

Birth of the Player Draft

Bell was proud of the player draft; he had proposed it in 1936, when he owned the floundering Philadelphia Eagles. The ostensible purpose was to give weak franchises an opportunity to bid for top-notch collegians without being swamped by New York or Chicago dollars. Bell claimed that aside from the Bears, Giants, Packers, and Redskins, other teams rarely made the championship game. He stated that between 1933 and 1946, the four top teams won 252 games and lost only 59 against the other six teams.[2] Because the best players wanted to play with winning teams, they gravitated to the top four clubs. Bell claimed, "The kids would play for less for the [them] than they would for us [Philadelphia]."[3] Bell persuaded the owners that the reverse-order draft, in which the "last shall be first," to quote the biblical injunction, would promote competitive balance. While he attributed the passage of the proposal to the willingness of wealthy owners to help their less fortunate brethren, economists suspect a more self-interested motive: the player draft forces collegiate players to negotiate with only one team, severely limiting the players' bargaining ability.

George Halas, like other owners, discounted the disparity in bargaining strength conferred by the draft; he testified that the system was "completely fair in that it permits a team to select a player for the position it needs the most. This gives to the player who is selected the privilege of playing rather than sitting on the bench and . . . not one of them wants to sit on the bench. The fact that a player has been chosen for a particular position to help strengthen the team which chooses him gives him a high bargaining power for his services." NFL Players Association lawyer Creighton Miller explained the draft's rationale differently: "He either plays with the club drafting him or he does not play professional football. . . . Depriving a professional entertainer of his right to choose his employer is an unusual exception to allow in the framework of an American economy which relies on free competition for the determination of where and for whom an individual shall be employed. It can be justified only if to depart from it would destroy the entertainer's livelihood — a possibility too remote to warrant consideration. This system is employed to equalize competition and minimize salaries." Miller, though, worried that without some sort of antitrust exemption, even if it "remove[d] one of the few legal remedies presently available to the players, it is apparent that, if this treble damage theory is misused, it can destroy professional football by bankrupting the owners."[4]

Bell also extolled the virtues of a secondary draft of players released from the sixty-man preseason rosters. Teams selected these castoffs in reverse order. Bell explained, "When a club selects a player, it must agree to take over the player's contract at the salary agreed to by the original club and pays $100 waiver price. Players not selected within 48 hours become free agents."[5]

Legislators Examine the Draft

During congressional hearings, Bell had to admit that the reverse-order player draft did not immediately bestow its blessings upon competitive balance. He cited the fact that some teams exerted scant effort in scouting collegiate players, and therefore fared poorly in the draft.[6] Craig Coenen showed that the downtrodden Steelers, Eagles, Cardinals, and Brooklyn Dodgers won just 35.2 percent of their games between 1932 and 1935; these same four teams won 29.1 percent during the first ten seasons with the draft. Only the Washington Redskins showed much improvement in the years following the institution of the draft. The owners themselves tacitly admitted the draft's inability to bolster weak clubs; they considered denying teams with stronger records their draft picks on rounds two through six, but tabled the proposal.[7] After the war, though, such teams as the formerly woebegone Philadelphia Eagles and Detroit Lions experienced surges in performance ("revivals" would be incorrect, as neither team had ever been "vived"). In the Lions' case, new owner D. Lyle Fife and coach Bo McMillin came to the realization that they would never transform the club with their usual tactics: "We've come to the conclusion that the only way to get players is in the draft. Heaven knows we've tried to beg, borrow or steal players this year from other clubs."[8] The actions of owners such as George Halas belied the owners' pious claims that the draft was intended to improve parity. Halas shipped a couple of expendable players to Bert Bell and the Philadelphia Eagles; in return, he wanted Bell to draft Heisman Trophy winner Jay Berwanger and then transfer him to the Bears. The joke was on Halas, as Bell drafted Berwanger but the youngster opted for a career in industry. On another occasion though, Halas's machinations paid off, as he landed quarterback Sid Luckman, who later became a star, in return for Edgar "Eggs" Manske.[9]

Economists are dubious about the reverse-order player draft's effect upon competitive balance.[10] The draft may help owners of teams in weaker markets capture the "economic rent" from their players' talents (under a free market, the player reaps most of the benefits from his talent), which may enable the owners to survive financially.

Certainly the draft's explicit purpose — to maintain or improve competitive balance — was plausible. NBA fans can remember the coin flip between the Milwaukee Bucks and Phoenix Suns, two expansion teams with weak win-loss records, with Lew Alcindor (later known as Kareem Abdul-Jabbar) as first prize and Neal Walk as second prize, or the infamous 1984 draft in which the Houston Rockets selected first and got Hakeem Olajuwon, while the Portland Trailblazers drafted second and got the ill-fated Sam Bowie. The NFL's initial experiences with the draft produced few dramatic moments and little change in the league standings by 1941.

The legislators were concerned that players might be forced to play with teams they didn't want to join. Bell and the owners testified that teams sent questionnaires to prospective players prior to the draft to see whether a player was interested in playing pro football and, if so, whether he would be willing to play for that team. Team officials also tried to ascertain a prospect's draft status — that is, his status in Uncle Sam's draft. Football legend Red Grange, himself signed as a free agent out of college, cited the case of Travis Tidwell. Tidwell indicated that he would only play for the Giants, so the other teams did not select him. Note that the NFL wanted it both ways with the draft: they claimed both that players had discretion over where they would play and that the draft promoted competitive balance.[11] Jack Jennings, just finishing up his NFL career, claimed, "I think they [college players drafted] are pretty honored to be with that club. I don't think it really hurts them very much."[12]

Bell opposed a system in which players would be required to give their written consent before becoming subject to the player selection. He quoted sports columnist Lewis F. Atchison of the *Washington Evening Star*: "As for a player's freedom being abridged, that's technically correct but usually not true. . . . As [Red] Smith [New York sportswriter] pointed out, teams don't like to waste draft choices. So it's a selfish motive, but the young man doesn't get picked by a team he won't play with."[13] Esteemed college coach Bud Wilkinson disputed the necessity of the reverse-order player draft, and he related tales about some of his players, who were drafted by teams they didn't want to play for.[14] In response to congressional pressure, or as Bell unctuously put it, "at the suggestion of those representatives in Washington who have been so helpful to us," the NFL owners inserted a clause in their constitution permitting a player with a valid reason to ask to be traded.[15] One assumes that the commissioner would determine what a "valid reason" was.

After World War II some of the wealthier owners wanted an occasional crack at the top choice in the draft, and the lottery was born. Unlike the NBA's draft lottery, in which only mediocre teams participated, the NFL version gave every team a chance at the "bonus pick," which was a choice made before the reverse-order draft. Once a team got a bonus pick, it was ineligible for another bonus choice until all the other teams had received one. The bonus pick belied the claims of altruism made by the owners of strong teams.[16]

Legislators disliked the bonus-pick lottery, but not because the lottery might dilute any palliative effects upon competitive balance. The legislators appeared to worry about the random nature of assigning players to teams via lottery. Bell backpedaled quickly from the lottery, stating unctuously, "We are perfectly willing to eliminate the bonus pick." By the time of the hearing, however, only the Chicago Cardinals had not received their bonus pick, so it was a convenient time to end the program. The NFL owners tried to retain the bonus pick at first, but could not agree on a way to do so that would not resemble a lottery.[17]

Another contradiction of the owners' stated intent of the draft was their willingness to move it up before the regular season ended when it suited their purposes in their competition with the AAFC, the Canadian leagues, and the AFL. A team that finished last after all the "returns" were in might have ended up with a less attractive draft position because of its partial-season record.[18] George Preston Marshall had strong opinions about this tactic (as he did on almost every issue): "I've been trying to get the league to abolish it for years. We might have done it last year, but I changed my vote because a club or two felt so intense about the thing. . . . One of the main [objections] I have is that it's such a burden on the coaching staffs. . . . Now, we just don't need it. Another factor I consider is that draft positions are apt to change. A lot can happen in this league in two weeks and the December 1 standings aren't any guarantee of the final standings." Marshall also thought owners were depriving themselves of the additional information supplied by players' performances in bowl games. Bert Bell pointed out that owners of weak teams were particularly worried about losing players to the Canadian teams if the draft were to be held at its normal time.[19]

NFL owners defended their draft not only by claiming they would not knowingly draft a player who expressed no desire to play for that team, but by asserting that pro football's reserve clause was not as binding as Major League Baseball's, as football's clause was interpreted as binding for the life of the contract instead of being perpetual. Bell cited a few cases in which he intervened to get the owners to transfer a player to a city of his choice, given sufficient cause. He claimed, "No ballplayer is any good to a club if he is dissatisfied mentally or in any other way."[20] He also stated (bragged?)

that, "We don't need to pay him a bonus, but when kids are just getting out of college and especially if they are married and they don't have a cent and they owe $400, $500, or $600, they usually get it." Bell mentioned that a few players got true signing bonuses, but the lack of bargaining leverage undoubtedly undercut most players' ability to get such bonuses.[21]

The owners' rationales, though, were specious. Baseball's Leslie O'Connor spelled out the true state of affairs: "If S. 2391 [granting an antitrust exemption to professional sports leagues] be enacted, its proponents ought to be congratulated or condemned, as the viewpoint may be, for an atavistic achievement. For that will be a denial of human rights, of labor's rights, and a throw-back of over six hundred years to the despotic first labor laws of England — the *Ordinance of Laborers* and the *Statute of Laborers*." He went on to outline the wrongs involved, including denying due process of law to the players, confiscating players' exclusive property rights to their skill, depriving players and owners their right of contract, and monopolistic coercion (because an individual owner's freedom of contract was abridged).[22] The owners, of course, presumably surrendered some individual rights of contract in order to gain increased bargaining leverage over amateur players. Years later, Charlie O. Finley, owner of the Kansas City/Oakland Athletics, and surely no patron saint of player rights, was more succinct: "[Major League owners] adopted a free agent draft to eliminate the excessive bonus bidding, thereby solving its own problem at the expense of the prospective player." Baseball differed from football in that many of baseball's draftees were just out of high school, and some were not yet eighteen years old. Such players might have been able to repudiate any contract at a later date.[23]

Did the draft help to make teams more evenly matched? As Bell admitted, the early drafts did not promote competitive balance. Why not? Unlike today, after decades of predraft analysis and hype, modern fans don't realize that they probably pay more attention and perhaps even devote more effort to the draft than did the owners in February 1936. If the draft did improve parity, it probably did so only over time. *Sports Illustrated*'s Tex Maule claimed that of the fifty to sixty rookies kept on NFL rosters, "only two or three a year in the entire 12-team National Football League are apt to be good enough to play first string. . . . Ordinarily, a team which must depend on more than one or two rookies in its starting lineup has little or no chance to go all the way to a title."[24] Maule's estimate of "only two or three a year" seems to be an exaggeration. If the average NFL career was only three or four seasons long, the turnover had to approximate 25 to 33 percent a season.

Students of NFL history are likely to recall Jay Berwanger as the first Heisman Trophy winner and the first pick in the NFL's inaugural draft. They may also know that Berwanger eschewed an NFL career with the hapless Philadelphia Eagles. What they are not likely to know is that the last-place Eagles were unable to sign any of their nine draft choices. Table 22 shows that owners often came up somewhat short in the early drafts. Player salaries did not so greatly exceed jobs in industry that talented players automatically opted for a pro career. Given that the vast majority of players were college graduates, often with better-than-average career choices, NFL owners were in the same dilemma as BAA/NBA owners of the 1940s and 1950s: they did not have enough gate receipts to guarantee sufficiently high salaries to entice talented scholar-athletes to play professional sports.

While Bell boasted of the draft's ability to bolster weak teams such as the Baltimore Colts, who went from being a weak, revived club to being the world champions between 1953 and 1958 — with a castoff quarterback named Johnny Unitas, who was picked up as a released free agent — he also claimed that player salaries increased 300 percent during the postwar period (while ignoring that revenues increased sharply, too) in an attempt to allay fears that the draft suppressed salaries.[25]

Paul Dixon, counsel for the congressional committee, cited an article by sportswriter Shirley Povich. Povich had interviewed a player who had wished to remain anonymous. The player stated that he didn't think the draft system was fair, as he couldn't seek the best offer from all of the teams: "The truths of that situation [college draft] when fully developed could be sufficient to jolt the Senators into wonderment how the pro football league has gotten away with their unconscionable draft of college boys all these years."[26] Bert Bell retorted, "98 percent of the players in the National League, with the salaries they are getting, would vote in favor of the player selection question." Bell didn't provide any evidence of such a poll, but

Dixon let it pass. Bell stated that if a player didn't want to play for the NFL team that drafted him, "He can go to Canada." He finally admitted under Dixon's questioning that the draft did not permit a player to market his abilities competitively: "That is right. It does not and when it does there won't be any more pro football because you go back to the days when I had a football team and there were four great teams. . . . The player selection system is the greatest thing that ever happened."[27] This was not Bell's shining moment. Dixon continued to press Bell. Bell finally claimed that without the draft, "the four top teams, financially speaking would sign each year at least 100 of the top ballplayers in the United States."[28] Given the thirty-five-player limit and the continued service of veterans, his statement was patently absurd at best.

Several witnesses expressed skepticism regarding the draft's efficacy in promoting competitive balance. Bud Wilkinson cited the Cleveland Browns' continued dominance as evidence of the draft's inability to level teams over time. "The idea that this is all that keeps the competition equal doesn't quite ring the same bell with me as it does with people who have a vested interest in professional athletics. . . . If that is the reason that has been given for Cleveland winning — because they got these fine players when they were in the All-America Conference — I would like to know how many of the men who played for Cleveland last year actually participated in the All-America Conference?"[29] Nine of the team's players had begun their careers in the AAFC; eight of the other players were starting their careers in 1956. Wilkinson also disputed Bell's claim of fabulous player salary increases. "The salary of a professional football player — who is drafted without compensation — is almost a fictitious sum of money. He doesn't get paid unless he survives the final cut before the season begins after putting in 2 months of work, even though he must finish the season to get his full salary."[30] Wilkinson disputed Bell's claim that football's more liberal reserve clause offset any unfairness inherent in the player draft; Wilkinson pointed out that young baseball players were able to sign with whichever team they wanted, so that baseball's more stringent reserve clause was mitigated.[31]

Wilkinson and his fellow college coaches who were called to testify, Duffy Daugherty of Michigan State University and Bowden Wyatt of the University of Tennessee, stated they did not believe that pro coaches and scouts could ascertain which players were the best. As Wilkinson put it, "I don't believe, first, that there is that much difference in football players, that the 1st choice is worth more than the 20th choice. I believe . . . that the success of the top 10 draft choices as pro football players has not been greater than the 20th and 30th choices. . . . I question whether there is any way that any one team could possibly tie up all the good athletes, particularly as long as they keep the rule that the squad must be cut to 35." When Senator Estes Kefauver asked, "If you had the job of choosing, say, the 5 best players, or if you had the right to call the 5 or 6 best players, would you have difficulty in deciding who they were?" Wilkinson responded, "I would have a tremendous amount of difficulty." He modified his statement by pointing out that a coach might be looking for a player to fill a particular skill or position, which might refine the search to between twenty-five and thirty players.[32]

Duffy Daugherty disliked the reverse-order draft, saying "the good Lord Jesus with all his omnipotence had one guy go astray among the disciples, and you never know when one Judas can upset the whole applecart and abuse these exemptions that you are going to give, and I think it is a dangerous trend." He went on to say that he would have difficulty choosing the first draft pick out of four hundred prospective college seniors. "If Bud [Wilkinson] and Bowden [Wyatt] and I each had the opportunity now to go throughout the country, maybe Bud and Bowden can do this, but we can't and pick out the 40 or 50 best freshmen. . . . I daresay that only 10 of the 50 or maybe one-fourth of them would came [sic] through and play football for us." He also mentioned the NFL's unheralded stars, who had never received much glory in college.[33]

The third college coach, Bowden Wyatt, provided somewhat contradictory evidence. He thought the draft was particularly unfair to the football specialists, such as kickers and punters. He testified that these specialists might be drafted by teams "who already have those certain types of specialists on the team, [and] are hurt." He didn't mention why a team with a good kicker or punter would draft another such specialist. He made greater sense when he mentioned the intangibles. Some players were slow starters or poor practice players. He confirmed that players received questionnaires about their desire to play pro football from NFL teams, but that the teams apparently ignored them and drafted uninterested boys anyway. He denied that the draft would affect competitive balance, because football depended on the morale factor. He concluded, "It would take a magician to pick the ability of certain football players."[34]

One player was not shy about testifying against the reverse-order draft. Retired quarterback George Ratterman stated, "I do not believe it can definitely be determined that such [dire effects] would be the result of eliminating the player draft. Professional baseball has existed for many years without a player draft similar to that of football." He asked the committee to ensure that any antitrust exemption would include safeguards for players' rights: "If the players cannot resort to the courts of this country, they must have some other body to which they can appeal."[35]

Why the Draft Was Not Effective in Equalizing Talent

In some cases, the owners' dismal draft records reflected their lackadaisical approach to researching potential players. While talented college players might appear in newsreels, or owners and their coaches might attend a few college games, they were operating in a world in which hearsay reigned. All-American lists, tips from friends in the college coaching ranks (who were sometimes paid by NFL owners) or fans, and serendipity guided many teams' choices in the 1930s. A few owners, such as George Halas, maintained an informal grapevine of informers, especially college coaches and former players, who recommended players from their home regions.[36]

Bert Bell testified that some teams used to buy scouting information from Norman Sper, who was out on the West Coast, in addition to consulting Grantland Rice's All-American list. Bell also mentioned that some owners paid college coaches $200 a year to scout for them.[37] Sper pressed for the owners to hire him to provide scouting information for the league, making him a one-man scouting combine. He requested $11,000 a year, a request he later dropped to $8,000. George Preston Marshall voiced his approval, but his fellow owners turned down Sper's proposal.[38]

Although George Halas had employed Frank Korch to scout college prospects before the war, Korch's was a lonely task, as no other teams appeared to have hired similar personnel. After the war, the Rams began a systematic compilation of information on prospective players. Since the drafts sometimes consisted of thirty or more rounds, teams needed information on three or four hundred prospects. The Rams decided to invest in a system of scouting prospective players. The team employed five scouts to watch other NFL games and fifteen to scour college talent. Eddie Kotal supervised the program for the Los Angeles Rams; it is said to have cost $20,000 per season. Prior to this system, many teams hired a scout at $20 per game on an ad hoc basis. Kotal drove his company car around the nation interviewing and watching players, their coaches, and reporters. He filed reports to the Rams, where Maurice (Clipper) Smith collated and organized the information. The Rams had a good track record with players from smaller colleges, including Andy Robustelli, Larry Brink, and junior college player Dick (Night Train) Lane; all three became All-NFL players.[39]

By the early 1950s teams were investing tens of thousands of dollars in scouting prospects. The Detroit Lions kept several college football assistant coaches on retainer as scouts. Some college conferences disliked pro football, but Bert Bell calmly explained, "We've got no quarrel with the colleges. . . . We have their best interests at heart. They're our farm system."[40]

Even if owners and coaches had developed more sophisticated scouting and selection techniques by the late 1930s, the military draft would have rudely disrupted any such systems. When the war ended, the AAFC was competing with the NFL for college players. Since an NFL team drafting a player now ran the risk of losing that player to an AAFC team or to Uncle Sam, the draft's efficacy in promoting competitive balance (whatever that might be) was jeopardized.[41]

For teams unwilling to spend much on scouting, playing the odds by choosing players from well-known powerhouses made sense. As late as 1959, Joe King pointed out that the Big Ten and a few other midwestern schools supplied twenty-four of the eighty rookies who made the pro rosters that season.[42] Although many owners focused on stars from major university and college programs, perhaps trusting that these players had proven themselves in tougher competition or perhaps figuring that their scouting dollars went further watching big-time programs, some teams began watching smaller (including black) colleges. Old-timers, such as George Halas, Curly Lambeau, and Steve Owen found good, even great, players at obscure programs or on sandlots. Halas often eschewed college

All-Americans, because such a player was "a marked man on a major college team is near the end of his effectiveness. He has hard, concentrated knocks for three seasons, and it shows in his pro playing."[43]

Even with the postwar integration (or reintegration) of the NFL and Paul Brown's success with African American players, NFL teams lagged in scouring the rich talent lode at black colleges and universities. Similar to baseball's Brooklyn Dodgers, who established a scouting system in the Caribbean, a few NFL teams began mining the black schools. Eddie Kotal was one of the first scouts to investigate historically black colleges, and one of his first signings was "Tank" Younger of Grambling. Kotal decided to take a risk with the player, even though most football men thought players at black schools couldn't compete in the pro game. Because the other teams were dubious about such talent, Kotal was able to sign Younger as a free agent.[44]

Some players developed late. New York Giants coach Steve Owens pointed out: "Lots of boys don't develop until their last year of college and hit the pros right at their peak. On the other hand, some burn out in college; they do all the work they can, and can't go further."[45]

In the early years of the draft, many owners and coaches relied on various college All-American lists. By the late 1950s, though, being a college All-American was almost a prelude to being snubbed in the draft. Sportswriter Tommy Devine queried pro officials on why the All-American label didn't sell with them. He noted that thirty-four players made various All-American lists in 1958, but only three were chosen in the first round, with a total of seven chosen through four rounds. Pro scouts and coaches pointed out that players who could succeed in college ball were sometimes too small to make the grade in the pros. Some college quarterbacks, such as Joe Kapp, played in offensive schemes that left the player unprepared for the pros. Kapp, of course, proved an exception. Although he was selected only in the eighteenth round, he had a lengthy career. Some pro officials thought college players depended on being well-rounded, while pro teams looked for specialists.[46]

Even possessing the bonus pick, which was the first pick in the draft, did not guarantee a quality player. The teams had surprisingly little success with their bonus picks. Aside from Philadelphia's choice of Chuck Bednarik and Green Bay's Paul Hornung, only one other bonus pick player, Leon Hart, ever achieved All-NFL status. Green Bay heard envious remarks about their lottery pick, Hornung. For once, the hype surrounding a bonus pick was justified. Packer coach Lisle Blackbourn boasted, "He is the best, he can do anything."[47] Hornung was a superb player, but the Cleveland Browns did handsomely with Jim Brown, the fifth pick in the first round. As sportswriter Joe King pointed out, most of the bonus picks were used to select quarterbacks.[48]

Gary Glick epitomized the lackadaisical approach to the draft and to the bonus pick. Pittsburgh selected Glick, who had been a quarterback at Colorado State. The other teams and sportswriters were perplexed: "Gary who?" Glick played for a number of years but surely the Steelers could have used the bonus pick for another player and still have gotten Glick later. The Steelers claimed they liked Glick's ability to run with the football and also his abilities as a kicker.[49]

Identifying productive players was an uncertain process at best. Table 23 shows the rounds in which the All-Pro players of 1950–60 were selected. Although the earliest rounds had the highest likelihoods of producing top players, almost half the All-Pro players went in the fifth round or later or were undrafted and signed as free agents.

The Bears, once perennial contenders, hit a rough patch in the early 1950s. Sportswriters attributed the team's struggles to the lack of a quarterback after the durable Sid Luckman retired, but also to poor first-round draft choices. Of the team's previous six choices, only two remained with the team during the 1953 season.[50]

Some teams lucked into star players. The San Francisco 49ers, typically a middling team, finished in a three-way tie for the second-worst record in 1951. The Chicago Bears owned Baltimore's pick, which was the first in the regular draft. The 49ers needed a quarterback and were considering Bobby Williams, yet another Notre Dame quarterback, and Y. A. Tittle. The Bears chose Williams, so the 49ers took Tittle. Williams proved to be a nonentity, while Tittle became a Hall-of-Fame quarterback.[51]

Even when teams drafted diamonds in the rough, they sometimes didn't recognize what they had. The Steelers drafted quarterbacks Frank Filchock, Johnny Unitas, and Len Dawson, but traded or released them before they blossomed. The latter two are in the Pro Football Hall of Fame, while Filchock was an All-NFL player.[52] The Steelers had traded their first-round pick in the December 1938 draft to the Chicago Bears, who selected Hall-of-Fame quarterback Sid Luckman.

The availability of players who later became All-NFL stars, even in the later rounds, indicated the difficulty of identifying talent. A pretty solid team could have been built on undrafted Hall-of-Fame players such as Emlen Tunnell and Night Train Lane, as well as Big Daddy Lipscomb. These African American players may have been neglected because of their race and because they didn't play for major college programs.

In the late 1950s George Preston Marshall advocated reducing the number of rounds from thirty to twenty-five or twenty, echoing a motion made in 1945. He pointed out that relatively few good players were left in those rounds. Joe King surveyed the current rosters and found that

> The 12 teams in the NFL obtained 44 percent of their strength in the first four rounds, and more than half, 51 percent, in the first five draws. The striking total of 71 percent of all active players was derived from the first ten rounds, which is only one-third of the draft. . . . From rounds 11 to 20, in the second third, a net of only 13 percent was realized. As Marshall asserted, the last third, from round 21 through 30, was inconsequential, with a showing of a mere 6.9 percent. Even free agents — players ignored in the draft — provided more strength, at 8.6 percent.

King also showed that there were sixty-one players currently playing that had been drafted in the first round, with an additional seven from the bonus pick. Of course, owners and coaches, desiring to save face, might have been more patient with first-round players, enabling them to remain on rosters longer. The owners eventually agreed to limit the draft to twenty-five rounds in 1958 and to twenty rounds in 1959.[53]

In touting the 1958 rookies, sportswriter Joe King again lauded the reverse-order draft. He argued that the fact that more first-round choices were in the league than any later round dispelled "the charge that the draft is merely a grab-bag, with the order of picking signifying little." King, however, did not demonstrate that the team with the first pick of each round did better than teams with later choices on every round.[54]

After the end of World War II released many players from military service, NFL owners refined their draft in response to competition from the AAFC and from their fellow NFL owners. To ensure an orderly process, the NFL owners resolved not to sign any players until their fellow owners had had a chance to draft them. Bell worked out a deal with the NCAA whereby the NFL owners would wait until a player's class graduated, while colleges would no longer block former pro players from becoming members of college football coaching staffs or keep referees from officiating both college and NFL games.[55] The question of what to do about players who did not intend to attend college or who wanted to play pro football before their class graduated remained a thorny one. NFL owners had long sought to cooperate with college coaches by not poaching players prior to graduation, but AAFC coaches had not shown such scruples, and World War II disrupted the normal college matriculation for many potential players. When the AAFC passed a similar resolution, these owners exempted players who had already been signed. Duffy Daugherty, Michigan State University coach, testified before the U.S. Senate committee that "I daresay there wouldn't be very many boys that would attract the pros' interest as undergraduates, sophomores, or juniors, and I don't think it would be enough to cause any hardship on the colleges."[56]

George Preston Marshall's success with the Redskins began to wane after World War II. He concentrated on drafting well-publicized college stars. A list of his first-round draft picks between 1946 and 1960 is a dismal one. The Redskins used their first-round pick in both the 1946 and 1947 drafts on Cal Rossi of UCLA, who never played in the NFL. They selected longtime quarterback Harry Gilmer with their 1948 bonus pick; their first round choice, Lowell Tew, played briefly in the AAFC. The team drafted Rob Goode with its 1949 first-round pick, and he performed full-time for four seasons as a running back. Their 1952 choice, Larry Isbell, never played in the NFL. In 1955, the team selected Ralph Guglielmi, star Notre Dame quarterback. He played for seven seasons but failed to make the All-Pro team. Then again, several other teams were captivated by glittering quarterbacks from Notre Dame who did not succeed as pros. In 1959 and 1960 Marshall selected two quarterbacks, Don Allard and Richie Lucas, who would cap fifteen years of draft futility. Neither quarterback played for

Marshall's Redskins; both had brief careers in the AFL. The team did not succeed in drafting good players on subsequent rounds either. As table 24 shows, Marshall's overall drafting strategy netted very few star players and undoubtedly contributed to the Redskins' lengthy mediocrity, a mediocrity that belied Bell's optimistic claims for the draft.

Table 25 shows that most teams kept a majority of the star players that they had drafted and signed for their entire careers or at least until near the end of their careers. Even teams in small cities, such as Green Bay and Pittsburgh, retained most of their drafted star players. The Cardinals and Redskins, though, did not keep the few stars they drafted and signed.

Some football players were all-around athletes and were coveted by baseball executives, as their managers "find that football players bring to the diamond initiative, fight, fast thinking and a disdain for injuries, which they call highly refreshing."[57] These players possessed bargaining leverage because they were multitalented. Georgia tailback Charley Trippi excelled at football and baseball. Although the Miami/Baltimore team had AAFC draft rights to him, these owners acquiesced in the AAFC Yankees' wooing the player to sign both football and baseball contracts, a position Dan Topping, owner of the Yankees both in baseball and in football, was in a unique situation to offer; if the football Yankees had signed Trippi, they would have sent two or three players to Miami/Baltimore. The NFL Chicago Cardinals had draft rights to Trippi, but they could only offer a pro football contract while possibly countenancing a simultaneous baseball contract. Because Major League Baseball teams were offering tens of thousands of dollars in bonuses, the NFL and AAFC owners were at a disadvantage. Charles Bidwell's Cardinals signed Trippi to a reported five-year, $100,000 contract and permitted him to negotiate with two minor league baseball teams.[58]

Some players chose industry over pro football. Dick Kazmaier opted to attend the Harvard Business School for an MBA, saying, "I think I can go farther in business than I can football." Many players who did opt for a pro football stint had business interests on the side.[59]

Other famous struggles for prime college talent involved Army's fabled Glenn Davis and Doc Blanchard. Although these two backs had to fulfill military duties in return for their education, pro owners salivated at the thought of employing such glamorous players.[60] Davis hoped to get permission to resign from the Army early; he indicated a preference for playing on the West Coast. The Rams, knowing his geographical preference and gambling on a favorable Army ruling, traded draft picks with Detroit, while the San Francisco 49ers held AAFC rights to him. He eventually played two seasons with the Rams.[61]

NFL owners also had to worry about prospective players' status regarding the military draft. A player who was married and had a child, or who had some injury or condition that disqualified him for the military (but not for football), was especially attractive to risk-averse coaches and owners. As one reporter put it, "There will always be the up-to-the-minute report on [a player's] military status."[62] Other teams were willing to draft a player and wait for his return from the military.

Teams used different approaches to the draft. Some, such as the Los Angeles Rams, stockpiled draft choices. The Cleveland Browns acquired extra picks in January 1951 from Green Bay, Detroit, San Francisco, and the New York Yanks.[63] Sportswriter Piers Anderton wrote, "Some owners, the most prominent of them [George Preston] Marshall, draft the big names, either the nationally publicized All-Americas or a profitable local drawing card."[64] The 49ers surveyed their current weakness in deciding which players to draft.

Some coaches, particularly Paul Brown of the Cleveland Browns, ignored all extracurricular considerations and drafted "to need." When the Browns' draft choice, Bobby Freeman, opted for Canada, leaving the team without a substitute for George Ratterman, Otto Graham came out of retirement.[65] As the Browns' core of championship players retired or left the team for various reasons, Brown reloaded via the draft. Hal Lebovitz wrote, "An analysis of the 35-man roster reveals what a great change has taken place in the Browns since 1955, when they were the world's champions. In addition to the dozen rookies there are three players who returned from the service. . . . Moreover, six of the 19 players who finished the '56 season with the Browns are sophomores in this bruising pro football business." The Browns also signed guard Vince Costello, who went undrafted. The key acquisition, though, was fullback Jim Brown.[66]

Another reporter observed how Giants' coach Jim Lee Howell traded his draft picks to teams like the Rams, swapping for such stalwarts as Andy Robustelli, Ed Hughes, and Harland Svare. Joe King wrote, "Although they swapped only ten [draft picks] in the six-year span, compared to 12 for Pittsburgh, coach Jim Lee Howell of New York risked an amazing number of high picks. He dealt off three No. 1 draws, a No. 2 and two No. 3s. No other club came close to that kind of gamble; the Steelers up to the present draft had lost only one No. 1 and one No. 2."[67] The flip side of the Rams' mania for draft choices was a rapid turnover in their roster and a distribution of former Rams players throughout the league, with ten of them playing for the Steelers and Eagles during the 1950s.[68]

Bert Bell worried about teams trading draft choices, and especially about weaker teams trading picks for immediate help. After the Pittsburgh Steelers' coach, Buddy Parker, traded several of his picks, Bell proposed a rule that "would forbid deals involving future picks after Labor Day. That date is, on the average, about four weeks before the season's opener." Bell hoped his proposal would force teams with a surfeit of talent from benefitting by "holding surplus players until the cutdown date, and would release them earlier for the benefit of teams suffering from the manpower pinch."[69]

Sportswriter James Murray thought the NFL could improve its draft by borrowing an idea from the National Basketball Association—the territorial draft. This system allowed teams a special draft pick for players graduating from colleges within a specified radius of a pro team. Murray explained, "This would give meaning to the competition and have the effect of heightening the emotional content of pro football, which, it seems to me, is its big lack at the moment." Murray went on, though, to describe the barren college football wasteland surrounding New York City: "Currently one of the invalids of pro football, the Giants' franchise is suffering from nothing more or less than the fact that collegiate football died a strangling death in New York a decade ago [as did its college basketball dominance in the wake of the point-shaving scandals]."[70]

By 1955 a level of sophistication had taken hold of the NFL player draft. Former player Herman Hickman described the process: "Today's professional football is certainly a far cry from the pro version of even 20 years ago when I was playing. Each club today has paid scouts all over the country checking outstanding players. They study closely the case history of hundreds of players, especially as to temperament and injuries. In the old days, it was more or less of a one-man operation for each team — a matter of personal contacts."[71] This is in contrast with Gil Brandt's recollections of teams coming in unprepared: "Guys would come in with rolls of quarters. . . . So they would have a pick coming up, and they'd run out to the pay phone and drop two dollars and twenty-five cents in . . . and call Pappy Lewis of West Virginia. 'Hey, Pappy, who is the best offensive lineman you played against last year?' And that's how this kind of stuff took place, as recently as the late '50s."[72]

Fans began paying attention to the player draft. The Baltimore Colts' general manager, Don Kellett, offered season-ticket holders a chance to delay resubscribing until they saw draft choices George Shaw and Alan Ameche. Some five thousand fans renewed immediately, and a sportswriter speculated the team might end up with twenty thousand season-ticket holders.[73]

While most players mouthed platitudes about "what an honor it is to have been drafted," a new sensibility had emerged by 1960. Mike Ditka, of all people, told reporters, "We draw about $80,000 into the stadium every Saturday, and we should get at least $30 a month for toothpaste and clean shirts." Other All-American players sharing the awards function with Ditka expressed dissatisfaction with their college experiences. Tee Moorman claimed he would not have played football if he had not needed the scholarship to get his undergraduate degree on his way to medical school. Wayne Harris said, "This is really nice. But after eight years (four as a high school player) I'm pretty well tired of football by now." Moorman and Harris did not play professional football. E. J. Holub, who would play professionally for ten seasons, stated, "It won't go to my head. My daddy says that for every lion there's a lion tamer."[74]

Conclusion

The NFL's reverse-order draft, at best, offered only an opportunity for lackluster teams to improve, but the draft could not guarantee competitive balance. Individual owners' and coaches' lack of attention, bad luck, and other factors transformed the draft into a stochastic process through which clever owners could maintain their team's superiority. Even had the draft worked in the way predicted by contemporary observers, it might not have had long-term effects upon competitive balance. Had the Pittsburgh Steelers or Green Bay Packers drafted Sid Luckman, for example, his ability to propel a team to the top of the division standings and to attract fans would have created an arbitrage opportunity: Art Rooney or the Packers' management might have faced lucrative offers from the Chicago Bears or New York Giants for the quarterback. Such a prospect would confirm many economists' belief that, at best, the reverse-order draft affords an opportunity for owners of teams in smaller cities to reap financial windfalls, but makes no long-term improvement in competitive balance.

9

GATE SHARING

The way in which competing teams split up the gate receipts from their game is a fundamental issue in professional sports. Many people believe that gate-sharing exists to redress inequalities in revenue. There is a strong presumption that New York teams end up paying out more to the Green Bays of the league than they receive from such teams, but this is only a presumption. Such a pattern might be dubbed a Robin Hood effect. In most industries, owners of successful firms often desire to drive out owners of less successful firms, so professional sports team leagues differ from most industries. Since the championship teams need rival teams to beat, there is a place for weak teams in the league and a rationale for subsidizing weaker teams.

If teams are forced to share part of their home gate receipts, the benefit (denoted by economists as the marginal revenue product, that is, the additional revenue) derived from signing a talented player could be reduced because of the sharing. Such a reduction would lower the incentive to sign the talented player. The reduced incentive to sign talented players might keep wealthy teams from signing too many such players; it could also suppress the demand for top players, which would hold down player salaries. This simple story, though, might not be accurate under actual circumstances, as a key assumption underlying many economic models was that the stronger a team was, the worse it drew on the road.

The subsidization aspect is dubious on another level. Owners, especially owners of successful teams, appear to disagree with the notion that they should subsidize owners of weaker teams. If you owned the Yankees, your attitude might be, "I should get a large piece of the pie when I visit Kansas City, since I'm bringing in a strong, well-paid, attractive club. When the

Royals start bringing in a strong, well-drawing club to Yankee Stadium, I'll be willing to share more revenue." The effect and the intent of revenue sharing, then, are ambiguous.

This chapter examines the experiences of two professional sports leagues with dissimilar gate-sharing plans during the 1950s: the National Football League (NFL) and baseball's National League (NL). The experiences of the two leagues provide useful contrasts with regard to the efficacy of their different plans.

Because congressional investigations required owners to divulge financial records for the 1952–56 seasons, this is a good era to study. With this financial information, we can examine whether the NL and NFL wanted gate-sharing rules simply to help poorer teams in smaller cities, or whether there were other motivations for such rules. Was the NL's revenue-sharing plan flawed by its seeming lack of generosity (in terms of proportions of home gate revenue shared) compared with the NFL's plan? In addition, the National League altered its revenue-sharing plan during the period examined. The change in the plan provides some clues as to the owners' attitudes regarding gate sharing. Finally, examining the gate-sharing experiences of the 1950s will shed light upon the debate concerning whether fans preferred absolute (opponents with the best records) or relative (opponents with similar records to the home team) quality in the visiting team.

Previous Commentaries on Gate Sharing

Baseball historian Harold Seymour and witnesses at the 1951 congressional hearings implied that gate-sharing rules were intended to redress revenue differences between teams that drew well and those that did not, but the owners often sang a different tune. Seymour wrote, "Appreciating the results of inequality of markets, the owners tried to compensate by sharing gate receipts."[1] He also chronicled the underlying animosity between owners of large-city teams and their peers. The National League had difficulties with its New York and Philadelphia clubs during its inaugural season of 1876. The large-city owners refused to travel west to play some clubs, and, instead, offered to pay the western clubs handsomely if they would come east. The National League eventually, but only temporarily, settled on a fixed guarantee of $125 instead of a percentage split in 1886. Owners of teams in the smaller cities favored the percentage split, with the Detroit manager complaining, "We should be nice suckers . . . to go to Boston or to Washington and put big money in their treasuries for $125."[2] Albert Spalding, owner of the Chicago team, retorted that wealthier clubs were "tired of carrying along a club like Detroit."[3]

Certainly, some sports historians believe such rules foster competitive balance. Leifer makes explicit his belief in the link between the NFL's generous gate-sharing rule and its competitive balance: "The main reason why the NFL did not experience high performance inequality, and early baseball leagues did, was the liberal revenue-sharing policies adopted by the NFL."[4]

Sports economists, however, debate whether gate-sharing rules have much effect upon competitive balance, though most agree that such rules may ensure the viability of teams in smaller cities. In addition, most economists assume that gate sharing redistributes money from wealthier teams, typically in larger cities, to poorer teams, typically in smaller cities, but some argue that increased revenue sharing should have little effect upon competitive balance and would merely serve to suppress player salaries. Some economists also share a belief that the "more equal the gate-sharing plan among the teams, the more equal the revenues."[5] Underlying their argument is the implicit assumption, embodied in their models, that the stronger the team is the more it draws at home but the worse it draws on the road (because the rival team is, ceteris paribus, weaker): "Intuitively, gate sharing lowers the value of an additional win-percent to a team because the team only captures a fraction of any increased revenue at home games. On the road, the team generally loses revenue because, on average, the win-percent of its opponent has fallen."[6]

Other economists developed models in which a team's ability to draw on the road was not necessarily inverse to its relative strength. Marburger altered this assumption and found that revenue sharing could enhance competitive balance under certain circumstances, a finding shared by Kesenne.[7] Later, Szymanski and Kesenne demonstrated plausible conditions under which certain forms of revenue sharing might reduce competitive balance. With respect to football, Vrooman suggested that the short schedule may reduce the importance of the attractiveness of the visiting team; that is, there may not be a strong relationship between a team's relative strength and its ability to draw on the road.[8]

There may be another motive underlying gate sharing. Canes argued that revenue-sharing and other league rules may help leagues because "their absence may encourage team owners to produce higher team quality than is socially efficient." He describes the externality problem thus: "Since the owner's profits are not affected by decreased demand for games in which his team does not play, he will not take such effects into account; that is, they will be external to the owner's cost and revenue calculations." While owners might compensate each other for revenue losses caused by fielding too strong a team, "this would require difficult decisions about which teams should be compensated and to what extent. Moreover, if not all team owners were party to the agreement, some could increase the quality of their teams and so displace the others, or could threaten to increase quality in order to be compensated not to do so."[9] Thus, a properly designed revenue-sharing plan can reduce the incentive (in terms of marginal revenue product) to overinvest in team quality and also to help owners sidestep the potentially disputatious need to determine the compensation described above.

Revenue-Sharing Rules

The National League required the home team to pay 22.5 cents per admission to the visiting team through 1953 and 27.5 cents through at least 1956.[10] Owners of wealthy teams resisted some forms of revenue sharing. Walter O'Malley, owner of the Brooklyn Dodgers, refused to share his television revenue with visiting teams, characterizing such sharing as socialism; to paraphrase the famous line in *A League of Their Own*, he seems to have espoused the mantra, "There's no socialism in baseball."[11]

Sports historians and other commentators have lauded the National Football League for its generous gate-sharing plan. Leifer believes that football chose a generous plan because of "early uncertainties in local support. . . . Generous revenue sharing allowed teams to work out mutually advantageous schedules, bringing football to wherever it might attract large audiences."[12] Craig Coenen, though, suggests a different and less benevolent motive for revenue sharing. He described how initial NFL commissioner Joe Carr hoped to transform the league from a collection of small-town teams into a set of teams concentrated in the larger cities. In order to discourage owners of teams in small towns, he pushed for increased franchise fees, a forfeit guarantee, and increased minimum visitors' guarantees.[13]

Michael MacCambridge suggests that Lamar Hunt got his AFL television revenue-sharing idea from baseball executive Branch Rickey. Rickey suggested a plan in which one-third of television revenue would go to the home team whose game was being telecast and two-thirds would be placed in a common pool. Hunt refined the plan to put all of the money into a common pool. MacCambridge also believes that Bert Bell was inspired by baseball impresario Bill Veeck Jr.'s fifty-fifty sharing of television revenues between the two teams playing in a particular game, which differed from putting television revenue into a common pool. Bell, however, "sensed quickly that . . . revenue sharing of television receipts could provide another mechanism to equalize the opportunity for each of the NFL's clubs to field a competitive team."[14] Years later, Pete Rozelle explained to Congress that League Think worked to benefit all of the teams. "[NFL prosperity] didn't just happen because of the T-formation or the speed of wide receivers. It is a product of a carefully studied set of policies designed to give each NFL team the opportunity to compete equally."[15]

While the NFL's gate-sharing rule of a 60-40 percent split is convenient to remember and seemingly more equitable than baseball's rules, the plan was less generous than its reputation. First, according to the NFL constitution, home teams deducted 15 percent of the gate receipts to cover stadium rental and other costs, whether or not the home team incurred such expenses. The home team then sent 2 percent (with a $400 minimum) of the remaining 85 percent of the gate receipts (1.7 percent of the original receipts) to the league. Finally, the home team paid 40 percent of the remaining 83.3 percent of the gate receipts to the visiting team.[16] In effect, then, the home team paid a minimum of one-third of the gate receipts to the visiting team. Second, most observers neglected to report a caveat to the simple 60-40 percent rule: the home team had to pay a minimum of $20,000 to the visiting team. The guaranteed minimum had been only $4,000 in 1935.[17] The guaranteed minimum increased through the years; although not all of the NFL constitutions were available, we can trace the progression. The minimum guarantee rose to $5,000 by 1938; $10,000 by 1946; $15,000 in

1948; and $20,000 by 1949, although the owners defeated a proposal to increase it to $25,000 for the 1958 season. The minimum continued to rise, reaching $30,000 in 1960.[18] Bell suggested that the owners might cut the minimum visitor's guarantee to $15,000 for the 1953 season, but nothing came of this suggestion.[19] These increases suggest that the team owners wanted a binding guarantee, not a symbolic one.[20]

Owners tied revenue sharing to scheduling during their 1946 meetings. While owners debated on which teams would get six home games instead of five, they also discussed raising the guarantee from $5,000 to $10,000.[21] On occasion owners were exempted from paying visitor's shares. For the 1946 season the Philadelphia Eagles and Boston Yanks shared a home-and-home series. The league stipulated that they would not have to pay each other visitor's shares for the 1946 season only.[22]

The AAFC adopted a $15,000 guarantee with an option of 40 percent of gate receipts after deduction of taxes and stadium rental, which was $5,000 more than the NFL required in 1946 (the NFL had the 40 percent rider, too).[23] Sportswriter Stanley Frank noted that the AAFC's revenue-sharing rules were not altruistic: "That $15,000 nut to the visiting team may be a tough one to crack for potential weak links in Buffalo, Brooklyn, Miami and Chicago. Los Angeles and San Francisco, conversely, are yelping that the guarantee is not sufficient to cover their heavy traveling expenses across the continent for six [sic] games."[24] The NFL responded the following season by abolishing the guarantees and relying upon the 60-40 percent split. The Los Angeles Rams had to pay an additional $5,000 in guarantee during this period (note that these arrangements do not coincide with the league constitutions, although the constitution's dates may not coincide with seasons). For the 1949 season, though, the NFL restored the minimum guarantee, this time raised to $20,000, in addition to the 40 percent rule.[25]

The NFL and National League Revenue Picture, 1952–56

Tables 26 and 27 give basic attendance and win-loss records for teams in the two leagues during 1952–56. Both leagues had clubs that were typically successful or unsuccessful, although every team in the NFL had at least one losing season during the period surveyed.

Over the five seasons, the standard deviation in win-loss percent was 0.081 for the NL. The standard deviation in win-loss percent for the NFL's twelve teams was 0.129 (ignoring the Dallas Texans and their one season of play); this standard deviation was larger than that in the National League, but one should recall that during this period National League teams played a total of 770 scheduled games compared with 60 scheduled games for the NFL. Using the Noll and Scully concept of "idealized standard deviation," a league with equally matched teams would have a standard deviation of .018 for 770 games and .065 for 60 games. The National League's standard deviation was four times greater than its idealized standard deviation, while football's standard deviation was only twice as large as its idealized standard deviation, implying greater parity between NFL teams than between National League teams.[26]

For the decade, Fort found that the NL had less competitive balance, as measured by the standard deviation ration of winning percent imbalance: 2.06 to 1.52.[27] The Gini Coefficients, another measure of distribution, were higher, on average, for revenue imbalance in the NL than in the NFL during the 1950s (0.180 vs. 0.151), but the NFL had a higher Gini Coefficient for payroll imbalance (0.194 versus 0.112).[28]

The attendance patterns are of more interest. Five teams in the National League essentially broke even under the revenue-sharing plan, as their home and away attendance figures were nearly equal. Indeed, revenue-sharing was essentially a transfer between just the three strongest clubs. If one subscribes to the Robin Hood interpretation of revenue sharing, the National League was indeed a perverse example.

These perverse results occurred primarily because the Brooklyn Dodgers attracted the largest crowds on the road. The New York Giants also did well on the road. Part of their high road attendance certainly occurred because the two teams' fans could easily travel to "road games" between them.

The attendance differences between teams in the two sports were, in some cases, compounded by differences in ticket prices. The average ticket revenue for the National League during the five seasons was $1.53 per admission. The home teams shared 16.8 percent of their revenue with the visiting teams, a rate roughly half that of the NFL. Average ticket revenues varied from $1.33 in Chicago to $1.65 in Brooklyn. The ratio between Brooklyn's and Chicago's average ticket revenues was 1.24:1. Thus, the Dodgers paid a lower proportion of their gate revenue, 15.4 percent, to the visiting team, while the Cubs paid the highest proportion of theirs, 19.1 percent.

Based on the game-by-game information for 1956, the average ticket revenue in the NFL was $3.08. Cleveland had the lowest average ticket revenue at $2.74, while Washington had the highest average ticket revenue at $3.42. The ratio of Washington to Cleveland's average ticket revenue was 1.25:1, similar to that of the top and bottom teams in the National League. Green Bay's higher-than-average ticket revenue partially offset the team's tiny stadium and small home attendance.

The NFL's gate-sharing plan, based on a percentage basis, promised to redress the situation found in baseball's gate-sharing plan, under which teams with higher average ticket revenues paid out smaller proportions of their gate revenues to the visiting team. However, the amount of the redress depended upon the prevalence of payments of the $20,000 minimum. Both leagues, then, had revenue-sharing plans with regressive features.

What were the initial disparities in revenue between NFL and NL teams? Tables 28, 29, and 30 are derived from financial data given to the congressional hearing in 1957. All dollar amounts are reported in nominal terms, as the Consumer Price Index was remarkably stable between 1952 and 1956, varying from 99.3 to 101.6. In addition to yearly data, football owners provided game-by-game data for the 1956 season. In general, the data appears accurate and consistent, with occasional errors in addition. The game-by-game data was consistent with the league's revenue-sharing rules.

The tables use the standard deviation of teams' shares of league revenue, top:bottom ratio, and first quartile:fourth quartile ratio to compare the revenue distributions of the two leagues. The National League appeared to have greater relative disparity in gate revenue than did the National Football League, especially as measured by the top:bottom and first quartile:fourth quartile ratios. The National League's standard deviations also appeared to be higher, but it only had eight teams instead of twelve.

The National Football League's media revenue was typically much more evenly distributed than that of the National League, where the Brooklyn Dodgers had more than four times as much as did four of its competitors. The Dodgers' owner, Walter O'Malley, led the resistance to any sharing of television revenue, and, given the dramatic disparities between media revenues in the National League, his stance is not surprising. Aside from 1952, the NFL typically had roughly a two-to-one ratio between the teams with the most and the least media revenue. However, during this era, media revenues comprised only about one-eighth of either league's total revenue.

The National Football League did have one source of revenue that was quite unevenly distributed: exhibition games. The San Francisco 49ers took in more than five times as much from this source as did either the Baltimore Colts or Green Bay Packers.

Thus, if gate sharing is not included, the two leagues had roughly similar disparities in income between the haves and the have-nots.

The National League's Experiences with Revenue Sharing

The National League's gate-sharing plan succeeded in reducing the standard deviation of team's shares of total league gate revenue, but the overall impression is that the redistribution toward poor teams was moderate at best (tables 29 and 30), especially when compared with the earlier effects of a similar plan.

Although teams did not report the amount of home revenue paid to visiting teams, the revenue-sharing rules make such calculations easy. A formula for a team's estimated gate revenue without gate sharing is: estimated gate revenue without gate sharing = home revenue reported + (0.225 or 0.275) (home attendance). Aside from discrepancies for Boston/Milwaukee in 1952–53 and Cincinnati in 1953, the calculations were consistent with the total away revenue reported.

Table 31 shows the amount of redistribution under the National League's gate-sharing plan in 1952. No team gained or lost more than $87,000. The Boston Braves gained $87,000 from gate sharing, raising their total gate revenue to $462,000; without gate sharing, the team would have had just $375,000 in revenue. Thus, gate sharing provided 18.8 percent of the Braves' actual gate revenue in 1952, but the pennant-winning Brooklyn Dodgers gained almost as much as the Braves did. To give the reader an idea of how significant these amounts were, consider this: in 1952, the Dodgers reported a team payroll of $505,139 (including managers and coaches, as well as players). The Braves reported a player payroll of $333,251. Thus, the $87,000 transfer was over one-quarter of that team's payroll. It was more than half of the difference between the Dodgers' and the Braves' payroll.

The Boston Braves discovered the baseball equivalent of El Dorado in Milwaukee, a result that shocked Major League Baseball owners. The team earned the least combined home and road revenue in 1952, but the relocated team had the greatest combined gate revenue for each of the four seasons 1953–56. Although other National League teams would occasionally lose small amounts of revenue because of the gate-sharing plan, the Braves essentially funded the redistribution, with either the Brooklyn Dodgers or the New York Giants gaining the most revenue from the plan in each season surveyed. The change in the gate-sharing rule from 22.5 to 27.5 cents per admission after 1953 primarily injured the Braves.[29] We cannot say whether the Braves were against the change. Ironically, the increase in the gate-sharing rate after the 1953 season did not greatly benefit any of the financially weaker teams in the league, while the Dodgers and, later, the Giants appeared to have gained the most from the increase.

As a sop to the weaker teams, the league's revenue-sharing rule was ineffective. The moribund Pittsburgh Pirates finished last every season between 1952 and 1955; the team improved to seventh in 1956. Over the five seasons surveyed, the Pirates gained a total of $30,000 (table 32 differs from table 31 due to rounding). The league's two other weak teams, Chicago and Cincinnati, also experienced minimal effects from revenue sharing. For four teams, the amounts transferred during the five seasons were *less than 1 percent* of their estimated home gate receipts. Milwaukee lost over 7 percent, while the Dodgers gained 6 percent.

Table 33 shows the team-by-team attendance and net transfers during 1956. The Dodgers attracted more fans on the road than at their stadium against every rival. Indeed, the Dodgers were the best road draw for five of their seven rivals. The Braves drew more at home than on the road against all of their rivals. The Giants benefited greatly by having the Dodgers in such close proximity; games with Brooklyn represented 38 percent of the team's home gate.

A look at the lower right corner of table 33's upper panel reveals that National League fans of weaker teams did not flock to games against other weak teams, showing that, for this season at least, fans appeared to prefer the absolute quality, instead of the relative quality, of the visiting team.

While the National League's gate-sharing plan was less generous than the NFL's, a more generous plan — for example, double the amount — wouldn't have redressed the situation. The lack of generosity simply was not the key factor driving the league's "perverse" redistribution toward the Dodgers and Giants. If home teams had to share forty-five cents in 1952–53 and fifty-five cents in 1954–56, the amounts shown in tables 31–33 would simply have doubled: the Dodgers and Giants would have gained twice as much, while the Braves would have lost twice as much. The weaker teams would have seen gains of roughly 1 percent of gross home gate revenue. Of course, it is possible that owners might have changed their ticket prices and promotions if they had had to relinquish more of the home receipts. In order for the National League's gate-sharing plan to have been more redistributive, the owners would have had to sever the link between a team's ability to draw on the road and its share of road revenue.

The NFL's Experiences with Revenue Sharing

What effects did the NFL's revenue-sharing plan have in 1956? The gate-sharing plan did reduce the standard deviation of the percent of the league revenue (net of the league share). With twelve teams, a typical team would receive 0.083 of the overall gate receipts. Without gate sharing, the standard deviation would have been 0.028 in 1956; in other words, two-thirds of the teams would have been within one standard deviation of 0.083, or between 0.055 and 0.111. Ninety-five percent of the teams would have been within two standard deviations of 0.083, or between 0.027 and 0.139. The gate-sharing plan reduced the standard deviation to 0.022.[30]

In table 34 we see that two teams experienced more than a $100,000 shift in gate revenue from the plan, but these transfers represented a larger proportion of gate revenue than can be found in the National League; for the Chicago Cardinals (38.3 percent) and Green Bay Packers (16.0 percent), the transfers comprised a significant proportion of their revenue from the gate (table 35). The two teams that lost the most dollars, the Giants and Lions, lost 11.5 percent and 6.1 percent of their gate revenues respectively. For most teams, though, the plan had minimal effects.

Table 36 shows that, for several NFL teams in 1956, attendance at games against intraconference rivals did not strongly depend upon the strength of the visiting team. Each team played its five intraconference rivals home-and-home. The remaining two games were against interconference teams.

Over the five seasons, the Packers were the biggest beneficiaries from revenue sharing. As shown in table 27, the Packers drew over 500,000 more fans on the road than at home, so they probably gained around $500,000 from revenue sharing. The Rams were the biggest losers. Still, the attendance differences shown in the table imply that few teams saw a change of even $50,000 per season. The woebegone Cardinals might have averaged a gain of $30-$40,000 per season.

The NFL's gate-sharing plan did not suffer from the flat-rate defect afflicting baseball's plan. The transfers would have been larger, but the $20,000 minimum gate-share rule diluted gate-sharing's redistributive effect. Philadelphia paid $20,000 for each of two home games, while Cleveland and Green Bay each paid $20,000 for one home game. The perennially weak Chicago Cardinals, however, paid out $20,000 per game for five of its six home games during 1956 even though the team enjoyed an aberrant season, winning seven of its twelve games. The Cardinals had won only ten times in the previous four seasons and would win only seven games during the next three seasons. The Cardinals' home games had receipts of $276,538.80, almost $164,000 less than Philadelphia, the team with the next lowest receipts. The Cardinals paid $121,193.60 to visiting teams, including $100,000 for the five games where they paid the minimum. Had the $20,000 minimum rule not been in effect, the Cardinals would have paid 33.2 percent of receipts, or $91,810.88, to the visitors. The rule cost the Cardinals almost $30,000. The Cardinals paid 43.8 percent of their receipts to the visiting team, the highest proportion in the league. No other team paid more than 35 percent of their receipts to visiting teams.

Although the NFL's percentage gate-sharing rule mitigated the varying average ticket prices received by its members, unlike the National League plan, the minimum payout requirement had regressive effects. The NFL owners did not provide game-by-game receipts for 1952–55, but attendance figures found in Maher and Gill show that the Cardinals probably had to pay the minimum two or three times each season.[31] In some cases, the minimum wasn't much higher than the 33.2 percent levy; still, the weak Chicago Cardinals lost some of the benefits from gate sharing. Of course, if when weak teams played each other they simply exchanged $20,000 minimums, the rule's deleterious effects would have been minimal, but in 1956 the minimums were not always paid to other weak teams.

The Chicago Cardinals had the misfortune of playing in the American Conference, which also included Cleveland, New York, Philadelphia, Pittsburgh, and Washington. The American Conference teams drew far fewer fans to games during the five years under study than did teams in the National Conference: 5.1 versus 7.2 million. Typically, the Cardinals played home-and-home series with their intraconference rivals. The remaining two games on the schedule were interconference games, usually one with the crosstown Bears and one with another National Conference club. Thus, while Green Bay drew fewer fans at home than did the Cardinals, their road attendance was much greater because they played against the four teams in the NFL with the most drawing power (Baltimore might have ranked sixth had the team played all five seasons). The Packers also benefited from playing the American Conference's best-drawing team, Cleveland, in three of the seasons.

In a sense, aside from the regressive effects of the gate-sharing plan that blunted the Cardinals' gains, the NFL's plan was the very model of a gate-sharing plan, as held by popular opinion: transfers from successful teams, mostly in the largest cities, to weaker teams in smaller cities.

How the AAFC's Plan Might Have Worked

The AAFC had a 60-40 percent plan with the usual deductions for stadium rental and league offices. Table 37 shows that the Cleveland Browns would have funded the revenue-sharing plan, and the Brooklyn Dodgers would have been the chief beneficiaries. The New York Yankees and Chicago Rockets would have received benefits, too. The Los Angeles Dons and San Francisco 49ers would have been modest payers under the scheme. The teams in the largest cities of New York and Chicago, then, did not prove the conventional wisdom for gate sharing.

The Moral Hazard Aspects of Revenue-Sharing Plans

Economists and politicians bemoan the potential demoralization of recipients of government transfer payments. During the 1980s and 1990s, people debated whether welfare blunted the incentive to work. Professional team owners, too, debate whether the incentives created under revenue-sharing plans led to undesirable outcomes. Economists label a situation in which people may not exercise due diligence because of perverse incentives as a moral hazard.

Why did the NFL have a guaranteed minimum? American League baseball owners were familiar with franchises that held "fire sales" of players, ostensibly in order to remain solvent. The St. Louis Browns sold most of their best players between 1947 and 1951. The owners, the DeWitt brothers, pleaded poverty, but some rival owners grumbled about the brothers being "parasites, who feed on the drawing power of the better teams while on the road and keep themselves weak and without support at home."[32] A local sportswriter observed: "The [DeWitt brothers'] theory is that a major league franchise has a certain minimum value that can't be reduced even if no players of established major league caliber go with it . . . [they] recognize they can't draw much more poorly with no big leaguers in their lineup than they have drawn with a few, and that they may as well take advantage of their rivals' prosperity and cash in while the cash is good."[33]

During the 1930s the Philadelphia Phillies sold many players and remained weak on the field despite the revenue sharing. The NFL's guaranteed minimum might therefore, have served as a deterrent for franchises tempted to strip their clubs, thereby reducing the potential for moral hazard problems. The National League was less likely to enact a minimum guarantee, given the inverse relationship between a team's win-loss record and its ability to draw on the road: if the Pirates killed the gate at Brooklyn's Ebbets Field, why should the Dodgers be penalized by having to pay a minimum?

Football's minimum guarantee and the National League's apparent unwillingness to alter its gate-sharing plan in order to truly help its ne'er-do-well clubs both suggest that some sports owners are suspicious of mindless redistribution of revenue. Instead, owners of strong teams appeared to use gate sharing as a stick: maintain a minimally decent team or pay a penalty. While the National League did not have a minimum team payroll during the 1950s, Major League Baseball did have a minimum player salary; these rules might have forced owners to field a minimum of talent. The baseball owners in both leagues appear to have stood Canes's negative externality of too strong a team on its head (and, goodness knows, football's Cleveland Browns and baseball's Yankees and Dodgers might well have exemplified his thesis): owners of strong teams accused owners of weak teams of exerting a negative effect upon the gate. One wonders whether the pennant winners secretly wished for a league where all rival teams were (slightly) above average (but not as good as their pennant-winning teams), creating good crowds for every game.

Conclusions

The two leagues' revenue-sharing plans did reduce the standard deviations of member teams' shares of total gate revenues by roughly similar amounts in 1956. The proportional decrease in the standard deviation was larger in the NFL than in the National League, but there was only one season's worth of data for the NFL. However, the leagues differed significantly in the nature of the redistribution and in the narrowing of the standard deviations.

In the National League, the reduced standard deviation was primarily the result of whittling down Milwaukee's impressive drawing power at home while enriching the (heretofore) richest teams in Brooklyn and New York. Weaker teams in the National League did get net transfers, but these were often smaller in both absolute and relative terms than those accruing to Brooklyn and New York. The National Football League's plan similarly reduced the standard deviation by helping the Green Bay Packers and Chicago Cardinals, who drew poorly, at the expense of New York, Los Angeles, and Detroit. Thus, the NFL's experiences corresponded more closely to the way most people think about gate sharing.

The National League failed to have the Robin Hood effect found in the NFL not strictly because of a lack of generosity, but because wealthy, strong teams, such as Brooklyn and New York, drew well on the road. Thus, even if the National League had approximated the 33.2 percent redistribution rate mandated by the NFL, which could have been achieved by doubling the flat rate to forty-five cents in 1952 and 1953 and fifty-five cents after 1953, only Milwaukee, Brooklyn, and New York would have been affected by more than $80,000 over the five seasons. The other five teams, including the truly wretched Pittsburgh Pirates, would have received smaller gains than would the Dodgers and Giants from a more ostensibly generous plan. To alter the distribution of gate revenue significantly, the National League needed to pool the road revenue and then split it evenly, thereby severing the link between a team's win-loss record and its ability to draw on the road. However, the National League owners did not appear willing to do so, and they settled on merely increasing the per-attendee amount paid after 1953.

The policy did curb Milwaukee's home attendance advantage, mostly to the advantage of the Brooklyn Dodgers. Since the Braves lacked the Dodgers' media revenue (revenue that Brooklyn did not have to share), the equity of the transfer is ambiguous. The moral of the National League's experience was the potential gains from relocating a moribund franchise, such as the Braves. Indeed, the NFL would eventually send the Chicago Cardinals to St. Louis. Green Bay would eventually prosper under Vince Lombardi's coaching and benefit from playing in a larger stadium. Even shifting some games to Milwaukee did not greatly bolster the team's home attendance. For the Chicago Cardinals, though, a shift to the other conference might have provided a significant boost to its gains from the revenue-sharing plan, as witness Green Bay.

The NFL's gate-sharing plan worked as pundits expected, as the amounts transferred were 12.9 percent and 10.8 percent of the Cardinals and Packers' total gross incomes in 1956. The league's policy of enacting a $20,000 minimum, though, blunted the redistributive aspect of its plan.[34]

Whether because owners feared moral hazard problems from an inapt revenue-sharing plan or because they simply didn't think too much about the outcome of existing plans, both the NFL and NL plans fell short of maximizing the leveling of revenues possible, given the amounts paid to visiting teams. A resort to a common pool promised to better redress the disparities between revenues, but such a radical plan probably did not appeal to a majority of the owners.

10

GILDED PEONAGE

Professional athletes needed their consciousness raised. Baseball players revolted against the owners periodically, as they did during the short-lived Players' National League of 1890. The years immediately following World War II saw a spike in players' efforts to fight for their rights. Perhaps never in professional sports history was a tougher crowd of players collected; many were veterans of the war, who had seen the world and who might not be easily cowed by owners.

The NFL and professional basketball bragged about having college men playing their games, thereby eradicating the image of the athletic bum, who was slightly above a carnival roadie in social status. The spawning of new leagues in 1946 — the Basketball Association of America, the Mexican (Baseball) League, and the AAFC — gave players leverage in salary negotiations.

Coaches were still quite authoritarian. Paul Brown was not alone in dictating dress codes and behavior off the field; Joe McCarthy, manager of baseball's New York Yankees, issued similar edicts. Brown wanted to elevate the professional game's image in the public eye: "College players had a good reputation, but the public perception of the professional football player . . . was of a big, dumb guy with a potbelly and a cheap cigar. That kind of person disgusted me, and I never wanted anyone associating our players with that image, so I always tried to make our pro teams collegelike."[1]

NFL owners were paternalistic and patronizing at best and outright abusive at worst. George Halas was notorious for paying his players as little as possible, perhaps because he was operating on a thin margin in some years; he was also lauded for helping players with loans and other assistance throughout their lives.[2] Owners passed a rule stipulating that 25 percent of a player's total salary be withheld from every paycheck. At the end of each season, they then sent a check covering the 25-percent withholding to players. The owners apparently worried that some players would blow their salaries before the season ended.[3]

Tentative Improvements for Players

Basketball and football players' relatively brief athletic careers militated against the formation of players' unions in basketball and football. Major League Baseball players took tentative steps toward forming a players' association in the late 1940s; it was led by labor relations authority Robert Murphy. The baseball owners co-opted the movement by recommending the association's legal advisor, Judge Robert Cannon, an action Marvin Miller claimed was a violation of labor practices. Leland Stanford MacPhail, then part owner of the New York Yankees, convinced his fellow owners to implement a player pension plan. The benign aspect of the plan masked an ominous ulterior purpose: to keep players in line via threats to strip them of their pension "rights." During the struggle to keep the proposed Continental League from becoming a reality, Major League Baseball owners used the pension to raise the cost of starting the new league.[4]

The NFL owners decided to revise the standard player contract immediately after World War II. The new contract specified "the obligations of the club and of the player and adds to the protection of the player. The contract is for one year, with an option on the player's services for the succeeding season at a specified price." While Bert Bell extolled the virtues of the new contract, he made an interesting statement: "This contract eliminates 'servitude.'" If he believed this, he was one of the few owners or officials ever to admit that players toiled under conditions of "servitude." The owners made the adjustments, which later turned out to be largely cosmetic, in the hope that the courts wouldn't rule the contracts invalid on the grounds of lack of mutuality; hence Bell's statement, "We have talked about the player. Now we talk about the player and the club, about their responsibilities to one another."[5] A cynical observer might see the owners' action as a calculated response to the AAFC's challenge and to potential legal battles between the leagues and with players.

Owners were aware of the dubious legality of the player contract.

Commissioner Bell introduced attorney Phil Gilbert to the owners at an April 1946 meeting. Gilbert examined the validity of the player contract: "Any Player Contract which had a forty-eight hour release clause, or a reserve clause similar to the same only of longer duration, in all probability would not stand up in court. He suggested that it was his belief that a contract similar to the one which Mr. Marshall presented without any release clause in all probability would stand up in court." Gilbert said owners might use two separate contracts — one for players they expected to retain for the season and the other for players likely to be released. Bell presented a new "Uniform Players Contract" the next day with the suggested adjustments, and the owners approved it unanimously.[6]

Despite this more "lenient" reserve clause, Bell and the owners maintained their patronizing attitudes. As mentioned earlier, during his testimony before various congressional committees, Bell referred to the players as "boys." Rather than establish formal rights, Bell preferred to operate by having his "boys" come in as supplicants. He reveled in helping them, but, as some congressional observers stated, there was no guarantee that a future commissioner would be so benevolent.

Player Rights

Despite the minor adjustments made by sports owners immediately after World War II, player rights remained weak.

Congressional committee members were shocked at the marked lack of regard for player rights shown by owners of professional sports teams. They prodded and poked the owners and their representatives about playing conditions, reserve clause, and the reverse-order draft. While players earned higher incomes than most Americans, there was no escaping their chattel-like status. Owners in all team sports worked very hard to establish the fiction that these violations of the players' fundamental rights to their labor were necessary to maintain competitive balance. The owners were assisted by the public's ignorance of the exploitation of the athletes, as the public was mesmerized by the fact that players earned above-average incomes for playing a game.

A highly touted college football star could look forward to being drafted by an NFL team. If he was fortunate enough to graduate between 1945 and

1948 or after 1960, he could entertain offers from multiple teams. He was otherwise constrained either to negotiate only with the team possessing his draft rights or to go to Canada. His negotiations might be reported in the local newspaper, and his contract might call for multiple years at $10,000 or more per year. He would be wise not to start spending his money.

The rookie and the veteran alike would report for training in August. While he was housed, military-style, in dormitories or barracks, the player sweated, studied, and was indoctrinated into a coach's style of play, all without pay. When exhibition games started, he might, at the whim of his owner, get fifty dollars per game. In the meantime, for several weeks he got per diem and maybe a little pocket change for laundry. No one seemed to care much about his wife and children, if he had a family; dependents were left to fend for themselves. If, and only if, he made the final roster, he began getting paychecks. If he was cut or was injured, in most cases his fancy contract was just a piece of paper to put in a frame and hang on the wall. No wonder many talented college players decided to start their careers in industry instead. Players who disliked uncertainty might well have turned down NFL offers to play for just $5,000 or $6,000, compared to a white-collar job that paid a definite $3,500. The postwar period after all, saw the birth of "the organization man" described by William H. Whyte; these college graduates were looking for solid, safe jobs.[7]

Once the regular season started and paychecks began coming in, the player only needed to take care not to get injured. He might think that NFL players were covered under state workers' compensation laws, but he would be mistaken. Owners also did not interpret player contracts as binding: if the player got hurt, why pay him? While many, if not most, owners honored the contracts, they did so out of the goodness of their hearts or to placate a star player. One player, John De Laurentis, lost a court case involving his leg injury. The Washington Redskins released him, although everyone, including De Laurentis, thought he was recovered. His leg subsequently required surgery. The Redskins paid the medical bills and paid him $2,800, which he interpreted as settlement for breach of contract. The player then sought redress from the District of Columbia Workmen's Compensation Commission for $4,750; the commission awarded him compensation, ruling that the money the Redskins paid was for breach of contract. The Redskins appealed and won a reversal and De Laurentis had to return $2,400.[8] In a later case, Frank McPhee sued the Chicago Cardinals on the grounds that the team released him because of injuries in 1956. McPhee sued for the remaining balance on his contract. The Cardinals denied liability and claimed McPhee had accepted $1,083 in full settlement of his salary "after he quit the team on Oct. 17." The Cardinals claimed he failed to perform his agreement. Bert Bell told reporters that the owners turned down a player demand that contracts contain financial guarantees for injured players, because he "did not know of a player who had not been 'compensated in full' after he had brought an injury to the league's attention."[9] Haldo Norman also filed suit, claiming the San Francisco 49ers failed to pay him after he broke a collarbone and was released. He settled for $4,500.[10] Injured players clearly had reason to bemoan their ambiguous legal rights, despite Bell's assurances to the contrary.

If a team participated in a playoff game to qualify for the league championship game, there was no guarantee players would be paid for the game. In 1949 the San Francisco 49ers threatened to strike if owners Tony and Vic Morabito didn't pay them $500 bonuses for playing against the New York Yankees in a playoff game, competing for the privilege of getting whipped by the Cleveland Browns. Vic Morabito told reporters, "The odd thing about this bonus demand, is that our players are the only ones, of the four teams concerned, making such a demand. They don't seem to understand that their pay comes from the championship game and, even if they should lose Sunday, they would get third-place money." O. O. Kessing, the AAFC commissioner, added, "It would seem to me that the players' action is a bit premature. They may not realize they will have a lawsuit on their hands if they go through with it. The contracts which all of them signed specified that they would participate in these play-off games." With that, Morabito refused to accede to the players' demand, and the strike fizzled. The players' standard contract undoubtedly contained such clauses, but owners had to worry about concerted player actions.[11] Few players, however, contested any of the clauses in their contracts.

As Bob Dylan sang a decade later, "The times, they are a'changin." In the wake of baseball's Mexican League–inspired increase in player salaries during the 1946 season, some baseball players began challenging the reserve clause. Danny Gardella, a journeyman player, filed a lawsuit against Major League Baseball. The baseball owners, every bit as adept at making dire predictions as their football peers, cried that without the sacred reserve clause, the game would collapse (and wouldn't that be too bad for the girls and boys of America). Sportswriter Dan Parker, both more perspicacious and more cynical than his fellows, wrote:

> Why baseball, and the other professional sports . . . should require a contract of this type in order to survive when every other branch of the entertainment field manages to get along without this special privilege, isn't immediately evident to anyone who gives the matter a bit of careful study. At best, only the outstanding players would be affected to any great extent by the new type of contract. Theoretically, the richest clubs would corner the best players. But baseball magnates, in such matters as getting around their own waiver law, have shown a surprising aptitude for effecting "gentlemen's agreements." Not even a multimillionaire magnate would be blind to the ultimate disadvantages to himself as a whole-hog policy that disregarded the welfare of the league as an entity.[12]

Parker was incorrect.

Athletes were not the only glamorous people being economically exploited. Until Olivia de Havilland and Bette Davis took on the motion picture studios, actors and actresses faced their own version of a reserve clause. Davis lost her lawsuit in 1937, but de Havilland won hers in 1944.[13] In both baseball and motion pictures, owners claimed that they invested significant amounts of money into developing their workers' talents, and that they would not invest without some form of property rights to these workers, much to the detriment of the quality of play or of acting.

On occasion, someone associated with the NFL would strip away the façade. Disgruntled coach Norman "Red" Strader, fired from the New York Yanks, sued team owner Ted Collins. In his affidavit, Strader "described the method of drafting college stars as 'illegal' and contended that the club owners have arbitrarily set up a 'football czar' to enforce the system." Strader won his case against Collins, but nothing came of his remarks against the draft.[14]

The New York Giants' Arnie Weinmeister decided to play for the Vancouver Lions after the Giants told him in a letter that he would be replaced in the coming season. Weinmeister told Wellington T. Mara that he would not be back for the 1954 season and signed with Vancouver for $15,000. The Giants promptly sued. Part of their claim was that Weinmeister was an "indispensable part" of the team. Weinmeister's attorneys, ironically, tried to demonstrate that fans came see to the backfield men perform, not lowly tackles such as Weinmeister. An interesting aspect of Weinmeister's case, in addition to Mara's letter, was Wellington Mara's confession that he had paid Weinmeister $1,000 more than his contract stipulated: "Weinmeister contends the contract figure of $11,000 approved by the NFL commissioner, was exceeded, voiding the contract." This novel legal argument — "Your honor, he paid me too much, so the contract is voided" — did not prevent Weinmeister from prevailing, as Mara's letter proved to be pivotal.[15]

Players retained Creighton Miller, a former Notre Dame halfback turned attorney, to represent them in negotiations with the commissioner and with club owners.[16] The players' main demand was for a player pension similar to that provided to baseball players. The players also hoped to get nominal payment for exhibition games, a minimum salary, and some other concessions. Aside from the pension, their demands were shockingly modest, which was also true of demands made by baseball and basketball players. Owners might have forestalled greater militancy later on by accepting these modest demands and recognizing the Players Association. Instead, some owners, such as George Preston Marshall, were outraged: "The proposals sound ridiculous and, from a practical standpoint, they don't deserve any recognition from me. It's a matter for Commissioner Bell." Edwin W. Pauley, co-owner of the Los Angeles Rams, heard the news with placidity: "I believe it will help pro football. It's the same as in any business. There is nothing to fear."[17]

The NFL Constitution allowed players to bring labor-related matters to the commissioner. Bert Bell exercised his authority largely to the satisfaction of both owners and players. On several occasions, he urged owners to placate players. Bell interpreted the constitution to mean that he was not bound to meet with any player representative, and if he did meet with such a personage, he might bring his own attorney. Sportswriter Joe King reported, "The players are not militant in their stand, but believe it is only reasonable to have a central figure, with legal training, to represent them in contractual matters. . . . The four points were recognition of the union, training camp expenses, provision for recompense to injured players and a pension plan." Kyle Rote, one of the player leaders, emphasized that the players were not "demanding anything" but simply wanted to "discuss beneficial practices which several clubs already had in effect, in order to achieve as much uniformity as possible."[18] The players did not include another one of their considerations: payment to drafted players who were cut loose after failing to make a team in training camp.

Whatever Bell's personal beliefs about player unions, he was the owners' hired hand, so he stonewalled recognizing the players' association, although he met for an "informal chat" with Rote, Norm Van Brocklin (who was later traded, but whether in retaliation for his testimony is unknown; he played through the 1960 season), and Creighton Miller. Bell told reporters that he "was not representing and had no right to represent the club owners."[19] He would contradict this claim later.

The players asked for a minimum salary of $5,000, expense money during training camp, twelve dollars a day minimum for board and lodging while on the road, an injury clause guaranteeing a full season's salary, a shorter training season, and formal recognition of the association. Since few players had salaries below $5,000, the first request was simply a formality. The owners refused to implement it, though. Bell said, "There is no player in the National Football League who does not receive over this minimum. If there is one, and he tells me about it, I'll see that it's corrected." Probably because many of the owners had already fulfilled the other requests, the owners agreed to adopt them in order to standardize fringe benefits across teams. The owners, refused to recognize the Players Association, however. Bell reiterated, "Any player or players have the right to meet with the commissioner at any time for the purpose of discussing any problems. The league believes that the circumstances and conditions affecting each club are different and distinct. It is submitted that if any problems now exist or hereafter arise, the player or players on each club should meet with their individual owners for the purpose of discussing and resolving their particular grievances." Never was "divide and conquer" put forth so blandly. The players immediately responded with a show of support for the Professional Football Players Association by displaying 304 member signatures.[20]

The players were fortunate in that a power greater than Bert Bell and the owners was coming to the rescue. The Congressional Antitrust Subcommittee of 1957 took keen interest in player-management relations throughout sports. If Shakespeare had been writing in the 1950s, he might have written, "The congressional committee doth make cowards of us all." Creighton Miller told reporters that the owners refused to meet with him, even though more than 90 percent of the players had joined the association. Facing congressional pressure, Bell did a volte-face and told the committee he was ready to begin negotiating with the association's officials and that he had the authority to recognize it. In the words of Dana Carvey's "Church Lady" on *Saturday Night Live* some decades later: "How con-*veen*-ient." Fortunately for Bell, George Preston Marshall gave him cover when he told reporters that recognition of the players' association was "a matter for the clubs to decide and not the commissioner."[21] Several days later, the players' association asked Bell to "put in writing his verbal agreement to recognize the league's new player association."[22]

Miller described his frustration in dealing with Bert Bell. Bell had initially indicated that recognition was forthcoming and implied that he, Bell, had authority to do so himself. Miller claimed that Bell had told player representatives that he [Bell] would not take the players' proposals to the owners unless the players publicly endorsed the option clause and the player draft. (This was during the William Radovich case.) He claimed Bell told him, "If you endorse the option clause, you won't have any trouble getting recognized. I'll be able to take this into the owners, and say this is a sign of good faith; the boys have done something for us." As Bell was becoming less enthusiastic about the Players Association, Miller and the players refused to sign the endorsement.[23] The congressional committee queried Bell on this point. He testified that he had urged the players to make the public endorsements and had told them that he would do his best to get the owners to recognize the association. He also indicated the owners' primary opposition to the association was their fear that it did not have the proper authority and that "they also believed individually that the players could do much better for themselves dealing individually with their own clubs." Bell told Kenneth Harkins, chief counsel for the committee, that although he had agreed to insert the $5,000 minimum salary clause into the players' proposal, he was against it:' "I think it was academic, because there was nobody in 1955 who received less than $5,000."[24] Baltimore Colts owner Carroll Rosenbloom stated that owners claimed that some of their players had told them the association didn't represent them. The biggest stumbling block was that the Chicago Bears players hadn't joined the association yet.[25] Of course the owners may have been reporting what they wanted to hear.

NFL quarterback Norm Van Brocklin, players' representative, read a prepared statement to the committee. The players cited the improving economic condition of the NFL — increased revenues and profits due to lower amusement taxes, increased ticket prices, and decreased transportation tax — in asserting that their demands were "fair" and that "there is a certain gratification in accomplishing something that will better the conditions of play for the college players who are yet to come into the pro league. Many of our representatives have only one or two years of play remaining and their contributions to our association are not based on selfish motives — but are rather designed to improve the conditions under which future athletes will play."[26]

Creighton Miller went on the attack during his testimony. He stated bluntly, "The professional football players' contract is a legal monstrosity. To better understand the unconscionable advantage it bestows upon the commissioner and owners, certain features of the contract, which contain clauses unfair to the player, should be discussed." He later quoted Judge Jerome N. Frank's opinion in Danny Gardella's lawsuit against Major League Baseball: "We have a monopoly which, in its effects on ballplayers like the plaintiff, possesses characteristics shockingly repugnant to moral principles that, at least since the War Between the States, have been basic in America as shown by the thirteenth amendment to the Constitution condemning involuntary servitude."[27] Players could be released at a moment's notice without compensation, a clear lack of mutuality. The contract also stripped players of their right of appeal.[28] Again, the fact that players earned more than most Americans did not blind the legislators to the unjust nature of the contract, although the legislators proved unwilling to tackle the reserve clause and player drafts directly.

Bell defended the player draft and the reserve clause. He stated that teams contacted players before the draft and queried them as to their willingness to play for them. If a player indicated he would not play for a particular team, Bell said, the team rarely selected him.

To buttress Bell's testimony, the Chicago Cardinals' owner solicited several of his players to send in testimonials. Some of the testimonials were vague. Donald Stonesifer wrote, "I would quit playing football if I could be bought and sold to the highest bidder—for two reasons: 1) I do not care to be bought and sold like a slave. 2) Football is a team and spirit game. You cannot play for yourself—you must play for the team, and what the team represents. To me the team represents the Chicago Cardinals and I have a deeper feeling for the Chicago Cardinals than for Northwestern University, where I played my college ball." Not every Cardinals player was enthusiastic about the campaign; one wrote anonymously and told the committee, "We were asked to send a reply, and although it wasn't compulsory for us to reply, our chances of staying with the team would probably be very slim. The way pro football is today the players have no chance for collective bargaining, which is an accepted American practice. . . . I don't feel that I can sign my name to this letter because it will definitely hurt my chances of staying with the Cardinals."[29]

NFL player George Ratterman disputed the necessity of a player draft, pointing out that Major League Baseball did not have a draft of amateur players (baseball did have a reverse-order draft of minor league players). He asked, "If football needs a player draft, why doesn't baseball?"[30] In the wake of the controversy over the draft as an inherent denial of players' basic civil rights, Bell wanted to insert a clause into the league constitution and bylaws that codified the informal "if the player doesn't want to play for you, don't draft him" policy.[31] As with many of the NFL's changes to grant players more of their civil rights, this rule came with a large loophole—the commissioner had the power to determine whether a request was reasonable—but NFL owners shouldn't be chastised too severely; almost any industry facing regulation attempts to mitigate the effects.

Bell also said players were free to come to him and discuss grievances. Some of the committee members pressed him about his neutrality in such situations, since the owners paid his salary. Bell professed to lean toward the players. He painted them as young and unaware of "the different angles and different situations" and claimed, "Eighty percent of the players do not even read their contract except for the amount of money that is on it."[32] Committee members, many of them lawyers, were bemused. They began asking players whether they read their contracts and the question, "Have you read your contract?" became de rigueur (instead of that other 1950s question, "Are you now or have you ever been a member of the Communist Party?"). In response to this question, Chuck Bednarik, a veteran player, confessed that, "I feel that I am fairly intelligent, but I never read the fine print. I just look at the amount of money are they going to pay me." He added that he thought 95 percent of the players acted as he did. Emanuel Celler was incredulous, especially when Bednarik said he had a degree in Business Administration from the University of Pennsylvania's Wharton School. He said he didn't read the fine print because "money was the big thing then. I didn't have a nickel then, and I looked at the figures to see if that was satisfactory to me." Bednarik touted Bert Bell's interventions on behalf of players. When Celler commented, "Well I hope Mr. Bell lives for many, many, many years," Bednarik agreed, "I do, too." Celler tried to raise the player's consciousness by asking what would happen if Bell was no longer the commissioner. Bednarik said he wouldn't want to continue playing then, although in reality he played for three seasons after Bell's death.[33] Creighton Miller said the players' failure to read their contracts was based on two factors: "They know about it from the veteran ballplayers" and "They cannot do anything about [their contracts]."[34]

Celler wasted no time voicing his disapproval of paragraph 11 in the standard player contract, which concerned a player's automatic waiver of his right to seek redress from the commissioner's decision: "I would say this, gentlemen. I think that section is void as against public policy. You cannot preclude a man from going into the courts to have redress of wrongs. . . . That is a pretty harsh section."[35]

One former player, though, had read his contract. George Connor, former Chicago Bears player and now assistant coach, told the committee he had read his contract carefully and consulted with a lawyer. "We had three clauses in the contract crossed out, and we had another thing written on the side, an injury clause, that if I was injured I would get paid for my full contract." He had stricken the "release clause," which meant they had to keep him on the team for all three seasons. He also had the "physical capabilities of the player are not up to standard" and "conduct" clauses crossed out. Connor contradicted Bell's claim that teams did not select players who didn't want to play for them. The New York Giants selected Connor in the draft; Ted Collins, owner of the Boston Yanks, wanted Connor. Connor told him repeatedly that he had no interest of playing for Boston and that he only wanted to play with Chicago. Collins obtained the player from the Giants but eventually traded him to the Bears. Connor said that he was fortunate in having a family friend, a circuit court judge in Chicago, review the contract, but that most players did not have or seek recourse to legal counsel.[36]

Creighton Miller highlighted the owners' handling of workmen's compensation ("workmen's" was the contemporary term). He stated that he was not aware of any player who had filed for workmen's compensation, explaining, "He is protected by workmen's compensation, but this does not insure his salary. Few players file for workmen's compensation because many clubs pay them their regular salary anyway, in order not to raise what is already a rather prohibitive premium because of the dangers involved in professional football." Miller testified that Bell opposed insertion of an injury clause into the players' contracts. Bell told him that insertion would lead to "a lot of minor [law] cases on our hands if somebody gets a sore thumb."[37]

Teams submitted information on workmen's compensation costs. The Chicago teams were not covered, while the Pennsylvania teams had been rejected by the state workmen's compensation board because the benefits were too small and the club paid the full costs resulting from injuries. The other eight teams paid between $1,500 and $18,236 in 1956, with five teams paying less than $9,000. Teams also reported on how many lawsuits players filed over salaries. Most teams had no lawsuits filed, but the Cardinals had four suits filed against them, the Packers had four, the Lions had three, and the Giants and Redskins each had one. The Lions' lawsuits included the Radovich case. Owners investigated getting a bond to cover workmen's compensation, so they would not have to participate in the program.[38]

The Reserve Clause

The hearing was notable in that Bell and the NFL owners tried to present their interpretation of the reserve clause and option year as kinder and gentler version than Major League Baseball's "in perpetuity" interpretation. He claimed, "We changed our contract because our players do not play nearly as long in football as the average baseball player does. Pro football is a means to an end to establish a youngster in business. So we can make changes that baseball could not make, and we tried to make them."[39] Bell took pains to claim that players could easily play out their option year and become free agents.

When pressed for names of players who had done so, however, Bell became vague. He mentioned Ed Modzelewski and George Kennard, but these players had either retired for a year or had left the team. Kennard returned to his team (Bell implied that players preferred to stay on their own team), while Modzelewski was negotiating with teams. Committee members, perhaps recalling Arthur Conan Doyle's Sherlock Holmes story, "Silver Blaze" and the importance of "the dog that didn't bark," wondered about the free agents who weren't signed. Bell later recalled that George Ratterman was pursuing free agency. Ratterman had refused to sign a contract with a reserve or option clause; Jim Breuil of Buffalo gave him a one-year non-holdover deal, but the next year Ratterman played for the New York Yanks. In a masterpiece of doublespeak, Bell told Senator Joseph O'Mahoney (who later thanked him for his testimony and was clearly sympathetic to the owners), "Ratterman had the bargaining power. This [reserve] clause gives the greatest bargaining power a player can have."[40]

Creighton Miller pointed out that originally a player was to receive 100 percent of his original contract during the option year but that the owners had changed this to 90 percent "to discourage players from becoming so-called free agents, as most players prefer to renegotiate their contract rather than take an automatic 10 percent reduction." Miller claimed there was, in the words of Emanuel Celler, "sort of a secret agreement by the owners not to hire a man that becomes a free agent."[41] Players, too, were hard-pressed to name any colleague who had successfully signed as a free agent after completing his option year. There were rumors that the owners maintained a blacklist against any free agents. Chuck Bednarik thought Bud Grant had been a free agent, but Grant's free agency entailed playing in Canada, not for another NFL team. Bednarik had played in the NFL since 1949, and he could not name a single player. Bednarik and fellow NFL player Jack Jennings denied that there was a blacklist, with Jennings claiming hypothetically that if George Halas needed a guard and a free-agent guard was available, "I am sure Mr. Halas would pick [him] up." Creighton Miller told the committee that two players had played out their option but no club signed them, "although many coaches expressed serious interest."[42]

George Ratterman became the focal point of the free agency discussion. Ratterman played three seasons with Buffalo's AAFC team. When the league disbanded, he ended up with the New York Yanks. He signed a one-year contract with the Yanks that contained the usual option clause.

> In May the option was supposed to have been exercised—by May of 1951. It was not exercised, in my opinion. I contacted the management of the New York Yanks in the middle of May and mentioned the fact to them that I believed I was a free agent because they had not exercised the option clause. It was necessary for them to notify me that they were taking up the option, and I said they had not done that. I was informed by the general manager of the New York Yanks [Frank Fitzgerald] at that time that I could not go any place and play anywhere. I said, "Why not? I am a free agent." He said, "Well, none of the other teams in this league would sign you."[43]

Ratterman played in Canada but settled with the Yanks and finished the season (since the NFL season extended past the Canadian League season). Then Bert Bell stepped in and told Ratterman he could not play for the Yanks until he appealed to Bell. Ratterman stated, "The commissioner said he did not care what the judge in New Jersey said, the league rules said he had jurisdiction, and I could not play in the National Football League until I sent him a telegram requesting a hearing under [my] existing contract." Bell fined Ratterman $2,000 for going to Canada. The next season, Bell came up to him and said, "Forget the rest of your fine and just be a good boy."[44]

In a harbinger of the future of player movement, San Francisco 49ers receiver R. C. Owens played out his option year and became a free agent. If there was an informal gentleman's agreement not to sign free agents, the Baltimore Colts ignored it and signed Owens (famous for the "Alley-Oop" pass play) for the 1962 season. The owners, aghast that their "generosity" in adjusting the reserve clause had actually created a free agent, promptly enacted a rule saying that a team signing a free agent had to provide proper compensation to the team losing the player. This rule naturally made signing free agents less attractive, so players received little benefit from playing out their option. Ollie Matson, Billy Barnes, and John Adams later played out their option season and became free agents; the first two re-signed with their original teams, while Adams signed with a new team, which gave up a draft choice to his original team.[45]

George Halas disputed Ratterman's claim of a blacklist against free agents. When told that Frank Fitzgerald claimed there was a blacklist, Halas tried to discredit Fitzgerald: "That is Ted Collins's son-in-law. He did not know very much about football, to be frank with you. He was just a son-in-law, who was put in there — trying to save a buck." Halas claimed he would be willing to sign a free agent.[46]

Players Association

Halas went on to testify that his players were ambivalent about joining the Players Association. He quoted an article in the *Washington Post and Times Herald*, dated February 14, 1957, in which Bears player Stan Jones said, "After talking it over, we felt we'd have nothing to gain by belonging to the association. Halas is more than generous with us, we feel. When you're being treated right, I don't think it's any time to be complaining." Jones went on to say that Halas already gave them most of what the association was bargaining for.[47]

The ever-mercurial George Preston Marshall told reporters in November, "Most of the things the Association promulgated at the last league meeting were ideas many of us in the league had tried unsuccessfully to put across. . . . Now we've stabilized and standardized training camp dates and procedures, the process of cutting players from the roster, pre-season games, transportation, equipment and so forth. I also think it helped to get the player limit boosted from 33 to 35. All these things are in the interest of establishing equality of competition." He remained adamant in his dislike of the association: "There are inherent dangers in a league association of players and I've always pointed them out. I think it is bad for players on one team to be in a position to tell players on another team what to do." In fairness to Marshall, he probably thought the same of one owner telling another owner what to do.[48]

At this point in the hearings, Bert Bell made his big announcement, his "long bomb," if you will: "Accordingly, in keeping with my assurance that we would do whatever you gentlemen consider to be in the best interest of the public, on behalf of the National Football League, I hereby recognize the National Football League Players Association and I am prepared to negotiate immediately with the representative of that association concerning any differences between the players and the clubs that may exist. This will include the provisions of our bylaws and standard players' contract which have been questioned by members of this committee." After being congratulated by Emanuel Celler and the other members of the committee, Bell repeated the owners' excuse that prior recognition had been lacking because they were not sure the association "was truly representative of the players in the league." After a couple of skeptics asked whether Bell had authority for his statement, he replied, "Mr. Chairman, I do not think there is anyone against this association. I think what they have to do is find out, exactly what it is and what it means, and so forth; and that is my job." Although it was not quite spoken in Casey Stengelese, Bell's last sentence was sufficiently vague to satisfy everyone for the moment. Shortly thereafter, Bell and Miller exchanged letters outlining the basic agreement between the players' agreement and NFL owners; these letters were entered into the committee's records.[49]

The players, emboldened by Congress' disapproval of owner activities, considered filing a $4.2 million lawsuit against the NFL, alleging antitrust violations, but Creighton Miller advised them to hold the lawsuit as a threat to get owners to comply with their demands. While no one was agitating for free agency, Miller said the $4.2 million figure in treble damages was based on the difference between what "the players are getting now and what they would be able to get if they were able to offer their services to an open market." How Miller ascertained the difference was not divulged; it would have been of great interest to economists. Considering the congressional scrutiny they had endured over the last few years, NFL owners might have decided that capitulation was the prudent course, so they unanimously granted all of the demands except recognition of the Players Association. Bell, however, exerted his leadership and told them they "would have to accept as a fait accomplishment [sic] his own recognition of the player organization which he had made before the Celler committee. Bell emphasized that the topic wasn't even on the agenda; it had been consummated." Sportswriter Joe King believed that the owners had undercut Bell the previous January, leaving Creighton Miller to doubt his reliability. No wonder Bell took credit for the outcome: "I recognized the Association before Congress and the owners today approved my action."[50]

At the next set of hearings, in 1958, the committee queried Bell as to the owners' actions. Bell was able to report that an injury clause had been attached to the players' contracts as of January 1958, although he admitted that the owners had not consulted with the players in the writing of the clause.[51]

Players still didn't completely trust the owners. The committee received a letter from "Unnamed Prominent Football Player." This player urged the committee to consider its decision on the reserve clause carefully: "If you give football 100 percent exemption from the antitrust laws you people will be betraying 420 men thereby giving them absolutely no recourse by law. I am a layman in regards to law but know every man has the right to sue when dissatisfied. If you give pro football exemption, a player wouldn't be able to appeal to anyone but Commissioner Bell. Mr. Bell does a fine job for the league but his natural leanings are toward the desires of the owners because they, the owners, determine his salary and retention." The player asked the pertinent question, "Why shouldn't a player perform with the team of his choosing?"[52]

The 1958 hearings included testimony from prominent college coaches, including Oklahoma's Bud Wilkinson, Duffy Daugherty of Michigan State, and Bowden Wyatt of Tennessee. Wilkinson and Daugherty thought the pro players should get more than fifty dollars per preseason game. Daugherty thought that players who were cut from the thirty-five-man roster should be free agents instead of being included on a draft list. He also thought that players who made the roster should have a guaranteed salary for the season, regardless of injuries or release. Using the coaches' logic, one could argue that college players should receive more compensation than they did, but none of the congressional committee members was so impolitic as to broach that topic.[53] Wilkinson stated that he knew that

> The contract in certain cases has been altered or another contract has been written privately to cover the boy beyond the form contract. . . . The advice that I would give anyone is, first, that he should find out exactly how much money he is worth. . . . Also, I think that normally speaking he should get as much professional advice on the contract as it is possible to get. And commensurate with his ability, now, he ought to ask that the "24-hour release" clause of the contract be voided, and things of that sort. . . . I would advise him to demand everything the traffic will bear.[54]

Of course the NFL owners' recognition of the Players Association hardly meant the end of labor strife between labor and management. A year later, Billy Howton, president of the association, clashed with owners over bubble gum contracts, as well as over extra pay for preseason games.[55]

The players' next goal was a player pension plan. Bell's ballyhooed claim that NFL players viewed playing pro football as a temporary avocation and not a career, as witnessed by the three-to-four year average playing stint, was used as an argument against implementing a pension: players simply did not stay long enough in the league to make a pension feasible. Such an argument might have been plausible if a pension had been intended to provide for a player's full retirement income. After the obligatory stonewalling by Bell and the owners, the pension plan moved forward. Carroll Rosenbloom preferred a different plan in which players or owners put money into an investment fund for future use, not necessarily for retirement income.[56] Insurance advisor Bill Dudley estimated that a modest pension could be started for $338,000, of which $125,000 would come from player contributions and the remainder might come from extra preseason exhibition games. Joe King wrote, "The plan, as devised by Dudley, would require at least 75 percent player participation, to be workable, and to be approved legally. The anticipated benefit would be $100 a month at age 65 for athletes who had worked in the NFL for five years. A six-year man would draw $110, a seven-year player $120, etc."[57] Dudley proved persuasive, and Bell and the owners did their usual turnabout. A few months later, the owners unanimously approved a noncontributory player benefit plan giving immediate insurance protection to current players and promising undefined monthly benefits to retired players at age sixty-five. In the league meeting minutes of April 23, 1959, Bell emphasized the favorable publicity to be had from initiating such a benefits plan. The package included a $5,000 life insurance policy, hospitalization and medical coverage for players and their families at league expense, and the pension. To qualify for the pension, a player had to serve five seasons in the league, defined as four full seasons and at least one game of a fifth season. The plan was to be financed by the increased television fees for the annual championship game.[58]

While NFL players had made progress, they still chafed under the owners' control, although they sometimes expressed their dissatisfaction ambiguously. In an article by Dick Schaap, John Reger, secretary-treasurer of the Players Association, stated, "There's nothing in the contract for the players, it's all for the owners. . . . [but] the owners are pretty fair to us." He then added, "There are some ballplayers making a lot more money than they're worth." Schaap claimed, "If there is one single factor that spawns revolt among professional football players, it is the option clause and the way it operates. Almost no one seriously disputes the necessity of some sort of option clause . . . the result would be chaos." Even the vaunted player pension was being used by owners to keep players from jumping leagues. The owners saw to it that the players who jumped leagues forfeited their pension. To combat potential abuses, Creighton Miller said, "We want a player representative on the pension board. We'd be happy if the owners picked one man and we picked another to work with Rozelle."[59]

Years later players would become adamant about obtaining real free agency. By then it would be a fight for Pete Rozelle and a somewhat different cast of owners. Perhaps fittingly from a historical perspective, several African American players would lead the fight to end the chattel-like status of NFL players.

Conclusion

Player rights advanced slowly in the postwar period. The increased leverage that coincided with the AAFC, Canadian football, and AFL combined with congressional scrutiny to enable players to achieve modest goals. The improved player rights certainly did not jeopardize the NFL's prosperity.

11

TELEVISION

After World War II a new sense of anxiety gripped the entertainment industry. To be sure, nascent anticommunist hysteria was simmering, but the specter of television perplexed professional team sports owners, the motion picture industry, and the radio industry. These three mass entertainment forms had followed each other and, in some cases, had augmented each other during the first half of the twentieth century. Television, which offered both sight and sound along with all the conveniences of being home, threatened to supersede the other forms.

An Initial Overview of Television and Professional Sports

Chroniclers of the NFL's history laud the league commissioners' and owners' "enlightened" attitudes toward television. These historians believe that the league adroitly used television as a way to become America's most popular and successful professional sports league. As a comparison, they point to Major League Baseball owners' individualism, which they claim led to the diminution of Minor League Baseball.

In a passage that is typical of the historians' viewpoint, Craig Coenen summarized the beginning of television's relationship with the NFL: "Although it only made up as little as 3 percent of a team's total revenue, television soon became an essential source of income for many NFL teams. In the early 1950s, money earned from local TV deals, the 'game of the week,' and play-off telecasts often meant the difference between profits or losses."[1] He repeated the arguments that television hurt Major League Baseball and Minor League Baseball and that football was better suited for television than was baseball. Furthermore, he believed that the growing disparity in television revenue between teams threatened the long-term stability and competitive parity of professional football. He credited Bert Bell with recognizing early on that the disparities needed to be addressed, and cited a John Lardner article in *Newsweek*, which stated that the commissioner needed to "implore the rich to stop trying to corner the market on TV deals and spread it around to the have nots."[2] In these accounts, the historians painted a portrait of NFL owners of successful clubs altruistically sharing their gains with those less fortunate, due in large part to the persuasive abilities of Bert Bell and Pete Rozelle. Baseball, by contrast, was reputedly dominated by a few selfish and shortsighted owners. You may certainly call baseball's owners many things — they were not a particularly sympathetic lot — but whether successful NFL owners were more altruistic remains ambiguous, as was shown in the chapter on revenue sharing.

Disentangling the effects of television from other factors that affected attendance at NFL games during the late 1940s and early 1950s is not easy. Television's role in the downward slide of movie attendance during the late 1940s is undoubtedly exaggerated, as movie theaters experienced general declines in audiences before television became widespread. By 1950 the number of television sets nationwide had just begun to exceed one million. Many areas of the southern and western parts of the nation lacked television stations, in part due to a moratorium on issuing new station licenses. Milton Berle became renowned as "Mr. Television," but some observers believed that his popularity peaked while television was largely relegated to the northeast quadrant of the country. His shtick, a mixture of Borscht-Belt sensibility and broad humor, might not have played as well in the rest of the country.[3]

Television may have simply reflected a changing attitude or preference with regard to leisure time. The notorious baby boom of the late 1940s through the 1950s may have made attending a game in person less attractive, as young males, now burdened with domestic responsibilities, found themselves with competing uses for their evenings and weekends. Rising incomes and more widespread car ownership opened up new possibilities for leisure activities.

Televisions also represented a major investment for many families. The early sets, primitive as they were, were far more costly in inflation-adjusted dollars or in terms of amount of hours worked needed to purchase one than they are today. A cheap nineteen-inch color television, if you can even find one at a big box store today, costs less than ten or twelve hours of labor at around $15 per hour. In 1946 a nineteen-inch set was a "big screen" television, frequently purchased by bar owners; most screens on home televisions ranged from five to twelve inches in size. At average hourly earnings of $1.08 for manufacturing workers, a $350 television in 1946 represented hundreds of hours of labor.[4] A modern television, of course, is vastly superior to the models available in 1946–50. The early televisions required owners to get up and change the channels manually. Older readers can recall the irritation when the picture rolled, requiring adjustment of the horizontal control. Photographs of 1950s American cities showed rooftops crowded with antennae.

Television's role in "killing Minor League Baseball" is also exaggerated. In the wake of the postwar boom in spending on sporting events, many entrepreneurs in absurdly small towns decided the time was propitious for forming new teams and leagues. When the boom proved ephemeral by 1948 and 1949, many of the teams in the small towns disappeared. The proportion of teams collapsing was similar whether there were very many or very few televisions in the vicinity of a team.[5]

The NFL owners' initial reaction to television was mixed, although some owners were hostile to the new technology. Radio proved an imperfect substitute for being at the ballpark, as it engaged only the auditory sense. Television, which stimulated both sight and hearing, promised to be superior to radio as a substitute for actual presence at the game. Still, the owners' fears were likely overblown. Readers must not compare today's NFL television experience to that of sixty years ago. Black and white described not only contemporary racial mores but also television pictures. The telecast-enhancing techniques of instant replay, split pictures, and isolation shots, to name a few, existed only in the imaginations of visionaries. It may have been true that if the weather was inclement or the game unattractive, television afforded fans a handy excuse to skip traveling to the stadium. Because the technology was rapidly evolving, NFL owners' hesitance to fully embrace the new medium is understandable; that they may have made missteps is also understandable. The scientists, engineers, and entrepreneurs developing television were confounded by the medium's effects, too.

Television Arrives (Sort Of)

Television technology was nearing readiness for consumer use in 1939. During the spring of that year, experimenters televised some baseball games. The television people turned to football in the fall. A review in the *New York Times* practically rhapsodized about the telecast.

> Football by television invites audience participation. The spectator at the gridiron does not have that intimacy with the players. . . . But by television the contest is in the living room; the spectator is edged up close. . . . The quarterback is heard calling the signals. . . . It is such information that makes the telecast as interesting as a broadcast, plus the picture. . . . Telecasting calls for action. That is why a prizefight has 100 percent television value. There is plenty of action on the gridiron and that is why football is classed as a "natural" for the camera.[6]

Ace Parker recalled the first NFL game ever televised: it was an October 22, 1939 game between the Eagles and the Brooklyn Dodgers at Ebbets Field. Parker said none of the players knew the game was being telecast. Announcer Allan Walz recalled, "We used two iconoscope cameras. I'd sit with my chin on the rail in the mezzanine and the camera would be over my shoulder. I did my own spotting and when the play moved up and down the field, on punts and kickoffs, I'd point to tell the cameraman what I'd been talking about and we used hand signals to communicate. The other camera was on the field, at the 50 yard line, but it couldn't move so we didn't use it much."[7]

Craig Coenen describes how the NFL attempted to instruct radio play-by-play announcers on the "correct" way to do things. The owners were publicity-conscious enough to want the league portrayed in a flattering light. Bert Bell would later use such techniques with television. Radio (and later television) announcers were not allowed to criticize referees, players, and coaches; to dwell on fights on the field; or to make the game more attractive than it was. The latter concern was especially important in the 1930s, when there was less action; there was more emphasis on ponderous running plays and there were relatively few razzle-dazzle pass plays.[8] Critics often accused Bell of censoring television announcers. Fortunately for

Bell's equanimity, he was long dead by the time Howard Cosell appeared on the league's telecasts.

The NFL's Uneasy Embrace of Television

Major League Baseball owners were divided as to the effects of radio broadcasts of home games on attendance. The New York City owners were among the last to permit radio broadcasts. Their hesitance ended when radio stations began bidding for the broadcasting rights. With the introduction of television, baseball owners scrambled to sign up television stations. Craig Coenen thought NFL owners were more welcoming of radio, with several owners allowing broadcasts of games, even though compensation, if any, was modest.[9]

Football owners considered a national radio broadcast of games in 1949. An interesting aspect of this national radio broadcast was Bell's claim that "no member club would receive less for the sale of said broadcast than they were getting the previous year and that the member clubs make no commitments after 1949." The sale of monopoly rights to radio broadcasts appeared lucrative enough for a single radio network to pay more than the total amount the clubs had previously received from individual contracts.[10]

NFL owners also wondered how television would affect the gate. The reader may sympathize with the owners as they faced such uncertainties. The owners certainly understood that gate receipts were their main source of sustenance and that television, at best, would be a handy secondary source. Few observers envisioned the medium's potential for spectator sports. One sportswriter, Arch Ward, quoted Fred Miller of Miller Beer, a prominent sponsor of sporting events: "I can see where the professionals would have more reason to fear television of football, because they have no alumni. No one ever graduated from the Chicago Bears. But the pros are beginning to realize the value of TV and the potentially great benefits it can bring them."[11]

Table 38 demonstrates that even before there were very many households with televisions to worry about, the NFL suffered a decline in per-game attendance. The 1948–51 figures would ordinarily have pleased the owners, but the boom years of 1946–47 altered expectations. The increases in per-game attendance in 1953 reflected, to some degree, the relocation of the weak Dallas team to Baltimore.

NFL owners were interested in television from the beginning. As early as April 1946 Bell signed an agreement with Televisual Productions to film the 1946 and 1947 championship games. NFL owners met with NBC executives early in 1947.[12]

The NFL initially decided upon a laissez-faire policy, similar to the one employed by Major League Baseball: individual owner discretion, as long as the telecast did not violate another team's territorial rights. The NFL's New York Giants signed with NBC to televise their home games for the 1947 season. Since New York City was initially the epicenter of television, the other teams could observe the Giants' experiences with television.[13]

Many, if not all, owners believed that televising home games would have an immediate adverse effect on home gate receipts, although an optimistic few hoped that telecasts would create new fans who would eventually traipse to the ballpark and buy tickets. Most probably understood and applauded Colonel Leland S. MacPhail, co-owner of the baseball New York Yankees, when he told reporters: "Actually, we never have had a complete World's Series sellout in the Stadium. I am determined to have one if we get into the classic. I want every possible help. And television does not come under that heading. I am not interested in furnishing a free show for every tavern with a television screen. I believe it would be harmful to the gate to televise World's Series games out of the Stadium. If the World's Series is to be sold to the television people, consideration of anything under $100,000 would be downright silly."[14] Given that World Series tickets ran between four and five dollars at Yankee Stadium, MacPhail's estimate implied a loss of twenty to twenty-five thousand attendees spread out over up to four home games.

George Halas embraced television early on; he was especially eager when the Pabst Brewing Company paid him $5,000 to telecast a season-ending game against the Cardinals. The game was sold out, but fewer than fifteen thousand fans came to watch because of rain. Halas, of course, pocketed the gate receipts from the fifty thousand tickets sold, but he was so nonplussed at the sight of so many empty seats that he forbade telecasts of Bears home games. This, then, was the evidence upon which he based his decision. On the other hand, he realized quickly that telecasting the Bears' road games would be beneficial; he also worked at creating a network of stations to show Bears games, home and road, outside a seventy-five-mile radius of downtown Chicago. Jeff Davis credits Halas for convincing Bert Bell that the league needed to erect a seventy-five-mile-radius blackout of telecasts of home games.[15]

Bell, himself, frequently spoke of his distrust and dislike of televised NFL games, and he worked to minimize television's damage upon the game. Given the low quality and lack of enhancements in the early telecasts of football games, sportswriter Stan Baumgartner's article is interesting in its sense of television's potential. He reported that the Chicago Cardinals coach, Jimmy Conzelman, was photographed looking at his own game on television. Baumgartner wasn't sure whether this was a publicity stunt or not, but he wrote, "Most football coaches will admit that one of the worst places to follow a game is from the bench. That is why they now station aides in the press boxes to keep in constant contact with the bench by phone. You can spot weaknesses in defenses much quicker from the press box. Now, with television at hand, the head coach can follow close-up players via the TV box at his side — if he so wishes." Bell told Baumgartner that the possibility of having television sets on the sidelines would be discussed at the league meetings. Bell also stated: "At present, our attendance is up even though we are televising games in Philadelphia, New York, Washington, and Chicago. But because of the small number of sets in use and the tremendous amount of money in circulation as well as the continued growth of professional football in popularity, it is difficult to judge."[16]

A year later the owners were still divided. The consensus was that telecasts "affected gate receipts adversely to some considerable extent," but teams in five cities televised their games.[17] After the 1948 season a backlash developed. The Philadelphia Eagles decided to ban telecasts of home football games. Team president James P. Clark told reporters that "great numbers of season ticket holders didn't renew their orders this year. We wrote them to find out why and they told us they'd rather stay home and watch the games on television." Of course the television executives disputed his evidence. They demonstrated that the Eagles had filled Shibe Park to its 35,000 seat capacity for just two games, but each of five college games at Municipal Stadium topped 70,000, even though the games were televised.[18] Clearly it was going to be difficult to get definitive evidence of television's effects on attendance. The Eagles had seven home games in 1947 with 221,847 in attendance (an average of 31,700); in 1948 they had six home games with 155,571 attendance (26,000 average); and in 1949 the figures were six home games with 167,059 attendance (27,800 average). The team's records were 8-4, 9-2-1, and 11-1-0. The refusal to telecast home games didn't appear to have boosted the gate much, although the team's sterling record in 1949 may have ended the "pennant race" early, accounting for the roughly 22,000 in attendance per game for the final three home games.

The New York Giants, after having televised games for the "last four seasons," which would have meant 1945–48, decided to terminate broadcasts of home games. The team was planning a midweek television program showcasing highlights of the previous weekend's games. The New York Bulldogs quickly followed suit, as did Philadelphia and Pittsburgh.[19] Giants official George H. Rohrs made one of the more astute comments regarding the new medium: "The club feels that no final decision on the effect of television at the gate can be given at this stage and that the long range effect of television on sports attendance involves just so much guesswork. Until answers to certain questions can be determined, the Giants will ban the cameras."[20]

The NFL had yet to address another issue associated with television: revenue sharing. Some observers predicted that the NCAA would need to create rules governing the sharing of television receipts with the visiting team.[21] Major League Baseball owners were sharply divided on the issue, with Bill Veeck Jr., then the owner of the hapless St. Louis Browns, arguing that since the visiting team was half the show, they should get some television money. The owners with lucrative television rights refused to share, although they ran the risk of alienating the owners without such agreements. Those owners could retaliate by denying a team such as the Yankees the right to telecast games on the road. In the histories of the NFL and football, surprisingly little has been said about such television revenue sharing; the authors concentrate on the NFL's attempt to get a national TV contract instead of sharing revenue from individual contracts, which might have leveled the disparities considerably. The NFL could have simply ruled that such revenue be split, perhaps along the same lines as gate receipts.

The National Basketball Association owners negotiated a national TV contract in the early 1950s. The contract differed from the famous one

Pete Rozelle would negotiate later in that the home team got a stipulated amount, while the visiting team got nothing. If a team did not appear on national TV, it received no revenue from this source. Before the reader gasps at the apparent unfairness of the arrangement, it is worth noting that not all of the owners wanted to have their home games televised nationally. One owner later admitted the league made a deliberate choice to televise the least attractive matchups, so as not to detract from the already precarious gate.[22] The NBA eventually telecast an equal number of games from each team's venue over a two-year cycle, thereby allowing equal sharing of revenue from national television broadcasts.

The NFL was edging toward its home-field television blackout policy by 1949. A Bears-Cardinals game was blacked out in Chicago, even though it was a sellout. The game had a large audience watching on television outside the city. Bert Bell said, "I feel that eventually television will be big for everyone. But we are sort of standing by and using our judgment, feeling our way, while it is developing." He mentioned that the league was promoting a weekly film of highlights, with former owner Harry Wismer as commentator. Green Bay and Washington were televising all of their games, while other teams were telecasting road games. Reporter Ed Prell ended his article by saying, "That $100,000 [payment for the NFL highlight show] of 1949 probably will look very small in a few years."[23] At the league meeting in 1951, the owners voted eleven to one to allow telecasts in home territory with the permission of both the visiting and home clubs. Visiting teams could telecast the game anywhere as long as it did not interfere with any other team's home game or any other team's road game that was being televised or broadcast back to the home audience.[24] The owners were clearly developing a policy designed to protect home gate receipts.

Bert Bell negotiated a contract with the DuMont Television Network to televise the league's championship game for the next five seasons. The league received $75,000 per season for these rights, with the money designated for the players' pool. Baseball was receiving $800,000 for the 1950 World Series and later signed a six-year contract for $6 million; some baseball owners groused that Commissioner Ford Frick had sold the rights too cheaply.[25] Football owners might console themselves that the World Series was, of course, from four to seven games long.

The Columbia Broadcasting System, the National Broadcasting Corporation, and the DuMont Television Network were developing coast-to-coast networks of stations and the ability to telecast across the country. Television commentator Jack Gould wrote, "The inaugural [sic] of coast-of-coast network television very likely will have a marked effect on the whole world of show business, though the details of such a development are only dimly discernible at this time." A month later, he announced the "televising in color of Saturday's football game between California and Pennsylvania was the first exhaustive test of video in different hues and, more specifically, the transmission method of the CBS, which is on the verge of commercial introduction." The initial results were disappointing: "Most noticeable was the fact that the colors were very erratic in quality and far from true. . . . There may be a big difference in watching color television for twenty minutes and watching it for 160 minutes. That is a new factor in the color situation about which apparently much has yet to be learned."[26]

In another experiment, the Los Angeles Rams pulled in 83,501 fans for a playoff game against the Bears in the Los Angeles Coliseum. The game was broadcast on radio but not telecast. Rams officials pointed out that an earlier game in the Coliseum that had been televised brought in just 18,213 fans. Sportswriter Frank Finch immediately fingered television as the culprit: "TV must take a big share of the blame for the September floperoo." The astute Rams arranged their television contract with the Admiral Corporation and NBC's local video outlet, KNBH, in such a way that if attendance fell off, these two companies would reimburse the Rams. The Rams' six regular-season home games garnered an audience of 158,845 in 1950, but this paled compared to the 269,327 in 1949.[27] The team had similar win-loss records in 1949 and 1950. Not all observers agreed with the "television hurt Rams attendance" thesis. Some fans wrote to the editor of the Los Angeles Times. One argued that the Rams' increase in ticket prices discouraged fans, while another blamed "lousy football and too much tariff. Do you think it good football when the Rams run up 60 and 70 points on other supposed expert pro teams? I wouldn't mind the high scores — if the Rams were making an effort to hold down the other team's score — but have they?" A third fan argued, "No, it's not television. And it's not the prices. It can be summed up in one word: CHEERLEADERS [caps in original]. Yes, cheerleaders. Those obnoxious creatures who cavort about the stadium like so many flea-ridden apes and by dint of the most asinine ruses and schemes, exhort their sheep-like adherents to a game-ruining frenzy."[28] Unfortunately, the Rams' ticket prices for 1949 and 1950 are not available to the author, so we cannot know whether the team raised ticket prices between the two seasons.

The Rams certainly were not helped by games with the lackluster Baltimore Colts, Green Bay Packers, and New York Bulldogs (later Yanks). The latter team was typically a sad-sack outfit, although it sported a winning record in 1950. The Colts, in particular, were an unattractive draw. On the day of the game between the Colts and the Rams, sportswriter Frank Finch wrote, "The kickoff's set for 2 p.m., and about 95,000 good seats are yet available. Baltimore's losing streak of 17 straight extends back to the middle of the 1949 season." Television station KNBH took out a large advertisement in the *Los Angeles Times* proclaiming, "See the 'Rams-Colts' Game Today—KNBH Channel 4."[29]

The Rams' 1950 experience with televising home games became the cornerstone of the league's argument for the seventy-five-mile blackout policy. Fortunately for the NFL, the federal antitrust attorneys did not comb the back issues of the *Los Angeles Times*. After the Bears-Rams playoff game in December 1950, Bert Bell boasted about the NFL's 1950 season and mentioned that the Rams' dropoff in live attendance was compensated for by the team's television contract. At the same time, a sportswriter reported:

> In six league games at the Coliseum this season the Rams drew a total of 158,045 patrons, including those for free. For the same number of games last season, when there were no telecasts, the total was 309,327, or nearly double the 1950 figure. "Of course, we let in a lot more kids for nothing last year," Reeves hastened to point out. The Los Angeles champs did about $340,000 at the gate for their league games here this season. The cosponsors of the telecasts, Admiral Corp. and NBC's local outlet, KNBH, roughly will pay $280,000 for the privilege. This includes guarantees which they made to visiting teams. "The Rams said their sponsors feel that the experiment was a success," the club president said, "and we hope to work out a deal whereby we can televise again next season. Personally, I think TV did a great job of selling the Rams to the public."[30]

Even as the Rams were experiencing a decrease in attendance after televising games, West Coast college football teams were assessing the effects of telecasts upon attendance. While the Pacific Coast Conference's attendance fell in 1950 from 1948 levels (there were few, if any, games telecast in 1948), most of the dropoff came at two schools: University of Southern California and Stanford. The USC Trojans experienced a lackluster season on the field, which was probably the main cause of the school's attendance decline. Other West Coast teams experienced increases in attendance. Disentangling television's effects from the schools' varying performances on the field was difficult.[31]

While owners gradually reduced telecasts of home games, many were finding themselves inextricably tied to the new medium. Some owners, such as George Halas and George Preston Marshall, while they did not show telecasts of home games within the seventy-five-mile radius of their stadiums, developed networks of stations to show such games beyond that boundary.[32] Some of the owners sorely needed the radio and television revenues, and Bert Bell told a Football Writers Association luncheon that such revenues had been "life savers."[33] Sportswriter Joe Williams, citing Bell's favorite example of the precariousness of NFL ownership — forty-three teams were called, but only twelve were chosen — suggested that the owners were finally learning how to profit from television. He described the Giants' experiment with telecasting only their road games: "They figure it can't hurt them, may, on the contrary, help, and what they get out of it (from $5,000 to $10,000 a game) is just so much velvet. Plus good will. What they get is about enough to stand off bad weather box office and in this high risk game one bad gate can mean the difference between red and black ink."[34]

Bert Bell, citing the deleterious effects of television, suggested to the owners that "they will have to gear their expenses to an average attendance of 16,000 to 18,000." In his down-to-earth description, Bell stated:

The movies took the public out of the homes and put them on the streets . . . gave them a mental urge to go places. Television has taken them back off the streets and put them in the home . . . and has given them a different mental approach. It is much easier to sit at home and watch the best actors, the best singers and see the finest plays than it is to go out. People are naturally lazy. . . . They leave home only for the best, a football game of importance. . . . The ordinary run-of-the-mine [sic] contest . . . does not have the power to pull people into parks and stadiums.

The article's author, Stan Baumgartner, quoted Bell as having said that usually an average attendance of twenty-four to twenty-six thousand was necessary to break even. NFL players might wonder whether the television bogeyman was being used to tamp down salaries. Bell also remarked on the necessity of providing adequate parking for the "sizable number of fans coming in from out town, lest fans stay away."[35] Bell's thesis, presumably, would mean that telecasts of playoff and championship games should not affect the gate as much as they would affect receipts for mundane regular-season games. No one seemed to test this.

Bell worked with the DuMont Network to promote NFL games. For the 1953 season he hoped to launch a series of Saturday night games in conjunction with the Sunday lineup. The plan would enable the NFL to televise more games and to boost revenues. The Westinghouse Electric Corporation agreed to sponsor the Saturday telecasts, which it estimated would cost $1,347,000.[36] A few days later, the league announced plans to bring televised games to the entire country in the 1954 season. The NCAA was displeased with the NFL's decision to stage games on Saturday night, as the collegiate organization viewed Saturday as its "territory." The NCAA complained vociferously. Bell told reporters that the league could not discuss Saturday night telecasts with the NCAA, because the Justice Department might construe formal talks "as a conspiracy in restraint of television . . . I don't believe the colleges own Saturday night."[37]

While owners grappled with learning how to coexist peacefully and profitably with television, the technology kept offering new (but not always improved) gimmicks. An experiment with "panorama (four-way) football television programming was a dud. The idea was to present fragments of four games simultaneously, but the viewers complained of being confused."[38]

By the mid-1950s sportswriters were applauding the NFL's handling of television. W. C. Heinz told *Saturday Evening Post* readers that "the N.F.L. has been able to shackle the [TV] monster to its own uses." He quoted Bert

Bell as saying, "I'm a great believer in TV. It creates interest, but it's only good as long as you can protect your home gate. You can't give a game to the public for free on television and expect them to pay to go to the ball park for the same game."[39] Heinz noted that the demise of the DuMont network temporarily disrupted the league's plan for Saturday night football.

In fact, the DuMont network's collapse created a speed bump for the NFL's relationship with television. Until the league could get one of the other national networks to assume a contract, it broadcasted using independent stations, of which it corralled sixty. Bell explained the problem with the independents: "The big networks, because of quantity purchasing, can buy a cable from the A.T.&T. at, say, 25 cents a mile. The independents who could carry our games would have to pay approximately four times that, or perhaps one dollar a mile. The cost on this basis is just too exorbitant and the sponsors couldn't handle it." Bell noted an irony: the Federal Communications Commission set the cable costs. He explained, "It isn't the loss of money that makes us angry. After all, a team that makes money hands 50 percent of it back in taxes. But the public wants to see pro football on TV and we would like to give it to them. To put it briefly, the government wants us to liberalize our TV policy, then makes it so expensive that we can't do it."[40]

Fortunately for the NFL, the Columbia Broadcasting System (CBS), the bellwether network in the country, agreed to telecast sixty-three NFL games during the 1956 season on its 187 stations. An anonymous reporter wrote, "Last year, although pro games were telecast only in regional circuits—by DuMont in the East, ABC in the Midwest, on little 'bastard networks' set up by some of the clubs themselves—it outdrew other Sunday afternoon programs almost everywhere." Bill MacPhail, a CBS official and brother of the baseball New York Yankees' Lee MacPhail (who was, therefore, very well connected in both the television and professional sports worlds) expressed pleasure with the league's telecasts. He would later be one of Pete Rozelle's confidants and allies when the NFL took a giant leap forward with television. In the midst of strong advance ticket sales and the CBS television arrangements with individual teams for regional network telecasts, Bell waxed optimistic. He even advised fellow league official, Maurice Podoloff of the NBA, "Get your games on television!" Bell gave television credit for helping induce women and children to become fans of pro football, as well as for prompting top college athletes to sign with NFL teams instead of taking jobs in industry.[41] The league was also fortunate that the New York Giants were returning to the championship game that season. Giants players certainly benefited from this proximity, as Frank Gifford and Pat Summerall became long-time announcers. Charlie Conerly became a "Marlboro Man," appearing in advertisements for the tobacco company even though he wasn't a cowboy, as were many of the other men who portrayed the "Marlboro Man."

Bell demanded that telecasters observe some NFL guidelines. While his concerns are understandable, some of his edicts appear heavy-handed. He warned telecasters against showing players fighting and recommended that telecasters refrain from criticizing coaches, players, or referees. The league reserved the right to approve, reject, or supersede any broadcasters. Bell strenuously denied that he was exercising censorship, since sports-writers could report on what they observed, positive and negative: "But the broadcasters are different. You might say that they are being paid by their sponsors through the league — or even by the league through their sponsors — and that makes them salesmen for football. You never heard of a salesman saying that his product was no good, did you? Well, we don't want any of our broadcasters saying or even implying that about football. That's what our code is designed to prevent." Bell absolutely prohibited any remarks that involved gambling.[42]

Despite these issues, the league was pleased with television. Bell told owners that "league publicity in newspapers and magazines was at least 15 percent greater than in the past. He said that the CBS-TV show in 1956 was the greatest sports coverage in history, reaching from Maine to Seattle. With 10 or 12 sponsors after the show the Commissioner said that the league is in an excellent position."[43]

During the congressional investigations of professional team sports, the NFL and Bert Bell received more publicity (or notoriety). Each year the committee focused on a key issue: expansion, player control, television, merger, or interlocking ownership. In 1957 some of the committee members worried about closed-circuit and cable television. The underlying assumption held by some legislators was that citizens had a right to see championship games for free on television. Baseball's commissioner, Ford Frick, had pointedly stated that Major League Baseball had no plans to put the World Series on a pay-TV basis. Although Los Angeles and San Francisco football owners were interested in their baseball counterparts' experiences with pay-TV, Bert Bell, too, declaimed piously, "I think the kids of this country deserve to see every sporting event they can without paying for it." A year later he related an anecdote before the Senate committee: "Many a man comes to me at Franklin Field (Philadelphia) now with his kid and introduces his boy and says, 'Well, you used to let me in for nothing. Now I have a little dough. I am bringing my kid with me.'"[44] The specter of pay-TV had induced Ford Frick to tell the Senate Antitrust Subcommittee, "Unless we handle the problem of free TV now, within 10 years there will be no TV problem . . . there will be no baseball."[45] Frick was clearly Bell's match for dire hyperbole. Years later, Pete Rozelle addressed the issue of pay-TV. He thought it would augment but not supplant network telecasts.[46]

Bell's edicts regarding radio and television announcers' behavior came under scrutiny. Bell claimed, "I instruct the radio people. They worked [sic] for football. We are trying in football to do the best to sell football for the players. . . . We do not believe that the television people should teach the kids of this country that a great ballplayer is fighting, and then have him go out and copy it. They follow the play to the end, and they lift the camera if there is a fight going on. . . . We are not selling injuries and we are not selling fights."[47]

Bell now credited television with almost-miraculous powers. He told congressional counsel Kenneth Harkins, "Without radio and television and preseason games, salaries would drop to $100 a ball game, if they would play." Here, Bell's imagination failed him, as he continued: "I don't believe . . . that the television and radio [revenue] will increase very much, for the simple reason that today the price of cables and pickups and the price of line charges and the price of time at the stations have increased so much that the sponsor . . . will not be able to pay more in rights fees than they do today."[48]

The NFL's blackout policy would draw fire from critics and politicians for years to come and would eventually invite congressional scrutiny. Michigan governor G. Mennen Williams and Michigan senator Charles E. Potter hoped that the NFL would lift the television blackout in Detroit of the Lions/Browns championship game. Bell dashed those hopes. The senator postured and asked the Justice Department to investigate the "dictatorial and arbitrary" decision, but Bell replied: "I don't think it is honest to sell tickets to thousands of people, then afterward, when all the tickets are gone, to give the game to television."[49] Other fans evaded the blackout by traveling beyond the blackout radius to watch the game on television. At least for San Francisco fans such a drive entailed going to Reno or Lake Tahoe; fans in other cities had to endure miserable winter driving conditions to escape the blackout.[50]

Warming up for the 1958 congressional committee's investigation into professional sports, Emanuel Celler told reporters that professional team sports owners were pressing for antitrust exemptions for their television policies, including anticipated pay-TV schemes: "The real reason behind the House-passed bill, is that they [baseball club owners] want to be free to continue to be unreasonable in the way they manage baseball's business." Celler may have singled out baseball, but owners from the other sports knew he had all of them in his sights. With the NFL trumpeting its success and prosperity, Celler would be doubly suspicious about the league's activities.[51]

In the wake of "The Greatest Game Ever Played," reporters queried Bell as to whether the league would implement pay-TV, as some suggested pro football was "a ready-made feature for pay-TV." Bell never wavered from his staunch opposition to pay-TV: "A great part of our success came about because through TV we were able to show the public the kind of game we play, and we can maintain our fan support best by continuing to send out our sponsored pictures."[52]

The 1959 congressional committee focused on television blackouts. *Broadcasting* offered an editorial that worried about Senate Bill 2545, which included the seemingly innocuous phrase, "within special geographic areas." The editorial writer worried that the geographic exemption was a potentially devastating loophole that created the possibility of "a total blackout of free TV."[53] Bell told the committee that the NFL:

> operated satisfactorily within the framework of Judge Grim's decision, whose decision was not appealed by the Government and is now the

law of the land. We assume that our regulation of broadcasting and tele-casting consistently with this decision would undoubtedly be deemed "reasonably necessary" by the FCC but we would, of course, be happy to be relieved of the necessity to go before the Federal Communications Commission and rejustifying those regulations. . . . We are hopeful that if the committee should approve this provision of S. 886, you would make an exception in the case of professional football, in view of the Grim decision.[54]

This was Bell's last appearance before the committee, as he died later in the year. How well he would have handled the national TV contract in a later legislative battle is difficult to say. Pete Rozelle proved adept at mar-shalling political support, and it is difficult to imagine how the outcome could have been bettered.

Bell and the owners knew that NFL games were a hit on television. Bell told the owners in January 1958, "In the opinion of people who know, the televised games this year were the hottest program on television. . . . Excit-ing, spectacular games with great spectator appeal made this possible. The League is at the crossroads of television and must not do anything to price itself out of range of the sponsors." With his usual Janus-style approach to television, Bell continued by cautioning, "CBS claims that unless our halftime shows improve we will lose the audience and the sponsors will not have a viewing audience. [He] will get ideas from CBS regarding what they want at halftime. CBS plans to write to teams regarding halftime shows which CBS believes need improvement."[55]

Television began to affect the NFL in unanticipated ways. In 1958 Bell admitted the existence of "television timeouts" for the first time and told reporters the conditions for calling such timeouts.[56]

The possibilities for the NFL and television seemed unlimited. ABC offered to televise Saturday night games at $50,000 per game. The own-ers also opted to contract with DeMet for videotape of league games at $200,000 a year for two years.[57]

One of Bell's last acts that involved television was the announcement that the league would televise taped reproductions of games. The best twenty-six regular-season games would be televised during a special series to air between January 20 and August 20. Most of the proceeds would go toward the players' pension plan.[58]

Table 39 reveals that while NFL teams were steadily increasing their television revenues, their broadcast revenues paled beside those of Major League Baseball. The relatively mild increases in general prices during the 1950s — 16.9 percent between 1952 and 1964 — eroded some of the gains in broadcast revenues during the period (using 1952 as the base year, the adjusted 1964 per-team figures are $846,000 per team instead of $989,000 in the NFL and $1,036,000 per team instead of $1,210,000 in Major League Baseball). The table uses data supplied to a 1977 congressional hearing. The NFL apparently did not provide information on its championship game television revenues. In 1960 the ratio between baseball and football per-team broadcast revenues peaked at 4.14, the highest ratio since 1952. In the years after Pete Rozelle became commissioner, the gap narrowed; by 1964, with the second big national TV contract, the NFL finally surpassed Major League Baseball on a per-team basis. While observers believe the NFL handled TV better than did Major League Baseball, the revenue figures up to 1960 lend scant support for that belief.

The AFL, Rozelle, and Television

Bert Bell had envisioned a national TV contract with revenues split evenly among the teams. Pete Rozelle would make Bell's hopes into reality, but only after an upstart league beat the NFL to the punch. Although historians excoriate Major League Baseball for its failure to implement a national TV policy or to reduce the disparities in television revenue, some baseball executives were just as visionary as their football peers. Detroit Tigers executive John Fetzer, who had considerable experience in the television industry, worked to create a Monday Night *Baseball* program during the mid-1960s.[59]

Bill MacPhail thought that Pete Rozelle understood television better than most people. Rozelle studied the industry, attending affiliate meetings and meeting executives of the largest stations. He also helped CBS promote the game. Since the New York Giants had many adherents on Madison Avenue, he had an easy time enlisting topflight talent.[60]

When Bell died, the twelve NFL teams had individual contracts with the networks, most with CBS. The individual contracts were becoming less attractive to the networks; Rozelle (and probably Bell before him) recognized that awarding monopoly rights to a single network would boost the value of any contract to well above that of a collection of individual team contracts. The deterring factor, of course, was how to do so without triggering adverse antitrust scrutiny.

Lamar Hunt and the AFL owners had sold their collective national TV rights to ABC. ABC was the weakest of the three major networks, but Roone Arledge and others saw professional football's potential to lift a struggling network to prominence. Theirs was clearly a symbiotic relationship. Before awarding the contract, AFL commissioner Joe Foss predicted bids "up to $2,500,000" or $312,500 for each of the eight teams. Harry Wismer, president of the New York Titans AFL franchise, boasted he had rejected a $1.5 million television offer, because it required the Titans to play home games on Saturday afternoons. Wismer had earlier suggested that television would provide a major advantage for the AFL that the defunct AAFC had lacked.[61]

In 1961 reporters quoted Foss as indicating that AFL teams were "doing business in 1961 solely by virtue of their television money." ABC was not only supplying necessary revenue but badly needed publicity.[62] The AFL might also have been presenting a more entertaining brand of football telecast. While its players were undoubtedly inferior to those in the NFL, Foss and the AFL owners allowed a more freewheeling telecast. A reporter asked Foss his thoughts on television policy regarding to player fights. Foss quipped, "I really haven't thought about it, but you never get anywhere backing away from a fight. It's all right with me."[63]

Bert Bell worried about growing disparities between the teams' television revenues as the 1950s waned. The disparities were not too disturbing in the mid-1950s, but later on they showed a marked increase not only in absolute dollars but in proportions. These disparities mirrored those in Major League Baseball, especially in the American League. Baseball, though, wasn't saddled with a tiny market such as Green Bay.

The NFL owners considered extending revenue sharing to television revenue at the 1951 meetings. Philadelphia and Pittsburgh officials moved that "the sums received by any club under a television contract for the actual live playing of a championship or non-championship contest between NFL members shall be paid sixty percent to the home club and forty percent to the visiting club. All of this article is effective for the year 1951 only." The owners split six-to-six on the motion, and they never appear to have considered it again. In addition to the two teams making the motion, Cleveland, Detroit, Los Angeles, and San Francisco voted for it.[64] Major League Baseball eventually enacted a television revenue-sharing plan, according to Kansas City Athletics owner Charlie Finley's testimony before the Senate committee in 1965. Visiting teams would receive 25 percent of the home team's television revenue.[65]

The NFL owners might have found themselves in a Prisoners' Dilemma situation with regard to televising home games. If televising a home game reduced gate receipts by $10,000, but the owner received, for example, $7,500 for telecasting rights, he would benefit from signing such a contract. The television revenue was not subject to the 35 percent league and visitors' shares. If all owners pursued similar policies, the league as a whole would have been worse off. Extending revenue-sharing rules to the television revenue would have prevented such a potentially deleterious outcome.

Pete Rozelle inherited Bell's concerns, but author Phil Patton thinks Rozelle brought a new perspective to the television issue. Patton writes, "Bell's view of the medium remained tied to the knothole theory. He had established the local blackout. Television, he said, was great for building interest in the game, but the live gate had to be protected at all costs. You can't give away what you are trying to sell, he said, enunciating what would remain the league's first television commandment long after selling television rights had become more important than selling seats."[66]

Concurrent with widening disparities in television revenue, CBS's Bill MacPhail warned Rozelle that the NFL's current reliance upon individual team television contracts was unsustainable. NFL TV games overlapped, which diluted audiences; several markets were individually unattractive to networks. Worst of all, although most teams used CBS, a few used NBC or regional networks. MacPhail told the owners that CBS was willing to pay $3 million for exclusive rights to NFL telecasts, to be divided as the league saw fit.[67]

At the March 11, 1960 league meeting, Pete Rozelle presented an overview of the league's television situation. He told the owners that CBS was willing to pay \$3.5 million for a monopoly on national telecasts of the league's games. He suggested a three-year contract but thought CBS might want a five-year contract. To deal with existing disparities in television revenue, he suggested a variation from the eventual equal shares policy: "One plan for distributing the package TV income that seems to meet with the greatest accord is having clubs keep their TV base for 1959, add to this a flat \$150,000 for Dallas as a new club and \$75,000 for the League office, subtracting these amounts from the total of \$3,500,000 and distributing the balance equally among the twelve clubs."[68]

Eleven of the teams had contracts with CBS. Baltimore and Pittsburgh had a joint contract with NBC, while Cleveland had its own regional network. Had one team (perhaps Baltimore or New York) resisted, the other owners might have outvoted them; if unanimity was required, the holdouts might have been offered a side payment. It also helped that the CBS offer of \$250,000 per team was close to the amount the team with the most lucrative contract was receiving under the status quo.[69]

The owners also considered potential antitrust implications.[70] The reader should realize that the NFL was planning to sell *monopoly rights* to CBS, which was a major reason why the network was willing to pay such a large amount.[71]

Rozelle told owners at the January 1961 meetings, "Much of the past year has been spent in developing a television plan for the future. The NFL has been credited with harnessing television and using it to greater advantage than any other sports activity. This position, however, will be lost without planning for the future."[72] Rozelle's ties with Dan Reeves and Vince Lombardi's ties with the Giants helped convince these owners of teams in the largest markets that the equal-shares approach ensured the survival of weaker teams and ultimately strengthened the league. Left unspoken was the fact that the Rams and Giants did not, apparently, have the best television contracts among the teams — the Baltimore Colts did. There was no New York dominance of media revenues, as there was in baseball's American League (and had been in the National League before the Dodgers and Giants headed west). Another possible factor was that unlike baseball's haughty Yankees, Dodgers, and Cardinals, whose owners basically knew only prosperity, longstanding NFL owners of teams in the larger cities had experienced occasional lean years. They knew that prosperity was fragile and perhaps ephemeral.

On January 27, 1961, Rozelle won a crucial vote empowering him to negotiate a television contract on behalf of the league, subject to maintaining the home blackout policy and telecasting road games back to home markets.[73] As New York's Wellington Mara put it, "We should all share, I guess. Or we're going to lose some of the smaller teams down the line, and we've all stuck together." Mara's line exemplifies the attitude that Michael MacCambridge believes was ingrained in the NFL to a higher degree than the other professional leagues: "There was also a sense in which the interior world of pro football — with its draft, salary cap, revenue sharing, stacked scheduling, and 'equity rule' — was a reflection of the best impulses of American egalitarianism."[74] The reader should recall, however, the earlier attempt to redress disparities in television revenue by applying the existing rule concerning the sharing of gate revenue to television revenues as well. The owners were not altruists, and Rozelle's initial halfway proposal to give each team their 1959 base television revenue showed why the equal-shares program eventually passed: the network package was large enough to leave almost none of the owners worse off under the equal shares proposal. Most NFL owners, too, had recently experienced shifting fortunes in their television revenues, as shown in table 11; they knew their existing lucrative individual television deals might dissipate if the team soured. Baseball's New York Yankees consistently made so much more money than their American League rivals that the $6.5 million pact proposed by Detroit Tigers owner John Fetzer was not enough, at least initially, to keep the Yankees from being worse off under an equal shares plan.

A few years later Fetzer worked on a Monday-night national telecast for Major League Baseball. The revenue from the telecast would be split evenly among all the teams. Some senators wondered why the New York Yankees would be interested in such a deal. Fetzer explained, "Ultimately we can increase the price [of the national package] to the extent that all ball clubs will be receiving more money, including the Yankees."[75] Fetzer was shrewd enough to recognize that a successful national television contract depended more on benefiting all the owners than on relying upon any latent altruism.

The actual NFL contract was even more lucrative than that suggested during MacPhail's presentation. Rozelle negotiated a two-year deal with CBS for $9.3 million. Each of the fourteen teams would receive $320,000 a year, which was more than enough, in most cases, to cover each team's player salaries. Rozelle said that only the Baltimore Colts would get less television revenue than in the previous year, but later articles in *Broadcasting* and *The Sporting News* stated that the Giants would be the sole team not getting an increase in television revenue as a result of the deal. As a comparison, the NCAA received $10.2 million for college football telecasts in a two-year deal with CBS.[76] Two months later, Rozelle announced that NBC had won the rights to the league's 1961 and 1962 championship games, with a "record sum of $615,000 for television and radio rights." *New York Times* reporter Val Adams mentioned that the payment was three times what the league had received under the previous NBC contract, and that the $615,000 was more than twice the highest amount previously paid for a single sporting event—a fight between Rocky Marciano and Joe Walcott in 1953.[77]

The courts quickly quelled NFL enthusiasm. Judge Allen K. Grim invalidated the deal on July 20. Judge Grim wrote, "By this agreement, the member clubs . . . have eliminated competition among themselves in the sale of television rights to their games. Clearly, this restricts the individual clubs from determining from which areas the telecasts of their games may be made, since defendants (the NFL) have by their contract given to CBS the power to determine which games shall be telecast and where."[78] Since Bell and the owners had not anticipated they would be looking at a national TV deal in the early 1950s, they never thought to ask for an exemption for such a possibility during the earlier antitrust suit. Grim's earlier ruling primarily covered blackouts. His current ruling threatened to cost the NFL owners over $2 million in lost television revenues; the NFL immediately petitioned the court asking the judge to delay enforcing his ruling, but the judge denied the petition.[79] Commentators wondered whether Judge Grim's ruling would affect existing exclusive contracts between ABC and the AFL and CBS and the NCAA. Had the ruling invalidated the AFL contract, for example, the NFL might have been poorer in television dollars but more likely to rid itself of competition from the AFL, with its attendant higher player salaries. The antitrust case threatened to leave the issue in limbo for too long a period, so Rozelle gambled on getting antitrust-exemption legislation. Once again a Senate panel investigated television and professional team sports.

Rozelle had foreseen that a national TV contract might incite the Justice Department to investigate antitrust issues. When the contract was halted, Rozelle immediately canvassed Washington DC. He garnered the support of such folks as Wisconsin representative John W. Byrnes, representing Green Bay, who wrote to the committee stating his concerns.[80]

Rozelle's proposal was also strengthened by the AFL's success in landing a national television pact with ABC. As Craig Coenen points out, "CBS claimed that only good teams in large markets had profitable telecasts. Soon thereafter, NFL officials made an appeal for a re-hearing. Rozelle thought they had a good argument because Grim's ruling gave the AFL a competitive advantage. Furthermore, Grim's judgment was not in the public interest because CBS's unwillingness to televise games in half of the league's markets meant millions of Americans would not get to watch pro football."[81]

Mostly, though, Rozelle did a good job selling himself and the NFL to the legislators. His statement emphasized growing costs for independent stations, costs which would make them unable to compete for the right to televise NFL games, and, as always, the NFL's "weakest link" theory. Rozelle insisted, "Only by grouping the weaker and stronger clubs and the clubs with more and less favored geographic locations can the league hope to achieve any control over the manner in which its games are telecast. This is the only way the league can maintain sponsorship interest in telecasts of National Football league games, restore order and stability to league television arrangements, equalize television income among the clubs, secure realistic values for television rights, and assure all member clubs of the league of continued access to television facilities and television income."[82] Rozelle cited the unique aspect of professional sports leagues in that "the members of a sports league are engaged in a joint venture where their business interests are closely intertwined and each club is jointly in business with every other club in its league."[83] He also emphasized that even successful teams such as Baltimore depended on television revenue to remain profitable, while Green Bay's survival was predicated on getting a proportional share of the television pie. Rozelle also claimed that "the National Football League, alone among existing sports leagues, is singled out for prohibitions on joint television contracts [unlike the AFL]."[84]

Herbert Maletz, chief counsel for the antitrust subcommittee, established that Judge Grim's earlier ruling in 1953 was predicated on "the theory that the telecasting of football games, resulted in a diminution of gate receipts and, therefore, if attractive games were to be allowed to be shown in another team's territory on the day that team was playing in that territory, a serious financial loss would inure to the home team."[85] Maletz's questioning clearly gave the NFL an opening: by focusing on the ability of such teams as Green Bay to survive financially, the league could provide the cover the legislators needed to endorse the exemption.

The committee entered into the record the revenue figures for radio and TV rights published in *Broadcasting* for 1960 and 1961. In 1960 the combined rights varied from Green Bay's $105,000 to New York's $340,000; in 1961, the combined rights ranged from Green Bay's $120,000 to New York's $370,000. Rozelle later sent Emanuel Celler a letter stating that the true (television only) revenues for 1960 were between $117,000 and $445,000, with all clubs totaling $2,577,000. Rozelle's figures did not identify individual clubs.[86]

Herbert Maletz also asked, "Not until it was prohibited from entering into a package network contract, the National Football League has been operating satisfactorily, has it not, within the framework of Judge Grim's 1953 decision?" Rozelle could only agree. Maletz then went on to quote Bert Bell's testimony from the 1958 hearings stating the NFL's satisfaction with the status quo provided by Grim's 1953 ruling, which has been cited earlier. Bell concluded, "Indeed, the National Football League would be glad to have Judge Grim's decision written into this bill if that would be satisfactory to baseball, basketball, and hockey."[87]

Rozelle had to explain why he had only negotiated with CBS without giving the other networks an opportunity to bid. Rozelle admitted that he had received a telegram from NBC in which the network objected to its exclusion from bidding. He explained his decision:

Realizing the importance of the single network-type contract for some time, we explored how we might bring this about. As of the 1961 season, one network, CBS, had contractual ties on, I believe 9 or 10 of our clubs. CBS was the only network that had firm ties on our clubs for 1961 and beyond. Their tie was a 1961 — a 1961 contract, firm, with 1962 and 1963 first refusal options. So, in effect, they had 9 or 10 of our clubs legally tied for a period of 3 years: 1961, 1962, and 1963. They were the only network that had such ties on any of our clubs.

Rozelle added that TV rights to the league's championship game were awarded through open bidding.[88]

The NFL's deal with CBS threatened to injure other parties interested in telecasting games. These parties, naturally, testified to the deleterious aspects of the proposed legislation. The National Association of Broadcasters asserted, through their vice president for government affairs, Vincent T. Wasilewski, that the CBS monopolization of games would mean that many areas would no longer get two or three NFL games to choose from, but would be limited to whatever CBS offered. Wasilewski also made the valid point, which was not explored, that if the NFL was worried about television revenue disparity, the teams could put their current television revenues into a common pool without needing a exclusive national TV contract with one telecaster.[89] Lee Loevinger, the assistant attorney general of the Antitrust Division, sent a telegram to the committee. He expressed the Justice Department's concerns about the legislation:

> The bill would place in the hands of a few private persons tremendous power over a popular and lucrative sport. . . . The CBS vice president in charge of sports telecasting testified that CBS paid about $1,500,000 to televise 80 percent of the NFL regular season games in 1960. Under the contract declared illegal it proposed to pay $4,650,000 for the television rights to 100 percent of the NFL regular season games in 1961. Thus, to acquire the remaining 20 percent of the games and hold exclusive telecasting rights to the games of all teams, CBS was willing to pay 200 percent of the price it paid for 80 percent of the games. This, to us, is a striking example of the evils of monopoly.[90]

Other witnesses raised concerns about the NFL's encroachment on Saturday and Friday nights, which might harm attendance at college and high school games. Reporter Dave Brady said the insertion of a clause prohibiting such telecasts helped allay such fears and paved the way to congressional approval. One aspect that did not receive too much publicity was the interlocking ownership between the NFL and other industries. William Clay Ford was named president of the Detroit Lions in November. The Ford Motor Company paid $2.5 million to sponsor the NFL, as well as giving new station wagons to NFL owners.[91] Herbert Maletz raised the possibility that the NFL could tie up all three major networks and keep a rival, such as the AFL, from getting television money. Rozelle admitted that the possibility existed, although nothing suggests that the NFL had plans to do so. Maletz later asked Commissioner Joe Foss whether it was possible for the AFL to tie up all three networks. When Emanuel Celler questioned Foss, the latter said his league could only negotiate with ABC, because CBS and NBC were already committed to the NFL.[92]

Sportswriter Jack Walsh wrote that NFL lobbyist Clinton Hester was optimistic about the bill's passage, citing the passage of the 1957 antitrust exemption bill by the House (the bill failed in the Senate). Hester thought Senator Estes Kefauver and Representative Emanuel Celler were sympathetic to the antitrust problems of professional football.[93] An anonymous reporter in the *New York Times* suggested that the NFL was doing an "end run" around the Justice Department.[94]

Rozelle and the NFL got their exemption. After President John F. Kennedy signed the sports televising bill on October 10, 1961, the Green Bay Packers played in the NFL Championship Game. Sportswriter Joe King wrote about the small town hosting the first "million-dollar game in pro football history," considering the gate receipts and NBC television rights.[95] Wherever they were, Bert Bell, Curly Lambeau, and Pete Rozelle must have savored the symbolism of the smallest town in all of major league sports having the honor of hosting such a game.

Rozelle would subsequently testify before Congress on several occasions. The 1964 and 1965 hearings centered on blackouts and Friday night football, but the stakes were not as high. His testimony in the 1966 AFL-NFL merger hearings proved another highlight, but the 1961 hearings would remain his finest hour.[96]

Conclusion

Television historian Benjamin Rader summarized the NFL's and television's synergy: "Televised professional football seemed to be perfectly suited to the needs of the growing white-collar and professional classes in the United States. According to the national public opinion polls, the game appealed most to the 'successful,' to those who had the benefit of a college education, who lived in the suburbs, held jobs in the professions, and enjoyed higher incomes than the national average. Pro football, while not offering the same hoary mystique as baseball, reflected its fans' work experiences." Rader went on to compare football's "clock oriented" nature, calling it a "corporate or bureaucratic sport."[97]

NFL owners were ecstatic with their 1962–63 deal, but their joy was trebled a few years later. Rozelle got CBS to pay $14 million per year. Some of his owners were incredulous, as Rader relates:

ROZELLE: Art [Modell, owner of the Cleveland Browns]? Art, CBS got it. For fourteen million.

MODELL: How much?

ROZELLE: Fourteen million, Art.

MODELL: [long pause] We-e-ell, it could be worse. I did expect a little better, but hell, Pete, seven million a year isn't half bad. We can make it.

ROZELLE: Art—Art—FOURTEEN MILLION A YEAR. Twenty-eight million for two years.

MODELL: [longer pause] Pete, you gotta stop drinking at breakfast.[98]

In another strong reaction, Vince Lombardi was convinced the television deals saved football in Green Bay.[99]

Television, though, could be a Janus-like master. NBC, losing out in the bidding, decided to retaliate by paying the AFL $42 million for five years. On a per-team basis, the money was reasonably close to the NFL's payout of $1 million per team. The NBC contract ensured the AFL's survival and enabled these owners to make stronger bids for college talent, culminating when the Jets signed Joe Namath.[100] NFL owners could assume that much of their increased television revenue would eventually end up in the pockets of the players, which, to some readers, may seem just. Television altered the way sports were played as well. The television time-out was one of the minor irritants, but the medium would come to dominate the games, dictating starting times of games and interfering in other ways.[101]

12

INNOVATION

By the 1940s Major League Baseball had an established product and team owners were loath to tinker with the game on the field. Not until the early 1970s, when American League owners worried about a dearth of offense, did they make a radical change to the playing rules in the form of the designated hitter.

Football was in a state of flux after World War II, both at the collegiate and professional levels. The game before the war would probably seem primitive and dull to modern eyes, although the game was physically tough. The modern passing game was in its infancy, with such purveyors as quarterbacks (sometimes referred to as throwing halfbacks) Sammy Baugh and Sid Luckman and receivers such as Don Hutson developing techniques and tactics. Why did the NFL owners change the rules of their game?

The NFL faced competition from college football. The NFL owners strove to promote their brand of football as superior, whether because only the best collegiate talent played in the NFL or because the league implemented rules that improved the game and proved more satisfying for the fans.

Businesspeople in general try to avoid having their product perceived by customers as "perfect substitutes" for another firm's product or service. If multiple firms are perceived as producing perfect substitutes — in other words, if their products are interchangeable — none of the firms has the ability to raise its prices without losing all its customers. Firms producing perfect substitutes have no price-setting power; they are at the mercy of the market forces of supply and demand, which determine prices.

In order to avoid the unenviable situation of being perceived as providing perfect substitutes, owners of many products try to create positive differentiability in their products. Coca-Cola and Pepsi officials have expended millions of dollars trying to convince consumers that their products are different and better. Athletes, too, work hard at honing a unique set of skills. All these efforts, if successful, can give the owner or athlete price-setting power.

NFL owners, then, hoped to differentiate their games by introducing a host of new rules designed to create excitement and crowd-pleasing scoring. By doing so, the owners could increase their price-setting power (in economic terms, they could make the demand for their product less price-sensitive or less elastic). As with any innovation, owners had to weigh the potential benefits against the potential costs. For instance, rules to make field-goal kicking easier might mean paying for more footballs. Greater specialization could result in larger playing rosters and attendant increases in player payrolls. Intangible costs had to be considered, as excessive scoring could reduce the game's credibility.

More Scoring

In the late 1960s, when the NFL was becoming the most popular professional sports league in America, Major League Baseball went through a scoring drought. Commentators wrung their hands as the scoring drought in the American League coincided with the decline of the Yankees. Overall American League attendance rose in 1966–68 compared with 1961–65. National League attendance peaked in 1966 before falling in 1967–68. According to many observers, following the NFL was more exciting than watching baseball teams stagger to a 2–1 outcome (shades of soccer). In the NFL's early days, its scores had often mimicked baseball scores.

During the 1930s the NFL had revised its playing rules to assist the passing game. They moved the hash marks in from the sidelines. They also streamlined the ball, which helped players pass it. By placing the goalposts at the front of the end zone instead of the back, the owners made field goal attempts more attractive.[1] Scoring soared, and shutouts became rare. The league's brand of football featured more passing and scoring than many college games. The forward pass enlivened the game. By 1950, though, some people thought the tilt toward the offense had gone too far. One sportswriter broached the heretical question, "How long will it be before the rules committees (pro and NCAA) are forced to legislate against the forward pass in order to preserve the game of football?" He cited evidence that NFL teams attempted fewer than thirty passes per game on average in 1936, but in 1949 the average was almost fifty-five. In addition to more pass attempts, quarterbacks completed a higher percentage of passes (45.6 versus 35.3). Of course, as passing became more efficient, teams had an incentive to resort to it more often. The Los Angeles Rams' coach, Clark Shaughnessy, bemoaned the lack of defensive backs who possessed speed and quickness.[2]

The NFL had succeeded in distinguishing its game from the college game by emphasizing a more open style. By 1948 Hy Turkin, a long-time chronicler of professional sports, wrote that scoring was higher than ever in the NFL. He claimed that "defense is becoming a forgotten phase of the game. But the fans love telephone-number scores, and that's what really counts — especially in the continuing war (for patronage) between the rival leagues."[3]

Table 40 shows the general trend in NFL, AAFC, and AFL games. The NFL's scoring may have increased because the game was speeding up. The league added a fifth official for the 1947 season; this official's tasks included watching men in motion and "dead spots" on the field. George Strickler, the league public relations man, claimed that the new official would quicken play and result in an additional six to twelve plays. His prediction appeared accurate. A year later, NFL officials could show that they averaged 166.6 plays per game, while the AAFC averaged 145. League officials denied that they had concocted the statistic just to downgrade the AAFC and said that such statistics had been calculated for years. Between speedier ball handling by the officials, the league prompting coaches to have their teams spend less time in the huddle, and the developing passing game, play was more rapid.[4] The statistics in table 40 likely differ from the numbers in Prell's article, as they include the actual rushing and passing plays and not other plays. The NFL's number of plays decreased as the 1950s ended and by 1962 the number hardly differed from the 1946 figure.

Lisle Blackbourn, the Green Bay coach, discussed the differences between the pro and college games in 1954. He thought that the evaluation of current players on the roster was fraught with greater risk in the pros. Once a player was cut, other pro teams could swoop in and sign the player, whereas a college player could be relegated to the "B team" but could be brought back to the varsity with little difficulty. Blackbourn believed the position of the hash marks made the field look "15 yards wider." After out-of-bounds plays, the college rules placed the ball 53.3 feet from the sidelines, while the pro hash marks were 60 feet in. Blackbourn commented, "You'd be surprised what a big difference, both in spreading the defense and in making the offense more dangerous, those few feet make."[5]

As table 40 reveals, scoring in NFL games jumped between 1946 and 1947, whether in response to the AAFC or to a greater reliance on pass plays. Both rushing and passing plays, though, averaged more yards per play in 1947 than in 1946. With the exception of 1946, NFL games featured more scoring than AAFC games, but the difference was usually within two and one-half points per game and may be ascribed to the greater number of plays. The AFL featured more scoring and more plays per game in 1961 and 1962 than did the NFL.

College football eventually caught up with the NFL. By the late 1950s college coaches were borrowing heavily from the pros. Forest Evashevski, Iowa coach, told a luncheon, "College coaches must open up their offenses to compete with the pros who are making tremendous inroads through the medium of television."[6] Today's college football fans, inured to rapidly scoring teams such as the University of Oregon and Wisconsin in 2010, would have found 1940s college football less action-packed, but those earlier fans were treated to a "touchdown orgy" in 1949. One reporter described the carnage: "major college teams are blasting away at a record tempo of approximately 40 points combined per contest. This aggregate scoring pace is almost double the touchdown rate for teams just ten seasons ago. The touchdown orgy has brought widely varying reactions from coaches, critics and fans."[7] Even NFL observers bemoaned the forward pass and increased scoring. Joe King reported that Bert Bell "shudders at the thought of [basketball-like scores]."[8]

The playing differences between the pros and colleges had ramifications for the NFL. Presaging the debate about college option quarterbacks' readiness for the NFL, some pundits thought the college coaches' preference for the split-T formation in the 1950s meant that many quarterbacks were not developed correctly for the pro style. As sportswriter Jack Walsh wrote,

"As more schools adopt the Split-T, the potential of good hurlers becomes scarcer."[9]

The college rules committee did go beyond the NFL in one respect. The rules committee voted in January 1958 to allow teams to attempt a two-point conversion instead of the point after touchdown. Sportswriter Robert Burnes reported that coaches initially opted for the two-point conversion on "approximately 55 percent of the touchdowns scored. But they successfully negotiated the two points only 52 percent of the time." Those coaches opting for the point after touchdown (PAT) must have had inept kickers, as Burnes claimed the PAT succeeded only 64 percent of the time, "which is about standard for this time of year. Most coaches agree that as the season progresses, the extra-point kicker will improve his proficiency to a national average of about 75 percent."[10]

Not every coach approved of the two-point conversion option. An anonymous coach whined:

It's horrible, and I shudder to think what it will do to the coaching fraternity. A coach is on enough of a spot already. But with that new rule he's in a totally untenable position. He has to order a two-point try after the first touchdown or else he has not guts. If it misses, the other coach can settle for a one-pointer when he scores a touchdown. And the coach will be blamed whether his team makes or misses a one-pointer or a two-pointer. There will be a new epidemic of ulcers in this business. . . . The most tragic part of this new rule, though, is that it is removing the foot from football. Placement kicking was a dying art in college ball anyway.[11]

NFL owners were lukewarm toward the two-point conversion rule. Because goalposts were on the goal line in pro football, PATs were easier than in the college game, in which the posts were ten yards back in the end zone.[12]

But if college coaches grappled with the volatile attractions of the two-point option and bemoaned the disappearance of the foot in football, NFL commissioner Bert Bell wanted to go a step further. Captain Ahab had his white whale; Bell's bête noire was the PAT. Professional kickers, apparently, had made the PAT almost automatic, succeeding on well over 90 percent of the attempts, unlike their younger brothers in college. Bell stressed that the PAT was automatic and it was dull. In later years, he also claimed that the PAT encouraged bookies and created injuries in the pileups that occurred during the attempts. Other observers thought he wanted to save the cost of footballs, which amounted to a few thousand dollars a season for the entire league. By the 1950s, though, with the NFL's newfound prosperity, it's unlikely that saving money on footballs was a compelling motive.[13] Bell did suggest that if the extra point was eliminated, then touchdowns should count for seven points and a sudden-death overtime rule should be enacted.[14] There was another aspect of the PAT: sometimes it was difficult for the officials to gauge whether the ball had gone through the uprights, which hypothetically extended to infinity. To help the referees, Los Angeles Rams' owner Dan Reeves wanted to extend the goalpost uprights by twenty feet. The sportswriter discussing Reeves's suggestion lobbied for his own solution: a wide-mesh net between the goalposts.[15]

Bell came close to realizing his desire to rid the pro game of the pesky PAT during the January 1952 meetings. The owners voted seven to five in favor of eliminating the PAT and making touchdowns count for seven points, but a supermajority of ten votes was needed, leaving Bell disappointed once again.[16]

Punters did well during the 1950s. Their punting averages ranged between 40.4 and 41.3 yards between 1951 and 1957. Because the defenses had become more adept at covering punts, the average runbacks declined from 10.1 to 5.4 yards. Punt returns for touchdowns had all but disappeared, dropping from fifteen in 1952 to just two in 1957. Baltimore Colts general manager Don Kellett pushed for a rule forcing the punter to be within ten yards of the line of scrimmage, making it more likely that his punts would be blocked and reducing the pressure on returners since the punting team would need to retain some players to protect their punter.[17] Some observers thought the Canadian League's rule of allowing the receiver "a zone of five yards in front of him free of tacklers when he makes the catch" would restore some balance.[18]

Field-goal kickers, meanwhile, were improving their distance kicking. Arthur Daley highlighted the NFL's use of specialist kickers: "When the collegians moved their goalposts ten yards behind the goal line, the pros didn't budge theirs. So the excitement of a pro game gets added stimulus from the phenomenally successful field-goal kickers. Rare, indeed, is a field goal in a college game. Rare is a pro game without one."[19]

Two-Platoon Football

Possibly in response to the nascent AAFC, the NFL modified its substitution rule before the 1946 season. The league had been experimenting with ever more liberal substitution rules in the hope of reducing injuries and keeping players fresher.[20] Now three players could come in at once while the clock was running, and unlimited substitution was possible when the clock was dead.[21] George Halas opposed unlimited substitution. The substitution rules had been liberalized during World War II in response to a player shortage. Halas worried that "the present free-substitution rule will do more to kill fan interest in the game than anything I know. It has taken the personality out of football. The first game I saw this fall players were going in and out in such a steady stream I couldn't identify them. I'm still trying to find out who did what."[22]

Coach Jim Conzelman believed that specialization also meant fresher players in the fourth quarter: "We're seeing in the fourth quarter now the kind of football we used to see in the first quarter. The boys wore out and the game became more of a tugging match." He stated that the corollary of the freshness was that a fourth-quarter lead was no longer as safe as in years past, making for a more exciting game.[23]

Another possible ramification was the trend toward behemoths. Football players always tended to be bigger than the average Joe, but with two-platoon ball, a truly huge man was more likely to endure in the game. Sportswriter Watson Spoelstra remarked on Les Bingamon's 300-pound weight: "During the 1954 season, Bingamon was the only player to admit to being such a weight. Nowadays, many linemen are well in excess of 300 pounds."[24] The Baltimore Colts' fabled defensive front four — Big Daddy Lipscomb, Art Donovan, Don Joyce, and Gino Marchetti — weighed 240 to 288 pounds each.[25]

With improved pay, two platoons, and more teams, more NFL players continued playing into their thirties. Whereas Sammy Baugh's sixteen seasons of play had been an oddity, by 1960 forty players were over thirty years old and at least 125 players had played for five or more seasons. These trends gave the league continuity and experience.[26] A year later, sportswriter Joe King elaborated on this trend of older, more experienced players in pro football: "The founding of the AFL has divided the rookie supply and made it possible for an old gent here and there to hold on an extra season. Intense specialization at each position on offense and defense makes it more difficult for the rookie to learn all the tricks of the trade and oust the knowing old pros."[27] Quarterbacks, in particular, were enjoying longer playing careers, perhaps because of higher pay and because they no longer had to play defense under the two-platoon system. By 1960 the average age of the top fifteen quarterbacks in the league was 30.1 years, compared with an average age of 25.5 for all players.[28]

The NFL and college football diverged sharply on the issue of two-platoon football. After the war, colleges allowed liberal substitution that was tantamount to two-platoon football, but by the early 1950s, the Football Rules Committee of the NCAA was advocating a change to the two-way players of the past and for limited substitution. For modern fans, the idea that specialists, such as kickers, had to play on all downs is almost as foreign as using a football that was more akin to a rugby ball. Many coaches, perhaps even a majority, opposed reverting to the old style. Athletic directors, "beset with budgetary problems caused by rising costs and generally declining receipts," proved amenable to the reversion. Sportswriter Joseph Sheehan pointed out, though, that "the rules committee's action basically represents a 'coup' by the administrative group."[29] Sheehan continued by listing the ostensible benefits of limited substitution: it eliminated the "ridiculous extremes" of specialization, restored spectator appeal, and helped the smaller colleges compete by requiring fewer players. The opponents of the reversion retorted that two-platoon football gave more players opportunities to play, reduced injuries, cut down practice time, improved the caliber of play, and lessened competition for top players. It is certain that cost saving was a crucial reason; one writer cited the fact that "about fifty colleges have abandoned football recently."[30] Columnist Arthur Daley lauded the restoration of single-platoon football. He admitted that economic forces provided the key impetus, but he saluted "this revolutionary step . . . taken by the football fathers with admirable unselfishness. Although they are representatives of 'big' schools, they considered the 'little' schools and acted solely for the greater good of the game." He termed the change "the best thing that has happened to the gridiron game since the abolition of the flying wedge." He attributed the attendance decline at college games to the growth of specialists: "Individual personality was stamped from the game in favor of mob scenes of faceless robots. Even the coaches couldn't keep track."[31]

The colleges would restore the unlimited substitution system by 1960. A clear majority — 392 out of 590 votes — favored the restoration, although the NCAA took halting steps toward a full restoration, beginning with a wild-card substitution rule allowing teams to send in one substitute after each play without affecting reentry.[32]

Sudden Death

NFL owners resisted sudden-death overtime throughout most of the postwar era. They voted down proposals for such overtime periods in 1945 and in 1946. There was one compelling reason to get rid of ties, as George Strickler, the league's publicity director, pointed out that since ties were not computed in the league race, determining the champion could get complicated.[33] The league rules committee eventually approved sudden-death overtime for playoff games, setting the stage for the 1958 championship game between the Giants and the Colts.[34]

A Motley of Innovations

In addition to sudden-death overtime, NFL owners also resisted such fan-friendly and inexpensive innovations as putting numbers and names on jerseys.[35] Owners favored the numbering of players during the January 1952 meetings, although George Preston Marshall cast the lone dissenting vote.[36] A decade later AFL owners decided to put names on their players' jerseys. Some owners cited baseball impresario Bill Veeck Jr.'s concern about placing names on home jerseys: doing so might reduce program sales. Veeck's concerns were misplaced, and scorecards continued to sell as well as before.[37]

Because of the evolving rules and the difficulty of understanding what penalties were involved in plays, one observer suggested hiring an official who would sit in the press box and explain the rulings. He quoted one (anonymous) referee, who maintained that most of the coaches didn't know all of the rules: "I wonder how many could pass that examination we have of 100 trick questions on football decisions. How many would get 25 percent on the exam?"[38]

While NFL coaches had a tacit agreement not to have players fake injuries in order to stop the clock, Commissioner Bell pushed for a rule whereby twenty seconds would automatically be run off the clock in the event of an injury to a player on a team that was losing or was tied.[39]

The AFL patterned its game after the successful NFL style, but, in an attempt to bolster the passing game, it introduced (just as the NFL had years before) a more aerodynamic ball: the Spalding JV-5. This ball was slightly longer and slimmer than the NFL Wilson model.[40]

Some coaches experimented with electronics. Paul Brown, never one to shy away from the innovative and always one who liked to exercise tight control over his quarterbacks, decided that inserting a radio receiver into his quarterback's helmet was just the thing. Brown, renowned for shuttling offensive guards bearing play calls in and out of games, decided direct (but one-way) communication was superior. The receiver added about a pound to the quarterback's helmet. Paul and his quarterback, George Ratterman, tried the receiver in an exhibition game in Akron. They declared it a success, although the system broke down in a later game.[41]

Brown also wanted to hook up by shortwave with some of his assistant coaches who were stationed high up in stadiums, so they could have instantaneous communication. The shortwave idea caught on, and several other teams introduced their versions. The wondrous innovation came with a flaw; New York Giants officials admitted that they had tuned in on the Browns' shortwave transmissions. The Giants had signed Gene Filipski, who had been "hidden" by the Browns in the Canadian Football League. Filipski knew the Browns' signals and could translate them for the Giants. The Giants won the game 21 to 9. As a result of the Giants' interception, the owners voted to bar such communication.[42] During that same season, the Los Angeles Rams used a closed-circuit television system so that coaches could instruct their teams between plays. The league wasn't Luddite about technology, though; at the same time, they established a game-film exchange between teams.[43]

The Chicago Cardinals presaged the Chicago Cubs' ill-fated experiment with multiple head coaches. After Jim Conzelman led the team to its greatest success, winning the 1947 title and being the runner up in 1948, owner Charles Bidwill replaced him with Buddy Parker and Phil Handler as co-coaches. The experiment last half a season, after which Parker was made sole head coach for the remainder of the season.[44]

Although Red Grange and the Chicago Bears went on a tour in which they played several games per week in 1925, the typical NFL schedule featured one game per week. Jock Sutherland, coach of the Pittsburgh Steelers, thought that teams could play two games a week, although they would need more players. He hoped that such a schedule (which would presumably lead to more games per season) would help bolster the NFL's sagging profits during its war with the AAFC. Nothing came of his idea.

One innovation the league didn't need at the time was drug testing. The pharmaceutical approach to football hadn't taken root in the NFL. In 1960 a player admitted to using Benzedrine to ward off fatigue.[45] Whether players used such recreational drugs as marijuana or heroin remains conjectural. Certainly the league did not see any need to implement testing policies. Many players probably self-medicated in some fashion, and alcohol was undoubtedly a popular means of escape.

Violence and Mayhem at the Old Brawl Game

While football is exciting, many fans are likely to watch because of the violence, the controlled mayhem. NFL owners understood this crucial part of the sport's allure. They also knew that dirty play would allow critics to brand the sport a "legalized brawl" and would sully the game's reputation. They further realized that injuries to marquee players were detrimental. The challenge, then, was to hew a fine line between sporting and detrimental violence.

Although sports fans are familiar with the iconic image of a professional hockey player sans teeth, NFL players could empathize (as could NBA players facing errant elbows). One reporter described the Philadelphia Eagles' "Bridge Club," a society of players who had lost their front teeth. "These toothless wonders agreed a football player wasn't really one until those front molars [sic] had been sacrificed at the altar of the sport."[46]

Bert Bell continually rebutted charges of "dirty play" by claiming, perhaps too vociferously, "Not in the National [Football] League." He did admit that tempers flared and "we have some scraps. . . . That's natural and they may exchange a few punches, but that's not dirty football. That is good, honest, real, go-get-'em spirit." As a former collegiate player, Bell certainly understood the game in a way that sportswriters and other observers did not. He insisted, "Professional football is rugged play by rugged men. It is also played by men who know how to take care of themselves. They have a code of their own. Any newcomer who plays dirty football learns quickly to cut it out, or they teach him. Players who play dirty don't last." He continued by lauding his referees and their efforts to regulate the violence. "Sometimes what looks like a foul from the stands is not a foul. It depends upon the angle from which it is seen."[47]

Some players, coaches, and owners were not shy about revealing some of the shenanigans that occurred during games. A few years after Bell's categorical denial described above, famed quarterback Otto Graham slyly insinuated that there were dirty players and every opposing player knew who they were: "I'm not suggesting that deliberately foul football is new. It isn't. But it has been increasing in recent years at a rate that worries a lot of people who love the game." Graham blamed the prevalence of the T-formation and the brush block that accompanied it, as it "has led to a lot of easily hidden dirty work." He suggested getting rid of the rule allowing ball carriers to get up after being tackled. In this case, he believed the college rule of an immediate dead ball would "put an immediate stop to some of the carnage that goes on."[48] This was one of the earliest *Sports Illustrated* articles on the NFL, and the editors may have been hoping for a bombshell article to garner attention. Graham appeared to be immune to the rough play, having played all 126 games on the regular schedule during his career.

A 1955 *Life* magazine story, entitled "Savagery on Sunday," went too far. Eagles' players Bucko Kilroy and Wayne Robinson sued for libel, and each won $11,500 settlements.[49]

Because Graham refused to name the dirty players, opposing players and coaches disputed his allegations. The New York Giants apparently took his insinuations to heart, since Graham's interview occurred after a game against the Giants in which he was knocked out. Giants owner

Wellington Mara challenged Graham to provide specifics regarding dirty play. Jim Lee Howell retorted that Graham's lengthy stint as quarterback belied his allegations, since it was "the easiest thing in the world to put a quarterback out of commission. . . . The fact that such quarterbacks as Baugh, Luckman, Waterfield, Graham, Conerly and others were able to play so many years as they did is proof this game is clean, and is a credit to the league." Howell continued by bemoaning Bell's claim that the game was the roughest around: "The commissioner is missing the boat. He is drawing record attendance because of superlative skill, not injuries. The pros no longer need to stress the stretcher."[50]

Howell had been a stalwart critic of unnecessary roughness and dirty play in the NFL. The previous year, he had encouraged Bell to instruct referees and the league to banish dirty players. Howell claimed, "Only a few of the men are really dirty. They don't belong." He anticipated Graham's argument that the T-formation and the accompanying brush blocks encouraged rough play. He also pinpointed something that would make even the flintiest owner flinch: "the unhappy experience of paying salaries to injured men in dry dock for the season."[51]

In response to this attack, Bell reaffirmed the NFL's commitment to "the hard-hitting type of football which has brought the pros national popularity and made them a better gate attraction now than at any time in the past." Bell recollected, "Not so long ago, they used to say the pros didn't try to play football, that they didn't block or tackle or hit. Now some are saying we are playing so hard we are trying to commit murder. . . . My figures indicate there have been no more injuries this year than last, and no more last year than the year before. I don't believe football is becoming more of a risk."[52]

A year later, Graham continued to maintain that dirty play persisted in the NFL, saying, "I think the commissioner and owners could do something about it if they wanted."[53] This time he was joined by sportswriter Melvin Durslag, who wrote, "Never have the pros played better, more exciting ball. Never have division races been tighter nor games more unpredictable. Yet hanging like a pall over the otherwise brilliant play are two nasty words: 'dirty football.'" Durslag described such rough players as the Los Angeles Rams' Don Paul. The previous year, an anonymous writer for *Time* magazine called Paul "the dirtiest player in the league. Pro football being what it is, Paul takes this judgment for what it is meant to be — sheer flattery."[54] Paul colorfully described the difference between his rough play and dirty players. He said that "villains" used a combination of brains and brawn: "We learn to rile backs methodically and slip in the last cuff, the last shoulder, or the last billy goat without getting caught. I guess you'd call it a coldly calculated plan of discouragement." Paul made a distinction between villains and dirty players: "A dirty player [a 'viper' in his words] is one who purposely tries to injure his opponent to get him out of the game. . . . No respectable villain will even talk to a viper. If I met one in an elevator, I'd spit in his face. . . . [A viper] will punch a player in the eye or knee him in the back just for meanness." Paul did not provide names of the NFL's den of vipers, although he slyly indicted himself: "It's a matter of principle with us ['villains'] that we must never break the rules unless, of course, the officials are looking the other way." Durslag mentioned casually that Paul had been thrown out of only three games during his career. "By studying the way plays form, he can usually anticipate the positions of officials and knows when he can pull a little something without getting caught. A good villain must always stay on the best terms with officials and must be courteous at all times. He can't afford to be a marked man."[55] Durslag's article presaged the edgy, hip journalistic style of Hunter S. Thompson and 1960s writers.

By 1956, after several seasons of debate, owner concerns about violence and injuries induced them to pass a rule banishing "piling on" the ball carrier when he went down. Part of the owners' hesitance to enact the rule revolved around defining when a ball carrier was down, with owners debating which of the two clauses, "in the grasp of" or "after contact," was more appropriate. Even George Preston Marshall, a seemingly callous owner, called for changes in the rule to prevent injuries.[56] Shirley Povich, Washington sportswriter, noted, "It was probably the Hugh McElhenny case that helped to bring the owners around. It became clear to them that what happened to McElhenny and the San Francisco 49ers, could also happen to their own big star." McElhenny tried for extra yardage, but the subsequent tackling and piling on injured him. Povich continued, "The senseless business of trying to get that extra yard is inviting further assault at a time when the ball carrier is often in a defenseless position."[57]

McElhenny's injury stymied a 49ers' drive to the division title. The rule made "the ball dead when any part of a ball carrier, other than his hands or feet, touches the ground after he has made contact with the opposition."[58] The year before the rule was enacted, though, Joe King had written that only twenty-four players had been placed on the inactive list (for injuries) in 1955, down from of thirty-two in 1954.[59]

The rule changes didn't end the carnage. Bell must have been chagrined to read the following description of the 1956 game between the Bears and Lions that determined the division champion: "The 49,086 fans were treated to some exciting, top-flight football today. It was when they turned their talents in other directions—punching, kneeing, kicking and shoving—that the entire program was threatened. Too often the players appeared intent on maiming one another." Apparently the mayhem was too much for some spectators, who decided to join the fun: "Toward the finish several hundred spectators rushed onto the gridiron, all anxious to join in the melee."[60]

Bell was certainly aware of the mayhem in the Bears-Lions game, as he awaited evidence concerning Bears defensive end Ed Meadow's hit on Lions quarterback Bobby Layne. Bell defended Meadows in the press, but Detroit coach Buddy Parker, perhaps overwrought by the disappointment of the Lions' loss, threatened to resign as coach. He claimed that the game "has gotten far out of line because of deliberate and flagrant infractions" before accusing George Halas and George Preston Marshall of running the league. One of the Lions' owners, Edwin J. Anderson, also accused Meadows. Although Meadows's hit put Layne out of the game with a concussion, Meadows wasn't banished from the game until he earned a later penalty for unsportsmanlike conduct against another Lions player. Meadows claimed the collision with Layne was accidental.[61] Detroit sports editor Lyall Smith wrote, "The Lions' own movies positively reveal that Meadows did not slug Layne, deliberately or otherwise. He did tackle him after Bobby had flipped a lateral pass." Another Detroit writer stated, "Photographs of the Layne matter could convict Meadows of running into the passer—a personal foul—but no slugging is apparent."[62] Concurrent with the Bears-Lions brouhaha was a controversy surrounding Redskins player Norb Hecker, who denied that he had taken part in a money pool "with the pay-off going to the player who 'got' Bobby Layne of the Lions."[63] Edwin Anderson didn't get his wish: Meadows was not banished from the league and continued playing for three additional seasons. Layne outlasted Meadows and played six more seasons.[64]

Once again Bell defended the NFL. After the Meadows-Layne collision, sportswriter Tex Maule, a staunch supporter of the NFL, asked Bell, "Do you think that pro football is dirty and getting dirtier?" Bell responded, "No. I don't believe there is dirty football. I never have. Sure, there are flare-ups. But I have never seen a maliciously dirty football player in my life and I don't believe there are any maliciously dirty players in the National Football League." Bell blamed inflamed tempers and passions arising from the fact that the improved competitive balance within the league made every game matter. Within the same interview, Maule asked why the NFL prevented TV cameras from concentrating on fights on the field. Bell responded, "I don't believe for the best interests of football or the best interests of the women and children who watch football it should be shown. We're selling a product just like, say, Atlantic Refining is selling one. You don't see them putting out a story about a bad situation or a bad month, do you? If people want to watch fights, let them tune in on Wednesday nights."[65] Readers may be excused for marveling at Bell's laser-like precision as he made the distinction between exciting and legal violence and violence best not shown to women and children.

Running back Ollie Matson put a positive spin on the violence. He denied that, as a black athlete, he was targeted for extra abuse, but he explained,

> I found out one thing—if you're a *good* [italics his] player, everybody is out to get you. Not dirty, just hitting extra hard. You find a few rookies attempting illegal tactics, but it gets around the league and everybody gets after him. You got to understand it is a job and you got a family, so you play hard but not dirty. . . . The writers sometimes make it appear dirty, but they misunderstand. It has come to my attention that the only ones who get injured are the ones goofing off, trying to get out of doing what they should.[66]

Perian Conerly related an incident in her husband's career. A Chicago Bears end hit Charlie Conerly with an elbow. Conerly took exception to the elbow, believing it intentional. After the game, the Bears player approached him and said the elbow was an accident, "because he didn't make enough money to risk wasting it paying fines." Conerly accepted this explanation.[67]

On another occasion, fans were not satisfied with vicariously sharing the violence on the field. During a key game between the Giants and the Cleveland Browns, thousands of fans stormed the field. The Giants were ahead 48–7 with less than two minutes left. The fans "rioted" in exuberance over the Giants' victory over the despised Browns. Jim Thomson, the superintendent of Yankee Stadium, denied that the fans rioted, saying, "Whatever it was, my men had it under control. Call it the action of an overzealous, elated crowd, but not a riot. Mainly, the drunkards and teen-agers were involved." In response, however, Thompson said the team planned to remove 1,495 temporary field seats and not use them again for football. These seats cost $5 apiece, so the Giants stood to lose $45,000 for the season, but Jack Mara approved the change. Thompson mused, "We had more than 500 ushers and special police, plus members of the grounds crew and attendants from the rest rooms. Ordinarily, we have about 350 men available. If that had been a riot, 5,000 city policemen would have had trouble controlling the mob."[68]

Other observers were not so quick to deny that a riot occurred. Giants coach Jim Lee Howell worried that the officials would forfeit the game to the Browns because the crowd refused to disperse for eighteen to twenty minutes. Paul Brown, Cleveland's coach, said "Even if we didn't play the last two minutes, I wouldn't have accepted a forfeit. I went to the dugout in back of our bench to keep from getting beat up. I never ordered the team into the club-house — I was only protecting my own chops, and I guess the players were doing the same thing." Sports columnist Arthur Daley wrote in a deadpan observation that nothing similar had occurred in the early days of the NFL, because "there were too few spectators to do any damages [and] the customers didn't care much who won." Daley thought the fans had become bloodthirsty: "It was a blood vendetta. So intense has been the rivalry between the Giants and . . . Browns . . . that the humiliation of the visiting team sent the spectators into raptures of delight." Daley said that Jack Mara responded quickly and presciently by summoning the special cops and ushers. Daley blamed a couple of small boys, who ran out onto the field and grabbed a football.[69]

Violence, legal and otherwise, continued to be an attraction and an occasional blemish upon the sport. Owners hesitated to clamp down too fiercely on what was perceived to be a key selling point of their product. Fifty years later, league officials would still be struggling to contain violence within tolerable bounds.

Officials

Bert Bell was a staunch advocate for NFL officials. He took umbrage at criticisms of his hand-picked staff. He was particularly aroused when crowds cheered as officials were injured during the course of two games: "Why should these fine, upstanding citizens be subjected to such abuse and ridicule?" He tacitly admitted that the officials did not make a lot of money for their efforts, as they were paid between $900 and $1,500 a season: "These men officiate only because they love the game of football. Our league spends $80,000 each season to officiate these games. . . . One thing we will not stand for is an official favoring the home-town team. In fact, I have statistics to show that our officials don't lean that way."[70] NFL home win-loss records were less skewed than those in the NBA during the 1950s. Some owners did not help the referees, given their constant grousing about officiating. One referee thought the crescendo of complaints in the late 1940s arose from the increasing closeness of many games; closer games meant that each call assumed more importance.[71]

NFL referees certainly did not earn enough money to make refereeing their "day job." In 1947 Bell suggested paying referees more money. He estimated that many of the referees in the NFL made just $1,200 per year from officiating league games. He pointed out that referees in college games might make $100 a game with gate receipts of $250,000. Bell opined, "If that is a good percentage for such an important job, my knowledge of percentages must be all wrong." He wanted his referees to be full-time, permanent employees of the league, similar to Major League Baseball's umpiring staff. Of course, a referee could be the "Otto Graham of referees," but no fan would pay to watch him perform.[72]

The league recognized that there were problems in recruiting and retaining competent referees. Bell proposed that referees be recruited from among former players, with a five-year waiting period between playing and refereeing. He remarked, "As it is now, we rely on people who do this work out of love for the game. The pay is not really an incentive. But don't misunderstand me. I can vouch for the personal integrity and ability of every man officiating in the NFL today." He went on to say that the NCAA's refusal to hire NFL referees made recruiting more difficult, as NFL referees couldn't get enough games to officiate as a vocation instead of an avocation.[73]

An NFL official's job was undoubtedly difficult. The league occasionally helped the officials by passing simpler rules. One example was the abolition of the tackle-eligible pass play. Some teams had stretched the rule to its limit by springing not only tackles but centers and guards for pass receptions.[74]

Bell also insisted that television commentators refrain from criticizing referees; he claimed that the commentators often incorrectly second-guessed the officials, which led to disrespect for the officials.[75]

Bell's successor, Pete Rozelle, recognized Bell's wisdom in supporting a professional cadre of referees. By 1960 the officials made $250 per game, but, as a sportswriter put it, "they've never served a tougher taskmaster."[76]

Gambling

Football fans crave action, "action" being a double entendre. They certainly enjoy the hard-hitting action on the field, but many find added enjoyment if they've placed a friendly wager on the outcome. Betting on sporting events is hardly endemic to professional football; however, the league never suffered a scandal commensurate with Major League Baseball's 1919 World Series calamity, in which eight players were banished for life after some of them conspired to throw the Series and others failed to report the conspiracy. Maintaining the public's belief in the honesty of the game was a top priority for the National Football League commissioners.

Shortly after assuming the commissionership, Bert Bell found himself confronting a serious gambling situation. Just prior to the New York Giants–Chicago Bears championship game in December 1946, Bell and other officials noticed a marked swing in the betting line. The Giants had decisively beaten the Bears during the regular season, but were not the favorites for the championship game. On the eve of the game, though, suspicious bets were placed on the Bears and the point spread increased to ten points.

The office of New York district attorney Frank S. Hogan eventually discovered that two Giants players, Merle Hapes and Frank Filchock, had been offered bribes of $2,500 plus $1,000 bets on the Bears to ensure a New York loss by more than the prescribed margin.[77] Filchock was the Giants' halfback and passer, recently acquired from the Washington Redskins. He had won All-NFL honors twice, including 1946. Despite being named All-NFL, he threw 25 interceptions in just 169 passing attempts during the 1946 season. Hapes was a halfback who had completed his second season with the team. Both players' careers had been interrupted by military service, but Filchock had turned thirty years old during the 1946 season and may have been at or past the peak of his career.

The NFL owners quickly empowered Bell to monitor and to punish players and team officials with regard to gambling. The new rules read:

> (1) Any knowledge of, or the attempt to offer a bribe to fix a ball game by players, coaches, directors, stockholders or anyone connected with a NFL club, must be reported to the coach or owner, who in turn must report it to the commissioner. Failure to do so will result in either a definite suspension, or indefinite suspension, or suspension for life. (2) That all questions pertaining to the conduct of players, gambling and the above legislation be displayed in large print in the dressing rooms of each of the league's ten teams. (3) That the teams be restrained from giving anything away at the ball park, or being directly connected with anything which might be construed as a lottery.[78]

The owners also gave Bell authority to hire private police to patrol the stadiums during games and to send copies of the revised rules prohibiting gambling to all of the players. Players and team officials were also now prohibited from accepting or giving gifts or rewards for defeating a competing club.[79]

Bell waited until after the trials and convictions of gambler Alvin J. Paris and other gamblers to issue his edict on Hapes and Filchock. He suspended the two players indefinitely, which observers interpreted as the end of their football-playing days. Hapes did not accept his punishment gracefully, retorting, "It's a bunch of baloney about hurting the league. All that they got against us is just not reporting the attempt. I don't think we did anything to hurt the league, but I'm through with professional football anyway."[80] Sportswriter Arthur Daley applauded Bell's decision. He noted that Bell cooperated with the district attorney's office in not announcing the players' punishments until after the conspirators were convicted. He also noted that the league did not have a specific rule against consorting with gamblers but had to resort to the "actions detrimental to professional football" clause in order to punish the players.[81]

Daley compared Filchock's and Hapes's actions with those of the 1919 Chicago White Sox. He observed that while the latter group of players accepted money and agreed to throw the series (with the exception of Buck Weaver, who simply did not inform on his teammates), they had a legitimate grievance against owner Charles Comiskey for his tightfisted ways. He claimed that Filchock and Hapes did not have such an excuse: "The Giants always have been the most generous and considerate of employers. They paid the two of them handsomely and sums in the vicinity of $10,000 or more for four-months' work must be considered at least a living wage. Furthermore, they were playing for a coach like Steve Owen. It may be significant that every athlete in the league eventually winds up with a hankering to play for both Owen and the Giants." He characterized Hapes as "not too quick on the uptake in what started as innocent dealings with men who happened to be gamblers," while Filchock "was too smart for his own good" and who was "back in Washington trying to get rich quickly by selling frozen custard."[82]

In the aftermath of the scandal, the Giants fell to last place in their division in 1947 and did not have another winning record until the 1950 season, when they were fortified by a number of ex-AAFC New York players. The team did not reappear in the championship game again until 1956. Filchock played for Canadian teams before being reinstated by Commissioner Bell in 1950; he played briefly with Baltimore. Hapes never played again in the NFL. The two players died within a few weeks of each other in 1994.[83]

Bell, like some of the owners, had been known to frequent racetracks and other gambling establishments in his younger days. He put his familiarity with the gambling industry to good use and ferreted out information regarding potential problems. He scrutinized betting lines to identify oddities. Bell also hired ex-FBI agents and other law enforcement officers to monitor activities in every NFL city, and instituted preseason talks with players regarding the dangers of associating with known gamblers. The owners endowed the commissioner's office with the power to suspend "for life" any player or team official involved in fixing games.[84] Bell watched televised NFL games and would call the announcers if the latter made remarks about the point spread. As he testified before Congress, "We don't want anything pertaining to gambling. We don't even allow our teams to give away tickets on a lucky number in their program."[85]

Years later, sportswriter W. C. Heinz described Bell's constant vigilance. Bell hired Austin Gunsel, a former FBI agent, to head the league's security efforts, which included retaining former FBI investigators in every league city. As he put it, the agents were "not to tail the players, though; to watch the gamblers. Also they check on the sales of any team stocks, new owners, new officials, news broadcasters." He also established "listening posts" to alert him to reports of large amounts of money appearing in betting on any particular team or game. "Each week during the season he receives the betting prices and point spreads on Monday, Wednesday, Thursday and Friday nights, Saturday morning and Saturday night." "One night," Bell said, "I got the price of a Cardinals-Cleveland game, and the next thing they said was that the spread had dropped to three points. I called Cleveland and found they'd just announced that Otto Graham wasn't gonna play."[86] In the same news release, Bell indicated that he had lists of all the big-time professional gamblers in each city where the NFL played. Because of situations such as these, Bell launched the league policy of reporting injuries and player availability for upcoming games that is so familiar to fans today, saying, "The gamblers know these things. I want the public to know them too. I don't care if people bet, because people are gonna bet. I just want to be sure they stay away from our ballplayers and don't spread rumors."[87]

Bell's forthright confrontation of the gambling issue won him plaudits from sportswriters. Joe Williams wrote in 1957, "Bell does not blanch at the mention of gambling, or resort to platitudinous flapdoodle, extolling the nobility of game and gamesters, in an attempt to discount its inherent

dangers. Instead, he forthrightly concedes a great deal of money unquestionably is bet on pro football. . . . 'Who are we to say a man must not bet
on our games? . . . These measures do not reflect distrust. They have been
installed to protect the players, and the game officials as well, from making associations and frequenting places which might lead to embarrassing
consequences, if not worse.'" Williams went on to say that Bell had his
security officials do background checks on prospective referees. Williams
also pointed out that honest bookies were among Bell's most ardent boosters, writing: "They want no part of a fix. They can get hurt that way. Their
percentage is sure, steady and richly nutritious. Bookies are rarely involved
in fixes. Almost invariably it's a smart guy outsider."[88] Another sportswriter
seconded Williams's observation by pointing out that the "nation's hottest
betting sport" was pro football, because "[bettors] know they'll get a fair
shake."[89]

Although Bell worked hard to allay suspicions, they did recur. Even the
league's "Greatest Game Ever Played," the 1958 championship game between
the Giants and the Baltimore Colts, generated rumors. Sportswriter Murray
Robinson wrote:

> The Baltimore Colts drew the leers of the skeptics in the 23 to 17 victory
> over the New York Giants. . . . They had gone into the game four-point
> favorites over the Giants. In the overtime period, instead of trying for
> an easy field goal for a 20 to 17 victory, the Colts elected to go for a more
> precarious touchdown. They made it, and the cry went up that they had
> chosen the six-point try to protect a whopping bet made on the Colts
> by parties close to the Baltimore club. A field goal would have lost the
> bet, pegged in the talk at $50,000.

Robinson quoted Bell as saying, "No such big bet could have been made,
because it didn't show up in the price." Bell elaborated by saying the initial
line was Colts by 3.5 points and only changed to Colts and 4 points by
game time.[90]

Some legislators were skeptical of Bell's antigambling educational lectures
and other efforts. In 1957 the congressional committee asked Eagles star
Chuck Bednarik whether he read his player contract past the stipulated
salary amount. They especially wanted to know whether he'd read Rule 6

pertaining to the commissioner's power to suspend and/or fine players who gambled or failed to report knowledge of nefarious gambling offers.[91] A year later, other congressional investigators castigated Bell's focus on potential player malfeasance, since some of the owners had ties with gambling. Bell defended Giants owner Tim Mara, who had liked to bet on horses in the past. Bell admitted that Mara used to make book, but he, Bell, had also gambled in the past. He strenuously defended Mara's honesty.[92]

Bert Bell's actions helped allay any residual suspicions regarding NFL play. His surveillance apparatus enabled his successor, Pete Rozelle, to limit bad publicity when Paul Hornung and Alex Karras admitted betting on NFL games in the early 1960s.

Conclusions

While most pundits rely on the television aspect of the NFL's rise to prominence in the sporting world, the efforts of Bell and the owners to improve their product on the field and to avoid unsavory gambling incidents were unsung factors in the league's growing popularity. As NCAA football officials fumbled with annual changes in substitution rules, NFL star players specialized and enjoyed longer careers. While the NFL had not created a perfect game, sportswriter Bill Furlong could point out that the 1959 National Football League record book had a small but significant notation: "1959 — for the first time since 1933 no changes were made in the playing rules."[93]

13

INTEGRATION

The players in today's NFL are predominantly African American, but it wasn't always so. Imagining an NFL history without the likes of Jim Brown, Night Train Lane, O. J. Simpson, Walter Payton, Jerry Rice, Lawrence Taylor, Tony Dungy, and legions of others is impossible. African Americans have greatly enriched professional football. Sad to say, professional football has not always reciprocated.

Younger readers will have difficulty comprehending the virulent racism that pervaded America in the postwar period. The Second World War provided an impetus for Americans to review their attitudes toward race after confronting Nazi Germany and Japan.

Economists identify various types of discrimination. One form is statistical discrimination, whereby a decision-maker relies upon group averages in making a choice. For instance, a basketball coach examining a group of students may select the tallest ones for the team, figuring that "you can't coach height." While it may be true that taller people make better basketball players on average, there is much overlap between the playing abilities of tall and short people; the rule of thumb in this case, height, is no guarantee of accuracy. The virtue of statistical discrimination is that such a method is usually cheap to implement.

In the world of sports, discrimination can arise from owner, fan, or teammate preferences. There can, of course, be overlap, as all three sources may hold similar preferences.

An owner who does not like African American people may choose not to hire any. While most professional leagues have never codified a racial barrier, apparently the "gentlemen's agreement" was fairly binding in the NFL, as it had been in Major League Baseball. In baseball, such maverick officials as Branch Rickey and Bill Veeck Jr. broke ranks with their fellow baseball decision-makers and reintegrated the game in 1947. If teammates have a preference as to the hue of a teammate's skin, then some teams might end up all white. A more pernicious example of discrimination would be seen if fans actively avoided teams with African American players; then an owner either caters to the fans' preferences or runs the risk of alienating them.

Economics of Discrimination

In a perfectly competitive market, where buyers and sellers have no ability to affect the price, owners pay a premium to indulge their preferences if they wish to discriminate. If one business owner desired to field a coed company basketball team, she might prefer to hire taller workers, even though height has nothing to do with the job. If many business owners desire to field company basketball players, the taller people would see their wages rise, while shorter people would see their wages fall. The owners pay more to exercise their preference. These owners are vulnerable to other owners who primarily care about green—the color of money—in their hiring decisions. If taller workers are receiving a premium, owners who don't care much about basketball may begin hiring the cheaper shorter workers (again, we're assuming height has no effect upon productivity on the job). These owners pay lower labor costs and may eventually drive out the owners desiring company basketball teams.

The above argument fails if there is an excess supply of workers (unemployment), or if basketball-loving owners can somehow get the government to outlaw hiring shorter workers. Then all employers pay the same, and the basketball-loving owners are not at risk. In some cases, if the preference is culturally ingrained, the basketball-loving owners may be able to maintain a boycott of shorter workers. The more likely scenario, though, is that these owners must get an outside authority to maintain what amounts to a conspiracy against shorter workers.

If fans demonstrate marked preferences, the result may be that an owner may indulge such preferences but the team's quality may falter. In the case of the NFL, if fans in southern cities refused to patronize home teams fielding African American players, then owners of those teams who acceded to fan preferences would field teams without African American players. If the excluded players were talented, then the southern team owner might have competed at a disadvantage. The Washington Redskins' experiences during the 1950s exemplify this result.

If players demonstrate a preference for white teammates, then players with that preference might tend to congregate on all-white teams. If African American players are just as talented as white players, or if they are more talented than white players, then the white players with a yen for playing with teammates of a similar hue are likely to be at a competitive disadvantage.[1]

In addition to segregated teams, discrimination could result in salary differentials. Given the paucity of data about individual player salaries for the 1946–60 era, whether black players received lower pay for similar productivity is an unsettled question. Economist Lawrence Kahn found that salary differences between white and black NFL players were at most 4 percent by the late 1980s.[2] Certainly the evidence that owners and coaches stacked African American players in certain positions seems pretty strong, as there were few, if any, black quarterbacks for years.

The NFL's Early Integration

African Americans had played in the National Football League from its inception until 1933, when they were quietly eased out. A similar process occurred in the National Basketball League, where African American players performed immediately after the war and then disappeared until after the merger with the Basketball Association of America that formed today's National Basketball Association.

Some observers believe that George Preston Marshall, the dynamic and innovative Boston/Washington owner, pressed for exclusion upon his arrival in the league, but the evidence is mixed.[3] Marshall looms large in the NFL's second reintegration process after World War II. Given that he bestowed the "Redskins" name upon his relocated Washington franchise, he did not give early indications of being progressive on racial issues.[4] Historian Charles Ross discusses the possibility that Marshall led the way in establishing a "gentlemen's agreement," perhaps arguing that given the Depression, it was bad public relations to fill an NFL position with a black man when there were several suitable white men available. Even if Marshall persuaded George Halas to go along with the idea, Halas may have still considered signing Ozzie Simmons in 1936 and Kenny Washington in 1939, but he could not convince his fellow owners to acquiesce.[5]

Other observers thought that Joe Lillard, a former University of Oregon player, proved too rebellious. His Chicago Cardinals coach, Paul Schlissler, made the novel argument that Lillard's presence marked himself and the team for special treatment: the "rest of the league took it out on us! We had to let him go, for our own sake, and for his, too!"[6]

Certainly some of the earliest African American players were extraordinary men. Fritz Pollard and Paul Robeson were two of the early black players in the NFL. Robeson, an exemplar of the renaissance man, played pro ball prior to getting his law degree and then moving on to the stage and movies. Pollard, also a man of many interests, became the first African American coach in the NFL. He recalled, "I coached at Akron. Elgie Tobinn was listed as the coach; but when I came, they were still using some old plays. So I said why don't we try some of the stuff we had been doing at Brown. The owner, Frank Neid told everybody that if they didn't want to listen to me, they could leave right then." Pollard is not listed as the coach of the Akron team, but Maher and Gill's *The Pro Football Encyclopedia* lists him as the coach of Hammond's team in 1925. Pollard and Robeson faced hostile opposing players and fans. Pollard said he learned from his college experience to "roll on his back when knocked down and cock his feet up, ready to kick any players who might want to pile on him." He recalled that his teammates would "take sides with me."[7]

Changing Cultural Norms

Marshall wasn't alone among his peers. If the owners were not virulent racists as a group, they shared many of the commonly held beliefs of 1940s America. Many white Americans were content to ignore the racial hypocrisy surrounding them, or they chose to view it as a uniquely southern problem. Given the rapid transformation in the antipathy toward the Japanese people immediately after the war, though, there was reason to hope for a change in the attitudes of whites toward blacks.

African Americans, too, were changing their attitudes and becoming more insistent in asserting their rights. They had served America loyally in two World Wars, despite treatment that ranged from condescension to outright brutality.

While motion pictures are hardly a perfect barometer of cultural mores, it is worthwhile to review war movies. After World War I (or as contemporaries remembered it, "The Great War," not being prescient enough to recognize that another world war was imminent), a movie such as *The Fighting 69th* established one of the American war-movie clichés: the "diverse" American platoon or company of infantrymen. In *The Fighting 69th*, James Cagney and Pat O'Brien are part of a unit comprised of Irish Americans, Italian Americans, southerners, midwestern farm boys, Bronx wise guys, and other soon-to-be-stock characters. This tradition continued through World War II movies, with the casts of *Battleground* and *A Walk in the Sun* exemplifying the diverse crowd of white Americans. The major update was the private from Brooklyn, who always inquired, "How's dem Dodgers doin'?" No black soldiers were portrayed, except as French colonials in the Humphrey Bogart film *Sahara*. Then again, black people were not alone in being left out, as there weren't any Asian American soldiers shown, either, just lots of stereotyped Japanese soldiers (with bad teeth and slanted eyes, usually grinning while they machine-gunned or bayoneted helpless American, British, and Chinese soldiers and civilians).

By the time of the Korean War black soldiers had started appearing in various movie combat units, reflecting President Truman's edict integrating the military. In Sam Fuller's *The Steel Helmet*, the wily Chinese captive tries to persuade the African American soldier to rebel, asking him why he fought for a racist America. In the more upscale *Pork Chop Hill*, Woody Strode, a former collegiate star and one of the earliest black players in the reintegrated NFL, played a malingering private. He explained to Gregory Peck's lieutenant that he was from what we would now call a disadvantaged background, so why should he fight for America? Peck gives him some words of wisdom, and orders another black soldier, played by James Edwards, to watch the Strode character. In *All the Young Men*, Sidney Poitier assumes command of a Marine platoon, where he battles the racist attitudes of the white soldiers. In all these movies, the African Americans are portrayed as "the other" almost as much as are the Chinese or Korean troops they were fighting. On the other hand, *The Steel Helmet* and *Pork*

Chop Hill featured sympathetic, even laudable Japanese American characters, especially Lieutenant Ohashi in the latter movie.

Poitier, of course, became the first major black movie star. His counterparts in the entertainment industry, such as Nat King Cole, were making tentative progress in television and music. Bill Cosby would be the first African American star of a television series, *I Spy*, in the mid-1960s, before becoming a cultural icon as Dr. Huxtable on the *Cosby Show* decades later.

For most Americans, though, African American faces became national figures in the entertainment industry through sports. Black boxers, track and field participants, and jockeys had already achieved fame during the first half of the twentieth century. Branch Rickey of baseball's Brooklyn Dodgers garnered most of the headlines for signing Jackie Robinson to play for the Dodgers' Montreal farm team before introducing him into the Major Leagues in April 1947. Blacks had played in organized baseball during part of the nineteenth century, before a "gentleman's agreement" barred them from further overt participation. Whether any of the Cuban players or even some of the ostensibly white players were of African descent is debated among researchers. Certainly no one had an incentive to reveal such ancestry, but given the racial mores of the times when even an eighth or a sixteenth or a thirty-second part of African ancestry labeled one as "Negro," it is likely that some players were, in the term of the time, of "mixed blood." By the twenty-first century, things had changed. Golfer Tiger Woods, whose ancestry was half Asian and one-quarter African, was regarded as African American — a neat twist on earlier racial mores.

NFL Integration, Part 2

Jackie Robinson's debut with the Brooklyn Dodgers ignited controversy. Some players and, apparently, most owners opposed his participation on the sacrosanct baseball field. Rickey had impressed upon Robinson the necessity of turning the other cheek, but no one could have possessed enough cheeks to have endured forever the taunts, spikings, and other mayhem perpetrated by rival players and even some teammates. Robinson's courage and grace under appalling conditions made him a hero for many people around the world.

Professional football had reintegrated several months before Robinson's major-league debut. While these players received some publicity, most labored in relative obscurity. The black pioneers in the NBL/NBA received even less publicity and adulation. These players faced conditions as repugnant as those Robinson endured. As Woody Strode commented years later, "If I have to integrate heaven, I don't want to go."[8]

Fortunately for African Americans, the first black pioneers included some exceptional talents. Robinson earned Rookie of the Year honors his first season. Football pioneers Bill Willis and Marion Motley helped establish the Cleveland Browns' dominance of the AAFC and, later, of the NFL.

Racism and other "isms" were common in postwar America. While Tiger Woods is perhaps one of the most recognizable athlete on the planet, in 1940s and '50s (and even in 1960s and '70s) America, he would have been doubly denied entry to many private golf courses: African and Asian Americans were not welcome. Neither were Catholic Americans, Jewish Americans or Hispanic Americans (and heaven forbid the acceptance of those who were open about their differing sexual orientation).[9] If the exclusive country clubs had been more meticulous, they would have overtly excluded Muslim Americans, too. Several European American groups were just beginning to be admitted.

At the other end of the social spectrum—bowling—racism was paramount. The horror of sharing a bowling ball no doubt inspired the American Bowling Congress (ABC) to exclude African American bowlers (along with people in the other groups mentioned in the previous paragraph). Sportswriter Dan Parker described the ABC in his expose about prejudice in the sports world, though he admitted, "It rates at least one tiny bow for not being underhanded about its position." He went on to say, "Of all the sports, boxing has the best record in its treatment of all the races. Cynics might put it: 'In the fight racket, all races are *mistreated* [italics his] to the same degree.'"[10] Parker snidely wrote, "A Chinese-American war hero was barred from a minor tournament. . . . Under its rules, redskins [sic] are barred, although they are the only 100 percent Americans in our Republic." The ABC, bereft of a sense of irony, had the temerity to state in its brochure that bowling was, "the greatest social leveler on earth . . . all are the same to the ABC." An ABC spokesperson decried the picketers outside a bowling event: "We're not going to be bullied into this thing by the CIO or any other pressure group. Many negroes have told me they don't want to join the ABC, where they would be so greatly outnumbered. Our only trouble comes from crusading newspapers and other publicity seekers."[11]

The owners of the Cleveland AAFC franchise hired Paul Brown before the war ended. He quickly began signing talent. Whatever Brown's attitudes toward race, he was perceptive enough to see that some black players were very talented. He signed fullback Marion Motley and guard Bill Willis to the Cleveland roster. The duo played eight seasons for the Browns, and they were both elected to the Pro Football Hall of Fame.

In the NFL, the Cleveland Rams transferred to Los Angeles after their 1945 championship season. The Rams wanted to use the publicly owned Los Angeles Coliseum, but the lease came with stipulations: they had to sign some African American athletes. The Rams grudgingly signed former UCLA stars Kenny Washington and Woody Strode in the face of opposition from their fellow NFL owners. Team backfield coach Bob Snyder admitted, "I doubt we would have been interested in [Kenny] Washington if we had stayed in Cleveland."[12] The duo had played in the Pacific Coast [Football] League after years of being snubbed by the NFL owners despite All-American honors in college; they sometimes received more pay per Pacific Coast [Football] League game than the top players in the NFL. The Hollywood Bears were proud of Washington and Strode and proclaimed on their ticket stubs: "The Hollywood Bears with Kenny Washington."[13]

NFL owners appeared to have a tacit agreement not to discuss integration. The author found no mention of integration in the NFL League Minutes between 1932, when George Preston Marshall entered the league, and 1960.

Both Washington and Strode, because of injuries and aging, were no longer the dynamic players they had been before the war. Strode played just sporadically, and he quickly realized that the Rams had signed him largely as a sidekick and roommate for Washington. At times the two players could not stay with their teammates in hotels or restaurants. Even a hotel in Chicago refused to let the two players stay there. The team gave them each $100 to find their own accommodations. Strode quipped, in that inimitable voice that became famous during his motion picture career, "Well, what the hell, let's be segregated!" They went to the Persian Hotel, which was the top black hotel in the city. The hotel had hired Count Basie to play in its nightclub. When white teammate Bob Waterfield eventually tracked them down at the Persian to inform them that the Stevens Hotel had rescinded its prohibition, Strode replied, "Forget that, boy. I'm going to be segregated, spend this hundred dollars, stay right here, and listen to the Count play his music."[14] While segregation occasionally paid handsomely, more often it was a nuisance and a humiliation. The Browns had to play a game in Miami during the AAFC's first season; because of the segregation laws, they left their two black players in Cleveland.[15]

If the players weren't welcome in hotels and restaurants, opposing players and fans weren't rolling out the welcome mat, either. At first, opposing players tried to intimidate African American players physically. While all rookies receive some hazing, Motley and Willis remember hazing that went beyond the usual. Willis recalled, "That kind of crap went on for two or three years, until they found out what kind of players we were. They found out that while they were calling us 'niggers,' I was running for touchdowns and Willis was knocking the shit out of them. They stopped calling us names and started to catch up with us."[16] Sometimes their teammates handled the retaliation because, as Motley observed, "If Willis and I had been anywhere near being hotheads, it would have been another ten years till black men got accepted in pro ball."[17] Given Willis's reputation for being one of the hardest-hitting, most physical guards in the league, this author suspects that opponents quickly learned not to rile him. Willis's and Motley's salaries were commensurate with those of their teammates, aside from quarterback Otto Graham. Both players earned more playing AAFC football than they had in their previous jobs, although none of the players, Graham included, were getting rich.[18]

Motley led the NFL in rushing in 1950, presaging such talents as Jim Brown, Gale Sayers, Walter Payton, Adrian Peterson, and other great African American running backs. Night Train Lane twice led the league in interceptions. Coaches initially viewed African American players as ideal candidates for the running back, receiver, and defensive back positions. For positions that supposedly required thinking or leadership, such as center, quarterback, and middle linebacker, coaches proved hesitant to employ black players. Given the plethora of talent in the historically black colleges, it is obvious that highly skilled African American players had performed at these positions. It would take decades for coaches to employ black play-ers at every position, let alone for owners to hire African Americans for coaching and front-office positions. African American players also noted an informal quota and an "even" system: teams used even numbers of black players, so they wouldn't have to integrate hotel rooms with white teammates, a pattern that persisted into the 1960s.[19]

For teams in the South that wanted an NFL franchise, the racial mores proved an impediment. The AAFC's Miami franchise lasted just one season, while the various Texas franchises skirted one racial incident after another. The short-lived NFL Dallas Texans employed George Taliaferro and Buddy Young, both very talented players. The teams' owners thought that the Texans' white fans eschewed the team because of its black players, while African Americans shunned the games because they were given inferior seats in a segregated section. The team had agreed to cooperate with the Dallas State Fairground officials who ran the stadium in the fairground's "Negro Day" in October (proving that the "Negro Day" in the musical *Hairspray* was not far-fetched). According to table 1, Dallas residents had lower per capita median incomes than residents of other NFL cities. Blacks in Dallas had a paltry per-capita income compared to blacks in large cities in the North or West. Perhaps the presence of the black players served to deflect scrutiny of the more likely culprit for the team's disastrous atten-dance: inept white teammates. The two African Americans ran for four touchdowns and more than 640 yards for a team finishing 1-11.[20]

Even in 1961 African American players faced outrageous situations. The San Diego Chargers team was told to leave a motion picture theater because the team was integrated. Coach Sid Gillman related the incident: "We were invited to this theater, but they didn't have a roped-off section for us. We wound up in the balcony. Then they wouldn't let our Negro players go down for popcorn. Then the manager or someone came and told me to ask my Negro players to move to the colored section. I told him I certainly would not do that, and I got the squad and we left the theater in the middle of the picture." Perhaps the most remarkable aspect of this story was Gillman's conclusion, "It's amazing to me to learn that things like that still happened in America." Unfortunately, such shenanigans persisted for years to come, although there was progress.[21]

The Rams' failure to sign younger African American players hurt them. They incurred the displeasure of their fellow owners (with whom they were already on strained terms due to their relocation to the West Coast), and they selected two players who were past their prime. Washington and Strode could not prevent the team's decline in the three seasons after the championship season of 1945.

In a sense, the Cleveland Browns' experience mirrored that of baseball's Brooklyn Dodgers. Motley and Willis fit in with a plethora of other talented players, including Otto Graham, Dante Lavelli, Lou Groza, and Mac Speedie, to make Cleveland pro football's dominant team for the next decade, just as Robinson helped transform the baseball Dodgers into the National League's best team for a full decade.

Historian Charles Ross believed that owners who integrated early reaped benefits at the box office. He cited a two-game home-and-home series between the Browns and the New York Yankees in 1947, where out of a combined attendance of 150,000, some 40,000 were black.[22]

Despite the Browns' success, rival AAFC and NFL owners hardly stampeded toward integration. Four AAFC teams integrated in 1947 (Brooklyn, Chicago, Los Angeles, and New York). In the NFL, the Rams remained the lone integrated NFL team during 1947. New York's Buddy Young proved a durable player, and the team improved in 1947, but the other clubs showed little improvement after hiring black players. Detroit and New York joined the Rams as integrated NFL teams in 1948, while the AAFC San Francisco team did so, too. Green Bay and the first Baltimore Colts team desegregated in 1950.[23] The AAFC teams also led the way in scouting small black colleges for talent.[24]

Michael MacCambridge makes the point that the 1950 NFL Championship Game between the Browns and the Rams, both pioneers in integration, featured nine of the fourteen African Americans in the NFL.[25] Sportswriter Wendell Smith lauded "Negro" players: "Professional football is having one of its greatest seasons this year and Negro players are doing more than holding their own in the highly competitive National Football League. Take, for example, San Francisco and Cleveland, two teams contending for top honors in their respective divisions."[26]

By 1952 the Bears, Cardinals, Steelers, and Eagles had also integrated their teams, leaving the Washington Redskins as the sole holdout. Even the NFL Dallas team had George Taliaferro, and the resurrected Baltimore team signed Mel Embree for the 1953 season. Integration was not permanent. A couple of NFL teams temporarily went back to an all-white roster in 1953 — Detroit and Pittsburgh (when Pittsburgh did not re-sign Jack Spinks for the season) — but the overall trend was clear. At the time, Marshall whined that he would "like very much to sign a colored football player. But it seems the other guys always beat me to them."[27] As Mac-Cambridge pointed out, by 2004 more than 70 percent of the NFL's players were African American.[28]

These historians, however, may have attributed too much to integration. Table 41 reveals that teams showed little change in either win-loss or attendance records in the season in which they integrated compared with the previous season. The Rams' jump in attendance was undoubtedly more reflective of the change in locale, although the Dons also showed a jump in attendance after integrating. Baltimore's 1953 increase was attributable to its reincarnation from the inept Dallas club. The one team that seemed to justify the historians' faith in the beneficial power of integration was the Washington Redskins: this was surely an ironic outcome. Table 1 shows why attendance was unlikely to be greatly increased by integration. Several of the cities with NFL teams had relatively small populations of African Americans, and, of course, African Americans had lower incomes than whites on average.

Bringing Up the Rearguard

The Washington Redskins, laggards in integrating their team, reflected their owner's maverick personality. George Preston Marshall was a bumptious fellow with a reputation for being frugal. One sportswriter, perhaps uncharitably, referred to him as "the last of the small-time spenders."[29] He also disliked the thought of a players' association and increasing salaries. He had some wonderful ideas that boosted the league, such as divisions and playoffs, but he was almost defiantly abrasive. Years before the embarrassment of watching Jimmy Carter, Jane Fonda, and Ted Turner doing the "Tomahawk Chop" during an Atlanta Braves postseason game, Marshall nicknamed his team the "Redskins." While people chafe as such monikers as the "Chiefs," "Indians," and "Warriors," "Redskins" would seem to be beyond the pale. Few people would willingly refer to themselves as such.[30] Marshall's intransigence regarding integration, therefore, was no surprise. He once boasted, "We'll start signing Negroes, when the Harlem Globetrotters start signing whites."[31] The fact that the team was playing in the nation's capital only ratcheted the embarrassment factor upward. The Soviet Union had been quick to castigate Major League Baseball on its attitudes toward blacks, but they didn't appear to use the Redskins as part of their propaganda effort.[32]

Even Marshall's co-owner Harry Wismer urged him to integrate the team to no avail. Wismer said, "Marshall told me to do the broadcasting and he would run the football team."[33] For years, people picketed the NFL and the Redskins over Marshall's practices.[34] Edward Bennett Williams, later an important owner in the NFL, was on the Redskins' board of directors and also encouraged Marshall to sign black players.[35]

The incoming Kennedy administration provided the critical push in forcing Marshall to integrate. While the President was frequently criticized for his timidity in pushing promised civil rights legislation, he backed his secretary of the interior, Stewart L. Udall, in requiring the team to integrate if it wanted to use the new, publicly financed stadium in Washington DC (which was eventually known as RFK Stadium). Because the stadium was publicly financed and was under the aegis of the Department of the Interior, Udall had the leverage to insist that the team be integrated. He also personally boycotted the team's games. He eventually granted Marshall a reprieve for the 1961 season, with the stipulation that the owner sign some African American players for the 1962 season.[36]

Marshall sarcastically rebutted Udall's charge of discrimination by saying, "If Udall would get us Lennie Moore we'd use him." He went on to explain his position: "We take most of our players out of Southern colleges and are trying to appeal to Southern people. Those colleges don't have any Negro players. I don't know where I could get a good Negro player now—the other clubs aren't going to give up a good one."[37] He also mentioned that he feared to offend his radio and television audiences by fielding an integrated team. He claimed that he had, in the past, hired Samoan, Hawaiian, American Indian, and Cuban players.[38]

Senator Kenneth Keating of New York criticized Udall's action, labeling it a "clever subterfuge to distinguish the administration's feeble civil rights record" and stating, "I cannot help but feel that governor [of Arkansas, Orval] Faubus and his cohorts need a little more attention than George Preston Marshall and company. The Redskins may be tough on a football field [?], but the administration apparently has decided that they are easy targets in the political arena."[39]

Udall took a misstep by allowing the segregated Georgetown University team to play in the stadium, although he provided the lame excuse that the team was comprised of amateur and not professional athletes. He reacted quickly when he discovered that the national park rangers were almost unanimously white, with just one black ranger out of 474.[40] According to Thomas Smith, some Americans felt that blacks played for other NFL teams, so why should Washington be forced to integrate and why would any blacks want to play for Marshall? A critic pointed out that there were plenty of other groups not represented on the Redskins (or most other teams, for that matter), including Asian Americans, Puerto Ricans, and women. As usual, Marshall turned the latter suggestion into a pungent joke, "Of course we have had players who played like girls, but never an actual girl player."[41]

Some civil rights advocates suggested that talented black players ought to shun the Redskins, but sportswriter Sam Lacy opposed this policy and suggested that a black player would have a "moral obligation" to sign with the Redskins if he were drafted because of the "importance of sacrifice for the sake of justice."[42]

Marshall's team, reflecting the economic prediction at the beginning of this chapter, missed out on many talented players. The team's record during the 1946–60 period was mediocre at best. A *Sports Illustrated* reporter predicted, "The Washington Redskins, principally because they do not employ Negro players, are a sensible choice for last."[43]

Marshall drafted Ernie Davis, Syracuse's star running back, but surreptitiously traded him to the Cleveland Browns for Bobby Mitchell.[44] The latter player had never meshed with coach Paul Brown. He became an instant star with the Redskins and led the league in receiving in 1962, so Marshall landed himself a Hall-of-Fame player. Readers can be excused for wondering at the justice of the league's most avowed traditionalist hitting the integration jackpot. The team drafted a few other black players. The world didn't end for Washington. Eighth-round draft pick fullback Ron Hatcher became the first black to sign with the team.[45] Southern fans of the team did not boycott. The team temporarily improved from 1-12-1 in 1961 to 5-7 in 1962.

Marshall still didn't get it. He wanted to stage an exhibition game with the Philadelphia Eagles at Norfolk, Virginia. The Eagles returned the contract unsigned and cited their "colored players'" refusal to play before a segregated crowd.[46]

Bobby Mitchell and John Nisby, two of the players who integrated the Redskins, had mixed feelings about Marshall. Since Marshall suffered a stroke in 1963 and turned the reins over to Edward Bennett Williams and Jack Kent Cooke, though, they had limited interaction with him.[47]

If Marshall's actions were reprehensible, he had plenty of company in the segregationist rearguard. As late as 1961, African American San Diego Charger players had to consider protesting segregation in the stands at Houston's Jeppesen Stadium. The team's general manager and coach, Sid Gillman, wasn't supportive and warned players that they could be suspended or fined if they refused to play. The players chose to play, but one can imagine their chagrin at being in the middle of the situation.[48]

Conclusions

While the evidence is scant as to whether the NFL's reintegration process helped popularize the game, that integration surely did not hinder the league's growing popularity. If owners' complaints that there were not enough good players available were to be believed, then the accession to a pool of an additional 10 percent of American males must have upgraded the overall quality of players in the league. If they had practiced more equitable treatment of African American players and fans, perhaps NFL teams could have increased their fan base and popularity even more.

CONCLUSION

THE NFL'S RISE TO PROMINENCE

The AFL's debut served to point out the NFL's success in establishing football as America's second most popular professional team sport during the 1950s. Pundits began whispering that the sport was even about to overtake Major League Baseball.

Commissioners

Historians sometimes use the "Great Man" approach to history, in which history is determined to a significant extent by the actions and personalities of great men. Caesar, Napoleon, Gandhi, Hitler, Stalin, and others are invoked as examples of great men (whether good or evil). While no one would dare suggest that Bert Bell, Pete Rozelle, Joe Foss, or any of the pro football commissioners are "great" in the same sense, they have had effects upon the NFL's development.

Bert Bell and Pete Rozelle each assumed the NFL commissionership as the league dealt with new competitors. Bell's NFL differed greatly from Rozelle's. Bell's NFL was still unsure of itself; Rozelle's NFL had enjoyed a decade of prosperity and consolidation. Bell thought in terms of survival and prosperity; Rozelle could envision greatness. Bell was older and, despite his wealthy birthright, projected an earthy, down-to-earth demeanor. He could, on occasion, use his social and political connections. Rozelle, a product of the burgeoning American middle class, learned suavity and diplomacy. He learned, too, to navigate the corridors of political power. He epitomized the modern American professional, smooth and affable. Had they changed places, the NFL's history would have been much different and possibly much less successful.

The owners recognized Bell's skills and contributions. They frequently voted to extend his contract and to give him pay raises and bonuses.[1] Two of Bell's key contributions to the NFL were his handling of the league's schedule and his Lincolnesque magnanimity toward the three AAFC franchises that joined the NFL.

In the first instance, the NFL owners, self-interested every one, needed his even-handed self-assurance and neutrality lest the disputes over scheduling and other league matters lead to divisive enmity. While newer owners would occasionally grouse that Bell favored his old cronies in the league, none of them seriously disputed his authority. The league's success and prosperity under his aegis squelched dissent.[2] Sportswriter Jack Orr thought that Bell's thorough knowledge of professional football was a major aspect of his success: "He knows more than they do. . . . He has been in the game for a long time and he knows every angle. The owners know he knows what he's doing and whatever it is, it must be good for football. I have seen the respect for Bert grow gradually over the years. They know he is square. He will fight and argue, but he doesn't hold a grudge. No matter how friendly you are with him, if he thinks you are wrong, he'll tell you. They know there wouldn't be big-league football today without him."[3] Bell may have had his favorites; given that he had known Halas, Rooney, Marshall, and a few others for decades and had shared the NFL's tribulations with them, it would have taken uncommon rectitude not to have held some bias.

Bell was adept at herding the owners in the direction he deemed best. After letting the owners exhaust themselves in deciding divisional lineups in the wake of the NFL-AAFC merger, Bell stepped in and solved the impasse quickly by threatening to act unilaterally. The owners quickly settled on an alignment — one that Bell was planning to recommend.[4]

His handling of the absorption of the AAFC teams displayed his ability to gain the loyalty and respect of even former adversaries. Bell had been offered a franchise in the AAFC, but once he cast his lot with the NFL he was an implacable and pugnacious foe of the AAFC. Arthur Daley marveled at Bell's graciousness and even generosity:

The originally suspicious All-American Conference owners became his firmest supporters. They came expecting the worst. They left satisfied. . . . One shudders to think what might have happened if a less firm hand than Bell's had been at the controls. He stepped on a few toes but no damage is as irreparable as it could have been if the magnates had been left to themselves. . . . His rulings during the football meetings have been so fair and sound that he saved the conclave from degenerating into a nasty mess. He emerged with vastly increased stature and pro football reflected that gain. The moral of it all probably is this: Never start trading punches with a guy whose name is Debenneville.[5]

Bell's staying power proved an advantage against his AAFC counterparts. The AAFC commissionership proved to be a revolving door, with James H. Crowley lasting until the end of 1946, when he joined the Chicago Rockets as coach and co-owner—which was a bad career move.[6] Admiral Jonas Howard Ingram, commander-in-chief of the Atlantic Fleet, enlisted as commissioner; within two years, he would resign, citing his age (sixty-three). He declared erroneously, "I still believe that peace [between the two leagues] is close."[7] Ingram was followed by O. O. Kessing.

Among Bell's other accomplishments was his prompt and judicious handling of the Frankie Filchock/Merle Hapes gambling scandal. His actions impressed the public and the owners.[8]

Bell recognized that by enabling owners of terms in smaller and less lucrative cities to survive and even prosper, he was creating stability and strength for the entire league. He summed it up thus: "We're a twelve-team league, let's keep it that way." On another occasion he noted, "It's because we got great owners [unlike baseball]. They argue and fight. Sometimes they can't even agree on when to adjourn for dinner, but when it comes down to helpin' the league, they vote right every time." But it was Bell who led the way to "the right." His empathy for the owners of weaker teams may have stemmed from his struggles with the Philadelphia Eagles. He persuaded owners of prosperous teams in New York and Chicago to forego short-term self-interest for the good of the league occasionally, although those owners' altruism was limited. While sports historian David Harris lauded Pete Rozelle's League Think, the concept was not new; Bell created a foundation for Rozelle to build upon. Rozelle understood and appreciated Bell's legacy.[9]

One can, however, exaggerate the league-think motive. Owners demonstrated self-interest in many ways. Even the proposals touted as revealing their altruism were often cloaked with self-interest. The player draft enabled all owners to have the whip hand in bargaining with players, even if it meant that owners of weaker teams had the opportunity to improve themselves. The battles over scheduling showed some resistance to helping the neighbors. The vaunted national television contract, too, revealed the depth of owner self-interest. Because only one team, at most, stood to receive less television revenue in the short run, it didn't take much altruism to go for the big network score.

Bell's ambivalence toward television augured ill for the league. He didn't appear to see television as the path to much greater popularity for the league. He urged caution by the owners in negotiating television deals. According to the league minutes of the May 1958 meetings, Bell "told members to take the attitude not to price themselves out of television. The Commissioner told members if they are offered a decent figure and a five-year contract for TV, to take it as it will be one of the smartest things they could do for their team, for their sponsor, and for the league."[10] Bell had earlier introduced Bill MacPhail, CBS-TV's sports director, to the owners. Given the difference between Bell's and Rozelle's ages and outlooks, it is difficult to imagine that Bell would have used MacPhail's abilities and eagerness to market the NFL to the same extent that Pete Rozelle did.[11] Bell expressed caution with regard to television at the January 1958 and January 1959 meetings. Somehow he seemed haunted by the NFL's years of scrounging for revenue and survival.[12]

Bell liked to portray himself as the players' friend. To some degree, he undoubtedly enjoyed helping the young men in the league, within the constraints of not antagonizing the owners too much. He testified before the antitrust subcommittee that players felt free to present grievances, and he tried to resolve the grievances informally if possible. While the committee members winced at his calling the players "boys" and treating them as "kids," this may have been a reflection of the growing age difference between himself and the players.[13] While players testified that Bell ultimately served the owners, many of them voiced satisfaction with, if not affection for, him.

Bell, however, appeared to be growing weary of the decades-long struggle to establish the NFL. He gave what can be seen in retrospect as a valedictory speech at the January 1959 meetings: "Don't argue among yourselves, it can only hurt us. I guess I am getting a little old and sentimental and mellow but I hate arguments between teams and between coaches. . . . I have no desire to run the League like a czar. Pro football is my life. . . . Build up the National Football League."[14]

Bell's sudden death came at an inopportune time for the league. The new league that he had touted at the congressional antitrust hearings during the summer of 1959 was becoming a reality. AFL leader Lamar Hunt had a relationship with Bell which, while it was not completely based on mutual trust, at least held potential to reach some sort of accommodation.[15]

Bell and Rozelle both scored triumphs in antitrust cases concerning television. Since television became a major source of revenues and prestige, their victories shaped the NFL we know today. Jack Orr credited Bell with assuaging congressional concerns about the NFL's practices: "Whatever he [Bell] said, he said it well. Emanuel Celler (D-Brooklyn), chairman of the Judiciary Subcommittee, who had had his back up about the running of professional sports, listened to Bell in person. After Bell's testimony, Celler said he was willing to modify his views."[16]

Pete Rozelle had over a decade of experience in marketing and professional sports, beginning in the late 1940s. Bell had selected him to help resolve a long-standing feud between the Rams' owners, and the young man succeeded so admirably that he became the Los Angeles Rams' general manager at the time of Bell's death in the autumn of 1959. The owners turned to Rozelle because they could not resolve the split between the supporters of Interim Commissioner Austin Gunsel, Bell's security officer, and Marshall Leahy, the league's legal counsel. George Halas, hoping to get expansion approved, remained neutral, trying not to incur enmity and jeopardize his proposal. Rozelle became an ideal candidate because no one had reason to oppose his surprise candidacy. The rival groups quickly chose to support him as a compromise candidate. The owners elected him commissioner on the twenty-third ballot.[17]

Almost concurrently with the NFL owners' selection of Pete Rozelle, the AFL chose Joe Foss, former fighter pilot and governor of South Dakota, to be its commissioner after University of Michigan coach Fritz Crisler rejected the offer. Foss's political background was a key inducement for the

AFL owners' approval of his candidacy. Both sets of league owners realized the AFL-NFL fight would spill over into Congress.[18]

Rozelle's ability to get along with people while still exerting an unshakable determination and authority proved invaluable. While Bell undoubtedly recognized the potential value of New York's Madison Avenue advertising industry, Rozelle was superbly equipped to exploit this potential to the fullest. Rozelle moved the league office to a prestigious address in New York City. As Michael MacCambridge put it, "In New York, Rozelle was close to the advertising, television, and publishing industries, a mass media community already galvanized by the rise of pro football and the concurrent Giants renaissance that would put them in six title games in eight seasons. Rozelle quickly solidified important friendships with key executives like Jack Landry at Philip Morris, one of the league's main advertisers, and Bill MacPhail, head of sports at CBS. Both were visionaries in their respective fields."[19] The Rozelle-MacPhail relationship would greatly enrich NFL owners in the years that followed.

When Rozelle testified before yet another congressional antitrust subcommittee in 1964, he told the members that the league's efforts to promote parity had "made it possible for Green Bay, a town of 62,000 people, to participate in a league on an equal basis with New York, a city of 8 million people." Bert Bell would have approved.[20] Rozelle again portrayed owners as "true sportsmen," who loved the game and the fans: "They'll do what's best for the fans. . . . None of them are out for the quick buck."[21]

The Game Itself

Pundits and historians trying to explain the NFL's rise during the 1950s may be giving short shrift to an obvious point. The owners had an attractive product to sell. NFL games were exciting, violent, and increasingly fashionable. The game was better suited for television, especially as the medium's technology improved. The owners' efforts to make the game more exciting paid off.

The other explanations fall short. The league's revenue sharing, while it did not create the perverse outcomes of baseball's plans, came with regressive elements that limited the transfers of revenue from the wealthy Cleveland and Los Angeles teams to the downtrodden Chicago Cardinals.

A switch from the intradivision home-and-home schedule to a round-robin format might have helped the Cardinals, Steelers, Eagles, and Redskins to a greater degree than did the gate-sharing plan, although such a change might have injured the Packers. The league's vaunted League Think was not much in evidence. Owners voted down a measure to apply revenue sharing to television revenues; the national TV contract did not require significant sacrifice on the part of any team, except possibly one. Owners decided relocation and territorial rights on the basis of payoffs to owners whose territory was being invaded. The reverse-order draft gave all owners strengthened bargaining power over players; the draft, at best, gave owners of downtrodden teams an opportunity for improvement (and a rather modest one, at that), but not a guarantee. Owners of wealthy teams lobbied for the lottery draft pick, belying their claims of willingness to help weaker teams. While the NFL featured a lower ratio of idealized to actual standard deviations than baseball, teams such as the Cleveland Browns dominated postseason play. Other teams, such as Washington, Pittsburgh, and the aforementioned Cardinals, stumbled and bumbled through the 1950s.

Bringing in the popular Cleveland Browns and San Francisco 49ers combined with the Rams' relocation to Los Angeles to give the league three very strong franchises. The eventual demise of weak teams such as the Boston Yanks and the eventual resurrection of the Baltimore Colts also helped create another strong franchise. The league had yet to fully resolve the problems of limited appeal and limited stadium capacities in Philadelphia, Pittsburgh, Green Bay, and Washington. The league's most pressing problem by the late 1950s, the Chicago Cardinals, moved to somewhat greener pastures in St. Louis.

The owners received increasing amounts of money from television, but their gains throughout the 1950s were no more impressive than those of Major League Baseball. Not until the league signed the national television contract did television become a major source of revenue. CBS's willingness to pay a large amount for the contract, of course, depended upon the league's having a good product to sell.

Throughout the postwar years, NFL owners tinkered with the game's playing rules. From two-platoon football to moving in the hash marks to streamlining the football itself, owners sought ways to create a more exciting game. The NFL product of the 1930s might not have proven as attractive to television audiences, given its slow, plodding games that often resulted in single-digit scores. In the 1935 season, no team scored 200 points during its twelve league games and four of the nine teams scored fewer than 100 points; by 1958, eleven of the twelve teams scored more than 200 points. The only team that failed to crack the 200-point barrier in 1958 scored 193. Both seasons featured twelve-game schedules (although two teams in 1935 played just eleven games). Although integration did not appear to directly boost teams' win-loss records and attendance, with the Browns being the possible exception (however, they had no prior season with which to compare), the enlarged pool of players undoubtedly improved the quality of the league's games.

By the celebrated 1958 championship game, then, NFL football had evolved into a game that captured the imaginations and hearts of millions of fans. The game's action was perfect for the improving television technology. The subsequent television bonanza and battle against the AFL demonstrated the game's burgeoning popularity.

APPENDIX OF TABLES

TABLE 1. Characteristics of NFL cities (1950)

Team	% black[1]	White median income[2]	Black median income[3]
Baltimore Colts	19.0	$2,399	$1,345
Chicago Bears/Cardinals	10.4	$2,695	$1,919
Cleveland Browns	10.2	$2,611	$1,743
Detroit Lions	11.8	$2,902	$2,290
Green Bay Packers[4]	0.0	N/A	N/A
Los Angeles Rams	4.9	$2,297	$1,627
New York Giants[5]	8.4	$2,554	$1,696
Philadelphia Eagles	12.6	$2,429	$1,548
Pittsburgh Steelers	5.9	$2,359	$1,608
San Francisco 49ers	6.2	$2,557	$1,865
Washington Redskins	22.7	$2,892	$1,843
POTENTIAL CITIES			
Dallas	13.3	$2,066	$1,018
Kansas City	10.7	$2,383	$1,407
Milwaukee	2.5	$2,535	$2,032
Minneapolis	1.1	$2,254	$1,652
St. Louis	12.3	$2,403	$1,402

1 Proportion of population fourteen years old and over that is black; based on Standard Metropolitan Statistical Area (Table 87).
2 Individuals, SMSA (Table 87).
3 Individuals, SMSA data (Table 87).
4 Green Bay not a SMSA.
5 New York portion of New York–Northeastern New Jersey SMSA.

Source: U.S. Department of Commerce, *Census of Housing*, 1952, II: (section and page) 5:463, 9:101, 13:336, 20:169, 22:335, 23:248, 25:293, 32:441, 35:499, 38:523, 43:591, 49:221.

TABLE 2. NFL attendance, 1946–60 (in 000s)

	BAL[1]	CHB	CHC	CLE	DET	GB	LA[2]	NY	PHI	PIT	SF	WAS	OTH[3]	TOTAL
1945	DNP[4]	140	32	DNP	156	110	78	314	183	96	DNP	209	33	1,424
1946	DNP	247	123	DNP	124	108	212	362	177	179	DNP	202	118	1,852
1947	DNP	229	176	DNP	155	164	200	190	222	207	DNP	215	122	1,880
1948	DNP	262	179	DNP	113	132	190	139	156	175	DNP	196	71	1,614
1949	DNP	258	169	DNP	104	100	299	137	167	153	DNP	167	48	1,602
1950	DNP	265	145	200	149	117	141	176	209	158	153	153	217	2,092
1951	DNP	227	106	231	214	105	293	174	120	134	187	147	47	1,987
1952	DNP	236	139	240	280	107	302	203	123	133	220	146	57	2,187
1953	170	218	121	275	316	127	328	147	148	158	208	145	0	2,360
1954	164	236	126	183	325	119	312	190	158	181	257	126	0	2,378
1955	237	255	151	252	310	153	383	154	183	176	270	155	0	2,680
1956	238	291	136	222	331	144	367	281	148	170	275	147	0	2,750
1957	280	267	136	324	334	161	446	291	130	169	334	158	0	3,030
1958	322	274	121	371	321	168	502	294	175	141	334	160	0	3,183
1959	343	268	160	338	280	190	444	390	216	160	331	170	0	3,292
1960	343	273	140	338	306	204	370	358	286	173	313	137	129	3,370
Total[5]	2,097	2,812	1,479	2,976	3,167	1,595	3,890	2,657	1,896	1,753	2,882	1,643	450	29,307

1 Baltimore is the second version of the team, 1953–60.
2 Played in Cleveland in 1945.
3 Includes Baltimore in 1950, Boston/New York Yankees in 1946–51, and Dallas in 1952 and 1960.
4 Did not play.

5 Total for 1950–60 seasons. 1950–60 are post-absorption years that include the three AAFC survivors.

Notes: League champions in boldface.

Paid attendance listed in U.S. House, *Organized Professional Team Sports*, 1957: 2551 reports lower attendance than the totals shown above, usually by 100,000–200,000 per season (1950–56). Teams had wildly different numbers of home games during 1945 (Giants with seven; Cardinals with two); one game played at a neutral field (Cardinals and Lions, 5,461) included in total.

Source: Maher and Gill, *Pro Football Encyclopedia*, 117–20.

TABLE 3. NFL ticket prices, earliest and latest reported prices for box and reserved tickets, 1941–61 (in dollars)

	First year[1]	First year Box/Res.[2]	1952 Box/Res.	1956 Box/Res.	Last year	Last year Box/Res.
BAL	1948	5.00/3.50	4.80/3.60[3]	4.50/3.50	1961	6.00/5.00
CHIB	1947	4.80/3.60	4.00/3.00	4.00/3.00	1959	5.00/4.00
CHIC	1949	4.00/3.00	4.00/3.00	4.00/3.00	1960	6.00/5.00[4]
CLE	1946	3.60/2.40	3.60/2.40	4.00/3.00	1961	5.00/4.00
DET	1945	3.50/2.00	5.00/4.00	3.50/—[5]	1961	3.50/—
GB	1952	4.80/3.60	4.80/3.60	4.75/3.50[6]	—	—/—
LA[7]	1941	2.00/1.65	—/2.00[8]	—/2.50	—	—/—
NY[9]	1939	3.30/2.20	4.00/3.00	5.00/4.00	1961	5.00/4.00
PHI	1948	4.00/3.00	4.00/3.00	5.00/4.00[10]	1959	6.00/5.00
PIT	1950	6.00/4.35	6.00/4.35	6.00/5.00	1960	6.00/5.00
SF	1949	3.75/3.00	3.75/3.00	3.75/—[11]	1961	4.50—
WAS	1943	2.20/1.65	4.80/3.60	4.50/3.50	1960	6.00/5.00

1 First year ticket prices listed in sources examined.

2 Single-game box seat and reserved seat prices.

3 Baltimore did not play in 1952; 1948 is for first Colts' team.

4 In 1960, Cardinals played in St. Louis. Last St. Louis price was 1958, $5/$4.

5 Beginning with 1955, Lions only listed one kind of reserved seating (normally $3.00 from 1949 through 1956). These seats increased in 1957 to $3.50.

6 Did not list prices for 1956 on; 1955 prices shown.

7 Cleveland through 1945; LA thereafter.

8 Rams only sporadically listed general admission ($2.00 1952; $2.40 in 1953–54; $2.50 in 1955).

9 New York Giants charged $3.30 and $2.20 until at least 1943.

10 Eagles did not list prices in 1956; 1955 prices were $5/$4.

11 49ers quit listing reserved but showed cheaper seats after 1953.

Sources: Media Guides and Team Programs at Joyce Sports Collection, Notre Dame University; Media Guides, Team Programs, and Team Files at Pro Football Hall of Fame Archives and information Center (for years, see bibliography); Advertisement in *Cleveland Plain Dealer*, October 3, 1946, 10.

TABLE 4. AAFC and NFL reported losses, 1946–49

	Losses[1]	W-L %	Home att.[2]	Per-g att.	Road att.	Per-g att.
Brooklyn[3]	1,050	0.214	247	12	540	26
Buffalo	800	0.472	672	25	654	24
Chicago	1,125	0.231	538	20	620	23
Cleveland	165	0.898	1,299	48	951	35
Los Angeles	1,425	0.481	857	32	777	29
Miami-Baltimore[4]	1,000	0.250	614	23	617	23
New York	835	0.667	760	28	893	33
San Francisco	80	0.722	944	35	878	33
League	6,480	0.500	5,931	28	5,931	28

NFL

	Losses	W-L %	Home att.	Per-g att.	Road att.	Per-g att.
Boston/NYB[5]	900	0.245	360	15	605	26
Chicago Bears	N/A[6]	0.755	997	42	881	38
Chicago Cardinals	15	0.691	647	31	898	35
Detroit	400	0.213	496	21	516	22
Green Bay	155	0.372	505	22	692	29
Los Angeles	825	0.596	901	39	786	33
New York	250	0.436	829	33	576	26
Philadelphia	N/A	0.734	721	30	722	31
Pittsburgh	N/A	0.511	713	31	598	25
Washington	N/A	0.447	779	32	674	29
League	2,545[7]	0.500	6,948	30	6,948	30

1 $ in 000s.
2 All attendance figures in 000s.
3 Brooklyn played three seasons (1946–48) before merging with New York Yankees (1949).
4 Miami (1946) and Baltimore (1947–49) combined.
5 Boston Yanks (1946–48) became New York Bulldogs (1949).
6 Not available.
7 Does not include profits for four teams.

Source: Ed Sainsbury, "Bitter Pro Football War Cost Magnates $9,000,000," Philadelphia Inquirer, December 25, 1949, 26.

TABLE 5. NFL net income before taxes, 1952–56 ($ in 000s)

Franchise	1952	1953	1954	1955	1956	Total	Per year
Baltimore Colts	—	-56	56	204	140	345	86
Chicago Bears	2	1	29	77	110	219	44
Chicago Cardinals	-78	-272	-162	-205	-81	-799	-160
Cleveland Browns	64	112	75	**137**	101	489	98
Detroit Lions	**115**	**247**	363	206	237	1,168	234
Green Bay Packers	-25	21	86	89	53	224	45
Los Angeles Rams	103	155	244	227	193	922	184
New York Giants	49	14	16	49	**123**	251	50
Philadelphia Eagles	-27	32	107	46	-12	146	29
Pittsburgh Steelers	-5	36	43	35	24	133	27
San Francisco 49ers	185	153	350	154	224	1,066	213
Washington Redskins	104	-6	-27	42	47	160	32
League	487	437	1,182	1,060	1,160	4,325	
Team average	44	36	98	88	97	73	
Standard deviation	78	130	152	116	96		

Note: League champions in boldface.

Source: U.S. House, *Organized Professional Team Sports*, 1957: 2562–65.

TABLE 6. NFL gross operating income, 1952–56 ($ in 000s)

Franchise	1952	1953	1954	1955	1956	Total	Per year
Baltimore Colts	—	659	673	926	947	3,205	801
Chicago Bears	1,051	1,027	1,159	1,194	1,512	5,943	1,189
Chicago Cardinals	632	540	658	668	825	3,323	665
Cleveland Browns	709	816	**811**	**1,009**	966	4,311	862
Detroit Lions	**843**	**1,013**	1,134	1,003	1,075	5,069	1,014
Green Bay Packers	478	576	631	684	681	3,050	610
Los Angeles Rams	829	906	1,059	1,161	1,194	5,148	1,030
New York Giants	601	569	709	753	**935**	3,566	713
Philadelphia Eagles	472	569	716	657	692	3,106	621
Pittsburgh Steelers	643	783	901	886	909	4,123	825
San Francisco 49ers	1,248	1,243	1,534	1,545	1,634	7,205	1,441
Washington Redskins	822	808	772	969	1,000	4,371	874
League	8,327	9,511	10,757	11,455	12,370	52,420	
Team Average	757	793	896	955	1,031	888	
Standard Deviation	236	223	274	260	292		
Top:Bottom[1]	2.64	2.30	2.43	2.35	2.40	2.36	

1 Team with highest gross operating income/Team with lowest gross operating income.

Note: League champions in boldface.

Source: U.S. House, *Organized Professional Team Sports*, 1957: 2562–65.

TABLE 7. NFL home game receipts, 1952–56 ($ in 000s)

Franchise	1952	1953	1954	1955	1956	Total	Per year
Baltimore Colts	—	318	343	493	499	1,654	413
Chicago Bears	643	578	704	742	862	3,530	706
Chicago Cardinals	324	249	245	331	285	1,434	287
Cleveland Browns	284	308	**294**	**412**	333	1,631	326
Detroit Lions	**414**	**418**	439	457	477	2,206	441
Green Bay Packers	182	245	225	269	255	1,176	235
Los Angeles Rams	322	369	419	522	498	2,130	426
New York Giants	216	171	229	209	**437**	1,262	252
Philadelphia Eagles	136	179	224	245	216	1,001	200
Pittsburgh Steelers	354	436	534	508	513	2,345	469
San Francisco 49ers[1]	654	599	696	763	795	3,506	701
Washington Redskins	428	427	365	505	489	2,213	443
League	3,958	4,299	4,720	5,456	5,662	24,096	
Team average	360	358	393	455	472	408	
Standard deviation	101	106	117	135	140		
Top:Bottom[2]	4.81	3.49	3.14	3.66	3.98	3.53	

1 San Francisco includes admission taxes.
2 Team with highest home game receipts/Team with lowest home game receipts.
  Note: League champions in boldface.
  Source: U.S. House, *Organized Professional Team Sports*, 1957: 2562–65.

TABLE 8. NFL home game receipts/attendance, 1952–56 ($ per attendee)

	1952	1953	1954	1955	1956	Avg.
Baltimore Colts	—	1.87	2.09	2.08	2.09	2.04
Chicago Bears	2.72	2.65	2.98	2.91	2.96	2.85
Chicago Cardinals	2.32	2.06	1.95	2.19	2.09	2.13
Cleveland Browns	1.18	1.12	**1.60**	**1.63**	1.50	1.39
Detroit Lions	**1.48**	**1.33**	1.35	1.47	1.44	1.41
Green Bay Packers	1.70	1.93	1.90	1.76	1.77	1.81
Los Angeles Rams	1.07	1.12	1.34	1.36	1.36	1.26
New York Giants	1.06	1.17	1.20	1.36	**1.56**	1.29
Philadelphia Eagles	1.10	1.21	1.42	1.34	1.47	1.32
Pittsburgh Steelers	2.67	2.76	2.95	2.88	3.01	2.86
San Francisco 49ers	2.97	2.88	2.71	2.83	2.89	2.85
Washington Redskins	2.94	2.95	2.89	3.25	3.33	3.08
League	1.81	1.82	1.99	2.04	2.06	1.95

Note: League champions in boldface.

Sources: Home game receipts from U.S. House, *Organized Professional Team Sports*, 1957: 2562–65; attendance from Maher and Gill, *Pro Football Encyclopedia*, 117–20.

TABLE 9. NFL away game receipts, 1952–56 ($ in 000s)

Franchise	1952	1953	1954	1955	1956	Total	Per year
Baltimore Colts	—	151	156	231	239	777	194
Chicago Bears	195	172	213	274	328	1,183	237
Chicago Cardinals	150	140	131	136	227	784	157
Cleveland Browns	171	170	**185**	**232**	169	927	185
Detroit Lions	**174**	**216**	252	234	260	1,136	227
Green Bay Packers	162	169	202	265	229	1,028	206
Los Angeles Rams	194	182	222	255	245	1,098	220
New York Giants	134	155	156	193	**201**	840	168
Philadelphia Eagles	122	137	201	168	181	808	162
Pittsburgh Steelers	149	142	139	174	206	811	162
San Francisco 49ers	230	237	251	247	238	1,204	241
Washington Redskins	120	149	128	177	181	754	151
League	1,802	2,021	2,237	2,586	2,705	11,351	
Team average	164	168	186	216	225	192	
Standard deviation	38	31	44	44	43		
Top:Bottom[1]	1.91	1.73	1.97	2.01	1.94	1.60	

1 Team with highest away game receipts/Team with lowest away game receipts.
Note: League champions in boldface.
Source: U.S. House, *Organized Professional Team Sports*, 1957: 2562–65.

TABLE 10. NFL exhibition game receipts, 1952–56 ($ in 000s)

Franchise	1952	1953	1954	1955	1956	Total	Per year
Baltimore Colts[1]	—	63	32	42	52	189	47
Chicago Bears	92	124	71	81	100	468	94
Chicago Cardinals	117	85	125	102	130	558	112
Cleveland Browns	98	137	**150**	**176**	270	831	166
Detroit Lions	**141**	**193**	194	156	153	836	167
Green Bay Packers	54	64	51	73	54	295	59
Los Angeles Rams	268	251	252	211	279	1,261	252
New York Giants	93	84	105	133	**118**	533	107
Philadelphia Eagles	89	91	110	113	132	536	107
Pittsburgh Steelers	78	101	72	98	85	434	87
San Francisco 49ers[2]	273	295	391	363	371	1,694	339
Washington Redskins	96	127	142	131	151	646	129
League	1,398	1,615	1,695	1,678	1,895	8,282	
Team average	127	135	141	140	158	140	
Standard deviation	74	75	100	84	98		
Top:Bottom[3]	5.10	4.71	12.10	8.70	7.07	8.95	

1 Baltimore only played four seasons, so ratio is overstated.
2 San Francisco includes visitors' share and admission taxes; 1954 and 1955 also include All-Star Game; 1956 includes All-Star Game and playoff game.
3 Team with highest exhibition game receipts/Team with lowest exhibition game receipts.
Note: League champions in boldface.
Source: U.S. House, *Organized Professional Team Sports*, 1957: 2562–65.

TABLE 11. NFL receipts from sale of television
and radio rights, 1952–56 ($ in 000s)

Franchise	1952	1953	1954	1955	1956	Total	Per year
Baltimore Colts	—	94	115	130	124	462	115
Chicago Bears	96	140	160	85	202	683	137
Chicago Cardinals	15	53	137	78	151	434	87
Cleveland Browns	100	147	**125**	**138**	150	660	132
Detroit Lions	**86**	**137**	212	125	149	708	142
Green Bay Packers	30	63	114	35	95	337	67
Los Angeles Rams	24	80	145	141	141	530	106
New York Giants	158	158	218	218	**179**	931	186
Philadelphia Eagles	90	125	145	85	120	565	113
Pittsburgh Steelers	53	95	150	100	100	498	100
San Francisco 49ers	58	69	139	116	165	546	109
Washington Redskins	60	80	104	112	145	502	100
League total	769	1,239	1,764	1,364	1,720	6,856	1,371
Team average	70	103	147	114	143	581	116
Standard deviation	42	36	36	45	31	156	30
Top/Bottom[1]	10.53	3.00	2.09	6.18	2.12	2.76	2.76

1 Team with the most television and radio receipts/Team with the least television and radio receipts.
Note: League champions in boldface.
Source: U.S. House, *Organized Professional Team Sports*, 1957: 2567.

TABLE 12. NFL gross operating expenses, 1952–56 ($ in 000s)

Franchise	1952	1953	1954	1955	1956	Total	Per year
Baltimore Colts	—	714	617	723	807	2,861	715
Chicago Bears	1,049	1,027	1,130	1,117	1,402	5,725	1,145
Chicago Cardinals	710	813	819	873	906	4,121	824
Cleveland Browns	645	704	**737**	**872**	865	3,822	764
Detroit Lions	**728**	**767**	771	797	837	3,901	780
Green Bay Packers	505	556	546	598	633	2,838	568
Los Angeles Rams	725	751	815	934	1,001	4,226	845
New York Giants	552	555	693	704	**811**	3,314	663
Philadelphia Eagles	499	537	609	611	704	2,960	592
Pittsburgh Steelers	647	747	859	851	884	3,988	798
San Francisco 49ers	1,063	1,090	1,184	1,391	1,400	6,128	1,226
Washington Redskins	718	814	798	928	953	4,210	842
League	7,842	9,074	9,577	10,398	11,204	48,094	
Team average	713	756	798	866	934	815	
Standard deviation	190	172	193	221	240		
Top:Bottom[1]	2.13	2.03	1.94	2.33	2.22	2.16	

1 Team with highest gross operating expenses/Team with lowest gross operating expenses.

Note: League champions in boldface.

Source: U.S. House, *Organized Professional Team Sports*, 1957: 2562–65.

TABLE 13. NFL administrative salaries, 1952–56 ($ in 000s)

Franchise	1952	1953	1954	1955	1956	Total	Per year
Baltimore Colts	—	27	45	45	52	169	42
Chicago Bears	71	73	88	97	144	473	95
Chicago Cardinals	12	14	16	26	57	125	25
Cleveland Browns	119	123	**126**	**134**	133	635	127
Detroit Lions[1]	**119**	**156**	174	166	188	803	161
Green Bay Packers	30	35	41	47	50	202	40
Los Angeles Rams	125	129	177	164	175	770	154
New York Giants	83	86	114	117	**144**	544	109
Philadelphia Eagles	7	7	7	10	10	42	8
Pittsburgh Steelers	90	122	143	139	156	650	130
San Francisco 49ers[1]	79	87	103	181	188	638	128
Washington Redskins	98	111	111	129	135	584	117
League	834	970	1,146	1,254	1,432	5,635	
Team average	76	81	95	105	119	96	
Standard deviation	42	50	57	59	61		
Top:Bottom[2]	17.93	20.94	23.84	18.14	18.79	19.20	

1 Detroit and San Francisco include coaches' salaries.
2 Team with highest administrative salaries/Team with lowest administrative salaries.
   Note: League champions in boldface.
   Source: U.S. House, *Organized Professional Team Sports*, 1957: 2562–65.

TABLE 14. NFL other expenses, 1952–56 ($ in 000s)

Franchise	1952	1953	1954	1955	1956	Total	Per year
Baltimore Colts	—	266	309	360	407	1,342	336
Chicago Bears	615	593	619	618	854	3,299	660
Chicago Cardinals	443	554	540	553	530	2,621	524
Cleveland Browns	246	302	**306**	**370**	360	1,585	317
Detroit Lions	**291**	**294**	274	297	296	1,452	290
Green Bay Packers	243	267	261	289	306	1,365	273
Los Angeles Rams	309	359	346	432	450	1,896	379
New York Giants	222	221	273	280	**325**	1,321	264
Philadelphia Eagles	272	293	348	344	398	1,655	331
Pittsburgh Steelers	348	389	462	469	449	2,118	424
San Francisco 49ers	741	753	774	885	880	4,034	807
Washington Redskins	402	458	450	558	542	2,410	482
League	4,131	4,750	4,964	5,456	5,797	25,099	
Team Average	376	396	414	455	483	425	
Standard Deviation	166	163	161	177	196		
Top:Bottom[1]	3.34	3.41	2.97	3.16	2.97	3.05	

1 Team with highest other expenses/Team with lowest other expenses.

Note: League champions in boldface.

Source: U.S. House, *Organized Professional Team Sports*, 1957: 2562–65.

TABLE 15. NFL player salaries, 1952–56 ($ in 000s)

Franchise	1952	1953	1954	1955	1956	Total	Per year
Baltimore Colts	—	222	231	356	294	1,104	276
Chicago Bears	291	287	341	318	343	1,580	316
Chicago Cardinals	253	243	262	294	318	1,371	274
Cleveland Browns[1]	279	275	**298**	**351**	368	1,571	314
Detroit Lions	**294**	**300**	312	315	330	1,552	310
Green Bay Packers	232	255	245	262	278	1,271	254
Los Angeles Rams	282	252	281	323	353	1,492	298
New York Giants	244	239	299	303	**324**	1,409	282
Philadelphia Eagles	219	234	238	253	283	1,227	245
Pittsburgh Steelers	209	236	254	242	277	1,219	244
San Francisco 49ers	243	250	307	325	333	1,457	291
Washington Redskins	217	245	237	241	276	1,216	243
League	2,764	3,038	3,305	3,584	3,778	16,469	3,294
Team average	251	253	275	299	315	1,396	279
Standard deviation	31	23	36	40	32	162	28
Top:Bottom[2]	1.41	1.35	1.48	1.48	1.33	1.30	1.30

1 Cleveland 1955 and 1956 includes All-Star Game.
2 Team with highest player salaries/Team with lowest player salaries.
  Notes: League champions in boldface.
  These figures do not include bonuses.
  Source: U.S. House, *Organized Professional Team Sports*, 1957: 2567.

TABLE 16. NFL Championship Game finances, 1945–59

Year	Attendance	Gross gate receipts	Players' pool	Winners' share	Losers' share
1945	32,178	$164,542	$ 95,261	$1,470	$902
1946	58,346	$282,955	$143,953	$1,976	$1,296
1947	30,759	$159,498	$ 83,887	$1,132	$754
1948	36,309	$223,622	$109,856	$1,541	$874
1949	27,980	$149,345	$ 77,541	$1,095	$740
1950	29,751	$157,078	$ 76,272	$1,113	$686
1951	57,522	$328,053	$156,551	$2,108	$1,483
1952	50,934	$314,319	$174,045	$2,275	$1,712
1953	54,577	$358,693	$188,403	$2,424	$1,654
1954	43,827	$289,126	$184,524	$2,479	$1,586
1955	85,693	$504,257	$276,665	$3,508	$2,316
1956	56,836	$517,385	$284,833	$3,779	$2,485
1957	55,263	$593,968	$335,708	$4,295	$2,750
1958	N/A	N/A	N/A	N/A	N/A
1959	57,545	$666,281	$389,020	$4,674	$3,083

Sources: National Football League (1945–57), NFL *Records and Rules Manual*; *The Sporting News*, January 6, 1960, Sec. 2, p. 3.

TABLE 17. NFL franchise sales and expansion fees, 1946–63

Franchise	Year	Price	Year	Price
Baltimore Colts	1948	$180,000	1964	$1,000,000[1]
Cleveland Browns	1953	$600,000	1961	$3,925,000
Dallas Cowboys	1960	$600,000		
Detroit Lions	1948	$185,000	1963	$6,000,000
Los Angeles Rams	1962	$7,100,000[2]		
Minnesota Vikings	1960	$600,000		
Philadelphia Eagles	1949	$250,000	1963	$5,505,500
San Francisco 49ers	1947	$100,000[3]		
Washington Redskins	1960	$350,000[4]		

1 Carroll Rosenbloom bought 31 percent of stock for $1,000,000.
2 Dan Reeves purchased team for imputed value of $7,100,000.
3 Tony Morabito bought out minority partners for $100,000.
4 Harry Wismer sold his 25 percent share for $350,000.
  Source: Quirk and Fort, *Pay Dirt*, 409–34.

TABLE 18. AAFC home attendance and win-loss records (in 000s)

	1946	1947	1948	1949	Total	W-L
Brooklyn Dodgers	98	77	72	DNP[1]	247	.214
Buffalo Bills	118	218	176	160	672	.472
Chicago Rockets	195	131	104	107	538	.231
Cleveland Browns	400	391	319	190	1,299	.898
Los Angeles Dons	141	304	280	132	857	.481
Miami/Baltimore Colts	49	200	206	159	614	.250
New York/Brooklyn Yankees	195	264	165	135	760	.667
San Francisco 49ers	186	242	286	230	944	.722
Total	1,381	1,827	1,610	1,113	5,931	

1 Did not play.

Sources: Maher and Gill, *Pro Football Encyclopedia*, 112–18. AAFC *Record Manual* (1949 Supplement, 84) lists similar but slightly different attendance figures. Differences are usually within 2,000 with the exceptions of Los Angeles 1948: 288, total 866; Baltimore 1949: 152, total 609; New York/Brooklyn Yankees 1949: 145, total 770. The league total differed in 1948 (1,619 vs. 1,610), 1949 (1,123 vs. 1,113) and grand total (5,947 vs. 5,931) (All-America Football Conference, AAFC *Record Manual*, 1949 Supplement, 4).

TABLE 19. Competitive balance in the NFL and AAFC, 1946–59

	NFL				AAFC			
SEASON	RATIO STDEV[1]	CHAMP[2]	RUP[3]	ATT/G[4]	RATIO STDEV	CHAMP	RUP	ATT/G
1946	1.333	CHIB	NYG	33.7	1.841	CLE	NY	24.7
1947	1.298	CHIC	PHI	31.3	2.277	CLE	NY	32.6
1948	1.891	PHI	CHIC	27.0	2.356	CLE	BUF	28.8
1949	1.785	PHI	LA	26.7	1.856	CLE	SF	26.5
1950	1.700	CLE	LA	26.8				
1951	1.633	LA	CLE	27.6				
1952	1.348	DET	CLE	30.4				
1953	1.871	DET	CLE	32.8				
1954	1.456	CLE	DET	33.0				
1955	1.212	CLE	LA	37.2				
1956	1.181	NYG	CHIB	38.2				
1957	1.174	DET	CLE	42.1				
1958	1.619	BAL	NYG	44.2				
1959	1.562	BAL	NYG	45.7				

1 Actual standard deviation/Idealized standard deviation of win-loss percentages.
2 Winner of league championship game.
3 Loser of league championship game (runner-up).
4 Attendance per regular-season game (ooos).
Source: Maher and Gill, Pro Football Encyclopedia, 256–68.

TABLE 20. Volatility in the NFL, 1946–59

Team	Seasons[1]	W	L	T	W-L%[2]	Range Low[3]	High[4]	Big loss[5]	Big gain[6]
BAL	1953–59	41	42	1	.494	.250	.750	.042	.208
BOS[7]	1946–51	18	48	5	.289	.125	.583	.417	.458
CHIB	1946–59	105	59	3	.638	.292	.833	.375	.375
CHIC	1946–59	65	98	4	.401	.125	.917	.375	.208
CLE	1950–59	88	30	2	.742	.417	.917	.375	.375
DET	1946–59	78	85	4	.479	.091	.833	.542	.500
GB	1946–59	56	108	3	.344	.125	.583	.292	.458
LA	1946–59	94	66	7	.584	.167	.750	.500	.208
NYG	1946–59	95	66	6	.587	.250	.833	.432	.333
PHI	1946–59	85	76	6	.527	.208	.917	.417	.375
PIT	1946–59	77	85	5	.476	.333	.667	.333	.208
SF	1950–59	63	54	3	.538	.250	.750	.292	.375
WAS	1946–59	67	95	5	.416	.250	.667	.208	.417

1 Seasons played in NFL.
2 (wins + 0.5 ties)/(wins + losses + ties).
3 Lowest W-L % for a season.
4 Highest W-L % for a season.
5 Biggest loss in W-L %. over two consecutive seasons.
6 Biggest gain in W-L %. over two consecutive seasons.
7 Boston/New York Yanks (Bulldogs in 1949).
Note: Baltimore (1950) and Dallas (1952) not shown. Both teams went 1-11-0 for their sole seasons.
Source: Maher and Gill, Pro Football Encyclopedia, 256–68.

TABLE 21. Greatest season scoring disparities, 1946–59

BEST RATIOS

Year	Team	League	Points	Against	Points: Points against	W-L record
1946	CLE	AAFC	423	137	3.088	12-2-0
1949	PHI	NFL	364	134	2.716	11-1-0
1948	CHIB	NFL	375	151	2.483	10-2-0
1948	PHI	NFL	376	156	2.410	9-2-1
1947	CLE	AAFC	410	185	2.216	12-1-1
1951	CLE	NFL	331	152	2.178	11-1-0
1950	CLE	NFL	310	144	2.153	10-2-0
1953	CLE	NFL	348	162	2.148	11-1-0
1954	CLE	NFL	336	162	2.074	9-3-0
1948	CLE	AAFC	389	190	2.047	14-0-0
1948	SF	AAFC	495	248	1.996	12-2-0
1949	CLE	AAFC	339	171	1.982	9-1-2

WORST RATIOS

Year	Team	League	Points	Against	Points: Points against	W-L record
1949	GB	NFL	114	329	0.347	2-10-0
1949	NYB	NFL	153	368	0.416	1-10-1
1952	DAL	NFL	182	427	0.426	1-11-0
1946	MIA	AAFC	167	378	0.442	3-11-0
1947	BAL	AAFC	167	377	0.443	2-11-1
1946	DET	NFL	142	310	0.458	1-10-0
1948	CHI	AAFC	202	439	0.460	1-13-0
1950	BAL	NFL	213	462	0.461	1-11-0
1948	BOS	NFL	174	372	0.468	3-9-0
1954	BAL	NFL	131	279	0.470	3-9-0
1954	WAS	NFL	207	432	0.479	3-9-0
1948	DET	NFL	200	407	0.491	2-10-0
1949	BAL	AAFC	172	342	0.504	1-11-0
1958	DET	NFL	193	382	0.505	1-10-1

Source: Maher and Gill, Pro Football Encyclopedia, 256–68.

TABLE 22. Number of players who played in NFL versus number drafted, 1936–38, 1950–52, and 1956–58

Franchise	1936–38 P^1-D^2	PCT.	1950–52 P-D	PCT.	1956–58 P-D	PCT.
Baltimore	DNP[3]	—	5- 5	1.000	9-15	.600
Brooklyn/NYY	12-17	.706	8-11	.727	DNP	—
Chicago Bears	11-15	.733	18-20	.900	14-15	.933
Chicago Cards	9-16	.563	12-15	.800	9-13	.692
Cleveland Browns	DNP	—	13-19	.684	12-18	.667
Detroit	5-14	.357	13-15	.867	10-11	.909
Green Bay	8-14	.571	10-12	.833	14-15	.933
Los Angeles[4]	8-11	.727	14-17	.824	21-29	.724
New York Giants	11-14	.786	14-15	.933	8-12	.667
Philadelphia	8-17	.471	8-13	.615	11-13	.846
Pittsburgh	8-11	.727	10-14	.714	11-12	.917
San Francisco	DNP	—	13-16	.813	11-15	.733
Washington[5]	7-15	.467	11-16	.688	10-15	.667
League	89-150	.593	149-188	.793	140-183	.765

1 Played in NFL.
2 Drafted by the team.
3 Did not play.
4 Washington played in Boston (1936–38).
5 Los Angeles played in Cleveland (1937–38).
   Note: For 1936–38 first fifty players selected; 1950–52 first 66, 70, and 61 players selected; 1956–58 first 61 players selected.
   Source: Carroll, Gershman, Neft, and Thorn, *Total Football*, 1481–500.

TABLE 23. Round drafted of All-NFL players, 1950–60

Rounds	Number[1]	Times All-NFL		
		Once	Twice	Three+
0[2]-1	35	13	7	15
2	21	8	5	8
3	15	4	4	7
4	8	5	1	2
5 to 10	29	8	10	11
11 to 30	29	14	6	9
Not Drafted	18	7	2	9
Total	155	59	35	61

1 Number of times a player was named All-NFL.

2 Bonus picks selected ahead of regular draft.

Note: Of the "not drafted," seven were signed by AAFC teams in 1946 and 1947 and were not drafted. Of the remaining eleven, Boyd, Davis, Lane, Lipscomb, Perry, and Tunnell were African American. Lane, Perry and Tunnell were elected to the Pro Football Hall of Fame.

Sources: Carroll, Gershman, Neft, and Thorn, *Total Football*, 1,481–506; for bonus pick information. Maher and Gill, *Pro Football Encyclopedia*, 35–39 for All-NFL data.

TABLE 24. Teams that drafted All-NFL players, 1950–60

		Times All-NFL			Seasons
	Players drafted[1]	Once	Twice	Three+	All-NFL
BAL 1[2]	4	3	1	0	5
BAL 2[3]	5	1	1	3	21
BKN	2	0	1	1	6
BOS/NYY	6	2	2	2	19
CHIB	14	4	6	4	35
CHIC[4]	7	6	0	1	11
CLE	12	4	1	7	41
DET	13	3	2	8	50
GB	13	4	3	6	40
LA (CLE)[4]	21	9	5	7	52
NYG	18	7	4	7	52
PHI	11	3	3	5	34
PIT	10	4	2	4	21
SF	9	2	3	4	25
WAS	5	4	0	1	8
Other AAFC	5	3	1	1	10
Total	155	59	35	61	430

1 Includes players not drafted but signed as free agents.

2 BAL-1 is the team that folded after 1950.

3 BAL-2 is the team that was resurrected in 1953.

4 Don Paul drafted by CHIC in 1950 and LA in 1948.

Sources: Carroll, Gershman, Neft, and Thorn, Total Football, 1481–506 for bonus pick information; Maher and Gill, Pro Football Encyclopedia, 35–39 for All-NFL data.

TABLE 25. Outcomes for teams that drafted All-NFL players, 1950–60

	Players drafted	Players signed	Entire career	All but last year
BAL 1[1]	4	4	2	0
BAL 2[2]	5	5	4	1
BKN	2	0	0	0
BOS/NYY	6	3	0	0
CHIB	14	12	5	3
CHIC[3]	7	5	1	0
CLE	12	11	4	2
DET	13	12	9	0
GB	13	11	5	2
LA (CLE)[3]	21	15	4	2
NYG	18	13	9	0
PHI	11	10	7	0
PIT	10	7	4	2
SF	9	9	4	0
WAS	5	2	0	1
Other AAFC	5	4	0	2
Total	155	123	58	15

1 BAL-1 is the team that folded after 1950.
2 BAL-2 is the team that was resurrected in 1953.
3 Don Paul drafted by CHIC in 1950 and LA in 1948.

Sources: Carroll, Gershman, Neft, and Thorn, *Total Football*, 1481–1506; Maher and Gill, *Pro Football Encyclopedia*, 35–39 for All-NFL data.

TABLE 26. NL attendance and win-loss records, 1952–56 (in 000s)

Team	Total att.[1]	Home att.[2]	Road att.[3]	Net att.[4]	W-L %[5]
Brooklyn Dodgers	13,171	5,520	7,651	-2,131	.630
Chicago Cubs	8,184	4,133	4,051	82	.440
Cincinnati Reds	7,531	3,676	3,855	-179	.490
Milwaukee Braves[6]	13,080	8,291	4,788	3,503	.549
New York Giants	9,931	4,405	5,526	-1,121	.527
Philadelphia Phillies	8,301	4,206	4,096	110	.510
Pittsburgh Pirates	6,391	3,154	3,237	-83	.352
St. Louis Cardinals	9,604	4,712	4,892	-180	.503

1 Home attendance + Road attendance.
2 Home attendance.
3 Road attendance.
4 Home attendance – Road attendance.
5 Win-loss record for 1952–56 (ties not counted in computation).
6 Braves played in Boston in 1952, Milwaukee 1953–56.

Note: Attendance figures may not sum due to rounding.

Sources: Thorn, Palmer, and Gershmann, *Total Baseball*, 76-77; The Sporting News, *Baseball Guides*, 1953–57; *Complete Baseball Record Book*, 2002 ed., 289, 292, 295, 299, 311, 319, 324, 328, 331–32.

TABLE 27. NFL attendance and win-loss records, 1952–56 (in 000s)

Team	Total att.[1]	Home att.[2]	Road att.[3]	Net att.[4]	W-L %[5]
Baltimore Colts[6]	1,658	799	859	- 60	.340
Chicago Bears	2,479	1,236	1,243	-6	.569
Chicago Cardinals	1,498	672	826	-154	.310
Cleveland Browns	2,137	1,172	964	208	.712
Detroit Lions	2,775	1,561	1,213	348	.678
Green Bay Packers	1,814	650	1,164	-514	.373
Los Angeles Rams	2,857	1,693	1,164	529	.614
New York Giants	1,867	975	892	82	.534
Philadelphia Eagles	1,642	760	882	-122	.500
Pittsburgh Steelers	1,715	819	896	- 77	.417
San Francisco 49ers	2,532	1,230	1,302	- 72	.552
Washington Redskins	1,484	719	765	- 46	.458
Dallas Texans[7]	230	57	173	-117	.083

1 Home attendance + Road attendance.
2 Home attendance.
3 Road attendance.
4 Home attendance – Road attendance.
5 Win-loss record for 1952–56 (ties not counted in computation).
6 Baltimore played 1953–56.
7 Dallas played during 1952.
  Note: Attendance figures may not sum due to rounding.
  Source: Maher and Gill, *Pro Football Encyclopedia*, 117–20.

TABLE 28. Five-year total sources of revenue
in the NFL, 1952–56 ($ in 000s)

Team	Gate[1]	Media[2]	X-games[3]	Gross[4]
Baltimore Colts	$2,431	$377	$189	$3,205
Chicago Bears	$4,713	$683	$468	$5,943
Chicago Cardinals	$2,218	$434	$558	$3,323
Cleveland Browns	$2,558	$660	$831	$4,311
Detroit Lions	$3,341	$708	$836	$5,069
Green Bay Packers	$2,204	$337	$295	$3,050
Los Angeles Rams	$3,228	$530	$1,261	$5,148
New York Giants	$2,102	$931	$533	$3,566
Philadelphia Eagles	$1,809	$565	$536	$3,106
Pittsburgh Steelers	$3,155	$498	$434	$4,123
San Francisco 49ers	$4,710	$546	$1,694	$7,205
Washington Redskins	$2,968	$502	$646	$4,371
League total	$35,437	$6,771	$8,282	$52,420
Top:Bottom	2.61	2.76	8.96	2.36
First:Fourth	2.09	2.02	4.13	1.95
St. deviation[5]	.027	.024	.051	.024

1 Home revenue and road revenue.

2 Sales of television and radio rights.

3 Revenue from exhibition games.

4 Gross operating income from home revenue, road revenue, exhibition games, sales of radio and
television rights, concessions, and other income.

5 Based on share of total league revenue; average team would have 0.833 share.

Source: U.S. House, Organized Professional Team Sports, 1957: 2562–65.

TABLE 29. Estimated gate revenue without gate
sharing in the NL, 1952–56 ($ in 000s)

	1952	1953	1954	1955	1956
Brooklyn	**$1,644**	**$1,787**	$1,745	**$1,833**	**$2,124**
Chicago	$1,309	$983	$1,009	$1,194	$992
Cincinnati	$830	$793	$1,105	$1,123	$1,798
Milwaukee[1]	$375	$2,629	$3,063	$3,108	$3,166
New York	$1,491	$1,264	**$1,818**	$1,482	$1,181
Philadelphia	$1,069	$1,241	$1,149	$1,485	$1,565
Pittsburgh	$1,037	$874	$762	$759	$1,515
St. Louis	$1,199	$1,216	$1,635	$1,359	$1,579
Top:Bottom[2]	4.384	3.315	4.020	4.095	3.192
First:Fourth[3]	2.602	2.649	2.756	2.625	2.434
St. deviation[4]	0.044	0.056	0.059	0.057	0.048
AMERICAN LEAGUE					
Top:Bottom	3.90	5.89	6.86	4.48	4.41
First:Fourth	3.23	4.62	4.18	2.55	2.26
St. deviation	0.060	0.069	0.059	0.045	0.046

1 Milwaukee played in Boston 1952.
2 Team with most gate revenue/Team with least gate revenue.
3 First quartile revenue/Fourth quartile revenue.
4 Standard deviation is based on each team's share of total league gate revenue (mean share = 0.125).
  Note: League champions in boldface.
  Sources: U.S. House, *Organized Professional Team Sports*, 1957: 354–56, 2046–47; Surdam, "'Not-So-Socialist' League," 273–74, for American League measures.

TABLE 30. Actual gate revenue (home and
away) in the NL, 1952–56 ($ in 000s)

	1952	1953	1954	1955	1956
Brooklyn	**$1,708**	**$1,857**	$1,909	**$1,994**	**$2,221**
Chicago	$1,224	$987	$1,032	$1,200	$1,040
Cincinnati	$840	$856	$1,098	$1,141	$1,792
Milwaukee[1]	$462	$2,434	$2,757	$2,808	$2,946
New York	$1,493	$1,312	**$1,836**	$1,586	$1,309
Philadelphia	$1,046	$1,248	$1,204	$1,439	$1,546
Pittsburgh	$990	$888	$803	$801	$1,495
St. Louis	$1,192	$1,247	$1,646	$1,374	$1,574
Top:Bottom[2]	3.697	2.843	3.433	3.506	2.833
First:Fourth[3]	2.459	2.460	2.543	2.473	2.200
St. deviation[4]	0.043	0.050	0.052	0.050	0.043
AMERICAN LEAGUE					
Top:Bottom	3.34	4.77	5.66	3.92	4.04
First:Fourth	2.88	3.83	3.77	2.42	2.24
St. Deviation	0.056	0.065	0.058	0.043	0.046

1 Milwaukee played in Boston 1952.

2 Team with most gate revenue/Team with least gate revenue.

3 First quartile revenue/Fourth quartile revenue.

4 Standard deviation is based on each team's share of total league gate revenue (mean share = 0.125).

Note: League champions in boldface.

Sources: U.S. House, Organized Professional Team Sports, 1957: 354–56, 2046–47; Surdam, "'Not-So-Socialist' League," 273–74, for American League measures.

TABLE 31. Estimated amounts transferred via
gate sharing, 1952–56 ($ in 000s)

	1952	1953	1954	1955	1956
Brooklyn	**$64**	**$70**	$164	**$160**	**$97**
Chicago	-$85	$3	$23	$7	$48
Cincinnati[1]	$10	$63	-$7	$19	-$6
Milwaukee[2]	$87	-$195	-$305	-$300	-$220
New York	$1	$48	**$18**	$103	$127
Philadelphia	-$23	$6	$55	-$46	-$19
Pittsburgh	-$47	$14	$41	$42	-$21
St. Louis	-$7	$31	$11	$15	-$6

1 In 1953, Cincinnati ($36,171) and Milwaukee ($4,178) had road revenue discrepancies; both teams reported more than $0.225 per road attendee.
2 Milwaukee Braves played in Boston during 1952.
  Note: League champions in boldface.
  Columns may not sum to one due to rounding.
  Source: U.S. House, *Organized Professional Team Sports*, 1957: 354–56, 2046–47.

TABLE 32. Summary of gate sharing's effects
on NL teams, 1952–56 ($ in 000s)

	Est. gate rev.[1]	Act. gate rev.[2]	Net rev. transfer[3]	% transfer[4]
Milwaukee	$12,341	$11,407	-$984	-0.076
Brooklyn	$9,133	$9,689	$556	0.061
New York	$7,238	$7,535	$297	0.041
St. Louis	$6,989	$7,034	$44	0.006
Philadelphia	$6,509	$6,482	-$27	-0.004
Cincinnati	$5,649	$5,727	$77	0.014
Chicago	$5,487	$5,482	-$4	-0.001
Pittsburgh	$4,947	$4,977	$30	0.006

1 Estimated home gate revenue without gate sharing.
2 Home and away gate revenue with gate sharing.
3 Amount transferred via gate-sharing plan.
4 Net revenue transfer/Estimated gate revenue.
  Note: Amounts may not agree exactly with figures shown in tables 29, 30, and 31 due to rounding.
  Source: U.S. House, *Organized Professional Team Sports*, 1957: 354–56, 2046–47.

TABLE 33. NL attendance and estimated gate-sharing payments, 1956

ATTENDANCE (IN 000S)
HOME TEAM

	BKN	MIL	CIN	STL	PHI	NY	PIT	CHI	Road att.
Road team	.604	.597	.591	.494	.461	.435	.429	.390	—
Brooklyn	—	343[1]	220	218	215	241	197	133	1,568
Milwaukee	252[1]	—	214	206	166	103	155	149	1,244
Cincinnati	179	349	—	150	133	61	149	82	1,104
St. Louis	144	208	195	—	134	74	144	109	1,009
Philadelphia	144	267	120	98	—	59	99	77	864
New York	216	304	138	127	105	—	117	85	1,092
Pittsburgh	153	230	114	131	96	61	—	85	869
Chicago	122	346	123	100	85	30	89	—	894
Home att.	1,210	2,046	1,124	1,030	935	629	950	720	8,644

NET REVENUE SHARING ($ IN 000S)

	BKN	MIL	CIN	STL	PHI	NY	PIT	CHI	Net
Brooklyn	—	25[2]	12	20	20	7	12	3	98
Milwaukee	-25[2]	—	-37	-1	-28	-55	-20	-54	-221
Cincinnati	-11	37	—	-12	4	-21	10	-11	-5
St. Louis	-20	1	12	—	10	-15	4	3	-6
Philadelphia	-20	28	-4	-10	—	-13	1	-2	-19
New York	-7	55	21	15	13	—	15	15	127
Pittsburgh	-12	20	-10	-4	-1	-15	—	-1	-22
Chicago	-3	54	11	-3	2	-15	1	—	48
Net	-98	221	4	6	19	-128	22	-48	—

1 Explanation of upper panel: Brooklyn drew 343,000 fans for games played in Milwaukee. Milwaukee drew 252,000 fans for games played in Brooklyn.

2 Brooklyn received $25,000 net from Milwaukee from revenue sharing. Milwaukee paid $25,000 net to Brooklyn for revenue sharing.

Note: May not sum due to rounding.

Source: Day-by-day tabulation of attendance recorded in box scores, in New York Times (checked against Des Moines Register). Daily totals were within 1,000 of the published season home and away totals except for Brooklyn home (off 3,817) and Cincinnati home (off 2,067); Milwaukee road (off 1,030), and Pittsburgh road (off 5,058).

TABLE 34. NFL revenue sharing, 1956 (attendance and revenue figures in 000s)

Team	Home att.[1]	Paid rev.[2]	Road att.[3]	Rec. rev.[4]	Net share[5]	W-L %[6]	Gross income[7]
Baltimore Colts	236	$247	238	$236	-$ 8	.417	$947
Chicago Bears	281	$285	281	$298	$13	.818	$1,512
Chicago Cardinals	99	$121	214	$227	$106	.583	$825
Cleveland Browns	208	$192	154	$169	-$23	.417	$966
Detroit Lions	316	$318	248	$260	-$58	.750	$1,075
Green Bay Packers	138	$155	221	$229	$74	.333	$681
Los Angeles Rams	299	$302	236	$245	-$57	.333	$1,194
New York Giants	266	$292	182	$191	-$101	.727	$935
Philadelphia Eagles	148	$151	173	$181	$29	.273	$692
Pittsburgh Steelers	170	$171	196	$206	$35	.417	$909
San Francisco 49ers	248	$265	233	$239	-$26	.455	$1,634
Washington Redskins	143	$163	175	$178	$15	.500	$1,000

1 Home attendance.
2 Gate-share amount paid to visiting teams.
3 Road attendance.
4 Gate-share amount received on road.
5 Paid rev – Rec. rev = Gain (loss) from gate-sharing. May not sum to zero because of rounding.
6 Win-loss record (ties not counted in computation).
7 Gross operating income, including "games at home," "games away," "exhibition games," "radio and television," "concessions (net)" and "other income."
Sources: U.S. House, Organized Professional Team Sports, 1957: 2552–56, 2564–65; Maher and Gill, Pro Football Encyclopedia, 119–20.

TABLE 35. Summary of gate sharing's effects
on NFL teams, 1956 ($ in 000s)

	Receipts[1]	Receipts w/gate shr.[2]	Transfer gate shr.[3]	Transfers/ Receipts[4]
Detroit Lions	$955	$881	-$58	-0.061
Los Angeles Rams	$906	$834	-$57	-0.063
New York Giants	$876	$760	-$101	-0.115
Chicago Bears	$836	$835	$13	0.015
San Francisco 49ers	$795	$755	-$26	-0.033
Baltimore Colts	$742	$722	-$8	-0.011
Cleveland Browns	$569	$536	-$23	-0.040
Pittsburgh Steelers	$513	$539	$35	0.069
Washington Redskins	$488	$495	$15	0.031
Green Bay Packers	$464	$531	$74	0.160
Philadelphia Eagles	$440	$462	$29	0.066
Chicago Cardinals	$277	$378	$106	0.383
Top:Bottom[5]	3.45	2.33		
First:Fourth[6]	2.32	1.91		
St. deviation[7]	0.28	0.22		

1 Actual gate receipts in 1956.
2 Receipts after gate share (less league share).
3 Transfers via gate-sharing plan.
4 Transfers/Receipts.
5 Team with greatest amount/Team with lowest amount.
6 First quartile revenue/Fourth quartile revenue.
7 Standard deviation of receipts.
   Note: Columns do not sum due to league share and rounding.
   Source: U.S. House, *Organized Professional Team Sports*, 1957: 2552–57.

TABLE 36. Attendance at intradivision NFL games, 1956

EASTERN CONFERENCE

		HOME TEAM						
		NYG	CHIC	WAS	CLE	PIT	PHI	Total
R O A D T E A M	NYG	—	21,799	26,261	60,042	31,240	16,562	155,904
	CHIC	62,410	—	25,794	25,312	24,086	36,545	174,147
	WAS	46,351	30,553	—	22,878	27,718	26,607	154,107
	CLE	27,707	20,966	23,332	—	35,398	25,894	133,297
	PIT	48,108	17,724	21,097	50,358	—	22,652	159,939
	PHI	40,960	22,609	22,333	20,654	31,375	—	137,931

WESTERN CONFERENCE

		HOME TEAM						
		CHIB	DET	SF	BAL	GB	LA	Total
R O A D T E A M	CHIB	—	57,024	53,612	45,221	24,668	69,894	250,419
	DET	49,086	—	46,708	42,622	24,668	76,758	239,842
	SF	47,526	55,662	—	37,227	17,986	69,828	228,229
	BAL	48,364	55,788	43,791	—	24,214	51,037	223,194
	GB	49,172	54,087	32,436	40,086	—	45,209	220,990
	LA	48,102	56,281	56,489	40,321	24,200	—	225,393

Note: Teams listed in order of finish in the conference. Cleveland and Pittsburgh tied; Green Bay and Los Angeles tied.

Source: Maher and Gill, *Pro Football Encyclopedia*, 119–20.

TABLE 37. AAFC road and road-home attendance (in 000s)

ROAD ATTENDANCE	1946	1947	1948	1949	Total
Brooklyn Dodgers	174	191	175	DNP[1]	540
Buffalo Bills	156	212	154	132	654
Chicago Rockets	156	167	163	135	620
Cleveland Browns	**206**	**270**	**268**	**207**	951
Los Angeles Dons	194	243	211	129	777
Miami/Baltimore Colts	164	161	166	126	617
New York/Brooklyn Yankees	173	334	215	171	893
San Francisco 49ers	159	249	256	214	878
Total	1,381	1,827	1,610	1,113	5,931

ROAD-HOME ATTENDANCE	1946	1947	1948	1949	Total
Brooklyn Dodgers	76	114	102	DNP	292
Buffalo Bills	38	-6	-22	-28	-18
Chicago Rockets	-40	36	59	27	83
Cleveland Browns	**-194**	**-121**	**-51**	**17**	-348
Los Angeles Dons	53	-61	-69	-3	-80
Miami/Baltimore Colts	115	-39	-40	-33	3
New York/Brooklyn Yankees	-22	70	50	36	134
San Francisco 49ers	-26	7	-30	-16	-66
Total	0	0	0	0	0

1 Did not play.

Note: League champions in boldface.

Sources: Maher and Gill, *Pro Football Encyclopedia*, 112–18. The AAFC *Record Manual* lists similar but slightly different figures. In most cases, differences were within a few thousand. The exceptions are Brooklyn 1946 (166 vs. 174), total (532 vs. 540); Buffalo 1946 (151 vs. 156); Chicago 1949 (128 vs. 135), total (615 vs. 620); Cleveland 1946–49 (213, 275, 271, and 213), total (972 vs. 951); league 1948 (1,618 vs. 1,610), 1949 (1,123 vs. 1,113), and total (5,947 vs. 5,931) (All-America Football Conference, AAFC *Record Manual*, 1949 Supplement, 84).

TABLE 38. Households with television versus
football attendance, 1946–60 (in 000s)

	TVs[1]	NFL Att.[2]	Per team	Per game	AAFC Att.[3]	Per team	Per game
1946	8	1,852	185.2	33.7	1,381	172.6	24.7
1947	14	1,880	188.0	31.3	1,827	228.4	32.6
1948	172	1,617	161.7	27.0	1,610	201.3	28.9
1949	940	1,602	160.2	26.7	1,135	162.1	27.0
1950	3,875	2,092	160.9	26.8			
1951	10,320	1,987	165.6	27.6			
1952	15,300	2,187	182.3	30.4			
1953	20,400	2,360	196.7	32.8			
1954	26,000	2,378	198.2	33.0			
1955	30,700	2,680	223.3	37.2			
1956	34,900	2,750	229.2	38.2			
1957	38,900	3,030	252.5	42.1			
1958	41,924	3,183	265.3	44.2			
1959	43,950	3,292	274.3	45.7			
1960	45,750	3,370	259.2	43.2			

1 Households with television sets (in 000s).
2 Attendance (in 000s) in NFL.
3 Attendance (in 000s) in AAFC.

Notes: NFL had 10 teams (1946–49), 12 teams (1951–59), and 13 teams (1950, 1960); NFL played 55 games (1946), 60 games (1947–49), 78 games (1950, 1960), and 72 games (1951–59).

AAFC had 8 teams and 56 games (1946–48) and 7 teams and 42 games (1949).

Sources: U.S. Department of Commerce, *Historical Statistics II*, 1975: 796 (Series 93–105); Maher and Gill, *Pro Football Encyclopedia*, 112–22.

TABLE 39. Broadcast revenues, MLB and the NFL, 1952–64 ($ in 000s)

Year	MLB				NFL			
	Local	League	Total	Team	Local	League	Total	Team
1952	4,165	N/A[1]	5,400	338	769	N/A	769	70
1953	4,741	N/A	5,952	372	1,239	N/A	1,239	103
1954	5,556	N/A	6,741	421	1,764	N/A	1,764	147
1955	6,123	N/A	7,308	457	1,364	N/A	1,364	114
1956	7,206	N/A	8,366	523	1,720	N/A	1,720	143
1957	5,290	1,750	10,290	643	1,958	N/A	1,958	163
1958	5,950	2,475	11,475	717	2,296	N/A	2,296	191
1959	6,315	3,225	12,790	799	2,634	N/A	2,634	220
1960	9,355	3,174	15,779	986	3,100	N/A	3,100	238
1961	10,780	2,666	16,696	928	3,510	N/A	4,200	300
1962	12,775	2,000	18,525	926	563	4,650	5,903	422
1963	13,000	2,225	18,775	939	710	4,650	6,486	463
1964	14,325	1,700	19,775	989	748	14,100	16,943	1,210

1 Not available or no national contract.

Note: MLB total includes World Series and All-Star Games; NFL total includes all playoff games and Championship Game.

Source: U.S. House, *Inquiry into Professional Sports*, 1977: 668.

TABLE 40. The game on the field, 1945–62

	Season	PER GAME Points[1]	PER GAME Plays[1]	% PASSING plays[2]	YARDS PER Rush[3]	YARDS PER Pass[3]	Int. %[4]	TD:Int.[5]
NFL	1945	37.0	114.9	36.8	3.4	6.8	9.1	.565
	1946	37.8	118.3	36.0	3.3	6.8	9.0	.597
	1947	43.9	121.2	41.1	3.9	7.2	8.4	.752
	1948	46.5	127.8	40.7	4.0	6.7	7.4	.845
	1949	45.0	131.9	41.4	3.9	6.5	7.5	.680
	1950	45.9	129.5	42.6	4.2	6.7	8.0	.641
	1951	43.9	128.9	41.8	4.1	6.8	7.4	.694
	1952	44.6	126.3	44.3	3.8	6.7	7.1	.760
	1953	43.0	126.2	47.0	4.0	6.5	7.2	.618
	1954	43.8	125.1	47.0	4.0	7.2	6.9	.735
	1955	41.7	126.7	41.9	4.0	6.6	6.8	.698
	1956	40.8	121.3	37.6	4.1	7.1	7.3	.675
	1957	39.6	117.9	39.3	3.9	7.4	6.9	.736
	1958	45.2	121.6	45.1	4.2	7.2	6.2	.868
	1959	42.7	119.7	43.1	4.2	7.2	6.0	.891
	1960	43.1	118.0	44.7	4.1	7.2	6.7	.807
	1961	43.0	116.3	46.4	4.2	7.5	6.3	.858
	1962	44.6	116.5	46.9	4.1	7.9	6.1	.923

	Season	PER GAME Points	PER GAME Plays	% PASSING plays	YARDS PER Rush	YARDS PER Pass	Int.%	TD:Int.
AAFC	1946	39.5	110.5	36.5	3.4	6.7	8.3	.711
	1947	42.4	110.7	37.1	4.3	7.1	7.1	.896
	1948	45.6	121.1	41.4	4.6	7.0	6.7	.893
	1949	42.6	119.2	39.2	4.2	7.1	7.3	.727
AFL	1960	43.1	118.0	44.7	4.1	7.2	6.7	.807
	1961	48.9	122.3	53.0	4.0	6.7	6.4	.784
	1962	46.2	120.4	51.3	4.3	6.8	7.0	.727

1 Points and plays by both teams per game.
2 Passing attempts/(Rushing attempts + Passing attempts).
3 Yards per rushing attempt and per passing attempt.
4 Interceptions/Passing attempts.
5 TDs/Interceptions.
Source: Carroll, Gershman, Neft, and Thorn, *Total Football*, 1,429–41.

TABLE 41. Integration on the field and in the stands

Franchise	Year[1]	WIN-LOSS RECORD			ATTENDANCE		
		Bef.[2]	Int.	Diff.	Bef.[3]	Int.	Diff.
CLE/LA[4]	1946	.900	.590	-.310	40	212	172
DET	1948	.250	.167	-.083	155	113	-42
NYG	1948	.250	.333	.083	190	139	-51
BAL I	1950	.083	.083	.000	159	98	-61
GB	1950	.167	.250	.083	100	117	17
CHIB	1952	.583	.417	-.166	227	236	9
CHIC	1952	.250	.333	.083	106	139	33
PHI	1952	.333	.583	.250	120	123	3
PIT	1952	.375	.417	.042	134	133	-1
BAL II[5]	1953	.083	.250	.167	54	170	116
WAS	1962	.107	.429	.322	208	290	82
CLE AAFC	1946	None	.857	—	None	400	—
BKN AAFC	1947	.250	.250	.000	98	77	-21
CHI AAFC	1947	.464	.071	-.393	195	131	-64
LA AAFC	1947	.571	.500	-.071	141	304	163
NY AAFC	1947	.750	.821	.071	195	264	69
SF AAFC	1948	.643	.857	.214	242	286	44

1 Year integrated.
2 Win-Loss record year before integration (ties count as one-half win, unlike Maher-Gill).
3 Attendance season before integration (in 000s).
4 Cleveland Rams played only three home games in 1945.
5 Dallas played only four home games in 1952 before resurrected in Baltimore for 1953.
  Note: Buffalo and Baltimore AAFC teams did not integrate.
  Sources: Ross, Outside the Lines, 165–77; Maher and Gill, Pro Football Encyclopedia, 112–25.

NOTES

Abbreviations

PFHOFAIC AFL LM   AFL League Minutes, 1959–60
PFHOFAIC NFL LM   NFL League Minutes, 1945–60
NYT   *New York Times*
OPTS   *Organized Professional Team Sports*
SI   *Sports Illustrated*
TSN   *The Sporting News*

Introduction

1. Commager quote found at www.americanheritage.com/articles/magazine/ ah/1976/5/1976, viewed December 31, 2010, 10:32 a.m.; "The NFL's Role in American History (Somebody's Gotta Be Kiddin')," *New Yorker*, November 3, 1975, 41–44.

2. The producer of the NFL films, Steve Sabol, grew up watching *Victory at Sea* and Leni Riefenstahl's *Olympia* about the 1936 Olympics. He loved the martial music and the sonorous narration (MacCambridge, *America's Game*, 183, 282).

3. On occasion in the contemporary press, sportswriters referred to the NFL as the "National League" and the AAFC as the "All-America Conference." For consistency, the text will adhere to NFL and AAFC.

4. Grantland Rice, "Rx for Pro Football," *Sport*, September 1949, 28–30, 90.

5. "Pro Football Pass for the President," NYT, August 23, 1945, 19.

6. MacCambridge, *America's Game*, 106–7.

7. Joe King, "Unitas Spurs Colts to Title in Overtime," TSN, January 7, 1959, sec. 2: 3, 4; Tex Maule, "The Best Football Game Ever Played," SI, January 5, 1959, 8–11, 60.

8. Tex Maule, "Here's Why It Was THE BEST FOOTBALL GAME EVER (caps in original)," SI, January 19, 1959, 52–60.

9. Harris, *League*, 5; MacCambridge, *America's Game*, 99, 112, 159; see also Coenen, *Sandlots to Super Bowl*, 164.

10. Arthur Daley, "Pros and Cons of Pro Football," NYT, November 20, 1955, SM17; Davis, *Papa Bear*, 73.

11. J. G. Taylor Spink, "Rickey Urges Action to Offset Growth of Other Pro Sports," TSN, January 28, 1959, 1, 8.

12. Bill Furlong, "Can College Football Stand Off the Pros?" *Sport*, November 1959, 16–17, 72–75.

13. John Devaney, "The Inner Workings of the NFL," *Sport*, December 1964, 14–16, 71–72.

14. Perian Conerly, "Pro Football Game Has Grown Up," NYT, December 4, 1960, S2. See Ms. Conerly's wonderfully witty and wry look at life in the NFL in *Backseat Quarterback*.

15. Perian Conerly, "When Play Is Done: Into Plenty of Pies, Including Pizza Men in Pro Football Put Their Fingers," NYT, September 25, 1960, S3.

16. Tex Maule, "A Classic Rematch," SI, December 14, 1959, 16–19.

17. Charles Burton, "Air Hostesses Promise Kiss to First Texan Scoring TD," TSN, September 13, 1961, sec. 2: 6.

18. "Russians Find U.S. 'Futbol' Rough Game, Designed to Create 'Bandits and Haters,'" NYT, November 19, 1952, 9.

19. Tex Maule, "The Old Quarterback and the Youngster," SI, December 7, 1959, 18–19, 100–101.

20. MacCambridge, *America's Game*, 354.

1. The Usurpers

1. Ed Prell, "Champ Rams Now Set for '46 Intra-Loop Battle," TSN, December 20, 1945, 21; "Pro Football Peak," *Business Week*, December 22, 1945, 32, 34, 36.

2. During the 1920s and 1930s NFL owners considered many applications to join the league. Over time the owners raised the application fee from $2,500 to $10,000 in 1933 (PFHOFAIC, NFL LM, February 6, 1926, 7; July 12, 1930, 1; July 8, 1933, 2; April 12, 1940, 4).

3. Francis J. Powers and Ed Prell, "George Halas: The Papa Bear," *Sport*, December 1948, 52–61; Carroll, *Red Grange*, 119–39; Davis, *Papa Bear*, 71–86. Historian Craig Coenen provides a well-researched examination of the league's early history and describes the league's "bush league" character (Coenen, *Sandlots to Super Bowl*, 7–9, 11).

4. Surdam, *Postwar Yankees*, 332 (table 4.1); Seagraves, *Drive-In Theaters*, 235; U.S. Department of Commerce, *Historical Statistics*, I:20, 210, 224, 401.

5. PFHOFAIC, NFL LM, January 14, 1946, 8.

6. Coenen, *Sandlots to Super Bowl*, 119; MacCambridge, *America's Game*, 13, 46. NFL owners ducked this challenge by relying on a clause in their League Constitution that prohibited any postseason contests (Allison Danzig, "Pro Giants to Play Seven Home Games," NYT, April 30, 1946, 27).

7. MacCambridge, *America's Game*, 47.

8. "Paul Brown Signs to Coach Pro Team," NYT, February 9, 1945, 20.

9. "Contracts for Soldier Field," NYT, February 14, 1945, 24.

10. "Film Stars Buy Grid Club," TSN, November 1, 1945, 21.

11. "Bell Admits Crowley Talk," NYT, January 17, 1946, 32; Coenen, *Sandlots to Super Bowl*, 122.

12. Arch Ward, "Is the New League Here to Stay?," *Sport*, February 1947, 40–41, 96–98.

13. William Richardson, "Tigers and Boston Merge for a Year," NYT, April 11, 1945, 27.

14. "All America Bankroll," *Newsweek*, December 17, 1945, 89.

15. "Football Giants' Head Is Surprised by Brooklyn Owner's Withdrawal," NYT, December 6, 1945, 38; Arch Ward, "Topping's Pro Eleven Joins All-America," *Chicago Tribune*, December 6, 1945, sec. 2: 1.

16. Quote from Roscoe McGowen, "Sees Topping Deal Aid to New League," NYT, December 12, 1945, 38; "Pro Football Peak."

17. Coenen, *Sandlots to Super Bowl*, 121.

18. William Richardson, "Giants Reach Peak against Redskins," NYT, December 7, 1945, 29.

19. "Football Giants' Head Is Surprised by Brooklyn Owner's Withdrawal," NYT, December 6, 1945, 38.

20. Sportswriter Ed Prell lauded the league for doing so (Ed Prell, "Far West Host to Grid Confab," TSN, April 4, 1946, 25; see also Ed Prell, "All-America to Open Play with 8 Teams," *Chicago Tribune*, January 5, 1946, sec. 2: 1).

21. Ed Prell, "New Loop's Open Play Steams Up Pro Grid War," TSN, January 10, 1946, 19. Topping wasted no time thumbing his nose at the Giants by making exaggerated statements of his success in signing Giants draft choices (Roscoe McGowen, "Football Owners Discuss Schedule," NYT, January 15, 1946, 18).

22. "Deal for Passer Sought by Giants," NYT, October 21, 1947, 31.

23. "Pro Football War Looms," NYT, September 1, 1945, 16.

24. "NFL Admits War in Barring a Player," TSN, November 1, 1945, 21. The situation presented elements of melodrama, as Jones had told the Clippers he needed to fly back East to visit his ailing mother.

25. "Contract with All-America Conference Bars Ed Jones from the Chicago Bears," NYT, October 28, 1945, S1, S4; PFHOFAIC, NFL LM, January 12, 1946, 6.

26. "Rival Football Loop Approaches 5 Bears," NYT, December 5, 1945, 35; "Filchock Return Is Held Unlikely," NYT, December 19, 1945, 19.

27. Ward, "New League Here to Stay?"

28. An article in the *Los Angeles Times* suggested that the Green Bay Packers, Boston Yanks, and Washington Redskins arranged working agreements with teams in the Pacific Coast [Football] League and the Dixie League: "Redskins to Form Pact with Hollywood Club," *LA Times*, January 14, 1946, pt. 1, 10.

29. Stanley Frank, "The Grid Is Hot!," *Collier's*, September 14, 1946, 92–93; H. G. Salsinger, "Salaries Zoom in War of Pro Grid Circuits," TSN, January 24, 1946, 21.

30. Lawrence Robinson, "Price of Grid Beef Soars on Bull Market," TSN, February 11, 1948, sec. 2: 1, 4; U.S. Bureau of the Census, *Historical Statistics*,I:210.

31. "New Pro League Held to 8 Clubs," NYT, January 5, 1946, 8.

32. Ed Prell, "DeGroot to New League, Raiding Cycle Completed," TSN, January 24, 1946, 21.

33. Coenen, *Sandlots to Super Bowl*, 120. On occasion, teams lost players for novel reasons — such as the opera ("Bangert off Pro Eleven," NYT, August 2, 1946, 26).

34. Roscoe McGowen, "Ban Is Reaffirmed by Football Loop," NYT, January 16, 1946, 31; PFHOFAIC, NFL LM, January 12, 1946, 8; and April 29, 1946, 5–6. Bell said there were ninety-seven suspended players in the AAFC, with Los Angeles (twenty-two) and the New York Yankees (nineteen) having the most (PFHOFAIC, NFL LM, November 4, 1946, 1).

35. "Crowley Critical of National Loop," NYT, April 10, 1946, 38.

36. PFHOFAIC, NFL LM, November 7, 1949, 5.

37. "New Draft Plan for All-America," NYT, January 6, 1946, F7, F9.

38. "Ram Eleven to Withhold Names of Men It Drafts," NYT, January 1, 1946, 30. NFL owners' secrecy is discussed in PFHOFAIC, NFL LM, January 17, 1948, n.p.

39. "Bertelli, Star Passer, Restrained from Playing with Boston Yanks," NYT, June 6, 1946, 35; "Bertelli Is Signed by Boston Yanks," NYT, May 23, 1946, 26; "Bertelli Case in Court," NYT, June 22, 1946, 23. Throughout June, July, and September, the *New York Times* contained many stories chronicling the legal wrangling.

40. "All-America Group Shelves Plan to Use Association's Ball Park," NYT, May 21, 1946, 27.

41. "Ted Fritsch Rejoins Green Bay and Signs after Jumping to the Cleveland Browns," NYT, August 11, 1946, 83.

42. "Cleveland Eleven Will Keep Adams," NYT, August 30, 1946, 28; "Smith on Browns Eleven," NYT, July 24, 1946, 34. Another lawsuit that demonstrated the ambiguous status of many players in the postwar era involved Gerard Ramsey ("Ramsey Is Warned to Quit Pro Cards," NYT, August 30, 1946, 28).

43. "Baseball Felicitates Pro Football," TSN, December 24, 1947, 12.

44. Ed Prell, "Rams' Move to Los Angeles Tops Grid Surprises," TSN, January 17, 1946, 21. Reeves claimed that he had been considering the Los Angeles area for

his team since 1937 (Sid Feder, "Los Angeles Gets Rams' Pro Grid Franchise," *LA Times*, January 13, 1946, pt. II, 5).

45. Bill Stern, "The Football Feud," *Sport*, September 1946, 38–39, 87–88.

46. Frank, "Grid Is Hot."

47. Stern, "Football Feud." NFL owners also investigated air travel (PFHOFAIC, NFL LM, April 29, 1946, 7).

48. Ed Prell, "Grid Yanks Defy Giant Schedule, Book 7 Games in Direct Conflict," TSN, March 7, 1946, 23.

49. Prell, "New Loop's Open Play." The reader should prepare to be confused. In addition to Topping's AAFC New York Yankees, Ted Collins nicknamed his team the Boston Yanks. When Topping chose the "Yankees" moniker, Collins balked and threatened a lawsuit. Yankees official Red Patterson harrumphed and said, "Does Collins want us to call our football team the New York Red Sox?" After Topping's team collapsed in the wake of the AAFC-NFL merger, Collins, having moved his team to New York, changed his team's nickname from the Bulldogs to the Yanks ("Eleven to Retain Name," NYT, June 13, 1946, 22). Given the generally lackluster records of Topping's and Collins's teams in 1948–51, perhaps the baseball Yankees should have sued for "impersonation of a major league team" (but wait a minute, Topping owned the baseball team, too). The AAFC scheduled games on various nights of the week (Davis, *Papa Bear*, 205; Maher and Gill, *Pro Football Encyclopedia*, 112–15).

50. PFHOFAIC, NFL LM, April 29, 1946, 8; January 17, 1948, 10.

51. Sportswriter Paul Zimmerman wrote in the *Los Angeles Times* that the Coliseum was charging the Rams fifteen percent of admissions, net of federal tax, but also 15 percent of media revenues and concessions. He pointed out that most renters paid the Coliseum ten to twelve percent and $2,000 cleanup. An article in the *New York Times* cited a rental figure of fifty-one percent, but this appears to have been a transposition error (Paul Zimmerman, "Rams Close to Deal at Coliseum," *LA Times*, January 18, 1946, pt. 1, 10). When the Dons eventually received some playing dates at the Coliseum, the *Los Angeles Times* did not report the terms of the agreement ("Dons Pro Grid Dates Arranged," *LA Times*, February 14, 1946, pt. 1, 10).

52. Maher and Gill, *Football Encyclopedia*, 112; MacCambridge, *America's Game*, 31.

53. "Report on the Pros," *Newsweek*, November 25, 1946, 92.

54. "Seahawks Face Charges," NYT, December 14, 1946, 20. Crowley claimed to have used league funds to cover $60,000 worth of unpaid player salaries ("Miami Wins; Faces All-America Ouster," *Chicago Tribune*, December 14, 1946, sec. 2: 21).

55. Joe Williams, "A Report on the Two Pro Football Leagues," TSN, November 12, 1947, sec. 2: 8.

56. "Browns Plan Challenge," NYT, October 23, 1946, 42.

57. Ward, "New League Here to Stay?"

58. Ward, "New League Here to Stay?"

59. "Baseball Intrigued by Football War," TSN, January 24, 1946, 12.

60. "All-America Conference Admits Truce Bid to National Football League on Players," NYT, March 3, 1946, S1. By December 1946, Bert Bell told his owners some AAFC owners wanted a secret pact on the draft and contracts (PFHOFAIC, NFL LM, December 16, 1946, 1).

61. "Dudley, Steelers, Offered for Sale," NYT, January 26, 1947, S1, S4.

62. William D. Richardson, "Rival Leagues Bid for 2 Army Backs," NYT, January 31, 1947, 18. The leagues' feud achieved great heights of pettiness (see Rube Samuelsen, "Stubbornness Costing Pro Owners Millions," TSN, October 1, 1947, sec. 2: 8).

63. Louis Effrat, "All-America Loop Blasted by Mara," NYT, November 19, 1947, 37; Maher and Gill, *Pro Football Encyclopedia*, 113.

64. "Rockets to Stay in Chicago," NYT, November 27, 1947, 53; "Rockets Owe U.S. $62,706," NYT, January 21, 1948, 33).

65. The AAFC attempted to redress the deleterious disparity in talent by giving the Chicago Rockets several players, including John Rapacz ("Rapacz of Rockets Denies Being Pro," NYT, February 17, 1948, 35; "Rapacz Admits Signing," NYT, February 18, 1948, 38).

66. Ed Prell, "AAC Here to Stay, '47 Records Testify," TSN, December 3, 1947, sec. 2: 2.

67. "Shift Rumors Hit by Dodger Owners," NYT, December 16, 1947, 49; "Conference Takes Colts' Franchise," NYT, March 9, 1948, 32.

68. Joe King, "Chucking Chuck Conerly Fits T to a T," TSN, November 2, 1949, sec. 2: 3.

69. "Football Giants Get Rights to Conerly," NYT, January 21, 1948, 32; Conerly, *Backseat Quarterback*, 10–11.

70. Joseph Sheehan, "Yankees Claim 24, Including 17 Backs," NYT, December 17, 1947, 44.

71. "All-America Maps Gridiron Schedule," NYT, February 18, 1948, 38.

72. Shirley Povich, "NFL Putting AAC on Spot," TSN, February 25, 1948, sec. 2: 8.

73. Herman Goldstein, "AA Bolstered, Outlook Bright," TSN, September 29, 1948, sec. 2: 7.

74. The Maher and Gill *Football Encyclopedia* showed about seventy thousand total attendance in five games (Maher and Gill, 110).

75. Al Stump, "Will Pro Football Get Smart — or Go *Bust*?" *Sport*, November 1948: 10–12, 74, 76. Urging peace with the AAFC was no sudden whim on Thompson's

part; see "Thompson, Eagles' Owner, Favors Common Draft for Pro Leagues," NYT, December 2, 1947, 39.

76. Stump, "Will Pro Football Get Smart?" Thompson called for a common draft at the January 1948 meeting but knew his efforts were futile; he didn't even attend the meeting at which his proxy made the motion (Joseph Sheehan, "Football Rules Satisfy National," NYT, January 15, 1948, 30).

77. "Eagles' Owner Drops Peacemaker Role, Declares War on All-America Clubs," NYT, October 23, 1948, 12.

78. "Radical Pro Football Shake-Up, with One 12-Club League Hinted," NYT, December 17, 1948, 42.

79. Both quotes in "Mr. Marshall Says 'No'!," NYT, December 17, 1948, 42.

80. "AAC Ready for Change," NYT, December 17, 1948, 42. The surviving Hornets used Chicago and Brooklyn players. Question: What do you get when you mix players from a 2-12 team with a 1-13 team? Answer: A 4-8 team.

81. Joseph Sheehan, "All-America Conference Will Carry On in 1949," NYT, December 18, 1948, 17.

82. "Dallas Reported Ready to Join All-America Conference If Rockets Drop Out," NYT, December 19, 1948, S7.

83. Jimmy Powers, "Open Letter to Tim Mara," Sport, December 1949, 15, 88–89.

84. "Warring Pro Football Factions Meeting Today for Peace Talks," NYT, December 20, 1948, 33; "Bell Denies Report of Pro Football Truce; Shift of Boston Yanks to New York Looms," NYT, December 19, 1948, S1.

85. Louis Effrat, "Rival Pro Football Owners Fail to Reach Agreement in Philadelphia Parley," NYT, December 21, 1948, 37; Stan Baumgartner, "Pro Grid Loops' Officials Talk — but That's All," TSN, December 29, 1948, sec. 2: 2.

86. Dan Daniel, "Grid Pros Heading into Another Year of War," TSN, January 5, 1949, sec. 2: 2.

87. "Pro Peace Parley on Jan. 20 Likely," NYT, January 9, 1949, S4.

88. "Future of Football Yankees Hinges on Results of New Peace Moves," NYT, January 12, 1949, 36.

89. Tim Mara and Joe King, "Why We Won!," Sport, February 1950, 10–11, 84–85; "Football Giants to Open Here Sept. 17 with Yank Assist," NYT, April 13, 1961, 45.

90. "Topping-Collins Talk Clears Way for Boston Yanks to Use Stadium," NYT, January 13, 1949, 29.

91. Louis Effrat, "Football Yankees and Dodgers Merge and Will Play Home Games at Stadium," NYT, January 22, 1949, 17. Effrat wrote several other articles on the topic during January 1949.

92. "Merger in Pro Football Is Impossible under Present Conditions, Bell Says," NYT, February 8, 1949, 34; "Tim Mara, Marshall Are Called Pro Football's 'Peace Blockers,'" NYT, February 5, 1949, 18.

93. Roscoe McGowen, "Rockets Become Hornets and Receive 29 Men in Division of Football Dodgers," NYT, February 2, 1949, 38.

94. Grantland Rice, "Rx for Pro Football," *Sport*, September 1949, 28–30, 90; Pat Livingston, "The Pittsburgh Steelers," *Sport*, October 1953, 44–47, 86–89.

95. Harry Sheer, "Pros Again in Bruising Battle of Bucks: Only 2 Teams Appear Sure of '49 Profit," TSN, October 12, 1949, sec. 2: 1–2.

96. "Deny Football Merger," NYT, October 25, 1949, 35.

97. Brown's remarks in Maxwell Stiles, "LA Rams Told to Quit at Pro Peace Session," TSN, October 26, 1949, sec. 2: 8; McBride's remarks in "No End to War Seen by McBride," TSN, November 30, 1949, sec. 2: 2.

98. "Colt-Redskin Settlement Talks Barred by Kessing, All-America Conference Head," NYT, December 3, 1949, 11.

99. "Major Professional Football Rivals Form 13-Club National-American League," NYT, December 10, 1949, 12; Stan Baumgartner, "Grid Pros Blow Whistle on Red Ink Battle: War Ends Abruptly after Four Long Years," TSN, December 21, 1949, sec. 2: 3, 7.

100. Quote in "Marshall Waiver Led to Settlement," NYT, December 10, 1949, 12; "Major Professional Football Rivals," NYT.

101. "Baltimore Drops Pro Football Franchise and Giants Get Rote in Bonus Pick," NYT, January 19, 1951, 36.

102. Mara and King, "Why We Won!," *Sport*.

103. Mara and King, "Why We Won!," *Sport*.

104. "No Chance for Play-Off," NYT, December 10, 1949, 12.

105. "Yankee-Bulldog Eleven Will Play Home Games at the Stadium in 1950," NYT, December 10, 1949, 12; Roscoe McGowen, "Topping Explains Football Actions," NYT, December 11, 1949, S1, S4.

106. Arthur Daley, "Sports of the Times: For Whom the Bell Tolls," NYT, January 26, 1950.

107. Despite Brown's grousing, events turned out fabulously for the Cleveland team on the field, but not in the stands (Louis Effrat, "Cleveland Browns Dislike New Plan for Pro Football," NYT, December 11, 1949, S1).

108. "Equitable Set-Up for Pros Promised," NYT, December 13, 1949, 48; Arthur Daley, "Sports of the *Times*: For Whom the Bell Tolls," NYT, January 26, 1950, 40 for comments on Bell's influence.

109. Stan Baumgartner, "Bell Slams Lid on Pro League Squabbles," TSN, February 1, 1950, sec. 2: 1, 2.

110. PFHOFAIC, NFL LM, January 20, 1950, 9–10.

111. Baumgartner, "Bell Slams Lid," TSN; Louis Effrat, "Pros Stage Draft of Football Stars as Bell Paves Way," NYT, January 22, 1950, 141; also PFHOFAIC, NFL LM, January 19, 1950, 3–4; January 20, 1950, 6–8; January 23, 1950, 16–17.

112. Bell quote in "Bell Notes Buffalo Bid," NYT, December 21, 1949, 42; "Buffalo Seeks Franchise," NYT, December 14, 1949, 46; PFHOFAIC, NFL LM, January 19, 1950, 2.

113. "Houston and Buffalo Considered for Places in New Set-Up by Pros," NYT, January 6, 1950, 29.

114. Cy Kritzer, "Buffalo Stampedes over All Obstacles to Keeping Its Bills," TSN, January 18, 1950, sec. 2: 2; Louis Effrat, "Football Club Owners Bar Entry of a Fourteenth Team in League," NYT, January 21, 1950, 24; PFHOFAIC, NFL LM, January 19, 1950, 1–4.

115. Shirley Povich, "Sparring at Grid Banquet Hints Brown-Redskin Feud," TSN, January 18, 1950, sec. 2: 2. The Redskins did, in fact, have their largest 1950 home attendance for the Browns game, although at only thirty thousand it probably wasn't as satisfactory as had been hoped.

116. Baumgartner, "Grid Pros Blow Whistle," TSN.

117. Joe Williams, "Grid War's Over, but Red Ink Still Threatens," TSN, September 27, 1950, sec. 2: 8.

118. PFHOFAIC, NFL LM, June 3, 1950, 11.

119. "Graham, Van Buren on All-Pro Eleven," NYT, December 17, 1948, 42; Hugo Autz, "Van Buren Paces Field in All-Pro Voting," TSN, January 12, 1949, sec. 2: 5.

120. AAFC, AAFC *Record Manual — 1949 Supplement*, front page.

2. Prosperity and Its Drawbacks

1. Tim Cohane and I. R. McVay, "Canadian Football — Will It Change Our Game?" *Look*, November 16, 1954, 84–89.

2. Ed Prell, "Low Overhead, High-Salaried U.S. Stars Spark Canadian Grid Boom," TSN, October 21, 1953, sec. 2: 1, 2.

3. "Rams Win Huffman Case," NYT, August 1, 1951, 27; "Canadians Sign Ettinger," NYT, July 12, 1951, 33; "Eagles Fail to Curb Armstrong," NYT, October 21, 1951, 159; "Second Ratterman Suit," NYT, July 12, 1951, 29. Ratterman described his experiences in Canada, as did Tex Coulter. Both players enjoyed their experiences (George Ratterman and Al Silverman, "I'd Rather Play in Canada," *Sport*, November 1951, 8–9, 54; Tex Coulter and Bob Snyder, "Canadian Football — Big League or Bush?" *Sport*, September 1954, 24–27, 82–83).

4. Booton Herndon, "Young Man, Go North!," SI, October 26, 1959, 84–86, 89–91,, 95–96.

5. W. C. Heinz, "Boss of the Behemoths," *Saturday Evening Post*, December 5, 1955, 46, 72, 74, 77.

6. Quote from Stan Baumgartner, "Bell Not Worried, Calls Rival Bids Healthy for Game," TSN, October 21, 1953, sec. 2: 2; Tommy Devine, "Canadian Pro Loops Step Up U.S. Raids," TSN, October 17, 1951, sec. 2: 1, 2.

7. Prell, "Low Overhead," TSN.

8. "National Football League Blasts Canadians for Signing Tactics," NYT, January 8, 1954, 26.

9. Stan Baumgarter, "NFL 'Voice' Tells Gridders of 'Life North of Border,'" TSN, January 20, 1954, sec. 2: 2.

10. "Vancouver Signs Weinmeister, Touching Off Pro Football Feud," NYT, January 22, 1954, 33; Prell, "Low Overhead," TSN.

11. Stan Baumgartner, "'War,' Yells Bell at Canada's Theft of Weinmeister," TSN, February 3, 1954, sec. 2: 4.

12. Baumgartner, "'War,' Yells Bell," TSN. Marshall's equanimity was sorely tested when the Calgary team signed two of his players: Dick Modzelewski and Bob Morgan ("Redskins File Law Suit," NYT, February 17, 1955, 35).

13. "Peace between U.S. and Canadian Pro Football Regarded Unlikely until 1956," NYT, February 3, 1955, 32; "Border Warfare," SI, January 24, 1955, 17.

14. Keith Munro, "Football from the North," SI, August 30, 1954, 30–31, 55–56; Coenen, *Sandlots to Super Bowl*, 177.

15. "U.S., Canadian Football Leagues Agree Tentatively on No Raiding," NYT, January 23, 1955, S1, S2. The NFL owners empowered Bell to negotiate a "just and honorable" peace with Canada. Whether they endowed him with a top hat and umbrella in order to get "peace in our time" was not stated (Joseph Sheehan, "Football League Would End Raids," NYT, January 27, 1955, 29).

16. If a player did not sign a contract by a certain date, the team could invoke the option clause and sign him to the renewed contract.

17. Allison Danzig, "Football Giants Select Heap of Notre Dame on First Round of College Draft," NYT, January 28, 1955, 22. The Toronto Argonauts threatened to sue the other three clubs in the Big Four League if those clubs attempted to oust the Argonauts, in response to the team's raids on NFL rosters ("Toronto Threatens Suit If League Ousts Club," NYT, January 30, 1955, S5).

18. "Redskins, Calgary Agree on 'No Raiding' as Hopes Rise for Pro Football 'Peace,'" NYT, February 25, 1955, 24; PFHOFAIC, NFL LM, March 28, 1955, 4.

19. "Bears Win in Court; Pro Raids May End," NYT, May 1, 1955, S7.

20. "Court Blocks Dublinski," NYT, July 31, 1955, S2; "$6,950 Award to Lions," NYT, January 19, 1957, 19.

21. "NFL, Canadians Near Agreement," NYT, February 16, 1956, 37.

22. Jack Walsh, "Marshall Raps NFL Stand of Keeping Eye on Canada," TSN, December 5, 1956, sec. 2: 6.

23. Quote in Booton Herndon, "Young Man, Go North!," SI, October 26, 1959, 84–86, 89–91,, 95–96; Art Morrow, "First Canadian Grid Game in U.S. at Philly," TSN, September 10, 1958, 17.

24. U.S. Senate, OPTS, 1959: 48. Bell apparently called Davey O'Brien, who was associated with the AFL efforts, and asked permission to mention the new league. As historian Michael MacCambridge points out, Bell was a good salesman, but perhaps he oversold the NFL's position: "The more football there is and the more advertisement of pro football, the better off we are. We are in favor of the new league." While Michigan senator Philip Hart was skeptical that Bell reflected the owners' view, the commissioner persuaded the committee not to tamper with NFL practices (MacCambridge, *America's Game*, 123).

25. PFHOFAIC, AFL LM, September 12, 1959, 2.

26. MacCambridge, *America's Game*, 120, 129.

27. Howard Tuckner, "Local American Football League Team Is Named Titans," NYT, October 29, 1959, 41.

28. "Rival Teams Will Perform to Same Arena in 3 Cities," TSN, September 7, 1960, 20.

29. Joe King, "New League Hurls Challenge at NFL — Drafts 'Name' Stars," TSN, December 2, 1959, sec. 2: 6; PFHOFAIC, AFL LM, August 14, 1959, 1–9 in particular.

30. "3 Groups Propose Gridiron Circuits," NYT, August 1, 1959, 11.

31. "New Pro Football League Formed with Six Members, Including New York," NYT, August 15, 1959, 12; "New Loop's Goal Is Debut in 1960," NYT, August 23, 1959, S3. Bert Bell's temporary replacement, Austin Gunsel, and AFL commissioner Joe Foss considered meeting informally in hopes of forestalling a bidding war for players (PFHOFAIC, AFL LM, January 26, 1960, 2; PFHOFAIC, NFL LM, January 20, 1960, 6, 10).

32. U.S. House, OPTS, 1957:,2592. College coach Bud Wilkinson thought there were sufficient players: see U.S. Senate, OPTS, 1958: 431.

33. Joe King, "Grid Loops Will Trigger Bidding Binge," TSN, November 11, 1959, sec. 2: 1, 2.

34. King, "Grid Loops," TSN.

35. Joe King, "NFL Brushing Off Rival-Loop Rumors — 'Just Let 'Em Try," TSN, February 4, 1959, sec. 2: 5.

36. "Minneapolis–St. Paul Accept 1960 Franchise in National Football League," NYT, November 23, 1959, 43; "Boston Gets Spot in Football Loop," NYT, November 20, 1959, 39.

37. Howard Tuckner, "American Football League Gives Franchise to Oakland," NYT, January 31, 1960, S1, S2; also PFHOFAIC AFL LM, October 28, 1959, 1–6; March 3, 1960, 2, 5.

38. Joe King, "NFL Brushing Off Rival," TSN.

39. Joe King, "New League Hurls Challenge"; "NFL Disputes New League on Texas," NYT, August 31, 1959, 27.

40. "Twin Cities Drop New League Plan," NYT, January 4, 1960, 40; also PFHOFAIC, AFL LM, November 22–23, 1959, n.p.; January 27, 1960, 6.

41. Howard Tuckner, "Foss Threatens Plea to Congress," NYT, January 8, 1960, 28.

42. "Kefauver Pledges His Support to Foss's New Football League," NYT, January 9, 1960, 16.

43. "American Football League's Draft Sets Stage for Bidding War with NFL," NYT, November 24, 1959, 48. The scene smacks of a group of "Fantasy Football" fans getting together one evening and stocking their teams.

44. "New Football Loop Drafts 264, Then Hastens to Sign Choices," NYT, November 25, 1959, 32.

45. "American Football League Drafts 161 Players," NYT, December 3, 1959, 51. The NFL would, on occasion, cooperate to help a fellow team land a particular college star, such as Gale Sayers (Bob Curran, "Turmoil in the AFL," Sport, April 1966, 16–17, 71–72).

46. Joe King, "War Drums Rumble as NFL Empties Grab Bag in Record Time," TSN, December 9, 1959, sec. 2: 6; "Won-Lost Records in Pro Grid Battle," TSN, January 27, 1960, sec. 2: 2; Dan Daniel, "Pros Raise Ante—Stars Rake in Chips," TSN, January 27, 1960, sec. 2: 1, 2.

47. "Rymkus to Coach Houston Eleven," NYT, January 3, 1960, S1, S3. Rozelle apparently signed Cannon before LSU's bowl game. He gave the player a $10,000 bonus check and $500 for expenses on November 30. A month later, Cannon returned both checks and claimed that he only tentatively agreed to enter into a contract after the Sugar Bowl on New Year's Day. Cannon pointed out that the NFL's own rules made the contract not binding "until after such time." Cannon signed a three-year contract with Houston for a reported $100,000 after the game ("Rams File Suit to Keep Cannon," January 12, 1960, 24; "Cannon Attacks Rams," NYT, February 17, 1960, 45; Furman Bisher, "Billy Cannon and the Pro Football War," Sport, June 1960, 24–27, 70–71).

48. "Court Free Cannon from Contract with Rams of National Football League," NYT, June 21, 1960, 41.

49. William Briordy, "Giants Ask AFL Head for Help," NYT, January 14, 1960, 41; "Flowers Is Freed from Giant Pact," NYT, June 24, 1960, 21.

50. "Pro Football Clubs Assailed by NCAA," NYT, August 4, 1960, 21.

51. Rozelle quote in Louis Effrat, "National League Says Rival's Secret Draft Discredits Professional Football," NYT, November 22, 1961, 41; "American Football League Admits Holding Secret Player Draft," NYT, November 21, 1961, 49; "American

Football League Voids Secret Draft but Titans Will Ignore Edict," NYT, November 23, 1961, S5; "Foss Favors Ouster of Wismer," NYT, November 24, 1961, 42.

52. "Bumper Crop of Campus Heroes," TSN, September 25, 1957, 19; PFHOFAIC, NFL LM, January 22, 1960, 15.

53. "Prospects Bright for Pro Football," NYT, August 28, 1960, S7.

54. Tex Maule, "The Fanciest Game in Town," SI, September 26, 1960, 44, 58–65; MacCambridge, America's Game, 195. Some of the NFL castoffs were actually talented players, including quarterback Len Dawson.

55. Jack McDonald, "NFL's Pete Rozelle Shows That He Has Mind of Own," TSN, October 5, 1960, sec. 2: 6.

56. PFHOFAIC, NFL LM, March 29, 1960, 48.

57. "New League Has 400 Players and a Gridiron for Each Team," NYT, March 4, 1960, 30; PFHOFAIC, AFL LM, September 12, 1959, 2.

58. "2 Franchises Rejected," NYT, November 28, 1959, 18; Harris, League, 105.

59. Joe King, "Briefcase Battle Brewing—Pros Call in Lawyers," TSN, January 27, 1960, sec. 2: 1, 6.

60. Howard Tuckner, "American Football League Tells NFL to Stay Clear of Dallas," NYT, January 28, 1960, 37; see also "Rozelle Reveals Parley with Foss," NYT, February 9, 1960, 37, about a meeting between Foss and Rozelle in which the two leagues agreed not to raid each other. The NFL considered expanding into Houston to combat Bud Adams's Oilers but could not find a satisfactory place to play (Joe King, "Dallas Grid Pros Strap on Six-Shooters," TSN, February 17, 1960, sec. 2: 1, 2).

61. Both quotes in "Kefauver Says Football Quarrel over Dallas Is a Private Battle," NYT, January 30, 1960, 15.

62. Tex Maule, "Pro Football: The Infighting Was Vicious," SI, February 8, 1960, 50–52.

63. "NFL Is Accused by Rival League," NYT, March 10, 1960, 42.

64. "U.S. View Awaited in Football Feud," NYT, April 6, 1960, 52.

65. Joe King, "Rival Loop No. 1 on NFL's List of Its Big Headaches," TSN, January 11, 1961, sec. 2: 1, 8.

66. "New Football Group Sues Rival League," NYT, June 18, 1960, 1, 17.

67. "Dismissal Asked in Football Case," NYT, March 14, 1962, 49; "Hunt Says NFL Fought New Loop," NYT, March 1, 1962, 34; "National Football League Fails to Get Dismissal of Rival's Suit," NYT, March 16, 1962, 36.

68. "Court Rules National League Is Not a Monopoly in Pro Football," NYT, May 22, 1962, 41.

69. Al Hirshberg, "Sound Off! Joe Foss Diagnoses the Pro Football War," Sport, November 1962, 46–49, 95.

70. "Rozelle Rejects AFL Playoff Bid, Citing $10-Million Suit," TSN, January 25, 1961, sec. 2: 6; McDonald, "NFL's Pete Rozelle," TSN.

71. Richard Shepard, "ABC TV May Sign Football League," NYT, April 23, 1960, 47. Harry Wismer, owner of the New York Titans, was the league's contact with the American Broadcasting Company. The owners voted a key article into the league bylaws by stressing that television revenues would be shared equally (PFHOFAIC, AFL LM, August 14, 1959, 7, 9; August 22, 1959, 6; October 28, 1959, 11; November 23, 1959, n.p.; January 26, 1960, 4; March 4, 1960, 6; April 29, 1960, 4).

72. Roy Terrell, "The New Pros Open Up," SI, September 12, 1960, 31–36; Joe Donnelly, "Will the New Football League Survive?" Sport, April 1961, 45.

73. Terrell, "New Pros Open Up," SI.

74. Terrell, "New Pros Open Up," SI. Bud Adams estimated that he spent $1,250,000 for the Oilers' first season, including $250,000 for the renovation of Jeppesen Stadium, which increased the capacity from twenty-two thousand to thirty-six thousand (Clark Nealon, "Vets Spark Oilers to Fast Start in AFL," TSN, October 5, 1960, sec. 2: 3).

75. Tex Maule, "Pro Football: Saturation in Dallas," SI, October 10, 1960, 87.

76. Joe King, "New York Gate Weak," TSN, November 9, 1960, sec. 2: 1, 2.

77. "Opener of Series Proposed for '61," NYT, January 15, 1961, S6.

78. Harris, League, 30.

3. Measures of the NFL's Popularity

1. Coenen, Sandlots to Super Bowl, 58. League owners agreed in 1934 to provide the league office with attendance and receipt information after each game (PFHOFAIC, NFL LM, June 30, 1934, 4; see also April 12, 1940, 4, for information regarding turnstiles, capacity count, ticket prices, and the settlement of gross receipts, including season ticket revenues).

2. Maher and Gill, Football Encyclopedia, 117–20; U.S. House, OPTS, 1957: 2551; Baltimore Colts, Media Guide, 1961, 59; Detroit Lions, 1961 Media Guide, 31.

3. Coenen, Sandlots to Super Bowl, 58–59.

4. Coenen, Sandlots to Super Bowl, 61; Joseph M. O'Brien Historical Resource Center, Naismith Memorial Basketball Hall of Fame, New York Knickerbockers program, December 3, 1949.

5. Peterson, Pigskin, 161; Coenen, Sandlots to Super Bowl, 58.

6. Craig Coenen cites the capital's lack of big-time college football and the large proportion of educated workers who were emigrants as factors in the team's popularity (Coenen, Sandlots to Super Bowl, 108, 110).

7. "1,918,631 Pro Football Fans Set All-Time Attendance Mark in '45," NYT, December 30, 35.

8. Joe King, "NFL Races to Hinge on Giant-Bear Tilt," TSN, November 11, 1956, sec. 2: 8.

9. "Rams Upset Cardinals, 27 to 7, before Record 69,631 on Coast," NYT, October 20, 1947, 30.

10. Ed Prell, "Record Throngs Greet Pro Grid Openers; Chicago Cards, Buffalo Early Threats," TSN, October 1, 1947, sec. 2: 6.

11. "Football Crowds Bigger This Year," NYT, December 10, 1948, 38.

12. Tommy Devine, "Colleges Playing to SRO, Pro Turnstiles Slump," TSN, November 17, 1948, sec. 2: 2.

13. Harry Sheer, "SRO as Cards Battle Bears for Division Title," TSN, December 8, 1948, sec. 2: 2, 8.

14. Tom Meany, "Pro Football Facing Million Loss in NY," TSN, November 24, 1948, sec. 2: 1–2.

15. "Sees Big Year for Pros," NYT, September 12, 1950, 40.

16. "Pro Football Dip Noted," NYT, November 3, 1950, 33; H. G. Salsinger, "Gates for Pro Games Shrink," TSN, November 8, 1950, sec. 2: 10.

17. Louis Effrat, "Lambeau Puzzled by Poor Pro Gates," NYT, November 14, 1950, 40.

18. Surdam, *Postwar Yankees*, 308–10; "Attendance Down at College Games," NYT, October 27, 1950, 33; "College Football Shows Slight Attendance Rise," NYT, December 11, 1953, 45. The 1953 article used an estimated price of $2.50 per ticket, which was comparable to the NFL's average gate receipt.

19. By the late 1950s, attendance at colleges still fielding football teams surpassed the peak year of 1949 and exceeded twenty million ("College Football Crowds Show Increase Except in East," NYT, December 2, 1955; "Ohio State Teams Averages 82,717," NYT, December 16, 1960, 48).

20. Frank Finch, "Pro Bowl Victory Caps Brown's Top Season," TSN, January 24, 1951, sec. 2: 5; "Pro Bowl Football at Los Angeles for All-Star Teams Is Authorized," NYT, June 4, 1950, S1, S7. The game would be held at the Coliseum for the next twenty years, but the attendance of the January 14, 1951 game would not be surpassed until January 12, 1958 (PFHOFAIC, NFL LM, June 2, 1950, 4–5; June 3, 1950, 7–8; January 28, 1955, 4).

21. "NFL Group Urges Few Rule Changes," NYT, January 22, 1953, 30; Joe King, "Bell Claims Kick Too Automatic, Asks NFL to 'Boot' Extra Point," TSN, January 19, 1955, sec. 1: 7, sec. 2: 7.

22. "Pro Record Is Set by Football Fans," NYT, December 14, 1955, 59.

23. Frank Finch, "Gillman Make-Do Marvel in Ram Flag March," TSN, December 21, 1955, sec. 2: 7.

24. Joe King, "Graham Gone, Tighter NFL Race Likely," TSN, September 26, 1956, 19, 20; Detroit Lions *Media Guide*, 1961, 4.

25. Tex Maule, "Y. A. Tittle Starts Another Season," SI, October 6, 1958, 36–40.

26. Art Morrow, "NFL Eyeing Gate Records; 1,500,000 in Advance Sale," TSN, October 8, 1958, sec. 2: 9; season ticket sales information from Baltimore Colts *Media Guide*, 1961, 64; Detroit Lions *Media Guide*, 1961, 4; PFHOFAIC, "San Francisco Team Files," *49ers Diggings*, May 1958, 5. The Chicago Bears, of course, sold quite a few season tickets; the team relied upon one woman, who kept track of seat assignments and sales in her head (Davis, *Papa Bear*, 354–56).

27. Green Bay Packers, *Yearbook 1960*, 43.

28. Art Morrow, "'TV Helping NFL to Record Gates'—Bell," TSN, October 10, 1956, sec. 2: 1, 2.

29. Rube Samuelsen, "'Frisco Feudin' May Go to Bell for Settlement," TSN, October 9, 1957, sec. 2: 1, 2.

30. Tex Maule, "Pro Parade," SI, November 18, 1957, 9.

31. Joe King, "New Gate Record Assured for NFL," TSN, December 11, 1957, sec. 2: 5.

32. Tex Maule, "All Hail the Lusty Lions," SI, January 6, 1958, 8–11.

33. Joe King, "NFL to Let Draftee Switch Clubs If He Offers Valid Reason," TSN, January 15, 1958, sec. 2: 10.

34. Hugh Brown, "Sports Parade: Lori Hoskins Baker—a Loco Brave," TSN, October 21, 1953, sec. 2: 10.

35. Jack Walsh, "Like Old Days When Giants, Skins Meet," TSN, October 8, 1958, sec. 2: 7, 8.

36. Joe King, "Eastern Teams in Comeback in NFL Gate Race," TSN, October 29, 1958, 1, 6; "Rich Get Richer, the Poor Falter in NFL Gate Derby," TSN, November 26, 1958, sec. 2: 2.

37. Tex Maule, "A Stout Wall for Johnny," SI, October 5, 1959, 36–37, 39–44.

38. "Football Crowds Up," NYT, December 24, 1959, 26.

39. Joe King, "Colts, Giants Rate Slim '60 Choices in NFL," TSN, September 21, 1960, 19, 20.

40. Walter Robertson, "Dallas Pulls All Stops in Grid War," TSN, October, 5, 1960, sec. 2: 1, 4.

41. PFHOFAIC, NFL LM, March 3, 1950, 10.

42. PFHOFAIC, NFL LM, February 1, 1957, 5.

43. PFHOFAIC, NFL LM, January 20, 1949, 4.

44. PFHOFAIC, NFL LM, January 24, 1947, 14; November 28, 1955, 5; November 26, 1956, 2; December 1, 1958, 2; also Harold Rosenthal, "NFL in Big-Bucks Ticket, TV Class for Playoff Game," TSN, December 27, 1961, sec. 2: 4.

4. Profits and Losses

1. "Shift to Stadium of Tigers Is Seen," NYT, January 27, 1945, 16; "Ebbets Field Open to Tigers in 1945," NYT, January 9, 1945, 24.

2. "New Eleven Signs for Ebbets Field," NYT, October 16, 1945, 28. The other AAFC teams used municipal and college stadiums ("New Eleven Signs," NYT.

3. "Green Bay Citizens Will Vote Tuesday on Bond Issue for New Packer Arena," NYT, March 30, 1956, 31.

4. "Bert Bell Makes Plea for New Packer Park," NYT, April 1, 1956, 166. See Harris for detailed examination of NFL owners' stadium games (Harris, *League*, 25).

5. "Football Giants Quit Polo Grounds for Ten-Year Lease of Yankee Stadium," NYT, January 28, 1956, 13; Joe King, "Pro Football's Gone — Polo Grounds Will Live Long in Memory," TSN, October 31, 1956, sec. 2: 9; "Stadium Contract Extended by Giants," NYT, February 4, 1961, 11.

6. "Focus: Contamination or Competition?" SI, March 3, 1958, 23.

7. "Redskins Sign to Play in Capital Till 1991," NYT, December 23, 1959, 31; Jack Walsh, "Giants' Defense Chills Unveiling of DC Stadium," TSN, October 11, 1961, sec. 2: 2.

8. "Pro Team to Play in Polo Grounds," NYT, September 13, 1959, S1, S4; William Conklin, "City Votes Study of a Stadium in Flushing for 3d League Team," NYT, October 23, 1959, 1, 32.

9. For a look at the costs of clothing a player, see John Geyer, "Snappy Togs for Squad Cost $5,586 Plus $1,960," TSN, November 3, 1948, 11.

10. Coenen, *Sandlots to Super Bowl*, 126, 131, describes the losses incurred by most pro football teams.

11. Craig Coenen suggests that the league's first decades were awash in red ink (Coenen, *Sandlots to Super Bowl*, 59; footnote 25 indicates a variety of newspapers). In some cases, the claims of losses were supported by bankruptcy filings and near-bankruptcies, such as that of the Chicago Bears (Coenen, *Sandlots to Super Bowl*, 76; Davis, *Papa Bear*, 100–103).

12. MacCambridge, *America's Game*, 53.

13. Maher and Gill, *Pro Football Encyclopedia*, 115.

14. MacCambridge, *America's Game*, 59, no useful sources cited; attendance figures from Maher and Gill, *Pro Football Encyclopedia*, 113. Ted Collins, too, was facing loss of his tax write-off loophole, despite continued losses (Joe King, "Fall Guy Collins Stacks Blue Chips," TSN, November 15, 1950, sec. 2: 5).

15. William Richardson, "Rival Leagues Bid for 2 Army Backs," NYT, January 31, 1947, 18; see also "Only Three Pro Grid Clubs Made Money This Season," TSN, December 29, 1948, sec. 2: 2.

16. Rube Samuelsen, "Rising Flood of Red Ink Engulfs Pros: Both Loops Doomed, If Peace Fails," TSN, November 23, 1949, sec. 2: 1, 8.

17. Tom Meany, "Pro Football Facing Million Loss in NY," TSN, November 24, 1948, sec. 2: 1–2.

18. Francis J. Powers and Ed Prell, "George Halas: The Papa Bear," *Sport*, December 1948, 52–61.

19. Les Biederman, "Expenses Toss Steelers for Loss Despite Near Million-Dollar Gate," TSN, December 29, 1948, sec. 2: 2.

20. Ed Prell, "Sellout for Redskins-Ram Pro Title Game Would Bring $300,000 Gate," TSN, December 13, 1945, 20.

21. Coenen, *Sandlots to Super Bowl*, 134.

22. If the Los Angeles Coliseum truly charged fifty-one percent of the gate plus cleaning expenses for rental as cited in chapter 1 (probably erroneously, in the *New York Times*), then the Rams and Dons would have been hard-pressed to turn a profit under any circumstance. The *Los Angeles Times*, though, reported a fifteen percent rental charge.

23. Ed Pollock, "Pro Football Finally Shakes off Red Ink; Ten Clubs in Black," TSN, January 17, 1951, sec. 2: 6.

24. Harry Keck, "Why Pro Football Owners Age Fast," TSN, November 12, 1952, sec. 2: 8.

25. Watson Spoelstra, "'Stop-and-Go' Springs Roll Up Yardage," TSN, December 10, 1952, sec. 2: 3. An article reporting the Lions' net income for 1952 tallied with the information presented to Congress in 1957 ("A Pride of Lions," *Time*, November 29, 1954, 56–58, 60–62). Tex Maule's 1957 article gives far more pessimistic figures than the data the team gave to Congress earlier that summer (Tex Maule, "Lambs into Lions," SI, December 2, 1957, 67–70; Tex Maule, "Look How the Owners Smile," SI, March 10, 1958, 46–47).

26. Bill Rives, "Budget of $800,000 Likely in First Year," TSN, January 30, 1952, sec. 2: 3.

27. Stan Baumgartner, "Bell Urges Economy, Despite Record Year," TSN, January 28, 1953, sec. 2: 3.

28. "Pro Football Structure Ripe for Revamping," *Chicago Tribune*, January 4, 1953, sec. 2: 3; Coenen, *Sandlots to Super Bowl*, 158.

29. "1953 Pro Football Best Financially," NYT, December 23, 1953, 29.

30. James Murray, "Pros Aweigh: Professional Football Is Off and Barreling towards Its Finest Season, So Herewith Some Advice from a Friend," SI, October 8, 1956, 44, 48–52.

31. Roger Kahn, "When the Pros Come Marching In," SI, November 8, 1954, 10–13.

32. U.S. House, OPTS, 1957: 2821.

33. Franklin Lewis, "Start Browns All Over Again? No — Not for McBride," TSN, November 19, 1952, sec. 2: 8; U.S. House, OPTS, 1957: 2733.

34. The correlation coefficient was 0.74. A simple regression equation, Net Income before Taxes = -176.76 + 1.20(Attendance) suggests that the break-even point occurred at roughly 147,000 or about 25,000 per game. The attendance variable was statistically significant at the 1% level, and the adjusted R2 was 0.542.

35. Murray, "Pros Aweigh," SI.

36. Al Silverman, "Will Pro Football Have Union Trouble This Year?" *Sport*, September 1957, 24–27, 96–98.

37. PFHOFAIC, NFL LM, February 1, 1957, 5.

38. PFHOFAIC, NFL LM, January 20, 1960, 7.

39. Green Bay Packers, *Yearbook 1960*, 44.

40. Harris, *League*, 5, 23.

41. Arthur Daley, "Sports of the *Times*: War on the Gridiron," NYT, December 7, 1945, 29.

42. U.S. House, OPTS, 1957: 2765; Joe King, "Look-Ahead Meet Called by Bert Bell," TSN, November 26, 1958, 1, sec. 2: 4.

43. PFHOFAIC, NFL LM, January 21, 1959, 4.

44. "Cost of Officials $35,000 Few Years Ago, $85,000 in 1952," TSN, January 7, 1953, sec. 2: 11.

45. "Pro Football Structure," *Chicago Tribune*.

46. Joe King, "Rising Costs and Court Fight Peril NFL," TSN, January 7, 1953, sec. 2: 11.

47. PFHOFAIC, NFL LM, November 28, 1955, 9–10.

48. PFHOFAIC, NFL LM, June 3, 1950, 9; January 20, 1951, 32.

49. PFHOFAIC, NFL LM, January 21, 1951, 43, see also 29, 31, 35. Years later, the Cardinals and Bears were still sparring over the schedule (PFHOFAIC, NFL LM, March 28, 1955, 5–7).

50. Tex Maule, "A Stout Wall for Johnny," SI, October 5, 1959, 36–37, 39–44; Howard Roberts, "It Cost 100 Gees for Bears to Open," TSN, October 19, 1960, sec. 2: 8.

51. Leonard Shecter, "Rational Rebel," SI, May 13, 1963, 81–82; U.S. House, OPTS, 1957: 2676. Perian Conerly describes how she and her close friend Betty Rote did not discuss their husband's salaries with each other (Conerly, *Backseat Quarterback*, 125). George Halas sometimes lied to his players, telling them they were the highest-paid on the team, when, in fact, they weren't (Davis, *Papa Bear*, 139–40).

52. Riess, "Social Profile," 229, 233. Riess points out, though, that in the 1950s a majority of players were from blue-collar families. Riess and Coenen believe that the striving for upward mobility helped induce NFL players to begin viewing their

playing experiences as a career instead of as a stepping-stone to jobs in industry. Riess believes that college graduation rates in the NFL peaked in the 1950s (Riess, "Social Profile," 230; Coenen, *Sandlots to Super Bowl*, 179).

53. Coenen, *Sandlots to Super Bowl*, 180.

54. A reprint of Van Brocklin's article in *Pro Football*, circa 1957, appeared in U.S. House, OPTS, 1957: 2815–17.

55. "New Federal Tax Setup Boon to Game," TSN, January 1, 1946, 12.

56. U.S. House, OPTS, 1957: 2594, 2677 has Norm Van Brocklin's recognition of this lack of bargaining leverage.

57. U.S. House, OPTS, 1957: 2699. In today's world of reams of statistics, many of which have never been scrutinized by human eyes, the lack of sophistication inherent in Halas's anecdote is almost refreshing.

58. Peterson, *Pigskin*, 116; "Court Salaries," NYT, December 11, 1938, 86.

59. Whittingham, *What a Game*, 173.

60. "Buffalo's Eleven Lists 14 Contests," NYT, December 14, 1945, 31.

61. Stanley Frank, "The Grid Is Hot!," *Collier's*, September 14, 1946, 92–93; Coenen, *Sandlots to Super Bowl*, 129.

62. Stan Baumgartner, "Ewart Bosses Boss Who Bosses Ewart," TSN, December 1, 1948, sec. 2: 10. For lovers of alliteration, this headline was a doozy.

63. Barney Kremenko, "Browns Need $1,100,000 to Break Even," TSN, November 3, 1948, sec. 2: 1, 4; Surdam, *Postwar Yankees*, 72.

64. Frank, "Grid Is Hot!," *Collier's*.

65. Stan Baumgartner, "Bell Not Worried, Calls Rival Bids Healthy for Game," TSN, October 21, 1953, sec. 2: 2. Craig Coenen described how NFL payrolls "soared to more than $200,000. . . . Philadelphia Eagles spent as much as $280,000 on payroll" (Coenen, *Sandlots to Super Bowl*, 130). If these figures are correct, the owners did not enjoy much respite in salary costs after the AAFC folded; according to salary data presented to Congress in 1957, teams averaged roughly $250,000 each in team payroll in 1952 (see table 15).

66. U.S. Senate, OPTS, 1958: 398.

67. Surdam, *Empty Seats*, 331 (table 17); U.S. House, *Organized Baseball*, 1952: 1610.

68. "'It's Wonderful,'" *Time*, December 19, 1949, 53; Coenen, *Sandlots to Super Bowl*, 136.

69. Joe Williams, "$25,000 to Sign, Pal? Lush Days Are Over," TSN, December 1949, sec. 2: 8. Williams's argument is specious on two accounts. DiMaggio made $8,500 in 1936 according to the New York Yankees financial records housed at baseball's Hall of Fame in Cooperstown. For argument's sake, though, $10,000 in 1936 was equivalent to $17,000 in 1949 (using the Consumer Price Index). In

addition, the New York Yankees of 1936 were profitable and generated much larger revenue than did NFL teams in 1949.

70. Tim Mara and Joe King, "Why We Won!," *Sport*, February 1950, 10–11, 84–85.

71. Natie Brown and Tom Davis, "How Wrestling Looks from the Inside," *Sport*, November 1954, 22–23, 91–93; Jeane Hoffman, "Lady Wrestlers Strike It Rich," *Sport*, June 1951, 36–38.

72. Baumgartner, "Bell Not Worried," TSN.

73. Quote in Watson Spoelstra, "Walker, Halfback in a Hurry, Playing on 3-Year Plan as Pro," TSN, October 31, 1951, sec. 2: 3; "Pride of Lions," *Time*. Near the end of Layne's career, reporter Myron Cope wrote, "his salary is at least $20,000." If so, Layne hadn't made much of a pay raise in the intervening decade (Myron Cope, "Free-Wheeling Layne — Steeler Firebrand at 33," TSN, October 5, 1960, sec. 2: 1, 2).

74. William Worden, "Tittle of the 49ers," SI, November 22, 1954, 34–35, 52–54.

75. It should be mentioned that Lou Groza played twenty-one seasons. Baugh once quipped, "Half of my salary went in taxes, and half in Texas" ("Long Haul," NYT, November 20, 1955, SM17).

76. Newhouse, *Million Dollar Backfield*, 73. The 49ers were the NFL's equivalent of baseball's Boston Red Sox in that their owners allegedly gave generous salaries to their star players and created what sportswriters liked to refer to as a "country club" environment (Jack McDonald, "49ers Strike It Rich with Ground Attack," TSN, October 28, 1959, sec. 2: 9).

77. Frank Finch, "Crazy Legs Calls It Quits after 17 Years," TSN, December 22, 1954, sec. 2: 5.

78. Tex Maule, "For the Defense: The Offense-Minded Pros Look to the Defensive Platoon to Win Games, and Championships," SI, November 16, 1959, 52, 54.

79. Levin, Mitchell, Volcker, and Will, *Blue Ribbon Panel*, 61–77.

80. U.S. House, OPTS, 1957: 2628–29; "Fantastic Situation?" *Time*, January 3, 1949, 31.

81. U.S. House, OPTS, 1957: 2630.

82. "Gridiron Profits Shared," NYT, July 3, 1947, 19. The Baltimore Colts implemented a "share the profit" plan in 1953 that covered all the players, but later changed it to a "merit award" plan, where players were given individual bonuses or had salary adjustments (U.S. House, OPTS, 1957: 2688–89).

83. "Packer Coach Fines Team for Poor Play," NYT, October 13, 1948, 34. Things could get rough in Green Bay. A little more than a year later, Lambeau himself was given the boot. He decided to jump onto the Chicago Cardinals' sinking ship (Ed Prell, "Lambeau Alone with Memories," TSN, December 19, 1951, sec. 2: 8; "Lambeau Leaves Green Bay to Become Coach of Football Cardinals," NYT, February 2, 1950, 36).

84. "Lions Drop Dorais as Gridiron Coach," NYT, December 17, 1947, 44.

85. Frank Finch, "Gillman, Firm but Fair, Instills New Ram Spirit," TSN, October 5, 1955, sec. 2: 7.

86. Martin Kane, "Otto's Big Goodby [sic]," SI, January 3, 1955, 50–53; Joe King, "NFL Title Game Gold Mine; Top Slices $3,508," TSN, December 19, 1956, sec. 2: 1, 2. In 1948, winning players received $1,541, even though a snowstorm reduced the crowd (Louis Effrat, "Eagles Win National Football League Title in Driving Snowstorm," NYT, December 20, 1948, 33).

87. Frank Finch, "Rams, Bears, Browns, Redskins Place Seven Apiece in Pro Bowl," TSN, December 21, 1955, sec. 2: 7.

88. "Pro Gridders Gummed Up in Mess over Royalties," TSN, November 26, 1958, sec. 2: 5; PFHOFAIC, NFL LM, January 16, 1956, 2.

89. "Proposed Pro Football League Plans to Beat NFL on Salaries," NYT, August 24, 1959, 25; Al Hirshberg, "Sound Off! Joe Foss Diagnoses the Pro Football War," Sport, November 1962, 46–49, 95.

90. "Leahy to Be General Manager of New Pro Team," NYT, October 15, 1959, 50.

91. Hirshberg, "Sound Off!," Sport.

92. Murray Olderman, "'Iron Man' Conerly Giants' Kingpin at 38," TSN, November 4, 1959, sec. 2: 3, 6.

93. PFHOFAIC, NFL LM, January 24, 1947, 9 and January 20, 1951 25–56.

94. Edward Prell, "Pro Football League Skips Economy Moves," Chicago Tribune, January 26, 1953, pt. 3, 2.

95. Allison Danzig, "Roster Increase for Pro Elevens," NYT, January 30, 1955, S1, S3; "Higher Player Limit Suggested in NFL," NYT, December 25, 1956, 32; "35-Man Limit Set for Pro Football," NYT, February 4, 1957, 35.

96. Louis Effrat, "2 Changes Voted by NFL Owners," NYT, January 24, 1960, S1, S2.

5. Perils and Triumphs of Ownership

1. The author is always amused by those antique trading shows in which Grandma's hundred-year-old cedar chest has quadrupled in value. The sellers are always pleased, but, using the "rule of seventy-two," this implies a two-percent annual rate of appreciation. But don't go telling antique collectors this; they won't appreciate this information.

2. "Yanks to Stay in Boston," NYT, November 20, 1948, 18.

3. Quirk and Fort, Pay Dirt, 35, 38–39.

4. Coenen, Sandlots to Super Bowl, 44–48.

5. Coenen, Sandlots to Super Bowl, 82–84; Peterson, Pigskin, 122; Davis, Papa Bear, 4–5.

6. PFHOFAIC, NFL LM, January 22, 1960, 13; U.S. House, OPTS, 1957: 2580l.

7. Peterson, *Pigskin*, 112, 129. Peterson's amount differs from the $200,000 cited in Quirk and Fort and shown in table 17 in this book. Franchise sales figures are, unfortunately, notoriously unreliable.

8. Al Stump, "Will Pro Football Get Smart—or Go *Bust*?" *Sport*, November 1948, 10–12, 74, 76.

9. Louis Effrat, "Rival Pro Football Owners Fail to Reach Agreement in Philadelphia Parley," NYT, December 21, 1948, 37; "Champion Eagles Sold for $250,000 to 100-Man Group," NYT, January 16, 1949, S1, S4. Pete Rozelle worried about the hundred-man group proposal, fearing that no one would be in charge and thus no one could be held accountable (Harris, *League*, 112–13).

10. PFHOFAIC, NFL LM, April 7, 1945, 4.

11. Joseph Sheehan, "Syndicate of Business Men Acquire Detroit Lions Football Club," NYT, January 16, 1948, 28.

12. "Yankees under One Head," NYT, August 29, 1947, 22.

13. "Pro Dodgers Sale Looms," NYT, January 2, 1948, 18.

14. "Taliaferro Goes to Yanks' Eleven," NYT, June 3, 1950, 11; also PFHOFAIC, NFL LM, January 20, 1950, 10; June 2, 1950, 2.

15. "Aligning the Divisions Problem for Bell," NYT, January 23, 1951, 31; MacCambridge, *America's Game*, 76.

16. "Browns' Sale Completed," NYT, July 17, 1953, 21; Harris, *League*, 36; "Two New Yorkers Gain Control of Cleveland Browns in $4,000,000 Deal," NYT, March 23, 1961, 42.

17. "Wisconsin Men Buy Braves for $5,500,000; Club Will Stay in Milwaukee," NYT, November 17, 1962, 19.

18. "Pauley Buys into Rams," NYT, December 17, 1947, 44; "Actors to Buy Shares," NYT, December 19, 1949, 31.

19. "Owners of Rams Split," NYT, May 27, 1956, 179; Bill Becker, "Reeves Repurchases Control of Rams," NYT, December 28, 1962, 8.

20. Joe King, "Tim Mara Dies—Led Pro Football's Climb as Owner of Giants," TSN, February 25, 1959, sec. 2: 4.

21. PFHOFAIC, AFL LM, October 28, 1959, 7; PFHOFAIC, NFL LM, January 15, 1946, 12; "Wismer, Titans' Owner, Is Ordered to Sell His Stock in Redskins," NYT, November 10, 1960, 66; "Wismer Accepts Bid," NYT, November 22, 1960, 44.

22. PFHOFAIC, Philadelphia Eagles Team Files, 1953–62, letter from Daniel F. Reeves to Frank McNamee, December 19, 1962; Quirk and Fort, *Pay Dirt*, 428.

23. Glick, "Professional Sports," 80.

24. PFHOFAIC, NFL LM, April 10, 1945, 20–21; January 12, 1946, 5; April 30, 1946, 10; also Coenen, *Sandlots to Super Bowl*, 112, 122; MacCambridge, *America's Game*, 15. Sportswriter Al Stump described the acrimonious exchange between Reeves and some

of the other owners, an argument that spilled into the hotel's men's room, concluding, "The Los Angeles Rams undoubtedly are the only big-time pro team ever born in a toilet" (Al Stump, "The Los Angeles Rams," *Sport*, September 1952, 32–33, 83–87). An advertisement in the October 1, 1957 *New York Times* demonstrates the greater costs of train travel to western cities. A round-trip ticket from New York to Buffalo was $38.20, to Cleveland $51.65, and to Chicago $81.50 (including Pullman accommodations). For an entourage of forty people, including players, coaches, and a few others, the differences in ticket prices amounted to $1,200–$1,800. The price of a round-trip ticket between New York and Los Angeles was not reported, as the Lackawanna Railroad did not go west of Chicago ("Go Lackawanna" advertisement, NYT, October 1, 1957, 4).

25. Bob Burnes, "NFL Expansion Stirs Envy of Majors' Bigwigs," TSN, September 22, 1954, sec. 2: 8.

26. Joe King, "Marshall Always Kindling Fires in NFL," TSN, January 9, 1952, sec. 2: 9, 10.

27. PFHOFAIC, NFL LM, April 7, 1945, 5; April 10, 1945, 18–19; January 20, 1949, 6; also Joe King, "Yank or Ranger! Tough Bronco to Ride," TSN, January 30, 1952, sec. 2: 1, 2; Coenen, *Sandlots to Super Bowl*, 134. Sportswriter Joe King chronicled Collins's woes in Boston and New York (Joe King, "Showman Ted Gets First Grid Hit," TSN, November 22, 1950, sec. 2: 5). Collins blamed the press, too (Jerry Nason, "Here's Why Collins Pulls Stakes," *Boston Globe*, December 19, 1948, 33).

28. Mara quote in Louis Effrat, "Football Yanks Bought by Dallas after Eight Lean Years for Collins," NYT, January 20, 1952, S1, S3; PFHOFAIC, NFL LM, January 18, 1952, 10; January 19, 1952, 12, 14.

29. Ed Prell, "Wade First Choice in Grid Draft, but Uncle Sam Waits," TSN, January 23, 1952, sec. 2: 5); Joe Williams, "Pro Football Tossed Ted for Million Loss," TSN, January 18, 1950, sec. 2: 8. Years later, Interim Commissioner Austin Gunsel announced that the league had paid the last of the $25,000 annual payments to baseball's Yankees for the lapsed lease of Yankee Stadium (PFHOFAIC, NFL LM, January 20, 1960, 7).

30. Joe King, "Fall Guy Collins Stacks Blue Chips," TSN, November 15, 1950, sec. 2: 5.

31. Louis Effrat, "Pro Football Loop Maps Details of Yank Sale to Dallas, Then Ends Meeting," NYT, January 21, 1952, 20.

32. King, "Yank or Ranger!," TSN.

33. MacCambridge, *America's Game*, 76–77. The $250,000 figure, though, may have included the $100,000 franchise fee (Charles Burton, "Texans Fold; New Group May Seek '53 Franchise," *Dallas Morning News*, November 13, 1952, pt. III, 4).

34. "Dallas to Return Football Franchise to League," NYT, November 13, 1952, 43.

35. "National Football League Takes Franchise Back from Dallas Club," NYT, November 15, 1952, 21. Edward Prell reported that the league lost $65,000 operating

the team (Edward Prell, "Things Popped Fast in '52 for Pro Football," *Chicago Tribune*, January 4, 1953, sec. 2: 6).

36. "Dallas Drops Efforts to Regain Franchise as NFL Refuses to Share Stadium Debt," NYT, November 19, 1952, 38.

37. MacCambridge, *America's Game*, 78; "Baltimore Meets Goal Set by NFL," NYT, January 1, 1953, 27; Harris, *League*, 48.

38. U.S. House, OPTS, 1957: 2569; MacCambridge, *America's Game*, 78–79.

39. "Redskins Get Offer," NYT, November 9, 1956, 39.

40. "Steelers Weigh Louisville Offer," NYT, November 10, 1956, 24.

41. Johnson quote in "Pirates Threaten Franchise Shift," NYT, November 15, 1956, 45; Rooney quote in "Steelers Are 'Vitally' Interested in Fairgrounds' Pro Grid Bid," *Louisville Courier Journal*, November 10, 1956, sec. 2: 4. Rooney quickly backtracked on his statement, saying, "Actually I never thought of leaving [Pittsburgh]" ("Eagles Will Hear F. G.'s Bid Today," *Louisville Courier Journal*, November 14, 1956, sec. 2: 8).

42. "Buffalo Makes Bid for Steeler Eleven," NYT, November 12, 1956, 41.

43. Ed Prell, "Dallas Takes Yanks' Place in NFL; Where Does That Put Cards?" TSN, January 30, 1952, sec. 2: 2.

44. PFHOFAIC, NFL LM, January 21, 1959, 5–6; Davis, *Papa Bear*, 105.

45. Joe King, "NFL Brushing Off Rival-Loop Rumors — 'Just Let 'Em Try,'" TSN, February 4, 1959, sec. 2: 5. Both Halas and the Wolfners claimed they had "standing offers" to each other to pay $500,000 to the team that relocated (Burnes, "NFL Expansion," TSN.

46. PFHOFAIC, NFL LM, March 13, 1960, 39–40.

47. "Chicago Cardinals Get Approval to Move to St. Louis This Year," NYT, March 14, 1960, 32; Ralph Ray, "Brewer's Big Pitch Lands Grid Giants," TSN, March 23, 1960, sec. 2: 3, 4; Harris, *League*, 231.

48. Burnes, "NFL Expansion," TSN.

49. For the town's efforts to retain their team, see Bill Furlong, "New Day in Green Bay," SI, December 12, 1960, 26–29, 94. As early as 1946, Bert Bell had to issue a statement that the Packers were staying in Green Bay (Edward Prell, "Packers Stay in Green Bay, Bell Insists," *Chicago Tribune*, December 12, 1946, sec. 4, 59).

50. Surdam, *Postwar Yankees*, 299–300.

51. U.S. House, OPTS, 1957: 2527.

52. Coenen, *Sandlots to Super Bowl*, 113; MacCambridge, *America's Game*, 13.

53. PFHOFAIC, NFL LM, April 7, 1945, 4; January 23, 1947, 4; January 15, 1948, 2; also William Richardson, "National Football League Weighs Twelve-Team Postwar Circuit," NYT, April 9, 1945, 15; Harris, *League*, 102.

54. Harris, *League*, 28. This tale proves a cautionary one for economists, showing that not all businesspeople operate as cool, calculating rational actors.

55. Joe King, "Bell Urges Two-Club Expansion in NFL," TSN, November 13, 1957, sec. 2: 1, 2.

56. Bell's quote in PFHOFAIC, NFL LM, February 1, 1957, 4; January 21, 1959, 3; Marshall's quote in Jack Walsh, "Marshall Raps Bell's 14-Team Plan," TSN, November 20, 1957, sec. 2: 1, 2. Marshall, ever fickle, had earlier supported expansion, but changed his mind because he worried that NFL expansion would harm college football ("Marshall Battles Expansion: 'Why Harm College Game?'" TSN, October 8, 1958, sec. 2: 8).

57. "Halas Bids NFL Add Texas Cities," NYT, August 30, 1959, S1, S6.

58. Jack Walsh, "'Easy on Expansion,' Says Marshall, Citing Campus Grid Effect," TSN, November 19, 1959, sec. 2: 2; "New Group Seeks NFL Franchise," NYT, December 21, 1959, 35; PFHOFAIC, NFL LM, January 22, 1960, 13.

59. David Condon, "600 G's Likely Tab for New NFL Franchise," TSN, December 16, 1959, sec. 2: 8. Baseball's National League charged expansion clubs at least $1.7 million in 1961 (Surdam, *Postwar Yankees*, 242). Setting the correct fee was difficult, as established owners had to balance their collective losses from expansion with the threat of overburdening a new team at the outset (Harris, *League*, 158).

60. Tex Maule, "Pro Football: The Infighting Was Vicious," SI, February 8, 1960, 50–52. Halas biographer Jeff Davis claims Halas backed Marshall Leahy but eventually embraced Rozelle; Davis does not emphasize Halas's efforts to get expansion approved (Davis, *Papa Bear*, 352–53).

61. Louis Effrat, "National Football League Admits Dallas for '60 and Twin Cities for '61," NYT, January 29, 1960, 18; MacCambridge, *America's Game*, 117–18; PFHOFAIC, NFL LM, January 17, 1960, 2; January 18, 1960, 3–4; January 28, 1960, 21–27.

62. Louis Effrat, "National Football League to Let Vikings Choose from List of 96 Players," NYT, January 25, 1961, 40; PFHOFAIC, NFL LM, March 11, 1960, 32–33. Louis Effrat agreed with Winter's complaints about the setup: "the expendables acquired by the Vikings for $15,276 apiece appeared to be overage, overweight or over the hill" (Louis Effrat, "Minnesota Selects Youso, Boll and Kimber, Linemen, from Football Giants," NYT, January 27, 1961, 26).

63. Quote in Joe King, "Rival Loop No. 1 on NFL's List of Its Big Headaches," TSN, January 11, 1961, sec. 2: 1, 8; Joe King, "Buck Squeeze Forces NFL to Seek Larger Package from Video," TSN, February 8, 1961, sec. 2: 5.

64. Effrat, "Minnesota Selects," NYT.

6. Antitrust Adventures

1. U.S. House, OPTS, 1957: 2725. For a detailed examination of professional team sports and the congressional hearings, see Surdam, *Big Leagues Go to Washington*.

2. Fort, *Sports Economics*, 134, 137.

3. Nathanson, "Sovereign Nation of Baseball," 75.

4. "Baseball Names a Defense Group," NYT, March 23, 1957, 22.

5. Committee chairman Emanuel Celler apparently was duped into believing this charade. He applauded Bell's presentation of the reserve clause NFL-style as "a refreshing statement to hear" ("Family Man," SI, August 5, 1957, 21). Apparently some owners had once afforded unique "terms" to players, but George Preston Marshall moved and got approval for a rule that required adherence to a regular league form of the players' contract (PFHOFAIC, NFL LM, June 30, 1934, 3).

6. Even though law firms might plead competitive imbalance with regard to win-loss records in their cases, their chances of getting a reverse-order draft of law school graduates are slender indeed.

7. U.S. House, OPTS, 1957: 2580l-2580m; PFHOFAIC, NFL LM, January 24, 1947, 15.

8. PFHOFAIC, NFL LM, January 11, 1946, 3; U.S. House, OPTS, 1957: 2733; U.S. Senate, OPTS, 1958: 399–400; for an early newspaper description of the rule, see "Dudley, Steelers, Offered for Sale," NYT, January 26, 1947, S1, S4.

9. U.S. House, OPTS, 1957: 2569, see also 2531, 2568; "Colts Must Pay $150,000," NYT, January 25, 1950, 42.

10. U.S. Senate, OPTS, 1959: 49.

11. "Ruthstrom Loses Suit Against Redskins in Test of Football Reserve Clause," NYT, December 21, 1949, 43.

12. "Pro Football Loop Files Brief in Anti-Trust Suit," NYT, December 23, 1951, S6; "Football League Denies Sherman Act Violations," NYT, February 24, 1952, S6.

13. "Pro Football Suit Is Resumed by U.S.," NYT, February 3, 1953, 29.

14. "'Death Knell' of NFL Predicted If Government Wins Court Action," NYT, February 25, 1953, 30; Bell's quote in "Bell Tells Court NFL Needs Curbs," NYT, February 26, 1953, 35; "Bell Hedges on TV Destroying NFL," NYT, February 27, 1953, 29.

15. "Bell Loop Faces Anti-Trust Suit," NYT, September 28, 1954, 36.

16. "U.S. Supreme Court Agrees to Hear Suit Charging Monopoly in Pro Football," NYT, October 9, 1956, 57.

17. "Texts of the Court's Majority Opinion and Dissents," NYT, February 2, 1957, 36. Three justices dissented, but the majority cited the desegregation cases of a few years back: "a unanimous court had no difficulty in demolishing the 'rule of stare decisis' when it overturned the entrenched holding of the court that statutes enforcing racial segregation in the public schools are constitutional" (Arthur Krock, "In the Nation: Now Congress Has the Ball—Foot, Base and Basket," NYT, February 28, 1957, 26).

18. "Ex-Lineman Says He's 'Vindicated,'" NYT, February 26, 1957, 36.

19. PFHOFAIC, NFL LM, November 7, 1949, 5.

20. Bell's question found in "Baseball Names Defense" NYT.

21. Hillings's and Keating's remarks in "House Gets Proposal to Place Baseball under Antitrust Laws," NYT, February 27, 1957, 43; Celler's remarks in "Immunity Sought for Four Sports," NYT, February 28, 1957, 34.

22. "Football 'Story' Goes to Congress," NYT, May 7, 1957, 45. Although Bell thought $900,000 was an impressive amount, he might have been advised to recall the quote attributed to Senator Everett Dirksen of Illinois: "A billion here, a billion there, and pretty soon you're talking about real money." (www.brainyquote.com/quotes/authors/e/everett_dirksen.hmtl, viewed 12/19/10).

23. U.S. House, OPTS, 1957: 2495.

24. U.S. Senate, OPTS, 1959: 31–32.

25. U.S. House, OPTS, 1957: 2497.

26. U.S. House, OPTS, 1957: 2733.

27. Allen Drury, "Pro Football Hits Antitrust Curbs," NYT, July 25, 1957, 13. Perhaps Bell was hoping to soothe some ruffled feathers when he reported in his prepared statement that "The twelve league teams annually raise over a half million dollars for charity" (U.S. House, OPTS, 1957: 2734).

28. U.S. House, OPTS, 1957: 2499.

29. U.S. House, OPTS, 1957: 2533–34. Owners considered raising the minimum ticket price to $2.00 at the January 1951 meetings, but they decided not to ("Player Limit Raised to 33 Men for National Football Loop Teams," NYT, January 21, 1951, 135). George Preston Marshall advocated changing the minimum "day of the game" price to $2.00 and enacting a $1.00 minimum for other ticket sales (exclusive of taxes); his fellow owners approved the change in 1944 (PFHOFAIC, NFL LM, April 19, 1944, 12; June 19, 1943, 21).

30. U.S. House, OPTS, 1957: 2662. If Harkins had been upset with NFL owners setting minimum prices, then he and Creighton Miller would have been aghast (but probably not surprised) had they discovered owners discussing a "gentlemen's agreement" to suppress publication of player salary information, which happened in 1939 (PFHOFAIC, NFL LM, July 22, 1939, 14).

31. Rottenberg, "Baseball Players Labor Market."

32. Major League Baseball owners used the same tactic during the 1958 hearings (U.S. Senate, OPTS, 1958: 24).

33. "Players Defend Football Draft," NYT, July 26, 1957, 38.

34. U.S. House, OPTS, 1957: 2664, 2734.

35. U.S. Senate, OPTS, 1958: 393.

36. U.S. Senate, OPTS, 1958: 389; U.S. Senate 1959, OPTS, 31.

37. U.S. Senate, OPTS, 1958: 401–2.

38. U.S. Senate, OPTS, 1958: 414–15; PFHOFAIC, NFL LM, January 21, 1959, 5.

39. "Bell Tells Congressional Hearing New Pro Football League Is Being Formed," NYT, July 29, 1959, 22; U.S. Senate, OPTS, 1959: 40–41. Whether Bell sincerely believed the owners' professions of good faith or whether he was dissembling for congressional consumption is difficult to ascertain. The author is inclined to think Bell believed his own testimony because he wanted to.

40. U.S. Senate, OPTS, 1959: 40.

41. U.S. Senate, OPTS, 1959: 34, 40.

42. U.S. Senate, OPTS, 1959: 35, 37.

43. U.S. Senate, OPTS, 1959: 36.

44. See Peterson, *Pigskin*, 124, 167 for some background.

45. Roscoe McGowen, "Cleveland Rams Transfer Eleven to Los Angeles," NYT, January 13, 1946, S7, S9.

46. Roscoe McGowen, "Coast Pro League in National Set-Up," NYT, January 14, 1946, 23; see "Scranton Farm for Steelers," NYT, April 3, 1946, 42.

47. "3 Top Minor Football Leagues in Alliance to Combat 'Jumping,'" NYT, March 25, 1946, 32.

48. "Pro Minor League to Have 14 Teams," NYT, February 9, 1947, 56.

49. PFHOFAIC, NFL LM, January 13, 1946, 8; April 29, 1946, 5–6; January 23, 1947, 6; July 20, 1947, 3; January 17, 1948, 8.

50. U.S. House, OPTS, 1957: 2528; U.S. Senate, OPTS, 1958: 396.

51. U.S. House, OPTS, 1957: 2529.

52. U.S. Senate, *Professional Sports Antitrust Bill — 1964*, 81–84, 90.

53. PFHOFAIC, NFL LM, January 21, 1951, 34, 36. Whether the owners noted the irony inherent in the fact that their recent victory over the AAFC now put them over the 75 percent mark is an interesting question; the NFL owners do not appear to have developed a sense of irony. Bell introduced the NFL's attorneys handling the antitrust case at a January 1952 meeting. He told them that the fee for the lawyers "would be $30,000 if the case is lost, and $75,000 if the case is won" (PFHOFAIC, NFL LM, January 18, 1952, 11).

54. "Bell Loop Faces Suit," NYT.

55. Quotes from "Radio Big Help to Pro Football, Station Operator Says at Trial," NYT, February 10, 1953, 34; "Station Manager Tells of NFL Ban," NYT, February 4, 1953, 37.

56. "Pro Football Suit Recessed to Feb. 24," NYT, February 11, 1953, 41.

57. "Government Establishes Two Important Points during Football Suit," NYT, January 28, 1953, 34.

58. "TV Station Head Witness at Trial," NYT, January 30, 1953, 18. According to Coenen, government attorneys did not know of the league's meeting minutes until

Art Rooney "reportedly turned over the documents to the prosecution and commented, 'Here, maybe you can make some sense out of all this . . . I sure can't'" (Pat Livingston, "The Pittsburgh Steelers," *Sport*, October 1953, 44–47, 86–89; Coenen, *Sandlots to Super Bowl*, 158). According to an earlier article, the NFL was selected for the suit because "it has the most definite rule limiting TV" ("Anti-Trust Suit Against Pro Football Opens Today," *Chicago Tribune*, January 26, 1953, pt. 3, 2).

59. "'Death Knell' of NFL," NYT.

60. "Bell Tells Court," NYT.

61. Both quotes from "Bell Hedges," NYT.

62. "Mistrial Motion by NFL Denied," NYT, March 3, 1953, 31.

63. "Football Giants Call TV Harmful to Attendance," NYT, March 4, 1953, 33; "Giants Ask TV Sellout Guarantee," *Chicago Tribune*, March 4, 1953, sec. 3: 1. According to Robert Peterson, Mara also submitted a brief to the court showing that the sales of reserved seats fell as television sets proliferated in the city, dropping from 91.5 percent of reserved seats in 1946 down to 62.5 percent in 1950 (Peterson, *Pigskin*, 198).

64. "Marshall Charges Anti-Trust Suit Is Inspired by Radio, TV Interests," NYT, March 5, 1953, 30.

65. The information supplied to Congress in 1957 and shown in tables 5 and 11 differs from Kerbawy's figures: $114,754 net income before taxes and $85,980 in radio and television revenues.

66. "Lions Official Traces Gate Drop to Video," *Chicago Tribune*, March 6, 1953, sec. 3: 5.

67. "Lion Football Broadcasts Brought $113,000 of $114,000 Profit Last Year, Court Told," NYT, March 6, 1953, 31.

68. U.S. House, *Telecasting of Professional Sports Contests*, 1961: 16–21 contains a copy of Grim's ruling in "United States v. National Football League."

69. "Court Limits Pro Football's Control of Television to the Area of Home Games," NYT, November 13, 1953, 30.

70. PFHOFAIC, NFL LM, January 27, 1954, 1–2.

71. PFHOFAIC, NFL LM, January 20, 1960, 9.

7. Competitive Balance

1. MacCambridge, *America's Game*, 43; for the NFL's early efforts to promote parity, see Coenen, *Sandlots to Super Bowl*, 88.

2. U.S. Senate, *Professional Sports Antitrust Bill — 1964*, 113. Up to the end of World War II, the divide between the Bears, Packers, Giants, and, to a lesser extent, the Redskins, and the rest of the teams was marked. The Bears' record for the first twenty-seven NFL seasons was 211-78-31, a win-loss percentage far in excess even

of that of the Yankees during their heyday, 1921–64 (Warren Brown, "What's Happening at Halas U.?" *Sport*, November 1954, 10–11, 87–90).

3. MacCambridge, *America's Game*, 41.

4. See Bell's testimony, U.S. House, OPTS, 1957: 2526; MacCambridge, *America's Game*, 51. While Brown was an enlightened person in many ways, his unstinting drive to win seems excessive. For examples, see MacCambridge, *America's Game*, 51; Franklin Lewis, "The Browns Are on the Spot," *Sport*, September 1950, 60–64.

5. Hal Lebovitz, "Eagles and Browns Loom as Pro Repeaters: NFL Titlists Show Power; All AAC Teams Toughies. Forty-Niners Again Appear to Be Chief Rival for Conference Champions," TSN, September 28, 1949, sec. 2: 7.

6. Lewis, "Browns on the Spot," *Sport*.

7. Harry Warren, "Browns Ride High On Win over Eagles," TSN, September 27, 1950, sec. 2: 7.

8. Frank Finch, "Browns Make Believers out of Diehards: Dramatic Victory over Rams a Real Convincer to NFL," TSN, January 3, 1951, sec. 2: 3, 6.

9. PFHOFAIC, NFL LM, January 24, 1947, 15. In the discussion to follow, ties count as one-half win for purposes of calculating percentages. The NFL sometimes did not count ties in determining champions or calculating win-loss percentages.

10. For a discussion of this measure of competitive balance, see Quirk and Fort, *Pay Dirt*, 1992, 244–46.

11. Quirk and Fort, *Pay Dirt*, 1992, 247.

12. The Browns' scoring dominance over several seasons, though, was unprecedented.

13. Jack Sher, "Of Green Bay: The Story of a Great Town and a Great Team," *Sport*, December 1946, 58–68, 64, 66.

14. Art Daley, "Green Bay Small? Yes — but It Has Plenty of Gold," TSN, November 10, 1948, sec. 2: 2. Because of the NFL's scheduling, Curly Lambeau pointed out that the Eagles had not played in Green Bay since 1940. In the same article, Lambeau also boasted that, "the Packers, in 28 years in the National Football League, have never lost money except in one or two years and that loss was only a few thousand dollars."

15. Dan Parker quote found in Coenen, *Sandlots to Super Bowl*, 147–48; Harris, *League*, 154.

16. Herb Heft, "Upsets Boost Return to Balance in NFL," TSN, October 19, 1955, sec. 2: 1, 2.

17. Alfred Wright, "Football: The Pros have Been Thrilling Crowds with Cliffhangers as the New Talent Proves Its Mettle and Livens the League," SI, December 12, 1955, 43; for Bell's goal, see "Pro League's Improved Balances Points to Exciting Title Races," NYT, August 23, 1959, S7.

18. Quote in "Western Conference," si, October 8, 1956, 51; Watson Spoelstra, "Sidelines Cited as Factor in Lions' Limp," tsn, November 9, 1955, sec. 2: 1, 2.

19. Tommy Devine, "Lions Sniff nfl King Role Again, Jockeyed by Whip-Cracking Layne," tsn, October 31, 1956, sec. 2: 2.

20. "Nobody in the Cellar," *Newsweek*, December 3, 1956, 67.

21. Tex Maule, "Run for the Money," si, October 7, 1957, 20, 25, 58, 60.

22. Joe King, "nfl Cellar-Dwellers See New Light," tsn, October 7, 1959, sec. 2: 1, 2.

23. Coenen, *Sandlots to Super Bowl*, 99; "Packers Conquer All-Stars, 19 to 7," nyt, August 31, 1945. The owners had earlier banned postseason exhibition games with independent teams to forestall potential embarrassment (Coenen, *Sandlots to Super Bowl*, 15, 92).

24. Arthur Daley, "Sports of the *Times*: Block That Kick!," nyt, August 21, 1947, 30; for results of later games, see "Cleveland Browns Down College Football All-Stars before 92,180 at Chicago," nyt, August 18, 1951, 15; Tex Maule, "Nice Boys, but No Match," si, August 24, 1959, 14–15, 58–60).

25. "Pro Football Men to Weight 2 Issues," nyt, July 18, 1948, s6.

26. John Lardner, "Could 7.4 Gorillas Lick Army?" *Newsweek*, December 17, 1945, 88.

27. Stanley Woodward, "Army Coach Red Blaik Says: The Pro Game isn't Football," *Collier's*, October 28, 1950, 18–19, 40, 42. As Ned Pepper retorted to Rooster Cogburn in *True Grit*, "I call that bold talk."

28. Frank Finch, "Red Blaik Black and Blue under Barbs: Army Coach Termed Pay Game 'Show,'" tsn, November 1, 1950, sec. 2: 1, 2.

29. Bob Yonkers, "Browns Block Out Blaik with Blast," tsn, November 1, 1950, sec. 2: 2, 8.

30. Joe Williams, "Blaik's Crack at Pro Football Stirs Critics," tsn, November 1, 1950, sec. 2: 2.

31. Ed Prell, "'Weakest nfl Could Beat Army,'" tsn, November 1, 1950, sec. 2: 8; for more rebuttals see the November 1, 1950 issue of tsn.

32. Arthur Daley, "Pros and Cons of Pro Football," nyt, November 20, 1955, sm17.

33. Harold Burr, "Grid Dodgers Eye New Look," tsn, February 18, 1948, sec. 2: 8.

34. "Redskins Protest Heller's Transfer," nyt, November 21, 1934, 25; "Protest on Heller Is Denied by Carr," nyt, November 22, 1934, 28; "Poll of Football League Club Owners Will Decide If Heller May Join Giants," nyt, November 23, 1934, 26; "Giants Not to Use Heller Tomorrow," nyt, November 24, 1934, 10; Coenen, *Sandlots to Super Bowl*, 91–92; pfhofaic, nfl lm, December 10, 1934, 2, 3; June 16, 1935, 2.

35. MacCambridge, *America's Game*, 26.

36. Lewis, "Browns on the Spot," *Sport*.

37. "Boston Yanks Get Brooklyn Players," NYT, December 15, 1945, 26; Louis Effrat, "Pros Stage Draft of Football Stars as Bell Paves Way," NYT, January 22, 1950, 141.

38. "Taliaferro Goes to Yanks' Eleven," NYT, June 3, 1950, 11.

39. "Deal for Passer Sought by Giants," NYT, October 21, 1947, 31.

40. Joe King, "Stunning Swaps Shape Torrid Races in NFL," TSN, November 8, 1961, sec. 2: 1, 2; "Giants Made Swaps with 11 of 13 Rivals in 7-Year Span," TSN, September 20, 1961, sec. 2: 3.

41. Ed Prell, "Record Throngs Greet Pro Grid Openers; Chicago Cards, Buffalo Early Threats," TSN, October 1, 1947, sec. 2: 6.

42. NFL player movement data tabulated from Maher and Gill, *Pro Football Encyclopedia*, 35–39; table available upon request. Surdam, "Coase Theorem and Player Movement," 201–21.

43. "Pro Owners' War," *Newsweek*, November 1, 1948, 72–73; Francis J. Powers and Ed Prell, "George Halas: The Papa Bear," *Sport*, December 1948, 52–61. For rock 'n' roll aficionados, Halas's collection of star quarterbacks is reminiscent of the Yardbirds, who had Jeff Beck, Eric Clapton, and Jimmy Page, although the three were never in the band simultaneously. Halas also had George Blanda on the roster, although he did not initially use Blanda as a quarterback.

44. Tex Maule, "Lambs into Lions," SI, December 2, 1957, 67–70; Joe King, "What Puts the Roar in Detroit Lions?" TSN, December 15, 1954, sec. 2: 3.

45. Tex Maule, "They Cry for Moore in Baltimore," SI, October 20, 1958, 56, 58–59.

46. "Eastern Conference," SI, October 5, 1959, 39; "Western Conference," SI, October 5, 1959, 44.

47. Heft, "Upsets Boost Return," TSN; John Steadman, "Steeler Castoff Unitas Now Rated Bargain Find as Baltimore Passer," TSN, October 23, 1957, sec. 2: 9. The Unitas story—cut by the Steelers without much of a chance to demonstrate his abilities, working on a construction job, playing for a semi-pro team, and then the phone call from Don Kellett—has a recent counterpart in the Kurt Warner saga (Warner stocked groceries for an Iowa store).

48. Joe King, "Colts Cashed In On 'Spend-Win' Plan," TSN, December 24, 1958, sec. 2: 1, 6.

49. Joseph Durso, "Baltimore Triumphs, 8–2, after Losing 8–5, in 10," NYT, September 21, 1964, 40.

50. "12 Packers Members of Castoff Club," TSN, November 2, 1955, sec. 2: 10.

51. For early signs that Lombardi would transform the Packers, see Joe King, "3-Club Races Shape Up in NFL Derby," TSN, September 23, 1959, 27, 28; Tex Maule,

"Vince Brings Green Days to Green Bay," SI, October 19, 1959, 56–58. For the author's father, a Nestlé Quik chocolate mix promotion proved a macabre coda to the Lombardi legacy. On the back of the canister that held the chocolate powder was a contest for children to enter. The contest's slogan was, "Join Coach Lombardi." Unfortunately for Nestlé (and for Washington's team), Lombardi died during the contest.

52. Brown, "What's Happening at Halas U.?" *Sport*. Jeff Davis claims Lujack quit the NFL because of Halas's chicanery in negotiations and that Halas used the injury as a cover for the true reason for the player's retirement (Davis, *Papa Bear*, 237).

53. Bob Yonkers, "Browns' Last Title? Guess Again!," TSN, December 24, 1952, sec. 2: 1, 2.

54. MacCambridge, *America's Game*, 85.

55. Angelo Angelopolous, "Can the Browns Win without Graham?" *Sport*, September 1954, 26–27, 90–91.

56. Hal Lebovitz, "8-Time Winner Browns May Be Greatest," TSN, December 9, 1953, sec. 2: 5; Hal Lebovitz, "What Put Zip into Browns? Newcomers Now Clicking," TSN, December 8, 1954, sec. 2: 7.

57. Brown's quotes in Herman Goldstein, "Paul Sees Next 10 Years as Harder," TSN, October 12, 1955, sec. 2: 1, 2; Franklin Lewis, "Brown Free Trader, Acquires 18 of 33," TSN, November 2, 1955, sec. 2: 10.

58. Hal Lebovitz, "Big Mo Giving Browns New Title Glow," TSN, November 16, 1955, sec. 2: 3; "Collins Maps Plan to Transfer Team," NYT, December 23, 1948, 28.

59. Herman Goldstein, "Paul Brown Reaches His Goal Winning Ten Straight Pro Crowns," TSN, December 14, 1955, sec. 2: 5.

60. Hal Lebovitz, "NFL Player Draft Called Big Cause of Browns' Skid," TSN, October 31, 1956, sec. 2: 1, 2.

61. Fort, *Sports Economics*, 135.

62. PFHOFAIC, NFL LM, January 20, 1949, 6; January 20, 1951, 27–31.

63. U.S. Senate, OPTS, 1958: 43.

64. MacCambridge, *America's Game*, 39. George Preston Marshall exemplified the owners' plaints: "it is absolutely vital to the interests of the Washington franchise that the Chicago Bears play in Washington. . . . We have been . . . very reasonable with Mr. Halas, and we expect him to be so with us" (PFHOFAIC, NFL LM, February 1, 1938, 13).

65. Stanley Frank, "The Grid Is Hot!," *Collier's*, September 14, 1946, 92–93.

66. Roscoe McGowen, "National Football League Season to Open Sept. 22 and Close Dec. 8," NYT, January 17, 1949.

67. "Yanks Buck Giants on Football Dates," NYT, May 18, 1946, 14.

68. Joe King, "Marshall Always Kindling Fires in NFL," TSN, January 9, 1952, sec. 2: 9, 10.

69. MacCambridge, *America's Game*, 40.

70. Tex Maule, "It's Up in the Air," SI, December 15, 1958, 12–15. Bell's effort to promote "parity" raises the question, "Is there a 'win-loss' illusion in sports similar to the 'money illusion' in economics?" Do fans of teams whose records are inflated by playing other weak teams really believe their team is as good as its record?

71. Joe King, "Giants Revive NY as Grid Gold Mine," TSN, November 24, 1954, sec. 2: 1, 2.

72. MacCambridge, *America's Game*, 39.

73. Coenen, *Sandlots to Super Bowl*, 24, 105.

74. Lawrence Robinson, "Bert Bell Key Man in Pro Gridiron War," TSN, January 28, 1948, sec. 2: 1–2.

75. MacCambridge, *America's Game*, 330–31.

76. Bill Stern, "The Football Feud," *Sport*, September 1946, 38–39, 87–88.

77. PFHOFAIC, NFL LM, April 30, 1946, 9; July 20, 1947, 6; also "NFL Will Hear Plan for Division," NYT, January 22, 1947, 26. Marshall trumped the proponents of the round-robin system by citing a clause in the league's constitution that required unanimity. Marshall flaunted the rule and said he would not approve the change ("Player Limit Raised to 33 Men for National Football Loop Teams," NYT, January 21, 1951, 135; Louis Effrat, "Pro Football Loop Maps Details of Yank Sale to Dallas, Then Ends Meeting," NYT, January 21, 1952, 20).

78. "Pro Clubs Haggle Over Home Games," NYT, January 27, 1947, 18.

79. Louis Effrat, "NFL Shuts Door on Common Draft With Rival Loop," NYT, January 18, 1948, S1, S3.

80. Gordon Cobbledick, "Pro Grid Goal? It's Showdown," TSN, September 28, 1949, sec. 2: 8.

81. "Pros Argue on Divisional Set-Up, Bears Would Switch to American," NYT, January 22, 1951, 22; "Pro Elevens Face Knotty Problem," NYT, January 18, 1950, 44.

82. Art Rense, "Bell Plans Move to Curb Criticism of NFL Officiating," TSN, December 8, 1954, sec. 2: 7.

83. "Plan Is Approved by Ballot of 12–1," NYT, January 24, 1950, 43. George Preston Marshall had his proxy vote against the schedule, as he may have wanted a home-and-home series with Baltimore.

84. "78-Game Schedule for Pro Football," NYT, June 28, 1950, 36.

85. "Bell to Prepare Slate," NYT, March 30, 1951, 37.

86. Bell's quote in "Aligning Divisions Problem for Bell," NYT, January 23, 1951, 33; Ed Prell, "Demands for Bears Stymie NFL Chart," TSN, January 31, 1951, sec. 2: 1, 4.

87. Prell, "Demands for Bears," TSN.

88. "Proposal to Drop Conversion in Favor of a 7-Point Touchdown Loses — Contact Rule Upheld — 33-Player Limit Is Retained," NYT, January 24, 1953, 30; U.S. House, OPTS, 1957: 2580q.

89. Joe King, "Bell Urges Two-Club Expansion in NFL," TSN, November 13, 1957, sec. 2: 1, 2.

90. King, "Bell Urges Two-Club Expansion," TSN; Joe King, "NFL Scraps Bonus Picks, Okays Study of Player Pensions," TSN, February 5, 1958, sec. 2: 4.

91. Edward Prell, "Pro Football League Skips Economy Moves," Chicago Tribune, January 26, 1953, pt. 3, 2.

92. Joe King, "Grid Loops Will Trigger Bidding Binge," TSN, November 11, 1959, sec. 2: 1, 2; Joe King, "Pro War Brewing Over '60 College Stars," TSN, November 30, 1960, sec. 2: 3, 4.

8. The Player Draft

1. "The Rookies Are Stealing the Football Show," SI, November 21, 1955, 23.

2. U.S. House, OPTS, 1957: 2520. MacCambridge described how Bell's futile effort to sign Stan "King Kong" Kostka triggered Bell's interest in a player draft. Both Peterson and MacCambridge blithely assume that the reverse-order draft promoted competitive balance without bothering to demonstrate that the balance was indeed better in the NFL compared to other sporting leagues, and, if so, whether the draft promoted that balance. The minutes of the league meetings merely stated that Bell proposed the reverse-order player draft, but no discussion was recorded (PFHOFAIC, NFL, LM, May 19, 1935, 3; February 8, 1936, 1).

3. U.S. House, OPTS, 1957: 2515.

4. U.S. House, OPTS, 1957: 2660 for Miller's quote and 2696 for Halas's quote. Peterson quoted Halas as having admitted that there was "some truth" in the arguments that owners liked the draft's potential to keep rookie salaries low (Peterson, Pigskin, 120). The owners allowed the league president some discretion in adjudicating situations in which a player did not want to play for a particular team. The player, though, remained the property of the team until he was transferred, and a motion made in 1939, which stipulated that if a player did not sign within two seasons he would become a free agent, failed (PFHOFAIC, NFL, LM, May 19, 1935, 3; February 9, 1939, 4).

5. U.S. House, OPTS, 1957: 2727.

6. U.S. House, OPTS, 1957: 2727.

7. Coenen, Sandlots to Super Bowl, 89–90; PFHOFAIC, NFL LM, March 26, 1942, 3.

8. Watson Spoelstra, "'Little Difference in College, Pro Ball — Need Players in Both to Win' — McMillin," TSN, October 13, 1948, sec. 2: 2.

9. Francis J. Powers and Ed Prell, "George Halas: The Papa Bear," *Sport*, December 1948, 52–61.

10. Fort, *Sports Economics*, 275–77.

11. U.S. House, OPTS, 1957: 2604.

12. U.S. House, OPTS, 1957: 2585.

13. U.S. House, OPTS, 1957: quote on 2728 and Bell's remark on 2738.

14. U.S. Senate, OPTS, 1958: 436.

15. "Players Receive Voice," NYT, January 14, 1958, 44.

16. U.S. House, OPTS, 1957: 2513. Apparently they passed the lottery without clarifying some key aspects. Was the bonus pick in lieu of a team's first-round pick in that draft or was it an extra selection? The owners had to revise their constitution and bylaws to indicate that it was the second interpretation (PFHOFAIC, NFL LM, December 16, 1946, 2).

17. Bell's quote in U.S. House, OPTS, 1957: 2513–14; "National Football League Drops Bonus Choice in Players' Draft," NYT, January 30, 1958, 28. Never mind the fact that a decade later, legislators would countenance a lottery system for the military draft, a lottery that was shown on prime-time national television and that consigned young men to Vietnam.

18. Tommy Devine, "QBs to Be Prize Plums in Pro Grid Draft," TSN, November 21, 1956, sec. 2: 1, 8.

19. Jack Walsh, "Pros Likely to Junk Early Draft," TSN, November 26, 1958, sec. 2: 1, 2.

20. U.S. House, OPTS, 1957: quote on 2514, 2728.

21. U.S. Senate, OPTS, 1959: 40.

22. O'Connor remarks from U.S. Senate, *Professional Sports Antitrust Bill—1964*, 358, 370.

23. Finley quote from U.S. Senate, *Professional Sports Antitrust Bill—1965*, 117; Veeck, *Veeck as in Wreck*, 274.

24. Tex Maule, "Survivors of the Turk," SI, November 2, 1959, 48, 50, 52. It was a stroke of programming genius when ESPN figured out that people would actually *watch* the draft on television—how Bert Bell would have marveled.

25. U.S. House, OPTS, 1957: 2539.

26. U.S. Senate, OPTS, 1958: 710.

27. U.S. Senate, OPTS, 1958: 406–8.

28. U.S. Senate, OPTS, 1958: 409.

29. Wilkinson testimony from U.S. Senate, OPTS, 1958: 438; Carroll, Gershman, Neft, and Thorn, *Total Football*, 1350.

30. U.S. Senate, OPTS,1958: 438. Readers might wonder who was exploiting talented athletes more: college coaches or professional owners.

31. U.S. Senate, OPTS, 1958: 428. Bell, himself, used the Browns' continued dominance as evidence of why the reverse-order draft was necessary. He ignored the obvious question: if the draft was an effective leveler, how did the Browns maintain their dominance (U.S. House, OPTS, 1957: 2726)?

32. U.S. Senate, OPTS, 1958: 429.

33. U.S. Senate, OPTS, 1958: 443.

34. U.S. Senate, OPTS, 1958: 451, 453–54.

35. U.S. House, OPTS, 1957: 2680.

36. "Competition Ups Rams' Scouting Bill to $20,000," TSN, November 19, 1947, sec. 2: 6; Ed Prell, "Coaches' Friendship Pays Off for the Bears," TSN, October 17, 1951, sec. 2: 3.

37. U.S. House, OPTS, 1957: 2746.

38. PFHOFAIC, NFL LM, April 7, 1945, 5; April 29, 1946, 8.

39. Frank Finch, "Spot Big Pro Stars at Small Schools," TSN, November 5, 1952, sec. 2: 8. Peterson indicates that the Detroit Lions may have been the first team to employ a scout, although Richard Whittingham confirms the Rams' early efforts (Peterson, *Pigskin*, 123; Whittingham, *Meat Market*, 39–40).

40. "A Pride of Lions," *Time*, November 29, 1954, 56–58, 60–62.

41. "280 Are Drafted by Pro Elevens," NYT, December 29, 1960, 29.

42. Joe King, "Small Colleges Producing Prize Pros," TSN, October 21, 1959, sec. 2: 1, 2.

43. Powers and Prell, "Halas: Papa Bear," *Sport*; Ed Prell, "Sandlots, Small Schools Spawn Pros," TSN, November 17, 1948, sec. 2: 1.

44. MacCambridge, *America's Game*, 56–57.

45. Joe King, "All-Americas Shaded by Unknown Pros: Many Stars Never Went to College," TSN, November 29, 1950, sec. 2: 1, 2.

46. Tommy Devine, "The All-American Label Doesn't Fool the Pros," *Saturday Evening Post*, November 28, 1959, 32–33, 89–90.

47. Hugh Brown, "Hornung Top Plum among 49 Plucked in Pro Grid Draft," TSN, December 5, 1956, sec. 2: 6; bonus pick information from Carroll, Gershman, Neft, and Thorn, *Total Football*, 1481–506.

48. Joe King, "Rising Pro Standards Reduce QB Field," TSN, November 19, 1958, sec. 2: 1, 2.

49. Hugh Brown, "Steelers Take Obscure Glick as Bonus Pick in Pro Draft," TSN, December 7, 1955, sec. 2: 4. MacCambridge claims Glick was a terrible pick, made sight unseen by Dan Rooney. After drafting him, they requested film of his college games (MacCambridge, *America's Game*, 88).

50. Gene Kessler, "Maybe Bears Just Too Nice," TSN, October 28, 1953, sec. 2: 8.

51. Jack McDonald, "Tittle's Passing Making 'Frisco Forget Albert," TSN, December 16, 1953, sec. 2: 5.

52. After Unitas became a star, some observers wondered why the Los Angeles Rams, as leaders in scouting, missed him. The Rams knew about Unitas, but they had much more information on George Shaw. Dan Reeves admitted that the Unitas case was "just one of those things which can be expected to happen" (John Steadman, "Big College Reps Smudged in NFL," TSN, October 4, 1961, sec. 2: 8).

53. Joe King, "Survey Proves Pros Pick 'Em Right in Draft," TSN, December 3, 1958, 1 and sec. 2: 4; PFHOFAIC, NFL LM, April 6, 1945, 2. Owners offered Ted Collins additional draft picks after the thirty-round regular draft was completed, but he declined the offer (PFHOFAIC, NFL LM, April 6, 1945, 2).

54. Joe King, "NFL Harvesting Bumper Crop of Brilliant Rookies," TSN, October 15, 1958, 1 and sec. 2: 2.

55. "Acts on Football Draft," NYT, November 5, 1946, 44; "NFL Bans Signing College Eligibles," NYT, July 21, 1947, 23.

56. U.S. Senate, OPTS, 1958: 443, 439; "Adopt Eligibility Rules," NYT, April 12, 1946, 21.

57. Dan Daniel, "Retiring Grid Stars Eyed by the Majors," TSN, January 14, 1952, 15.

58. John Drebinger, "Trippi, Georgia Ace, Talks Terms with Football, Baseball Yankees," NYT, January 12, 1947, S1, S2.

59. Stan Baumgartner, "Kazmaier to Snub Pro Football," TSN, January 16, 1952, sec. 2: 1, 6; Braven Dyer, "Otto an Orchestra as Well as Gridder," TSN, February 3, 1954, sec. 2: 8.

60. Perhaps owners were astute (or pro football fans gullible) in focusing on college All-Americans and Heisman Trophy winners. Even if the highly touted college stars couldn't or wouldn't adjust to the pro level of play, their selection might be justified if enough eager fans would attend those players' early games in order to see them play.

61. "Pro Football Eyes Famous Shavetail," NYT, December 24, 1947, 17.

62. Piers Anderton, "Pay-Off for the Pros," SI, February 21, 1955, 26–27, 36–37.

63. "Baltimore Drops Pro Football Franchise and Giants Get Rote in Bonus Pick," NYT, January 19, 1951, 36.

64. Anderton, "Pay-Off," SI.

65. Anderton, "Pay-Off," SI; "Eastern Conference," SI, September 5, 1955, 57.

66. Hal Lebovitz, "Greenies Give Browns Blue-Ribbon Tint," TSN, December 4, 1957, sec. 2: 3.

67. Joe King, "Rams Snare Nine to Lead College Draft," TSN, December 10, 1958, sec. 2: 4, 6.

68. "Ram Kids Crowd Veterans; 21 LA Draft Picks Let Go," TSN, December 10, 1958, sec. 2: 4.

69. Joe King, "Bell Seeks to Curb Draft Pick Deals," TSN, November 6, 1957, sec. 2: 1, 2. Bell and Mara had earlier favored a rule that would have kept teams from selling or trading a drafted player until the player had signed a contract with the team and practiced with them for a week (PFHOFAIC, NFL, LM March 26, 1942, 4).

70. James Murray, "Pro Aweigh: Professional Football Is Off and Barreling towards Its Finest Season, So Herewith Some Advice from a Friend," SI, October 8, 1956, 44, 48–52. Owner Mandel of Detroit suggested implementing a territorial draft pick at the 1940 meetings; the other owners demurred, stating that such a territorial pick would dilute the purpose of the reverse-order aspect of the draft (PFHOFAIC, NFL LM, December 9, 1940, 2). The territorial selection might have helped the gate temporarily, but sometimes choosing the local player backfired, as when the Rams chose local USC star Jon Arnett instead of Jim Brown (Mac-Cambridge, *America's Game*, 107–8).

71. Herman Hickman, "Now and Then: In the Draft, the Names Got the Nod," SI, February 7, 1955, 46–47.

72. MacCambridge, *America's Game*, 88.

73. Joe King," Irish Again Dominate Draft Picks," TSN, February 2, 1955, sec. 2: 1, 2.

74. Howard Tuckner, "All-America Stalwarts Still Love Football, but . . . ," NYT, December 11, 1960, S1, S4.

9. Gate Sharing

1. Seymour, *Baseball: Golden Years*, 8.

2. Seymour, *Baseball: Early Years*, 209.

3. Seymour, *Baseball: Early Years*, 209.

4. Leifer, *Making the Majors*, 103.

5. Quote from Scully, *Business of Major League Baseball*, 80; see also Rottenberg, "Baseball Players' Labor Market"; Quirk and Fort, *Pay Dirt*, 287–92; Scully, *Market Structure of Sports*, 68–70.

6. Fort and Quirk, "Cross-subsidization, Incentives, and Outcomes," 1287.

7. Kesenne, "Revenue Sharing and Competitive Balance"; Marburger, "Gate Revenue Sharing."

8. Szymanski and Kesenne, "Competitive Balance and Gate Revenue Sharing"; Vrooman, "General Theory of Sports Leagues."

9. Canes, "Social Benefits of Restrictions," 92, 94, 95.

10. U.S. House, OPTS, 1957: 1448; *Sporting News Official Baseball Guide* 1954, 110.

11. Clifford Kachline, "'Socialism Threatens Game'—O'Malley," TSN, December 22, 1962, 1–2; Shirley Povich, "He Saighs Over Foes' TV Take," *Baseball Digest*, August 1951, 35–36.

12. Leifer, *Making the Majors*, 103.

13. Coenen, *Sandlots to Super Bowl*, 22–23. The NFL meeting minutes reveal discussion of gate sharing as early as June 1922. There was at least a simple $800 guarantee to the visiting club. In 1923, owners argued over increasing the guarantee to $1,200 and/or forty percent of gross receipts after park rental. These characteristics would remain part of gate-sharing plans. The owners raised the guarantee several times (PFHOFAIC, NFL LM, June 24, 1922, 1; July 28, 1923, 2; January 24, 1925, 3; July 16, 1927, 3; June 30, 1934, 3; February 12, 1937, 2; February 19, 1938, 3; February 9, 1939, 5; April 6, 1943, 6; April 19, 1944, 22).

14. MacCambridge, *America's Game*, 131–32.

15. Harris, *League*, 15.

16. U.S. House, OPTS, 1957: 2580ai, 2580k; PFHOFAIC, NFL LM, January 24, 1947, 13; NFL *Constitutions*, various years. NFL historian David Harris, at least, recognized this adjustment, but he did not discuss the league minimum, probably because it was not binding in the post-AFL period that he was examining (Harris, *League*, 24). Reporter Allison Danzig mentioned that "one of the minor changes put through gives the league 2 per cent of the gate receipts after a 15 per cent payment for rental of the park," in a 1955 article; however, the league's constitutions mentioned the two-percent league fund throughout the years (Allison Danzig, "Roster Increase for Pro Elevens," NYT, January 30, 1955, S1, S5).

17. NFL 1935, *Constitution*, 28. The league meeting minutes showed an increase in the league fees from $200 per annum and one percent of gross receipts in 1926 to $600 per annum and four percent of gross receipts by 1944 (PFHOFAIC, NFL LM, February 6, 1926, 7; April 12, 1940, 9; April 19, 1944, 9, 11).

18. NFL, *Constitution*, 1938, 28–29; 1946, 26; 1949, 26, 1950, 28; 1968, 42; PFHOFAIC, NFL LM, January 11, 1946, 3; January 17, 1948, 4; January 20, 1949, 4; January 22, 1960, 15. Preseason games required a $15,000 minimum guarantee (U.S. House, OPTS, 1957: 2580ap). George Preston Marshall claimed that before the 1940s, "all game contracts were a matter of bargaining," and that he, Marshall, had led the fight to get a uniform rule implemented (Joe King, "Marshall Always Kindling Fires in NFL," TSN, January 9, 1952, sec. 2: 9, 10).

19. Edward Prell, "Football Pros Speed Player Draft," *Chicago Tribune*, January 21, 1953, sec. 3: 1.

20. Owners of teams participating in playoff games to decide division champions in case of a tie would split the gate fifty-fifty after deducting the league share (PFHOFAIC, NFL LM, January 20, 1949, 4).

21. PFHOFAIC, NFL LM, April 7, 1945, 5 and April 8, 1945, 6. Boston and Brooklyn agreed to accept five home games, but Cardinals owner Charles Bidwill later balked. He agreed to only four home games, but did not realize the guarantee was going to remain at $5,000. Pittsburgh would take four games if the guarantee was $5,000, but opposed $10,000 for 1945. Philadelphia, recipient of six home games, offered to pay a $10,000 minimum.

22. PFHOFAIC, NFL LM, April 29, 1946, 4.

23. "New Gridiron Loop Boosts Guarantee," NYT, April 22, 1945, S1, S2.

24. Stanley Frank, "The Grid Is Hot!," *Collier's*, September 14, 1946, 92–93. Giants owner Tim Mara related an interesting anecdote about the possibility of raising the guarantee to $25,000 in 1950, with some owners arguing that if newcomers Buffalo and Baltimore could not draw enough fans to meet the guarantee, they should fold. "It's hard enough to escape losers, without taking in more. In the '49 season, Baltimore proved to me it could draw . . . I was for Baltimore" (Tim Mara and Joe King, "Why We Won!," *Sport*, February 1950, 10–11, 84–85).

25. "National Football Loop Tables San Francisco's Franchise Bid," NYT, January 25, 1947, 9; "Dudley, Steelers, Offered for Sale," NYT, January 26, 1947, S1, S4.

26. Scully, *Business of Major League Baseball*, 88–93; Quirk and Fort, *Pay Dirt*, 245.

27. Fort, *Sports Economics*, 172, 174.

28. The Gini Coefficient is a statistical measure often used in describing the pattern of income distribution. If all incomes were equal, the Gini Coefficient would be zero; if one person had all of the income, the Gini Coefficient would equal one.

29. Surprisingly, there was little mention of this rule change in *Sporting News*, *New York Times*, or *Chicago Tribune*; there was just a one-sentence mention in *Sporting News Official Baseball Guide* (1954, 110).

30. The smaller standard deviation in the NFL than the NL for 1956 appears to be significant. The F-statistic for the NFL's and NL's variances in shares of league revenue without gate sharing was 2.94, implying that one can reject, at the 10% level, the hypothesis that the variances are equal.

31. Maher and Gill, *Pro Football Encyclopedia*, 117–20.

32. Francis Stann, "It's 'Buy-the-Browns' Time Again," *Baseball Digest*, March 1951, 35–36.

33. Gordon Cobbledick, "Why Browns Get Fantastic Prices," 59–60.

34. Surdam, "Tale of Two Gate-Sharing Plans," 945.

10. Gilded Peonage

1. Peterson, *Pigskin*, 158.

2. Halas was not alone in loaning money to players. Bert Bell estimated that owners had $400,000 in outstanding loans to players in 1958 (Tex Maule, "Y. A. Tittle Starts Another Season," SI, October 6, 1958, 36–40).

3. Conerly, *Backseat Quarterback*, 32–33.

4. Miller, *Whole Different Ball Game*, 6–8; Dan Daniel, "Game's Prestige Growing with Pension Plan," TSN, July 25, 1962, 7.

5. Allison Danzig, "Pro Loop Changes Player Contract," NYT, May 1, 1946, 43.

6. PFHOFAIC, NFL LM, April 29, 1946, 6, 8; April 30, 1946, 10. The player contract had been changed in 1933; the original contract stipulated six days' notice, but the owners had unanimously approved a forty-eight hour notice (PFHOFAIC, NFL LM, December 16, 1933).

7. Les Rodney, "Life of a Pro Gridder — Gets Dough Hard Way," TSN, December 3, 1947, sec. 2: 8; William Whyte, "The Class of '49," *Fortune*, June 1949; Players Association lawyer Creighton Miller testified about the $50 per game payments in 1957 (U.S. House, OPTS, 1957: 2634).

8. "Redskins Upheld in Payment Appeal," NYT, December 12, 1953, 25.

9. "M'Phee [sic] Claim Disputed," NYT, March 9, 1957, 22.

10. "49ers Settle Norman Suit," NYT, April 23, 1957, 38.

11. Quotes in "Forty-Niners Reconsider Strike Threat on Bonus Demand," NYT, December 1, 1949, 45; "Threat of Strike Ended, 49ers Resume Practice," NYT, December 2, 1949, 39.

12. Dan Parker, "Baseball's Bombshell," *Sport*, April 1949, 12–13, 80, 82–83. Parker, of course, hadn't met George Steinbrenner.

13. "Bette Davis," Wikipedia, http://en.wikipedia.org/wiki/Bette_Davis, viewed May 24, 2011, 6:26 p.m.; Fred Stanley, "Hollywood Mulls Court Decisions," NYT, March 26, 1944, x3.

14. Quote in "Strader Suit Hits as Football Draft," NYT, September 19, 1951, 42; "Strader Wins Pay Suit," NYT, February 29, 1952, 29.

15. "Giants Sue Weinmeister," NYT, May 19, 1954, 40.

16. "Football Players Form Pro Bargaining Group," NYT, November 29, 1956, 45.

17. "NFL Players Organize, Pick Voice," TSN, December 12, 1956, sec. 2: 1, 2.

18. Joe King, "Showdown Near on NFL Players' Union," TSN, January 9, 1957, sec. 2: 1, 2.

19. "Players' Unit in Talks," NYT, January 29, 1957, 37.

20. Quotes in "NFL Rejects Expansion and Players' Association," NYT, February 3, 1957, listed as 159 and 2, but probably 1 and 2; "Pro Players List 304 as Members," NYT, February 6, 1957, 31. During the Great Depression, owners agreed to provide $2 per diem, aside from lodging expense. Some players were getting $6 a day for meal money; the Bears paid $5 a day in meal money in 1946, but most players

would get $9 by 1957 (William Fay, "Bears Follow Old Routine on Way to Battle," *Chicago Tribune*, December 14, 1946, sec. 2: 21; PFHOFAIC, NFL LM, July 9, 1932, 1; U.S. House, OPTS, 1957: 2643). How far did $6 a day for meals go? The *New York Times* ran advertisements for Manhattan restaurants. In October 1957, players could avail themselves of a seven-course dinner from $2.50 at the Restaurant Dubonnet, although the Chateaubriand offered "distinguished French Cuisine" from $5.00 for dinner. For players with more plebian palates, Manny Wolfe's, self-proclaimed as the "Roast Beef King," advertised a seven-course dinner, including cocktail, for $3.95 ("Restaurant Guide," NYT, October 1, 1957, 28). While $6 might not purchase three lavish meals, it did provide sustenance.

21. Allen Drury, "Bell Recognizes Football Union," NYT, August 2, 1957, 7; "Pro Football Union Weights NLRB Plea," NYT, August 1, 1957, 20; U.S. House, OPTS, 1957: 2502.

22. "Bell Will See Lawyers on Written Union Pact," NYT, August 11, 1957, 154.

23. U.S. House, OPTS, 1957: 2635–36.

24. U.S. House, OPTS, 1957: 2509–11.

25. U.S. House, OPTS, 1957: 2688.

26. U.S. House, OPTS, 1957: 2817.

27. U.S. House, OPTS, 1957: 2653.

28. U.S. House, OPTS, 1957: 2644–45.

29. U.S. House, OPTS, 1957: first quote on 2578, anonymous quote on 2586. The players' letter-writing campaign backfired, as wary legislators asked who orchestrated the effort, suspecting owner coercion.

30. Ratterman eventually became an attorney and became general counsel for the AFL Player Association. He also fought corruption in Newport, Kentucky, site of a famous Robert Kennedy battle with vice operations (U.S. House, OPTS, 1957: 2682).

31. Joe King, "NFL to Let Draftee Switch Clubs If He Offers Valid Reason," TSN, January 15, 1958, sec. 2: 10.

32. U.S. House, OPTS, 1957: 2503–4.

33. U.S. House, OPTS, 1957: 2583, 2588.

34. U.S. House, OPTS, 1957: 2649.

35. U.S. House, OPTS, 1957: 2589.

36. U.S. House, OPTS, 1957: 2609, quote on contract on 2611–12; Davis, *Papa Bear*, 220–21.

37. Quotes from U.S. House, OPTS, 1957: 2647–48.

38. U.S. House, OPTS, 1957: 2822–30; PFHOFAIC, NFL LM, January 24, 1947, 11.

39. U.S. Senate, OPTS, 1958: 396.

40. Quote from U.S. Senate, OPTS, 1958: 404; U.S. House, OPTS, 1957: 2494, 2728, 2750; Joe King, "New York Rattles the Rafters for Ratterman," TSN, November 8, 1950, sec. 2: 5.

41. U.S. House, OPTS, 1957: 2659.

42. First quote in U.S. House, OPTS, 1957: 2590; second quote in U.S. House, OPTS, 1957: 2660. Two former players, Jim Sid Wright and Robert Nelson, sent letters detailing their frustration over their free agent experiences; Bert Bell disputed their descriptions (U.S. House, OPTS, 1957: 2837–47). These two players went to Canada for the 1953 season. They returned to their original teams in 1954.

43. U.S. House, OPTS, 1957: 2683.

44. U.S. House, OPTS, 1957: 2685.

45. Dick Schaap, "Why Pro Football Players Revolt," Sport, January 1964, 6–8, 73–74. From the owners' perspective, the free-agency situation was a Prisoners' Dilemma situation: if each owner rationally pursued his self-interest, the collective could be worse off. The rule requiring compensation solved the dilemma. The compensation rule, dubbed "the Rozelle Rule," was overturned by court decision in 1976 (John Mackey vs. NFL).

46. U.S. House, OPTS, 1957: 2707. If this had been a situation comedy, there would have been the usual laugh track insertions at "just a son-in-law" and "trying to save a buck."

47. U.S. House, OPTS, 1957: 2711. Halas apparently paid his players for exhibition games and offered other modest generosities, thereby giving his players reason to think they would have something to lose by joining the association. The Bears held out against joining the association until 1962 (Davis, Papa Bear, 376–77).

48. Jack Walsh, "Marshall Raps Bell's 14-Team Plan," TSN, November 20, 1957, sec. 2: 1, 2.

49. U.S. House, OPTS, 1957: 2691, 2832–36.

50. Miller quote in "Players' Group Plans $4,200,000 Suit against National Football League," NYT, November 22, 1957, 39; other quote in Joe King, "NFL Magnates Back Bell on Player Demands," TSN, December 11, 1957, sec. 2: 5.

51. U.S. Senate, OPTS, 1958: 417.

52. U.S. Senate, OPTS, 1958: 711, also quoted on 406.

53. U.S. Senate, OPTS, 1958: 433, 446, 449.

54. U.S. Senate, OPTS, 1958: 430–31.

55. "Bell Is Assailed by Players' Unit," NYT, November 21, 1958, 40.

56. U.S. House, OPTS, 1957: 2689.

57. Joe King, "NFL Considers Player Pension Plan for $100 a Month at 65," TSN, January 28, 1959, sec. 2: 6. Using the Consumer Price Index, $100 in 1960 would

be about $750 today (http:/inflationdata.com/inflation/Consumer_Price_Index/ HistoricalCPI, viewed 12/23/10 at 10:30 a.m.).

58. "Bell Alters View on Pension Plan," NYT, January 23, 1959, 28; PFHOFAIC, NFL LM, April 23, 1959, 2 and January 22, 1959, 1–3, 5–9. Bell boasted at an earlier meeting, at which the Players' Association representatives were present, about how generous the NFL owners were; he concluded, "There isn't one owner in this League who is in football to make a living out of it. . . . They are fans. There never were twelve greater guys in the world to work for or with than the twelve in this room" (PFHOFAIC, NFL LM, January 22, 1959, 3).

59. Schaap, "Why Players Revolt," *Sport.*

11. Television

1. Coenen, *Sandlots to Super Bowl*, 156, 160.

2. Coenen, *Sandlots to Super Bowl*, 186; John Lardner, "A Czar's Ultimatum," *Newsweek*, December 15, 1958, 105.

3. Frank Rich, "The Lives They Lived; TV Guy," NYT, December 29, 2002, from http://www.nytimes.com/2002/12/29/magazine/the-lives-they-lived-tv-guy, viewed January 29, 2011, 1:34 p.m.

4. U.S. Department of Commerce, *Historical Statistics*, I:169; Cox and Alm, "Time Well Spent," 16.

5. Surdam, "Television and Minor League Baseball," 66–74.

6. Orrin E. Dunlap, "Television Forward Passes Football to the Home," NYT, October 15, 1939, 150; Peterson, *Pigskin*, 125 uses Dunlap's account. Roone Arledge compared television's compatibility with baseball and football, with football being an "ideal partner" for television (Roone Arledge and Gilbert Rogin, "It's Sports . . . It's Money, It's TV," *Sports Illustrated*, April 25, 1966, 92–106, quotes on 97 and 100; Patton, *Razzle-Dazzle*, 61).

7. Whittingham, *What a Game*, 193; Peterson, *Pigskin*, 124.

8. Coenen, *Sandlots to Super Bowl*, 100–101.

9. Coenen, *Sandlots to Super Bowl*, 100; for radio revenue in 1951, see his table 5.1 on page 154. Peterson, *Pigskin*, 127 for radio broadcast of 1940 championship game; for baseball's uneasy relationship with radio, see Surdam, *Empty Seats*, 197–218.

10. PFHOFAIC, NFL LM, January 20, 1949, 4.

11. Arch Ward, "We want football on TV," *Sport*, November 1952, 18–19, 93–94.

12. PFHOFAIC, NFL LM, April 29, 1946, 6; January 24, 1947, 11.

13. PFHOFAIC, NFL LM, January 24, 1947, 12; January 17, 1948, n.p.; January 20, 1949, 5; June 2, 1950, 10; "NFL Bans Signing College Eligibles," NYT, July 21, 1947, 23; Coenen, *Sandlots to Super Bowl*, 153. For the Chicago Bears' early experiences with television, see Peterson, *Pigskin*, 196. The NFL's policies during its first five or

six years with television contradicts Benjamin Rader's assertion: "From the earliest days of television, professional football was more successful in managing the medium than were most other sports." The NFL owners' willingness to transfer authority to Bert Bell evolved only in the early 1950s (Rader, *In Its Own Image*, 85).

14. "Col. MacPhail and Television," TSN, September 3, 1947, 12.

15. Davis, *Papa Bear*, 269–70.

16. Stan Baumgartner, "Television Endangers Coaching, Crowds," TSN, November 19, 1947, sec. 2: 1, 6.

17. "Dallas Reported Ready to Join All-America Conference If Rockets Drop Out," NYT, December 19, 1948, S7.

18. "Eagles to Ban Telecasts of Games at Shibe Park to Lift Attendance," NYT, June 2, 1949, 36. Baltimore decided to stop telecasting Colt games for the 1950 season; see "Colts Ban Television," NYT, August 16, 1950, 36.

19. "Giant Eleven Bans Video," NYT, June 7, 1949, 34; Sidney Lohnman, "News and Notes on Television," NYT, June 12, 1949, X9; "Bulldog Eleven Bans Video," NYT, June 22, 1949, 40.

20. "Radio and Television," NYT, June 25, 1949, 28.

21. Tommy Devine, "Television 'Take' Demand for Split, College Problem," TSN, October 26, 1949, sec. 2: 2.

22. Joseph M. O'Brien Historical Resource Center, Naismith Memorial Basketball Hall of Fame, "NBA Bulletin #33a," October 21, 1949; Pluto, *Tall Tales*, 23.

23. Ed Prell, "Grange Carrying Ball Again — This Time as Pros' TV Star," TSN, October 26, 1949, sec. 2: 2.

24. "Pros Argue on Divisional Set-Up; Bears Would Switch to American," NYT, January 22, 1951, 22.

25. Tom Swope, "Chandler Wraps Up $6,000,000 Video Deal," TSN, January 3, 1951, 4; for DuMont's early involvement with televising professional football, see Patton, *Razzle-Dazzle*, 35; MacCambridge, *America's Game*, 69.

26. Jack Gould, "Television Season: New Programs Will Be Relatively Few," NYT, August 26, 1951, X9; Jack Gould, "Radio and Television: California-Pennsylvania Football Game in Color Proves a Disappointment," NYT, October 1, 1951, 30. In another experiment, NFL owners saw a demonstration of pay-TV in 1952 (PFHOFAIC, NFL LM, January 19, 1952, 11).

27. Frank Finch, "Ram Playoff without TV Pulls 83,501," TSN, December 27, 1950, sec. 2: 8; see Frank Finch, "Rams Draw Millions to Games — by Video," TSN, September 27, 1950, sec. 2: 7 for how Rams estimated the contract figures; Peterson, *Pigskin*, 191; MacCambridge, *America's Game*, 67, 69. Peterson gives an account of this debacle, claiming that Admiral paid $307,000 to make up the shortfall in

attendance; his account does not completely coincide with the attendance figures shown in Maher and Gill's *Pro Football Encyclopedia* (Peterson, *Pigskin*, 197).

28. Quotes in W. G. Caldwell, MD, "Is It Good Football?" *LA Times*, November 19, 1950, pt. II, 17; Joe Brooks, "Pros Preferred," *LA Times*, December 3, 1950, pt. II, 14; Richard Joseph, "End to Debate," *LA Times*, November 19, 1950, pt. II, 17.

29. Frank Finch, "Rams Picked to Whip Winless Colts Today," *LA Times*, October 22, 1950, pt. II, 15; "See the 'Rams-Colts' Game Today," *LA Times*, October 22, 1950, pt. I, 23 (advertisement).

30. Quote in "Rams-Bears Game Drew Record Crowd," *LA Times*, December 19, 1950, pt. IV, 2; "Bert Bell Says NFL Enjoyed Greatest Year," *LA Times*, December 6, 1950, pt. IV, 3.

31. Paul Zimmerman, "SC Sole TV Team under 1948 Gate," *LA Times*, December 5, 1950, pt. 4, 1; "College Football Attendance Drops," *LA Times*, December 7, 1950, pt. IV, 3.

32. Peterson, *Pigskin*, 197.

33. "Pro Football Crowds Increasing but Few Clubs Profit, Bell Says," NYT, October 14, 1952, 42.

34. Joe Williams, "Pro Football Finding a Way to Live with TV," TSN, October 29, 1952, sec. 2: 1.

35. Stan Baumgartner, "Public Demands Special Events — Bell," TSN, December 3, 1952, sec. 2: 1, 2.

36. "Plan Pro Football TV," NYT, May 4, 1953, 29; "More TV Football Seen This Season," NYT, May 14, 1953, 43. The irony of the NFL's relationship with the DuMont Network was that football could not save the network, despite some impressive audience ratings (Rader, *In Its Own Image*, 87). A decade later, the AFL would be a major contributor to ABC's success.

37. Bell quote in "Bell Confirms Position," NYT, January 6, 1955, 32. Some fantastical rumors floated about the league, including a report of $8 million, which was more than the league's collective gate receipts. League teams received about $125,000 each for radio and television in 1953 ("Commissioner Bell Gets New 12-Year National Football League Contract," NYT, January 30, 1954, 11). Even after the NFL prevailed in the legal fight over home territory blackouts, Bell warned owners against hubris in the wake of the Grim ruling (PFHOFAIC, NFL LM, January 29, 1954, 9).

38. John Wray, "Panorama TV Gets Panning," TSN, November 11, 1953, sec. 2: 10.

39. W. C. Heinz, "Boss of the Behemoths," *Saturday Evening Post*, December 5, 1955, 46, 72, 74, 77.

40. Hugh Brown, "Cable Costs Tie Knot in NFL TV," TSN, October 12, 1955, sec. 2: 8.

41. "The Pros Spread Wide," SI, October 8, 1956, 48; Bell's quote in Art Morrow, "'TV Helping NFL to Record Gates' — Bell," TSN, October 10, 1956, sec. 2: 1, 2; see also Frank Finch, "NFL Bigwigs Seek More TV; Loop Set Gate Mark in '55," TSN, January 25, 1956, sec. 2: 4. Robert Peterson thinks this concatenation of factors proved a boon for the NFL, boosting its profile among the advertising and publicity executives on Madison Avenue, a process that culminated in Rozelle's moving the league's headquarters to New York City. Players began to get lucrative endorsement opportunities (Peterson, *Pigskin*, 201; Patton, *Razzle-Dazzle*, 42).

42. Art Morrow, "Bell Draws Code for NFL Aircasters," TSN, October 5, 1955, sec. 2: 1, 2. Bell had long urged league control over broadcasters (PFHOFAIC, NFL LM, December 9, 1940, 2). In one case, Bell even admonished an NFL owner, Walter Wolfner of the Cardinals, for using film to criticize officials ("Bell Is TV Censor, Card Official Says," NYT, December 22, 1956, 22).

43. PFHOFAIC, NFL LM, February 1, 1957, 5. Bell introduced a consultant who was to help the league obtain television contracts at the January 1956 meetings. He also introduced Bill MacPhail, CBS executive, to the owners at the 1957 meetings (PFHOFAIC, NFL LM, January 17, 1956, 10; February 1, 1957, 7).

44. Quotes from U.S. House, OPTS, 1957: 2525; U.S. Senate, OPTS, 1959: 47. Bell repeated this refrain in Art Morrow, "NFL Eyeing Gate Record; 1,500,000 in Advance Sale," TSN, October 8, 1958, sec. 2: 9.

45. "Pay TV-Baseball Tie-Up Seen," *Broadcasting*, August 25, 1958, 78.

46. Jim Beach, "What Pay TV Will Mean to the Fan," *Sport*, June 1964, 18–19, 70–71.

47. U.S. House, OPTS, 1957: 2605–6.

48. U.S. House, OPTS, 1957: 2524; see also Tex Maule, "Look How the Owners Smile," SI, March 10, 1958, 46–47.

49. Bell's quote in "TV Blackout Rule Kept for Play-Offs," NYT, December 26, 1957, 35; "TV Inquiry Requested," NYT, January 1, 1958, 34.

50. Tex Maule, "Three for the Money," SI, December 16, 1957, 14–17; Maule also described an unruly crowd seeking to get a few thousand general admission tickets on the morning of the game.

51. Quote in "Celler Hits Sports Bill Lobby," *Broadcasting*, July 28, 1958, 76, 78; U.S. Senate, OPTS, 1958: 749.

52. "Sports Exemption: New Measure Offered for Antitrust Relief," *Broadcasting*, August 24, 1959, 70–71; see also "Joker Found in Sports Bill: Eight Hidden Words Would Give Professional Leagues Vast Control and Permit Pay-TV," *Broadcasting*, August 17, 1959, 70, 72.

53. Joe King, "Bell Opposes Pay-TV for Pro Football Tilts," TSN, January 14, 1959, 1 and sec. 2: 1. Bell told owners that forty million people watched the 1958

League Championship Game and that 49% of the radios in New York City were tuned to the game (PFHOFAIC, NFL LM, January 21, 1959, 5).

54. U.S. Senate, OPTS, 1959: 38; see also page 44 for his additional testimony on television blackouts.

55. PFHOFAIC, NFL LM, January 29, 1958, 6, 7.

56. "Time-Out for Commercial," NYT, September 14, 1958, S2.

57. PFHOFAIC, NFL LM, January 21, 1959, 5; January 23, 1960, 7.

58. "Football Series on TV," NYT, August 15, 1959, 37.

59. Surdam, *Postwar Yankees*, 130–31. Whether Howard Cosell would have been one of the announcers is unknown; of course, he later irritated baseball fans with his overt love affairs with NFL football and Muhammad Ali.

60. Harris, *League*, 13.

61. "Foss Predicts $2,500,000 TV Offer: New Football Loop's Head Says 8 Clubs Will Split Take," NYT, December 2, 1959, 27. David Harris claims that Lamar Hunt got his inspiration for the equal shares television contract from baseball's Branch Rickey and Bill Veeck Jr. Rickey, however, refused to share television revenues when he ran the Brooklyn Dodgers, while Veeck was not seeking equal shares, just a visiting team's right to some of the television revenues (Harris, *League*, 14; for Rickey's and Veeck's view, see Surdam, *Postwar Yankees*, 176–78).

62. "Football Gets $12 Million from Radio-TV," *Broadcasting*, August 28, 1961, 40–41, 44. A year later, ABC received stark evidence about the AFL's growing popularity. ABC and the AFL had had their "Heidi" moment years before the infamous 1968 NFL game. The New York Titans were playing Dallas, and the game was taking too long. ABC went to "The Walt Disney Show" and its switchboards lit up with protests. Moore later reflected, "I knew then that the AFL was very much among the living" (Patton, *Razzle-Dazzle*, 84).

63. "Joe Never Ran from Fight — So He Approved 'Em on Video," TSN, September 13, 1961, sec. 2: 3.

64. PFHOFAIC, NFL LM, January 21, 1951, 39. In 1942, Washington suggested that "all contracts for broadcasting and televising of football games shall be made by the Commissioner. The moneys derived from such contract shall be divided equally among the members of the League." Apparently the other owners were lukewarm, so Washington withdrew the motion (PFHOFAIC, March 26, 1942, 5). A year later, the league's executive committee recommended that "all receipts of the game" be redefined to include "receipts from program advertising and sale and also include any money derived from television" (PFHOFAIC, NFL LM, April 6, 1943, 2). No action was taken.

65. U.S. Senate, *Professional Sports Antitrust Bill — 1965*, 120.

66. Patton, *Razzle-Dazzle*, 50.

67. MacCambridge, *America's Game*, 171, cites League Minutes, January 24, 1961.

68. PFHOFAIC, NFL LM, March 11, 1960, 33.

69. PFHOFAIC, NFL LM, March 12, 1960, 36; March 13, 1960, 38; March 29, 1960, 44–45. MacCambridge claims Baltimore was receiving $600,000 per year from NBC, but this is not collaborated by the *Broadcasting* or Rozelle figures; Baltimore's figure might have included radio revenue. MacCambridge and Patton then claim that, in 1960, the revenues with CBS ranged from $75,000 to $175,000 (Green Bay and New York respectively), which does not seem too dire a spread (MacCambridge, *America's Game*, 171 cites Patton, *Razzle-Dazzle*, 53, who does not cite anyone).

70. PFHOFAIC, NFL LM, March 12, 1960, 35, 38.

71. The monopoly aspect was a major selling point of baseball's John Fetzer's plan to sell a Monday Night Baseball package in 1965 (Surdam, *Postwar Yankees*, 131–36).

72. MacCambridge, *America's Game*, 171, cites League Minutes, January 24, 1961.

73. Joe King, "Buck Squeeze Forces NFL to Seek Larger Package from Video," TSN, February 8, 1961, sec. 2: 5; MacCambridge, *America's Game*, 171.

74. MacCambridge, *America's Game*, xvii.

75. U.S. Senate, *Professional Sports Antitrust Bill — 1965*, 64.

76. "Each Club to Get $320,000 a Year," NYT, January 11, 1962, 54; "Football Gets $12 Million," *Broadcasting*.

77. Val Adams, "NBC Bids Record for Sports Event," NYT, April 6, 1961, 67.

78. Val Adams, "TV Football Pact Voided by Court," NYT, July 21, 1961, 1, 47.

79. Val Adams, "Court Ruling to Cost Football Teams, $2,264,000," NYT, July 31, 1961, 41.

80. Harris, *League*, 15; U.S. House, *Telecasting Sports*, 1961: 71.

81. Coenen, *Sandlots to Super Bowl*, 202; Harris, *League*, 14.

82. U.S. House, *Telecasting Sports*, 1961: 5, see also 4, 9.

83. U.S. House, *Telecasting Sports*, 1961: 6.

84. U.S. House, *Telecasting Sports*, 1961: 9–10.

85. U.S. House, *Telecasting Sports*, 1961: 10–11.

86. U.S. House, *Telecasting Sports*, 1961: 58, 73; "Football Gets $12 Million," *Broadcasting*.

87. U.S. House, *Telecasting Sports*, 1961: 28.

88. U.S. House, *Telecasting Sports*, 1961: 33. As a comparison with the NFL-CBS plan, Fetzer hoped his plan would bring in $6.5 million per year in 1965 (Surdam, *Postwar Yankees*, 131).

89. U.S. House, *Telecasting Sports*, 1961: 52, 61.

90. U.S. House, *Telecasting Sports*, 1961: 69.

91. Dave Brady, "Package TV Bill Gaining New Support," TSN, September 20, 1961, sec. 2: 4; Melvin Durslag, "Football Bad for the Rich," TSN, November 15, 1961, sec. 2: 10; U.S. House, *Telecasting Sports*, 1961: 36.

92. U.S. House, *Telecasting Sports*, 1961: 35, 44, 46.

93. Jack Walsh, "Top Attorney Carries Ball for Pro Gridders," TSN, January 6, 1960, sec. 2: 5, 6.

94. "NFL Gains Right to Pool TV Pacts," NYT, October 1, 1961, S1, S5.

95. Joe King, "Pigskin Punts: Green Bay Site for NFL's First Million-Dollar Tilt," TSN, December 13, 1961, sec. 2: 10.

96. For highlights of his statements, see U.S. Senate, *Professional Sports Antitrust Bill—1964*, 77–78; U.S. Senate, *Professional Sports Antitrust Bill—1965*, 199; U.S. House, *Professional Football League Merger*, 1966, 31-80, 110-130.

97. Rader, *In Its Own Image*, 94. Comedian George Carlin, while not spoofing Rader, certainly presaged Rader's comments in his sketch about baseball and football.

98. Rader, *In Its Own Image*, 91.

99. Rader, *In Its Own Image*, 92.

100. Rader, *In Its Own Image*, 91–92.

101. Richard L. Ottinger, "A Congressman's Battle Plan to Stop TV from Taking Over Sports," *Sport*, September 1967, 22–25, 75–76.

12. Innovation

1. Coenen, *Sandlots to Super Bowl*, 85.

2. Dick Hyland, "Rules Curb on Passers' Runaway Looms," TSN, October 11, 1950, sec. 2: 1, 2.

3. Hy Turkin, "Cards, Browns Pack Pro All-Star Selections; Baugh Still Among Best," TSN, December 22, 1948, sec. 2: 9.

4. Ed Prell, "Play Speedup in NFL Cited," TSN, February 11, 1948, sec. 2: 8; Edward Prell, "NFL Waves Statistics at Rivals," *Chicago Tribune*, January 23, 1948, sec. 2: 1. The AAFC had used a fifth official during its inaugural season. The fifth official was a sideline judge responsible for calling backfields in motion (John B. Old, "$250,000 Airlines Pact Signed by Pro Gridders," TSN, April 18, 1946, 33).

5. Chuck Johnson, "Player Limit Is Chief Problem for Coaches in NFL — Blackbourn," TSN, December 1, 1954, sec. 2: 7.

6. Tex Maule, "Y. A. Tittle Starts Another Season," SI, October 6, 1958, 36–40.

7. Tommy Devine, "'49 Touchdown Spree Gate Headache in '50," TSN, November 23, 1949, sec. 2: 2.

8. Joe King, "Defense Tipping Scales in NFL Power Battle," TSN, November 27, 1957, sec. 2: 5.

9. Jack Walsh, "Split-T Spoiling Passes, Pro Charge," TSN, November 10, 1954, sec. 2: 1, 6.

10. Robert Burnes, "Conversion Option Keeps Coaches in Air," TSN, October 8, 1958, sec. 2: 1, 2.

11. Arthur Daley, "Sports of the *Times*: Comes the Revolution," NYT, January 14, 1958, 44.

12. John Rendel, "Pro Officials Expect No Revision of Game Because of College Act," NYT, January 14, 1958, 44.

13. "Pro Football Code Keeps Extra Point," NYT, January 10, 1945, 20; Stan Baumgartner, "Bell Asks 'Death' of Extra Point," TSN, November 7, 1951, sec. 2: 1; for the cost of footballs see Lyall Smith, "NFL May Drop Extra Point to Save Pigskins," TSN, January 9, 1952, sec. 2: 11.

14. Bert Bell and Ed Pollock, "Let's Throw Out the Extra Point!," *Sport*, October 1953, 24–25, 62–63.

15. Maxwell Stiles, "Styles in Sports: Higher Goal Posts Possibility in NFL Next Year," TSN, October 26, 1953, sec. 2: 8.

16. "Dallas Group Seeks to Buy Yanks as Pro Football Men Gather Here," NYT, January 17, 1952, 31.

17. Joe King, "Rule Proposals in NFL Aimed at More Action," TSN, December 21, 1955, sec. 2: 1, 2.

18. Joe King, "Sky-High Punts Leave Receiver Tortured Target," TSN, December 10, 1958, 1 and sec. 2: 6.

19. Arthur Daley, "Pros and Cons of Pro Football," NYT, November 20, 1955, SM17.

20. Peterson, *Pigskin*, 137, 191.

21. Louis Effrat, "Football Coaches Cannot Agree on Unlimited Substitution Rule," NYT, November 2, 1948, 37.

22. "Halas Wants Pro Football League to Ban Free-Substitution Rule," NYT, January 6, 1946, F7.

23. Bob Broeg, "Old Pro Likes Modern Game," TSN, November 5, 1952, sec. 2: 8.

24. Watson Spoelstra, "Lions' Bingaman Tips Scales at 349 Pounds," TSN, October 6, 1954, sec. 2: 7; Joe King, "NFL Lines Ride Crest of Prime Beef Boom," TSN, November 30, 1955, sec. 2: 3.

25. Joe King, "Pros Put Sights on 300-Pound Linemen," TSN, October 14, 1959, sec. 2: 3, 6.

26. Joe King, "NFL Oldsters Thumb Noses at Father Time," TSN, October 5, 1960, sec. 2: 2.

27. Joe King, "NFL Gaffers Find Fountain of Youth," TSN, September 27, 1961, sec. 2: 1, 2.

28. William Furlong, "Wise Old Men of Pro Football," NYT, November 20, 1960, SM34, 36, 38, 44, 46.

29. Joseph Sheehan, "Outlawing of Two-Platoon System Stirs Controversy in College Football Circles," NYT, January 16, 1953, 27; "College Elevens to Launch Drills," NYT, August 30, 1953, S3.

30. "End of Platoon Two," NYT, January 17, 1953, 14.

31. Arthur Daley, "Sports of the *Times*: No More Mob Scenes," NYT, January 16, 1953, 26.

32. Joseph Sheehan, "NCAA Will Give Ruling Next Week," NYT, January 6, 1960, 40.

33. "Pro Elevens to Vote on Sudden Death Play and Abolition of the Try for Extra Point," NYT, January 6, 1945, 8.

34. "Dallas Group Seeks Yanks," NYT.

35. Louis Effrat, "Rival Leagues Continue Impasse in Spite of Pro Football Peace 'Feelers,'" NYT, January 21, 1949, 27.

36. "Dallas Group Seeks Yanks," NYT. It was okay to call his players "Redskins" but to depersonalize them by identifying them with numbers was too much even for Marshall.

37. Morton Moss, "AFL Teams Steal Veeck Idea, Sew Player Names on Jerseys," TSN, September 28, 1960, 16.

38. Cy Kritzer, "Fifth Grid Official Needed in Press Box," TSN, December 1, 1948, sec. 2: 10.

39. Stan Baumgartner, "NFL to Ballot on Important Rule Changes," TSN, January 27, 1954, sec. 2: 2.

40. MacCambridge, *America's Game*, 161.

41. "Browns' Radio Fizzles but Eleven Is on Beam," NYT, September 23, 1956, 201.

42. "12-Man Huddle," SI, October 8, 1956, 24; Joe King, "Bell Bans Use of Short-Wave Radios in NFL," TSN, October 24, 1956, sec. 2: 9.

43. "Rams Using Television to Coach during Game," NYT, October 31, 1956, 41.

44. Ed Prell, "Two-Coach System Not in Cards," TSN, November 9, 1949, sec. 2: 3. Prell should be commended for not using the "two heads aren't better than one" cliché.

45. George Walsh, "Our Drug-Happy Athletes," SI, November 21, 1960, 27–28, 33–34, 37–38. T. J. Quinn, writing for ESPN, reports that Sid Gillman had his players use Dianabol, an anabolic steroid in 1963 (T. J. Quinn, "Pumped Up Pioneers," http://sports.espn.go.com/espn/otl/news/story?id=3866837, viewed May 25, 2011, 11:00 a.m.).

46. Ed Prell, "Boom in Grid Face Mask Sales to Reduce Injuries," TSN, October 12, 1955, sec. 2: 7. Perian Conerly describes the changes wrought by the introduction of face bars on helmets (Conerly, *Backseat Quarterback*, 20).

END

47. J. G. Taylor Spink, "The Fifth Quarter: 'Pros Who Play Dirty Don't Last' — Bell," TSN, November 8, 1950, sec. 2: 10.

48. Otto Graham, "Football Is Getting Too Vicious," SI, October 11, 1954, 26, 50–52.

49. "Savagery on Sunday: Professional Football Play Gets Rougher as Fists and Elbows Fly," Life, October 24, 1955, 133–34, 136, 138.

50. Joe King, "Grid Pros Rocked by 'Dirty' Play Blasts," TSN, November 23, 1955, sec. 2: 1, 2.

51. Dan Daniel, "Blames Officials for 'Dirty Play,'" TSN, October 27, 1954, sec. 2: 1, 2.

52. Joe King, "Bell Hits Back at 'Dirty Play' Charge," TSN, October 20, 1954, sec. 2: 1, 2.

53. "NFL Play Vicious, Graham Charges," TSN, November 16, 1955, sec. 2: 10.

54. "A Pride of Lions," Time, November 29, 1954, 56–58, 60–62.

55. Melvin Durslag, "Pro Football Is Plenty Rough," SI, November 28, 1955, 32–33, 59–61.

56. Joe Williams, "Marshall Says Football Needs 'Error Column,'" TSN, November 16, 1955, sec. 2: 10.

57. Shirley Povich, "This Morning with Shirley Povich: Players Owe Bell Debt for 'Pile-On' Ban," TSN, January 25, 1956, sec. 2: 8; PFHOFAIC, NFL LM, January 16, 1956, 2.

58. "Pros Adopt Rule to End 'Piling On,'" NYT, January 17, 1956, 39.

59. Joe King, "Rule Proposals in NFL Aimed at More Action," TSN, December 21, 1955, sec. 2: 1, 2.

60. "Bears Win Western Title by Beating Lions in Rough Football Game," NYT, December 17, 1956, 40.

61. "Parker Threatens to Quit as Pro Football Coach," NYT, December 18, 1956, 53.

62. "Films Will Guide Giants for Bears," NYT, December 19, 1956, 55.

63. "Lions' Directors Discuss Contract," NYT, December 21, 1956, 30. Hecker's admission will not shock today's readers, given the New Orleans Saints' recent "bounties" scandal.

64. "As You Sow . . ." SI, January 7, 1957, 16.

65. Tex Maule and Bert Bell, "'I Don't Believe There Is Dirty Football,'" SI, January 21, 1957, 26–28.

66. Tex Maule, "Run for the Money," SI, October 7, 1957, 20, 25, 58, 60.

67. Conerly, Backseat Quarterback, 163.

68. Louis Effrat, "Stadium Field Seats Will Be Removed to Prevent Riots," NYT, December 9, 1959, 63.

69. Howell quote in "Forfeit Threat Halts Roisterers," TSN, December 16, 1959, sec. 2: 2; Arthur Daley, "Sports of the *Times*: Too Much Enthusiasm," NYT, December 8, 1959, 61.

70. Hugh Brown, "'It Ain't Right,' Clangs Bert Bell at Fans Razzing His Hand-Picked Officials," TSN, November 5, 1952, sec. 2: 3.

71. Ed Prell, "Sizing Up NL Refs — Also Their Problems," TSN, November 23, 1949, sec. 2: 10.

72. "Bell Suggests More Pay for Grid Officials," TSN, November 19, 1947, sec. 2: 6. The referees' low pay raises the possibility that one or more could have been susceptible to inducements to affect the outcomes of games, but no allegations have surfaced.

73. Art Rense, "Bell Plans Moves to Curb Criticism of NFL Officiating," TSN, December 8, 1954, sec. 2: 7.

74. "Bell's Salary Raised to $40,000 as Commissioner of Pro Football," NYT, January 20, 1951, 23.

75. Art Morrow, "Bell Draws Code for NFL Aircasters," TSN, October 5, 1955, sec. 2: 1, 2.

76. Gene Ward, "Rozelle Insists on Top-Drawer Officials in NFL," TSN, December 14, 1960, sec. 2: 8.

77. Alexander Feinberg, "'Fixer' Jailed Here for Bribe Offers to Football Stars," NYT, December 16, 1946, 1.

78. "NFL Head Plans Anti-Bribe Rules," NYT, January 23, 1947, 28; PFHOFAIC, NFL LM, January 23, 1947, 1–3. The league apparently did not see the contradiction involved with its lottery selecting the lucky team for each season's "bonus pick" and lotteries at the ballpark. The owners had earlier passed a rule stipulating banishment for any player or team official who placed wagers on NFL games (PFHOFAIC, NFL LM, December 10, 1934, 2).

79. William D. Richardson, "Pros Delay Choice of a Commissioner," NYT, January 29, 1947, 32. His counterpart in the AAFC, Admiral Jonas Ingram, also warned players of the dire ramifications should they transgress ("Conference Issues 'No Gambling' Rule," NYT, March 26, 1947, 33).

80. "Pro Careers End for 2 Giant Backs," NYT, April 4, 1947, 27.

81. Arthur Daley, "Sports of the *Times*: Bell Rings the Bell," NYT, April 4, 1947, 27.

82. Daley, "Sports of the *Times*," 27.

83. "Ban on Filchock Removed by Bell," NYT, July 14, 1950, 34; "Merle Hapes, 75, Ex-Giant Fullback," NYT, July 21, 1994, B11; Filchock's death date can be found in recent football encyclopedias.

84. MacCambridge, *America's Game*, 49.

85. U.S. House, OPTS, 1957: 2742.

86. "Acts Against Gamblers," NYT, July 16, 1947, 30.

87. W. C. Heinz, "Boss of the Behemoths," *Saturday Evening Post*, December 5, 1955, 46, 72, 74, 77. Bell was highly educated, and one can speculate whether his pronunciation errors were an effort to project an earthy common-man persona.

88. Joe Williams, "FBI-Trained Men Help Keep Pro Grid Fix-Proof," TSN, December 4, 1957, sec. 2: 8.

89. Murray Robinson, "Pro Grid Tilts Get Big Rush of Bet Fraternity," TSN, October 14, 1959, sec. 2: 8.

90. Murray Robinson, "Bell Keeps Sharp Eye on Gamblers," TSN, January 21, 1959, sec. 2: 10.

91. U.S. House, OPTS, 1957: 2587.

92. U.S. Senate, OPTS, 1958: 413.

93. Bill Furlong, "Can College Football Stand Off the Pros?" *Sport*, November 1959, 16–17, 72–75.

13. Integration

1. Fort, *Sports Economics*, 233–41; Becker, *Economics of Discrimination*.

2. Kahn, "The Effects of Race," 295–310.

3. Thomas G. Smith, "Outside the Pale," 260; Thomas G. Smith, "Civil Rights on the Gridiron," 194.

4. For readers wanting a more comprehensive examination of NFL integration, Ross, *Outside the Lines*, and Smith, "Outside the Pale," are good sources. Neither author cited the NFL's league minutes.

5. Ross, *Outside the Lines*, 46–47.

6. Smith, "Outside the Pale," 257. University of Oregon archives held little information on Lillard.

7. Al Harvin, "Pollard, at 84, Reflects on His Days of Glory," NYT, February 7, 1978, 7, 9.

8. Ross, *Outside the Lines*, opening epigraph; cited in Strode and Young, *Goal Dust*, 155.

9. The private golf associations were so snooty that the National Women's Golf Association didn't accept entries from public or municipal courses.

10. Dan Parker, "How Democratic Is Sport?" *Sport*, September 1949, 41–43, 96–98.

11. Parker, "How Democratic?" *Sport*.

12. Smith, "Outside the Pale," 277; Coenen, *Sandlots to Super Bowl*, 123.

13. Ross, *Outside the Lines*, 67. On occasion, Jackie Robinson, himself a talented football player, performed for rival Pacific Coast [Football] League teams (Smith, "Outside the Pale," 274).

14. Ross, *Outside the Lines*, 88, cites Strode and Sam Young, *Goal Dust*, 1990, 148. Strode played in two games in Chicago, both as a substitute. His late-night entertainment did not appear to detract from his readiness to play.

15. MacCambridge, *America's Game*, 32.

16. MacCambridge, *America's Game*, 33.

17. Smith, "Outside the Pale," 278.

18. Ross, *Outside the Lines*, 86.

19. Ross, *Outside the Lines*, 145.

20. Fay Young, "Fay Says," *Chicago Defender*, November 29, 1952, 27; Ross, *Outside the Lines*, 129; Coenen, *Sandlots to Super Bowl*, 173.

21. "Chargers Leave Theater after Segregation Request," TSN, September 20, 1961, sec. 2: 4.

22. Ross, *Outside the Lines*, 110; Coenen, *Sandlots to Super Bowl*, 125. Ross cited the *Cleveland Call and Post* of October 11, 1947 for the first game but gave no citation for the second game. Unless seating was segregated, it is difficult to see how the officials would have known the racial makeup of the crowd. The *New York Times* accounts of the two games confirmed the overall attendance figures but said nothing about the racial composition of the crowd ("New Yorkers' Bid Is Stalled, 26–17," NYT, October 6, 1947, 30; "Graham's Passes Feature 28–28 Tie," NYT, November 24, 1947, 33).

23. Historian Thomas G. Smith mistakenly wrote that, "By 1952 only the Redskins and Detroit Lions had failed to desegregate," but Melvin Groomes and Bob Mann played for the Lions in 1948 and later (Smith, "Civil Rights on the Gridiron," 194).

24. Smith, "Outside the Pale," 280.

25. MacCambridge, *America's Game*, 71.

26. Wendell Smith, "Negro Stars Shine with Pacemakers," TSN, November 19, 1952, sec. 2: 8.

27. Ross, *Outside the Lines*, 126, 130–31.

28. MacCambridge, *America's Game*, xvii; Ross, *Outside the Lines*, 130–31.

29. Smith, "Civil Rights on the Gridiron," 191.

30. Robert Murchison, son of owner Clint Murchison, wanted to get Russell Means, the leader of the American Indian Movement, to stage a protest of the "Redskins" nickname as a practical joke. The joke was stillborn, though, as Means proved to be not only an NFL fan but a fan whose favorite team was the Redskins, proving that NFL football makes for strange bedfellows (Michael MacCambridge, *America's Game*, 263).

31. "Speedster," *Newsweek*, October 15, 1962, 98.

32. Harry Schwartz, "Soviet's 'Beizbol' Bitter Jest Here," NYT, September 21, 1952, sec. 2: 6; "New Soviet Envoy to U.S. Plans to Witness 'Beizbol,'" NYT, September 19, 1952, 19.

33. "Football Bias Charged," NYT, January 4, 1957, 14.

34. "National Football League Teams Complete College Draft at Annual Meeting," NYT, February 1, 1957, 40.

35. Smith, "Civil Rights on the Gridiron," 202.

36. "Udall Will Shun Redskins' Games," NYT, October 6, 1961, 40; "Redskins Pledge No Bias in Hiring," NYT, August 15, 1961, 36; Smith, "Civil Rights on the Gridiron," 189, 197, 203. Smith provides a thorough examination of the situation.

37. David Halberstam, "Football Team Told to Avoid Hiring Bias," NYT, March 25, 1961, 1, 11.

38. Smith, "Civil Rights on the Gridiron," 200.

39. Smith, "Civil Rights on the Gridiron," 208.

40. Smith, "Civil Rights on the Gridiron," 202.

41. Smith, "Civil Rights on the Gridiron," 200.

42. Smith, "Civil Rights on the Gridiron," 203.

43. "An Overall Estimate of the League," SI, September 26, 1960, 64.

44. "Davis, Syracuse Back, Is First Negro to Be Drafted by Redskins," NYT, December 5, 1961, 56. Ernie Davis never played in the NFL due to a fatal form of leukemia. One can imagine him teamed with Jim Brown in a legendary backfield.

45. "Redskins Sign Hatcher, Their First Negro Player," NYT, December 10, 1961, S1, S3. Even here, Marshall created controversy, as he refused to pose with Hatcher for photographs commemorating the signing, saying this would be exploitation. Hatcher played three games with the Redskins; in a photo he was shown wearing an "Indian headdress," surely sending mixed signals of some sort.

46. Ross, *Outside the Lines*, 154.

47. Ross, *Outside the Lines*, 156, 158; Smith, "Civil Rights on the Gridiron," 204.

48. "Bias Protest Weighed," NYT, November 29, 1961, S1.

Conclusion

1. "Commissioner Bell Gets New 12-Year National League Contract," NYT, January 30, 1954, 11.

2. Tex Schramm of the Los Angeles Rams became Pete Rozelle's mentor and close confidant. At times, he chafed under Bell's leadership: "It was the old guard, and every ruling would be in favor of them. That shit got old fast" (MacCambridge, *America's Game*, 103).

3. Jack Orr, "The Commissioner Who Commissions," *Sport*, December 1958, 28–29, 92–94.

4. Jack Walsh, "Bert Tells Bosses Off, Runs Show," TSN, February 1, 1950, sec. 2: 2.

5. Arthur Daley, "Sports of the *Times*: For Whom the Bell Tolls," NYT, January 26, 1950, 40; for Daley's earlier view of Bell, see Arthur Daley, "Sports of the *Times*: Change in Commissioners," NYT, January 14, 1946, 23.

6. "Crowley Resigns All-America Post," NYT, December 31, 1946, 21.

7. "Veteran of Navy New League Head," NYT, February 27, 1947, 29; Louis Effrat, "Football Yankees and Dodgers Merge and Will Play Home Games at Stadium," NYT, January 22, 1949, 17.

8. Stan Baumgartner, "Grid Pros' Bell — Blunt Scrapper, Born Leader," TSN, February 8, 1950, sec. 2: 7.

9. "Bell Gains Vote of Confidence after Scoring NFL Bickering," NYT, December 2, 1958, 48; W. C. Heinz, "Boss of the Behemoths," *Saturday Evening Post*, December 5, 1955, 46, 72, 74, 77; Harris, *League*, 24.

10. PFHOFAIC, NFL LM, May 18, 1958, 4.

11. PFHOFAIC, NFL LM, February 1, 1957, 7.

12. PFHOFAIC, NFL LM, January 28, 1958, 6; January 21, 1959, 4.

13. U.S. House, OPTS, 1957: 2504, 2730.

14. PFHOFAIC, NFL LM, January 21, 1959, 5. Al Hirshberg provided a good summary of Bell's tenure as NFL commissioner (Al Hirshberg, "He Calls the Signals for Pro Football," NYT, November 23, 1958, SM 28, 30, 32, 35, 37).

15. MacCambridge, *America's Game*, 127.

16. Orr, "Commissioner Who Commissions," *Sport*.

17. Harris, *League*, 10–11 provides a good overview of Rozelle's ascent to the commissioner position; contemporary news articles include "Bert Bell, Pro Football Head, Dies after Collapsing at Game," NYT, October 12, 1959, 1, 23; Tex Maule, "Pro Football: The Infighting Was Vicious," SI, February 8, 1960, 50–52; John Devaney, "The Inner Workings of the NFL," *Sport*, December 1964, 14–16, 71–72.

18. "Crisler Rejects Offer to Head Proposed Pro Football League," NYT, October 26, 1959, 37; "'Connections' in Capital Called a Factor in Foss's Football Post," NYT, March 1, 1962, 34.

19. MacCambridge, *America's Game*, 156. A decade earlier, George Preston Marshall had advocated opening a league publicity office in New York City (PFHOFAIC, NFL LM, June 2, 1950, 11).

20. U.S. Senate, *Professional Sports Antitrust Bill — 1964*, 112.

21. Jim Beach, "What Pay TV Will Mean to the Fan," *Sport*, June 1964, 18–19, 70–71.

BIBLIOGRAPHY

Archival Materials

Pro Football Hall of Fame Archives and Information Center

AFL League Minutes, 1959–60 (denoted as PFHOFAIC AFL LM in notes).

NFL League Minutes, 1945–60 (denoted as PFHOFAIC NFL LM in notes).

NFL Media Guides

Baltimore Colts: 1948–49, 1950, 1953–55.

Buffalo Bisons: 1946.

Cleveland Browns: 1950–53.

Detroit Lions: 1952–53.

New York Giants: 1945, 1946, 1953.

San Francisco 49ers: 1950, 1957–59, 1961–63.

Washington Redskins: 1950, 1951.

NFL Programs

Chicago Cardinals: September 26, 1949; October 7, 1951; November 23, 1958.

Cleveland Browns: October 24, 1948; October 30, 1949.

New York Giants: October 27, 1959; November 16, 1961.

Pittsburgh Steelers: November 13, 1949; November 12, 1950.

NFL Team Folders

Chicago Bears: "1946–50," *Bear News*, various issues; "1951–55," *Bear News*, various issues.

Chicago Cardinals: "1950–54," *The Big Red*, February 1952 and June 1953.

Detroit Lions: "1945–45," loose pages (material is dated 1944–46 but erroneously filed in this folder); "1946–50," "Detroit Lions Season Ticket Information, 1948," brochure.

Green Bay Packers: *Yearbook*, 1960.

Los Angeles Rams: "General," *Ram Rumblings*, September 1941.

New York Giants: "1941–50," 1945 *New York Football Giants — Official Review and Roster*.

Philadelphia Eagles: "1943–52," loose pages.

San Francisco Team Files: "1946–60," *49ers Diggings*, May 1958.

Washington Redskins: "1942–51," photocopy of 1943 information.

Joyce Sports Collection, Notre Dame University

National Football League. 1935, 1938, 1946, 1949, 1950, and 1968. *National Football League Constitution*. Various cities: National Football League.

NFL Media Guides

Baltimore Colts: 1953–61.

Chicago Bears: 1952–53.

Chicago Cardinals: 1948, 1955–57, 1960.

Cleveland Browns: 1952, 1957, 1959–60.

Detroit Lions: 1948–61.

Green Bay Packers: 1950, 1953–54.

Los Angeles Rams: 1953–56, 1958–61.

New York Giants: 1952–53, 1957.

Philadelphia Eagles: 1952.

Pittsburgh Steelers: 1952–60.

San Francisco 49ers: 1949, 1952–56.

Washington Redskins: 1949–61.

NFL Programs

Baltimore Colts: September 17, 1950; October 31, 1953; September 18, 1954; September 16, 1956; October 4, 1958.

Chicago Bears: November 14, 1948; September 20, 1953.

Chicago Cardinals: September 7, 1952; September 29, 1952, September 27, 1953; September 15, 1954; October 2, 1955; October 7, 1956; October 6, 1957.

Cleveland Browns: November 25, 1951; September 28, 1952; December 19, 1954; September 1, 1956; September 20, 1958.

Detroit Lions: November 5, 1950; September 26, 1954; October 9, 1960.

Green Bay Packers: August 23, 1952; September 5, 1953; October 4, 1953; August 21, 1954; August 31, 1954; August 27, 1955; August 25, 1956.

Los Angeles Rams: 1952–55.

New York Giants: October 22, 1939; October 27, 1946; October 12, 1948; November 6, 1949; October 14, 1951; October 19, 1952; October 18, 1953; October 17, 1954; October 16, 1955; October 21, 1956.

Philadelphia Eagles: October 12, 1952; August 16, 1953; September 17, 1953; October 17, 1953; August 14, 1954; August 26, 1955; October 4, 1959.

Books, Articles, and Other Sources

All-America Football Conference. AAFC *Record Manual*. Edited by Joseph Petritz. New York: AAFC, 1947–49.

Becker, Gary S. *The Economics of Discrimination.* 2nd ed. Chicago: University of Chicago Press, 1971.

Canes, Michael E. "The Social Benefits of Restrictions on Team Quality." In *Government and the Sports Business,* ed. Roger G. Noll, 81–113. Washington DC: Brookings Institution, 1974.

Carroll, Bob, Michael Gershman, David Neft, and John Thorn, eds. *Total Football: The Official Encyclopedia of the National Football League.* New York: HarperCollins Publishers, 1997.

Carroll, John M. *Red Grange and the Rise of Modern Football.* Urbana: University of Illinois Press, 1999.

Coenen, Craig R. *From Sandlots to the Super Bowl.* Knoxville: University of Tennessee Press, 2005.

Conerly, Perian. *Backseat Quarterback.* New York: Doubleday, 1963. Reprint, Jackson: University Press of Mississippi, 2003. (Page numbers in notes refer to the 2003 reprint.)

Cox, W. Michael, and Richard Alm. "Time Well Spent." *1997 Annual Report: Federal Reserve Bank of Dallas.* 2–24. Dallas: Federal Reserve Bank of Dallas, 1998.

Davis, Jeff. *Papa Bear: The Life and Legacy of George Halas.* New York: McGraw-Hill, 2005.

Fort, Rodney D. *Sports Economics.* 2nd edition. Upper Saddle River NJ: Pearson Prentice Hall, 2006.

Fort, Rodney D., and James Quirk. "Cross-subsidization, Incentives, and Outcomes in Professional Team Sports Leagues," *Journal of Economic Literature* 33 (1995): 1, 265–99.

Glick, Jeffrey. "Professional Sports Franchise Movements and the Sherman Act: When and Where Teams Should Be Able to Move." *Santa Clara Law Review* 23, no. 1 (Winter 1983): 55–94.

Harris, David. *The League: The Rise and Decline of the NFL.* New York: Bantam Books, 1986.

Kahn, Lawrence M. "The Effects of Race on Professional Football Players' Compensation." *Industrial Labor Relations Review* 45, no. 2 (January 1992): 295–310.

Kesenne, Stefan. 2000. "Revenue Sharing and Competitive Balance in Professional Team Sports." *Journal of Sports Economics* 1, no. 1:56–65.

Leifer, Eric. *Making the Majors: The Transformation of Team Sports in America.* Cambridge MA: Harvard University Press, 1995.

Levin, Richard C., George J. Mitchell, Paul A. Volcker, and George F. Will. *The Report of the Independent Members of the Commissioner's Blue Ribbon Panel on Baseball Economics.* July 2000. http://www.mlb.com/mlb/downloads/blue_ribbon.pdf.

MacCambridge, Michael. *America's Game: The Epic Story of How Pro Football Captured a Nation*. New York: Random House, 2004.

Maher, Tod, and Bob Gill. *The Pro Football Encyclopedia: The Complete and Definitive Record of Professional Football*. New York: Macmillan USA, 1997.

Marburger, Daniel R. "Gate Revenue Sharing and Luxury-Taxes in Professional Sports." *Contemporary Economic Policy* 15 (1997): 114–23.

Miller, Marvin. *A Whole Different Ball Game: The Inside Story of Baseball's New Deal*. New York: Fireside, 1991.

Nathanson, Mitchell. "The Sovereign Nation of Baseball: Why Federal Law Does Not Apply to 'America's Game' and How It Got That Way." *Villanova Sports & Entertainment Law Journal* 16, no. 1 (2009): 49–98.

National Football League. *National Football League Constitution*. Various cities: National Football League, 1935, 1938, 1946, 1949, 1950, and 1968.

National Football League. NFL *Records and Rules Manual*. Composed by George Strickler (1946) and Joseph T. Labrum (1947–58). New York: NFL, 1946–58.

Newhouse, Dave. *The Million Dollar Backfield: The San Francisco 49ers in the 1950s*. Berkeley CA: Frog, 2000.

New York Yankees Baseball Club. *General Ledger and Cash Books*. Cooperstown NY: National Baseball Hall of Fame, 1913–44.

Patton, Phil. *Razzle-Dazzle: The Curious Marriage of Television and Professional Football*. Garden City NY: The Dial Press, 1984.

Peterson, Robert W. *Pigskin: The Early Years of Pro Football*. New York: Oxford University Press, 1997.

Pluto, Terry. *Tall Tales: The Glory Years of the NBA*. New York: Simon & Schuster, 1992.

Quirk, James and Rodney D. Fort. *Pay Dirt: The Business of Professional Team Sports*. Princeton: Princeton University Press, 1992.

Rader, Benjamin G. *In Its Own Image: How Television Has Transformed Sports*. New York: Free Press, 1984.

Riess, Steven A. "A Social Profile of the Professional Football Player, 1920–82." In *The Business of Professional Sports*, ed. Paul D. Staudohar and James A. Mangan, 222–46. Urbana: University of Illinois Press, 1991.

Ross, Charles K. *Outside the Lines: African Americans and the Integration of the National Football League*. New York: New York University Press, 1999.

Rottenberg, Simon. "The Baseball Players' Labor Market." *Journal of Political Economy* 64, no. 3 (1956): 242–58.

Scully, Gerald W. *The Business of Major League Baseball*. Chicago: University of Chicago Press, 1989.

———. *The Market Structure of Sports*. Chicago: University of Chicago Press, 1995.

Seagrave, Kerry. *Drive-in Theaters: A History from Their Inception in 1933.* Jefferson NC: McFarland and Co., 1992.

Seymour, Harold. *Baseball: The Early Years.* New York: Oxford University Press, 1960.

Seymour, Harold. *Baseball: The Golden Age.* New York: Oxford University Press, 1971.

Smith, Thomas G. "Civil Rights on the Gridiron: The Kennedy Administration and the Desegregation of the Washington Redskins." *Journal of Sport History* 14, no. 2 (Summer 1987): 189–208.

———. "Outside the Pale: The Exclusion of Blacks from the National Football League, 1934–1946." *Journal of Sport History* 15, no. 3 (Winter 1988): 255–81.

The Sporting News. *Complete Baseball Record Book.* 2003 edition. St. Louis MO: The Sporting News, 2002.

———. *The Sporting News Official Baseball Guide.* St. Louis MO: Charles Spink, 1953–57.

Surdam, David G. "The American 'Not-So-Socialist' League in the Postwar Era: The Limitations of Gate Sharing in Reducing Revenue Disparity in Baseball." *Journal of Sports Economics* 3, no. 3 (August 2002): 264–90.

———. *The Big Leagues Go to Washington: Congress and Sports Antitrust, 1951–1976,* unpublished manuscript.

———. "The Coase Theorem and Player Movement in Major League Baseball." *Journal of Sports Economics* 7, no. 2 (May 2006): 201–21.

———. *The Postwar Yankees: Baseball's Golden Age Revisited.* Lincoln: University of Nebraska Press, 2008.

———. "A Tale of Two Gate-Sharing Plans: The National Football League and the National League, 1952–56." *Southern Economic Journal* 73, no. 4 (April 2007): 931–46.

———. "Television and Minor League Baseball: Changing Patterns of Leisure in Postwar America." *Journal of Sports Economics* 6, no. 1 (February 2005): 61–77.

———. *Wins, Losses & Empty Seats: How Baseball Outlasted the Great Depression.* Lincoln: University of Nebraska Press, 2011.

Szymanski, Stefan and Stefan Kesenne. "Competitive Balance and Gate Revenue Sharing in Team Sports." *Journal of Industrial Economics* 52 (2004): 165–77.

Thorn, John, Pete Palmer, and Michael Gershman, editors. *Total Baseball: The Official Encyclopedia of Major League Baseball.* 7th edition. Kingston, NY: Total Sports Publishing, 2001.

U.S. Department of Commerce. Bureau of the Census. *Census of Population: 1950. Vol. II, General Characteristics of the Population.* Washington DC: Government Printing Office, 1952.

U.S. Department of Commerce. Bureau of the Census. *Historical Statistics of the United States: Colonial Times to 1970*. 2 vols. Washington DC: Government Printing Office, 1975.

U.S. House of Representatives. *Inquiry into Professional Sports. Final Report of the Select Committee on Professional Sports*. House Report No. 94-1786. 94th Congress, 2nd Sess. Washington DC: Government Printing Office, 1977.

U.S. House of Representatives. *Organized Baseball: Report of the Subcommittee on the Study of Monopoly Power of the Committee of the Judiciary*. House Report No. 2002, 82nd Cong., 1st Sess. Washington DC: Government Printing Office, 1952.

U.S. House of Representatives. *Organized Professional Team Sports. Hearings before the Antitrust Subcommittee of the Committee on the Judiciary*. Serial no. 8. 85th Cong., 1st Sess. Washington DC: Government Printing Office, 1957.

U.S. House of Representatives. *Professional Football League Merger. Hearings before Antitrust Subcommittee of the Committee on the Judiciary*. Serial no. 22. 89th Cong., 2nd Sess. Washington DC: Government Printing Office, 1966.

U.S. House of Representatives. *Telecasting of Professional Sports Contests. Hearings before the Antitrust Subcommittee of the Committee on the Judiciary*. Serial no. 13. 87th Cong., 1st Session Washington DC: Government Printing office, 1961.

U.S. Senate. *Organized Professional Team Sports. Hearings before the Subcommittee on Antitrust and Monopoly of the Committee on the Judiciary*. 85th Cong., 2nd Sess. Washington DC: Government Printing Office, 1958.

U.S. Senate. *Organized Professional Team Sports. Hearings before the Subcommittee on Antitrust and Monopoly of the Committee on the Judiciary*. 86th Cong., 1st Sess. Washington DC: Government Printing Office, 1959.

U.S. Senate. *Professional Sports Antitrust Bill — 1964. Hearings before the Subcommittee on Antitrust and Monopoly of the Committee on the Judiciary*. 88th Cong., 2nd Sess. Washington DC: Government Printing Office, 1964.

U.S. Senate. *Professional Sports Antitrust Bill — 1965. Hearings before the Subcommittee on Antitrust and Monopoly of the Committee on the Judiciary*. 89th Cong., 1st Sess. Washington DC: Government Printing Office, 1965.

Veeck, Bill. *Veeck as in Wreck*. New York: Putnam, 1962.

Vrooman, John. "A General Theory of Sports Leagues," *Southern Economic Journal* 61 (1995): 971–90.

Whittingham, Richard. *The Meat Market*. New York NY: Macmillan, 1992.

———. *What a Game They Played: An Inside Look at the Golden Era of Pro Football*. Lincoln: University of Nebraska Press, 2001 [1984].

INDEX

Adams, Chet, 19, 20

Adams, John, 220

Adams, K. S. ("Bud"), 50, 52, 355n60, 356n74. *See also* Houston Oilers

Adams, Val, 248

admission taxes, 70, 81, 127, 370n22. *See also* revenue

African American players, 109, 182, 224; and Canadian football, 40; and integration, 4, 155, 180, 280–82, 284–93, 401n45; intimidation of, 287; and the Pacific Coast Football League, 133; as percentage of NFL players, 290; and salaries, 281, 287; and specialized positions, 287–88. *See also* integration

All-America Conference. *See* All-America Football Conference (AAFC)

All-America Football Conference (AAFC), 3, 11–12, 14, 28, 31; and attendance, 21, 22, 23, 24, 25, 27, 28, 60, 61, 62–63, 79–80, 83, 106, 145, 320, 338; and competitive balance, 26, 145–46, 147, 148, 158, 168, 321; conciliation efforts of the, with the NFL, 26–31; debut game of the, 22; and the draft, 18–19, 26, 155, 183,

348n60; and exhibition games, 15–16; formation of the, 1, 13–15, 20–21; and franchise sales, 104; and franchise values, 15; and gate sharing, 194, 201; and integration, 155, 286, 287, 288, 289, 342; merger of, with the NFL, 31–38, 63, 135, 155, 159, 165–66, 296–97; and number of plays per game, 257; and owners' wealth, 13, 20–21; and profitability, 22–23, 78, 79, 83, 306; and publicity, 21; and quality of play, 13, 16, 23, 34, 37, 344n6; and "raiding" of players, 16–18, 19, 24, 25; and salaries, 17–18, 36–37, 91, 93, 94–95, 209, 287; and scheduling, 15, 21–22, 164; and stadium leases, 13, 14, 21–22, 29, 347n51, 359n2. *See also* National Football League (NFL)

Allard, Don, 183–84

Ameche, Alan, 13, 158, 187

Ameche, Don, 13

American Association, 134, 135. *See also* minor leagues, football

American Broadcasting Company (ABC), 238, 242; and the AFL, 54–55, 244, 249, 252, 356n71, 390n36, 392n62. *See also* television

American Football Conference, 56,
201. *See also* American Football
League (AFL); National Football
League (NFL)
American Football League (AFL), 3,
69, 77, 89, 193, 258, 299–300; and
antitrust lawsuit, 49, 53–54, 131–32;
and attendance, 55–56, 69; debut
season of the, 55; and the draft,
49–51; formation of the, 45–47,
48, 49–50, 115, 117, 131–32; and
gate sharing, 55; and innovations,
263, 264; merger of, with the NFL,
56; and player raiding, 52; and
publicity, 244; and salaries, 50,
98–99; and scheduling, 47; and
season length, 119; and stadium
leases, 46–47, 55, 75; and television,
5, 54–55, 56, 244, 248–49, 252,
253–54, 356n71, 390n36, 392nn61–
62. *See also* National Football
League (NFL)
American League, 11
Anderson, Edwin J., 269–70
Anderton, Piers, 185
antitrust issues, 4, 120, 213, 371n53;
and the AFL lawsuit, 49, 53–54,
131–32; and baseball, 121, 122, 127,
128, 137, 370n32; and commissioner
duties, 122, 124–25, 128–29; and
draft, 120, 122–23, 128–29, 132–33,
169, 175–78; and profitability, 81,
87, 121; and the reserve clause, 120,
122, 126–27, 128–30, 131, 132–33,
214, 222, 369n5; and television, 81,
120, 124, 125–26, 131, 136–42, 235,
239–42, 244, 246, 248–52, 371n58;
territorial rights, 3, 120, 122,

123–24, 128. *See also* Congressional
hearings; players' rights
Arledge, Roone, 244, 388n6
Armstrong, Neill, 39, 40
Artoe, Lee, 18
Association of Professional Football
Leagues, 134. *See also* minor
leagues, football
Atchison, Lewis F., 172
Atkins, Doug, 159
attendance, 31, 53, 85, 304–5, 329, 337,
351n115; and the AAFC, 21, 22, 23,
24, 25, 27, 28, 60, 61, 62–63, 79–80,
83, 106, 145, 320, 338; and the
AFL, 55–56, 69; in the American
Conference, 201; and baseball,
58, 59, 60, 61, 64, 195, 198, 256,
328, 334; calculating, 58, 59–60,
356n1; and championship games,
11, 23, 61, 66–67, 79, 98, 318; and
college football, 64–65, 236, 263,
357n19; and competitive balance,
61–62, 145, 189, 191–92, 200;
declines in, 58, 61–64, 119, 229;
and gate receipts, 58, 71, 77–78,
150, 310; and gate sharing, 189–90,
191–92, 200–201; increases in, 58,
60–61, 65–68, 69, 71, 77, 80; and
integration, 289, 290, 400n22;
in the National Conference, 201;
and the Pro Bowl, 65, 357n20; and
profitability, 63, 77–78, 80, 83,
361n34; and revenue sharing, 167,
195, 203, 335; and rivalries, 62, 68,
78, 162; and scheduling, 165; and
stadium capacity, 67–68, 74, 83;
and television, 63, 64, 66, 139–41,
226, 231–32, 234–37, 339, 372n63,
389n27. *See also* gate receipts

the AAFC and NFL, 13, 16, 23, 34, 344n6; between the AFL and NFL, 54; and attendance, 11, 23, 61, 66–67, 79, 98, 318; and competitive balance, 147–48; and gambling, 273–74, 277; and gate receipts, 11, 61, 98, 252, 318; "Greatest Game Ever Played," 5, 241, 263, 277, 391n53; and salaries, 98, 209, 224, 364n86; and sudden-death overtime, 263; and television, 5, 142, 224, 230, 233, 248, 251, 252, 391n53

Chandler, Happy, 127

Chicago Bears, 15, 16, 43, 77, 89, 152, 156–57; and attendance, 61, 62, 67, 78, 83, 329, 337; and championship games, 6, 23, 61, 145, 273–75; and competitive balance, 145, 156–57, 159, 372n2; and dirty play, 269, 270–71; and the draft, 181, 182, 324, 326–27; and gate receipts, 84, 309, 310, 311, 330, 336; and integration, 289, 342; and profitability, 27, 78, 83, 102–3, 359n11; and salaries, 92, 95–96, 317; and scheduling, 21, 162, 166, 265, 361n49, 376n64; and season ticket sales, 65, 78, 358n26; and television, 113, 114, 230–31, 313, 330; and ticket prices, 84, 305

Chicago Cardinals, 25, 41, 50, 61, 89, 98, 173, 184, 215, 265, 386n29; and attendance, 62–63, 67, 78, 82, 329, 337; and championship games, 6, 147; and competitive balance, 67, 152, 156, 157, 170, 301; and franchise relocation, 48, 67, 109, 113, 367n45; and gate sharing, 199, 200–201, 204, 336; and integration, 289, 342; and lawsuits, 209, 217; and profitability, 82, 104, 112–13;

relocation of, to St. Louis, 114; and salaries, 17, 317; and scheduling, 21, 166, 361n49, 384n21; and television, 113, 313, 330

Chicago Hornets, 30–31, 32, 33, 349n80. *See also* Chicago Rockets

Chicago Rockets, 19, 24–25, 26, 28, 156, 201, 297, 348n65; and attendance, 62–63, 338; become the Chicago Hornets, 30–31; and publicity, 21. *See also* Chicago Hornets

city size, 13, 59, 111, 164, 297, 300, 303; and baseball, 44; and competitive balance, 144, 149–50, 154; and expansion teams, 45, 48–49, 110–11; and gate sharing, 192–93; and minor league systems, 19; and spatial preemption, 45, 57, 101. *See also* stadiums

Clark, James P. ("Jim"), 30, 103, 231

Cleveland Browns, 26, 84, 85, 271, 350n107; and attendance, 24, 61, 66–67, 68, 106, 145, 320, 329, 337, 338; and championship games, 23, 34, 66–67, 79, 98, 146, 148, 159, 160–61, 289; dominance of the, 22, 23, 26, 28, 34, 38, 49, 144, 145–46, 148, 149, 159–61, 176, 285, 289, 301, 373n12, 380n31; and the draft, 185, 324, 326–27; and franchise value, 105; and gate sharing, 200, 201, 336; and gross operating expenses, 89; and integration, 155, 286, 287, 289, 342; join the NFL, 32, 104, 159; and player acquisitions, 16, 19–20, 158, 185; and profitability, 22, 27, 79, 82; and salaries, 32, 93–94, 97, 98, 317; and television, 246, 313, 330; and ticket prices, 196, 305

dates of the, 128; and the draft, 92, 120, 121, 127, 132–33, 169, 170–73, 175–78, 207, 214–15; and expansion, 114–15, 116, 117; and financial reporting from the NFL, 69, 82–83, 90, 190; and minor leagues, 135–36; and player contracts, 207, 277–78; and players' rights, 207, 213–19, 220–21, 222–23; and profitability, 69, 75, 81–83, 87, 89, 360n25; and the reserve clause, 120, 121, 129, 130, 131, 132, 207, 217–19, 222, 369n5; and revenue sharing, 121, 190, 193, 196; and salaries, 90, 91, 92, 97, 362n65; and television, 131, 239–43, 249–53; and territorial rights, 120, 123–24, 128; and ticket prices, 129, 131, 370n29. *See also* antitrust issues

Connor, George, 216–17

Consumer Price Index (CPI), 12, 17, 70, 93, 196, 387n57

contracts, player, 23–24, 214, 216, 348n60, 369n5; changes to, 206, 222, 385n6; and injuries, 209, 216, 217, 222; legality of, 206–7, 214, 216–17; and the option year, 42–43, 52, 122, 129, 131, 213, 218, 219–20, 352n16. *See also* players' rights; salaries, player

Conzelman, Jim ("Jimmy"), 231, 261, 265

Cook, Beano, 9

Cooke, Jack Kent, 293. *See also* Washington Redskins

Cooper, Ralph, 43

Cope, Myron, 363n73

Cosell, Howard, 229, 392n59

Costello, Vince, 185

Coulter, Tex, 41, 351n3

Cox, William D., 73

Crisler, Fritz, 299

Crosby, Bing, 13, 105

Crowley, James ("Jim"), 14, 15, 16, 18, 22, 23–24, 297, 347n54

Daley, Arthur, 86–87, 152, 271, 275, 296–97; on specialist players, 260–61, 262–63

Dallas Cowboys, 50, 53–54, 56, 58, 69, 115–16; formation of the, 46, 116, 118, 119

Dallas Rangers. *See* Dallas Cowboys

Dallas Texans (AFL), 8, 47, 56, 149

Dallas Texans (NFL), 104, 137, 168, 229, 288, 290, 366n35; folding of the, 109–10, 111, 149; relocation of the, from New York, 80, 167. *See also* Miller brothers; New York Yanks

Daniel, Dan, 29

Daugherty, Duffy, 176–77, 183, 222

Davis, Ernie, 51, 292, 401n44

Davis, Glenn, 24, 153, 184–85

Davis, Jeff, 231, 368n60

Dawson, Len, 161, 181–82, 355n54

DeGroot, Dudley Sargent, 18

De Laurentis, John, 208–9

Dempsey, Frank, 43

Detroit Lions, 43, 84, 148, 171, 252; and attendance, 63–64, 66–67, 80, 329, 337; and championship games, 66–67, 157; and competitive balance, 144–45, 150–51; and dirty play, 269; and exhibition games, 109, 312, 330; and expenses, 88–89, 314–16; and franchise value, 103, 104; and gate sharing, 199, 336; and integration, 289, 290, 342, 400n23; and lawsuits, 126–27, 217;

Detroit Lions (*continued*)
ability, 80, 82, 140–41, 360n25; and
salaries, 95, 97, 317; and scouting,
179, 380n39; and season ticket
sales, 65, 69, 80; and television,
140–41, 313, 330, 372n65; and ticket
prices, 70–71, 84, 305
Devine, Tommy, 61–62, 151, 180
discrimination, racial. *See* racism
Ditka, Mike, 187
Dixie League, 18, 134, 135, 346n28. *See
also* minor leagues, football
Dixon, Paul, 52–53, 131, 132–33, 175–76
Dobbs, Glenn, 156
Donaldson, Gene, 159
Donovan, Art, 158, 261
Dorais, Gus, 98
draft, player, 4, 169, 213, 301, 324–27,
354n45; in the AAFC, 18–19, 26,
155, 183, 348n60; in the AFL,
49–51; and the All-American
lists, 180, 381n60; and antitrust
hearings, 120, 122–23, 128, 132–33,
169, 170–78, 214–15, 222–23; and
the bonus pick, 172–73, 180–81,
182, 379n16, 380n49, 398n78; and
Canadian football, 40–41, 43; and
common pool (between AAFC and
NFL), 27–28, 29, 32–33, 349n76;
and competitive balance, 2, 26, 67,
122–23, 132–33, 143, 144–45, 151–52,
155, 157–58, 161, 168, 169, 170–72,
174–75, 176–78, 179, 184, 187–88,
378n2; dispersion, 155; fan interest
in the, 187, 379n24; and free
agency, 170; and integration, 180,
182, 292–93; and lawsuits, 210; and
merger between AAFC and NFL,
32–33, 35, 36–37, 155; and military

status, 172, 185; and number of
rounds, 179, 182, 381n53; origins
of the, 169–70, 175, 378n2; and
players' rights, 170, 172, 174, 176,
207–8, 210, 214–15, 298, 378n4;
and salaries, 3, 36–37, 92, 122–23,
133, 174, 175–76, 207–8, 378n4; and
scouting, 159, 170, 176–77, 178–80,
186–87, 380n39; and secret drafts,
18–19, 26, 48, 51, 57; strategies, 159,
178–82, 183–87; territorial, 186,
382n70; and timing, 49–50, 118,
173, 183, 186, 382n69; violations in
the, 50–51, 354n47
Dublinski, Tom, 42, 43, 151
Dudley, Bill, 223
DuMont Television Network, 141,
233, 234, 237, 238, 390n36. *See also*
television
Dupre, L. G., 158
Durslag, Melvin, 267, 268
Durso, Joseph, 158

Eastern Conference, 67, 68, 118, 168,
337
Ebbets Field, 73, 75, 78, 228. *See also*
stadiums
Embree, Mel, 289
Epes, W. Perry, 137, 139, 140
Etcheverry, Sam, 41
Ettinger, Don, 39
Evashevski, Forest, 258
Ewart, Charley, 93
Ewbank, Weeb, 158
exhibition games, 63, 109, 293, 374n23;
AAFC vs. NFL, 15–16; and college
football, 152–54; and revenue,
85–86, 197, 312, 330; and salaries,
208, 211, 387n47

gate sharing (*continued*)
197–99, 202–4, 331, 333–34, 384n30;
and city size, 191, 192–93; and
competitive balance, 189–90, 191;
economic models of, 189, 191–92;
and minimum guarantee to visiting
teams, 74, 77, 81, 193–94, 200–201,
202–3, 204, 383n13, 383n16, 383n18,
384n21, 384n24; origins of, 192–93,
383n13; and playoff games, 383n20;
and scheduling, 194, 384n21; and
stadium rental, 193, 383n16; as
subsidization, 189–90. *See also*
gate receipts; profitability; revenue
sharing
Gatski, Frank, 159, 160
Gifford, Frank, 239
Gilbert, Phil, 207
Gillman, Sid, 98, 288, 293
Gilmer, Harry, 183
Gini Coefficients, 195, 384n28. *See
also* revenue sharing
Glick, Gary, 181, 380n49
Glick, Jeffrey, 106–7
Goldstein, Herman, 26, 160
Goode, Rob, 183
Gould, Jack, 234
Graham, Otto, 36, 155, 159, 160, 161,
185, 276, 287, 289; on dirty play,
266–67
Grange, Harold ("Red"), 11, 90, 92,
130, 172, 265
Grant, Bud, 41, 218
"Greatest Game Ever Played," 5,
241, 263, 277, 391n53. *See also*
championship games
Green Bay Packers, 84, 144, 184, 300,
346n28, 367n49; and attendance,
66, 68, 83, 150, 200, 204, 329, 337;
and championship games, 252;
community ownership of the, 102;
and competitive balance, 144, 145,
149–50, 152, 155, 156, 158, 372n2;
and exhibition games, 85, 197, 312,
330; and expenses, 88, 314–16;
and gate sharing, 199, 200, 201,
204, 336; and integration, 289,
342; and lawsuits, 19–20, 217; and
profitability, 74, 83, 86, 114, 373n14;
and salaries, 90–91, 97–98, 317;
and scheduling, 162; and season
ticket sales, 66; and television, 86,
233, 253, 313, 330; and ticket prices,
70, 196, 305
Grier, Roosevelt, 7
Griffith, Calvin, 75
Grim, Allen K., 81, 124, 125–26, 131,
132, 137, 138, 140, 141, 142, 248–49,
250
Grimes, Billy, 159
gross operating expenses, 86–89, 314.
See also profitability
gross operating income, 83–86, 88,
96–97, 308. *See also* profitability;
revenue
Groza, Lou, 159, 160, 289, 363n75
Guglielmi, Ralph, 183
Gunsel, Austin, 86, 142, 276, 299,
353n31, 366n29

Halas, George, 11, 14, 89, 107, 219, 220,
269, 299, 368n60, 375n43; and the
AAFC, 26, 28; and the Chicago
Cardinals, 113–14, 118, 367n45;
and the draft, 50, 159, 169–70, 171,
378n4; and expansion, 48, 54, 117,
118; and integration, 282; and loans
to players, 205, 385n2; paternalism

of, 205; and publicity, 6, 21, 152; and rule changes, 261; and salaries, 92, 95, 156–57, 205, 361n51, 376n52, 378n4, 387n47; and scheduling, 161, 166, 168, 376n64; and scouting, 178, 179–80; and television, 230–31, 236; wealth of, 102–3. *See also* Chicago Bears

Hall, Parker, 18

Handler, Phil, 265

Hapes, Merle, 156, 274–75

Harkins, Kenneth, 97, 129, 135, 213–14, 240, 370n30

Harris, David, 6, 86, 103, 116, 297, 383n16, 392n61

Harris, Oren, 127

Harris, Wayne, 187

Hart, Leon, 36–37, 80, 94–95, 181

Hatcher, Ron, 293, 401n45

Hecker, Norb, 269

Heinz, W. C., 237–38, 276

Heller, Warren, 155

Henry, Bill, 112

Hester, Clinton, 252

Hickman, Herman, 186–87

Hillings, Patrick J., 127

Hilton, Barron, 56, 99

Hirsch, Elroy ("Crazy Legs"), 96

Hirshberg, Al, 54, 99

Hodges, Gil, 7

Hoernschemeyer, Bob, 156

Hogan, Frank S., 274

Hollywood Bears, 21, 286. *See also* Pacific Coast [Football] League (PCFL)

Holub, E. J., 187

Hope, Bob, 105

Hornung, Paul, 181, 278

Houston, Lin, 159

Houston Oilers, 50, 52, 354n47, 355n60, 356n74

Howard, Sherman, 109

Howell, Jim Lee, 185–86, 267, 271

Howton, Billy, 223

Huffman, Dick, 39

Hughes, Ed, 186

Hunsinger, Chuck, 157

Hunt, Lamar, 49, 50, 52, 54, 56, 117, 193, 299; and founding of the AFL, 45–46, 47, 48, 68; loyalty of, to other AFL owners, 52, 56; and television, 244, 392n61. *See also* American Football League (AFL); Dallas Texans (AFL)

Hutson, Don, 255

Ingram, Jonas, 16, 25, 26, 28, 297, 398n79

innovations, 4, 263–65, 278, 301–2; ball design, 264; and field goals, 256, 260–61; forward passing, 61–62, 256–57, 258; and "perfect substitutes," 255–56; and player size, 261; and the point after touchdown (PAT), 259–60; and punting, 260; and scoring, 256–61, 302; sudden-death overtime, 263; two-platoon football, 260–63; and uniforms, 263, 396n96; and violence, 265–72

integration, 4, 180, 279–80, 281–82, 284–86, 289–91, 302, 342; in the AAFC, 155, 286, 287, 288, 289; and attendance, 289, 290, 400n22; in baseball, 279–80, 284, 289; and college football, 291, 292; and the economics of discrimination, 280–81; and hazing, 287; and pop culture, 283–84; and segregation,

fan rioting, 271; and franchise value, 105; and gate sharing, 199, 336, 384n24; and gross operating income, 83–84; and integration, 289, 342; and profitability, 27, 37, 79–80; and salaries, 25, 41, 317; and scheduling, 15, 21, 29, 161, 162; and season ticket sales, 65, 69; and stadium leases, 7, 14, 73, 74; and television, 86, 139–40, 230, 232, 236, 239, 248, 313, 330; and territorial rights, 32, 108; and ticket prices, 70, 305

New York Giants (baseball), 16, 195, 198–99

New York Titans, 51, 56, 75, 99, 105, 244, 356n71

New York Yankees (AAFC), 23, 26, 29, 32, 35, 39–40, 78, 104, 148, 184, 201, 347n49; and attendance, 21, 24, 25, 62, 63, 79–80, 320, 338; folding of the, 64; founding of the, 14–15; merger of, with the Brooklyn Dodgers, 30–31; and profitability, 22, 79–80; and scheduling, 21, 161

New York Yankees (baseball), 73, 74, 104, 144, 247, 362n65, 366n29

New York Yanks, 78, 147, 185, 210, 218, 219, 235, 347n49; folding of the, 110, 148, 149; relocation of, to Dallas, 111, 112; and scheduling, 161. *See also* Dallas Texans (NFL); New York Bulldogs

Nisby, John, 293

Noll, Chuck, 159

Nordlinger, Bernard, 137–38

Norman, Haldo, 209

Nussbaumer, Bob, 169

O'Connor, Leslie, 174

officials, 87, 183, 257, 263–64, 272–73, 394n4; and dirty play, 266, 267, 268; and salaries, 98, 272, 273, 398n72

Olderman, Murray, 99

O'Mahoney, Joseph C., 131, 218

O'Malley, Walter, 107, 192, 196–97

option year (contractual), 42–43, 52, 122, 129, 131, 213, 218, 219–20, 352n16. *See also* contracts, player

Orr, Jack, 296, 299

Owen, Steve, 153, 179, 180, 275

Owens, R. C., 8, 219–20

owners, team (AAFC), 16–18, 19, 78, 348n60; and merger with the NFL, 33–35; wealth of the, 13, 20–21

owners, team (AFL), 46, 48, 52, 55

owners, team (NFL), 8–9, 23, 82, 135, 260, 295–96, 297–98, 348n60; and the AAFC, 14–16, 17, 18, 26–30, 32–35; and the AFL, 45, 47–49, 52, 53, 57; and antitrust issues, 4, 120–22, 123–25, 142, 174, 221; and Canadian football, 40, 42–43; and concessions revenue, 73, 84; and the draft, 4, 122–23, 171–74, 178, 182–83, 185, 187–88, 298, 301, 379n16, 381n53, 382n70; and exhibition games, 15–16, 85, 153; and expansion, 35–36, 44, 48–49, 52, 115–19, 368n56; and financial reporting, 69, 76, 370n30; and franchise relocation, 106–14, 365n15; and franchise values, 3, 82, 101–3, 105–6, 116; and gate sharing, 192, 193–94, 202–3, 204, 383n20; and income taxes, 76, 78, 88, 108, 359n14; and innovations, 256, 260,

326–27, 380n49; and gate sharing, 336, 384n21; and integration, 289, 290, 342; and profitability, 31, 78–79, 83; and salaries, 92–93, 317; and stadium leases, 60, 67, 68, 70, 74, 83, 112, 167; and television, 232, 246, 313, 330; and ticket prices, 60, 70–71, 84, 305

player movement, 16–17, 118, 126, 133–34, 154, 155–56; and the AFL, 49–51, 52; and blacklisting, 37–38, 40, 53, 126, 218–19, 220; and competitive balance, 143, 154–61; and lawsuits, 19–20, 42, 43, 122–23, 125, 126–27, 132–33, 210–11, 346n42; and "raiding," 16–18, 19, 24, 25, 39–41, 42–43. *See also* draft, player; players' rights; reserve clause; salaries, player

Players Association, 97, 211, 212–14, 220–22, 223, 387n47. *See also* players' rights

Players' National League of 1890, 205

players' rights, 178, 187, 205, 215–17, 221–22; and the draft, 170, 172, 174, 176, 207–8, 210, 214–15, 378n4; and injuries, 208–9, 212, 217, 222; and lawsuits, 208–9, 210–13; and pension, 206, 211–12, 223–24, 243, 387n57; and the Players Association, 97, 211, 212–14, 220–22, 223, 387n47; and the reserve clause, 217–20. *See also* player movement

Pollard, Fritz, 282

Pollock, Ed, 80

Polo Grounds, 29, 46, 61, 74, 75, 78, 108, 154, 162. *See also* stadiums

Potter, Charles E., 240–41

Povich, Shirley, 26, 36, 175, 268

Powers, Francis J., 78

Powers, Jimmy, 28

Prell, Ed, 78, 108, 156, 233, 366n35; on the AAFC, 25; on the Chicago Cardinals, 112–13

Prisoners' Dilemma situations, 124–25, 245, 387n45

Pro Bowl, 65, 98, 357n20

Professional Football Players Association. *See* Players Association

profitability, 2–3, 20, 27, 31, 37, 77, 81–83, 86, 100, 306–8, 360n25; in the AAFC, 22–23, 77, 79, 83; and attendance, 63, 77–78, 80, 83, 361n34; and bankruptcies, 359n11; calculating, 75–83; and dividends, 82; and expenses, 76–81, 82, 86–89, 306, 314–16; and franchise values, 3, 72, 82, 101–6, 116; and gross operating income, 83–86, 88, 96–97, 308; and salaries, 76–77, 80, 89–99; and stadium leases, 72–75, 78, 79, 80, 83, 94, 112, 360n22; and ticket prices, 3, 33, 72, 80. *See also* gate receipts; revenue; revenue sharing

promotions. *See* publicity

publicity, 6, 21, 37, 64, 239, 244; and College All-Star games, 152–54; and promotions, 59–60, 67–68, 69

Pyle, C. C. ("Cash and Carry"), 11

Quirk, James, 102, 147

racism, 75, 109, 279–80; in bowling, 285–86; and economic discrimination, 280–81; and pop culture, 282–84; and segregation,

San Francisco 49ers (*continued*)
pionship games, 34; and the
draft, 181, 185, 324, 326–27; and
exhibition games, 85–86, 197, 312,
330; and gate sharing, 201, 336;
and gross operating income, 84,
85–86; join the NFL, 32, 33, 115, 301;
and profitability, 22, 27, 78, 82–83;
and salaries, 96, 209, 317, 363n76;
and season ticket sales, 65, 69; and
ticket prices, 66, 84, 305

Sarkisian, Alex, 160

Sayers, Gale, 287, 354n55

Schaap, Dick, 224

scheduling, 34–35, 36, 125, 265, 296,
361n49, 377n83; and the AAFC, 15,
21–22, 164; and the AFL, 47; and
competitive balance, 161–67, 168,
376n64, 377n70; and expansion,
116, 168; and gate sharing, 194,
384n21; and stadium availability,
21–22, 29, 73, 74, 108, 162–63; and
transportation costs, 165, 167

Schetsley, Paul B., 139

Schissler, Paul, 139

Schlissler, Paul, 282

scouting, 170, 176–77, 186–87, 381n52;
development of, 178–80, 380n39;
and integration, 180, 289. *See also*
draft, player

season ticket sales, 27, 36, 65–66, 68,
69, 80, 110–11, 187, 358n26; and the
AAFC, 78; in the AFL, 54, 55, 56;
and franchise relocation, 112, 114;
and ticket prices, 60, 71. *See also*
gate receipts

Sebo, Steve, 99

segregation, racial, 286–87, 288. *See
also* integration

Seiler, James W., 137–38

Seley, Hal, 105

Seymour, Harold, 190

Sharkey, Ed, 158

Shaughnessy, Clark, 257

Shaw, George, 158, 187, 381n52

Sheehan, Joseph, 104, 262

Sheer, Harry, 31

Shepard, Richard, 54–55

Sher, Jack, 150

Shibe Park, 141, 168, 231. *See also*
stadiums

Shofner, Del, 156

Shula, Don, 158

Silberman, Saul, 105

Silverman, Al, 85

Simmons, Ozzie, 282

single-entity cooperation, 120–21. *See
also* owners, team (NFL)

Smith, Gaylon, 19

Smith, Lyall, 269

Smith, Maurice ("Clipper"), 179

Smith, Red, 172

Smith, Thomas G., 292, 400n23

Smith, Wendell, 289

Snyder, Bob, 286

Snyder, Robert, 41

Soviet Union, 8, 291

Spalding, Albert, 191

"spatial preemption," 45, 57, 101. *See
also* city size

Speedie, Mac, 41, 159, 289

Sper, Norman, 178

Spinks, Jack, 290

Spinney, Art, 158

Spoelstra, Watson, 150–51, 261

stadiums, 20, 34; and the AAFC, 13,
14, 21–22, 29, 347n51, 359n2; and
the AFL, 46–47, 55, 356n74; and

Televisual Productions, 230
Terrell, Roy, 55
territorial rights, 108, 113, 133–34; as
    antitrust issue, 3, 120, 122, 123–24,
    128; and expansion, 115; and
    television, 123, 124, 230. *See also*
    owners, team (NFL)
Tew, Lowell, 183
Thompson, Alexis ("Les"), 26–28,
    29–30, 83, 94, 103, 150, 349n76. *See
    also* Philadelphia Eagles
Thomsen, Roszel C., 54
Thomson, Jim, 271
ticket prices, 66, 84, 196, 305; AAFC
    vs. NFL, 33, 79; and admissions
    taxes, 70; in baseball, 195–96;
    and city size, 59; decreases in,
    70–71; increases in, 70, 71; and
    the price elasticity of demand, 59;
    and price-fixing, 129, 131, 370n29;
    and profitability, 3, 33, 72, 80; and
    promotions, 59–60; and season
    ticket sales, 60, 65–66; and seat
    classification, 59; and stadium
    capacity, 60, 71; and territorial
    rights, 3. *See also* gate receipts
Tidwell, Travis, 172
Tittle, Y. A., 8, 96, 156, 181
Topping, Dan, 18, 27, 30, 32, 62,
    79–80, 107, 345n21, 347n49; and
    the Brooklyn Dodgers (NFL), 15,
    170; and the New York Yankees
    (baseball), 34, 73, 104, 184; and
    Yankee Stadium, 14–15, 29, 34, 73,
    75, 109. *See also* New York Yankees
    (AAFC)
Torgeson, LaVern, 151
Toronto Argonauts, 42, 43, 352n17
Trans-America League, 47

transportation costs, 33, 77, 79, 89, 95,
    107, 365n24; and the AAFC, 21; and
    scheduling, 165, 167
Trippi, Charley, 184
Tunnell, Emlen, 182
Turkin, Hy, 257
two-platoon football, 260–63. *See also*
    innovations

Udall, Stewart L., 291, 292
Unitas, Johnny, 158, 175, 181–82,
    375n47, 381n52
United Football League, 136

Van Brocklin, Norm, 90, 130, 212, 214
Veeck, Bill, Jr., 67, 193, 232, 263, 280,
    392n61
Vessels, Billy, 40

Walker, Doak, 80, 95, 96, 109
Walsh, Jack, 252, 258–59
Walton, Joe, 156
Walz, Allan, 228
Ward, Arch, 13, 14, 17, 23, 152, 229
Warren, Harry, 146
Washington, Kenny, 282, 286–87, 289
Washington Redskins, 18, 25, 77,
    105–6, 346n28; and attendance,
    60, 63, 68, 329, 337, 351n115; and
    championship games, 79, 145;
    and competitive balance, 145, 156,
    372n2; and concessions revenue,
    84; and the draft, 170–71, 183–84,
    324, 326–27; and exhibition games,
    85, 312, 330; and gross operating
    income, 84; and integration,
    290–93, 342, 400n23, 401n45; and
    lawsuits, 42–43, 125, 208–9, 217;
    name of the, 290–91, 400n30;

and profitability, 27, 83; and promotions, 67–68; relocation of, from Boston, 107–8; and scheduling, 162, 376n64; and season ticket sales, 68; and stadium, 67, 75, 83, 111–12; and television, 140, 233, 313, 330, 392n64; and territorial rights, 29, 32, 33, 124; and ticket prices, 70, 71, 84, 129, 196, 305

Wasilewski, Vincent T., 251

Waterfield, Bob, 267, 287

Watner, Abraham, 33, 104, 110, 111. *See also* Baltimore Colts (AAFC and NFL)

Webster, Alex, 41

Weinmeister, Arnie, 41, 210–11

Western Conference, 67, 68, 116, 167, 337

Western Interprovincial Football Union, 43

White, Byron ("Whizzer"), 92–93

Wilkinson, Bud, 172, 176–77, 222–23

Williams, Bobby, 181

Williams, Edward Bennett, 291, 293. *See also* Washington Redskins

Williams, G. Mennen, 240–41

Williams, Joe, 37, 85, 154, 236; on gambling, 276–77; on salaries, 94–95, 362n65

Willis, Bill, 155, 159, 285, 286, 287, 289

Winter, Max, 118, 368n62. *See also* Minnesota Vikings

Wismer, Harry, 46, 56, 75, 105–6, 233, 244, 356n71; and draft violations, 51; and the Washington Redskins, 85, 105–6, 291. *See also* New York Titans

Wolfner, Violet M. Bidwill (Mrs. Walter Wolfner), 48, 67, 113–14, 367n45. *See also* Chicago Cardinals

Wolfner, Walter, 113–14, 367n45, 391n42. *See also* Chicago Cardinals

Worden, William, 96

World Series, 73, 74, 147–48, 230, 233, 240. *See also* Major League Baseball (MLB)

World War II, 1, 12, 58, 103–4, 372n2; and player availability, 13, 183, 261

Wright, Alfred, 150

Wyatt, Bowden, 176–78, 222

Yankee Stadium, 14, 29, 34, 46, 73, 74, 75, 108; and rental fees, 7, 78, 109, 110, 366n29. *See also* stadiums

Young, Buddy, 109, 288, 289

Young, George, 159

Younger, "Tank," 180

Zuppke, Bob, 154